Chronicles of Lake George

Journeys in War and Peace

Also by Russell P. Bellico

Sails and Steam in the Mountains:
A Maritime and Military History of
Lake George and Lake Champlain

Chronicles of Lake George

Journeys in War and Peace

Russell P. Bellico

PURPLE MOUNTAIN PRESS
Fleischmanns, New York

J. E. Butterworth

To my father, Russell Bellico,
who has always encouraged
my interest in history.

First Edition, 1995
published by
Purple Mountain Press, Ltd.
Main Street, P.O. Box E3
Fleischmanns, New York 12430-0378

Library of Congress Cataloging-in-Publication Data

Bellico, Russell P. (Russell Paul), 1943-
    Chronicles of Lake George : journeys in war and peace / Russell P.
Bellico. -- 1st ed.
        p.   cm.
    Includes index.
    ISBN 0-935796-62-2 (alk. paper). -- ISBN 0-935796-63-0 0 (pbk. :
alk. paper)
    1. George, Lake, Region (N.Y.)--History--Sources.   I. Title.
F127.G3B45   1995   95-17347
974.7'51--dc20   CIP

Manufactured in the United States of America. Printed on acid-free paper.
2 3 4 5 6 7 8 9

Front cover and title page:
"Fort William Henry Hotel." Painting by James Edward Buttersworth, ca. 1870. (Adirondack Museum)

Back cover:
Detail of "A Perspective View of Lake George" in 1759 with the radeau *Invincible* and sloop *Halifax*.
Drawing by Captain-Lieutenant Henry Skinner, published in the November 1759 issue of *The
Universal Magazine*. Reproduced from a hand-colored original in the collection of Stephanie Pell
Dechame. (Fort Ticonderoga Museum)

Contents

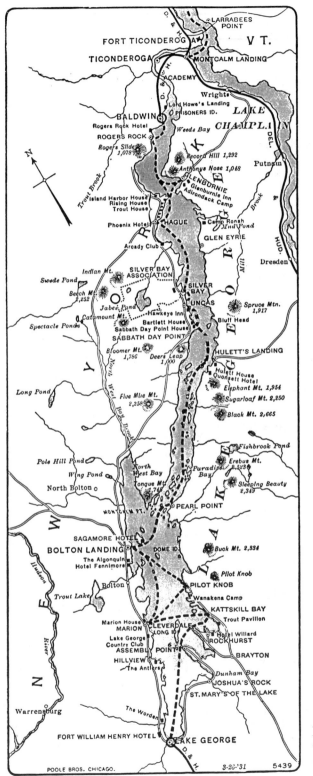

Lake George Steamboat
Company map (1931).
(Author's collection)

Acknowledgments

I WOULD LIKE TO GIVE SPECIAL RECOGNITION to Wray and Loni Rominger of Purple Mountain Press for providing the idea for *Chronicles of Lake George* and their support of the book. Their commitment to the publication of new regional history books and the reprinting of important older volumes is laudable.

The dedicated staffs of many libraries have assisted me in locating documents relating to Lake George: The New York State Library and Archives in Albany; the Bailey/Howe Memorial Library at the University of Vermont; the Fort Ticonderoga's Thompson-Pell Research Center; The University of Massachusetts Library at Amherst; the Boston Public Library; the National Archives of Canada in Ottawa; the Crandall Library; the Amherst College Library; the Smith College Library; the New York State Historical Association; the Lake George Historical Association; the American Antiquarian Society; and the Massachusetts Historical Society. In addition, I appreciated the help with illustrations that I received from the Adirondack Museum; New York State Historical Association; Albany Institute of History and Art; Continental Insurance Company; Fort Ticonderoga Museum; Fort William Henry Museum; National Archives of Canada; Bolton Historical Society; Ticonderoga Historical Society; the Library of Congress; and Gary S. Zaboly. I am also grateful for the research help from Gary S. Zaboly, Joan Fuller, Bruce Cole, Scott Padeni, Bruce Moseley, and Nicholas Westbrook.

I am especially indebted to Helen Lent, an administrative assistant at Westfield State College, for her unwavering help in typing and making innumerable changes in the manuscript. I am very appreciative for the assistance of two work-study students, Joy Nadone and Tara Nimblett, who transcribed my drafts onto a word processor. Much credit is due to John Morytko, director of photographic services at Westfield State College, for technical advice and the printing of the black and white photographs. I am likewise thankful to Jane Mitchell, reference librarian at Westfield State College, for her prompt and persistent efforts in obtaining interlibrary loans. I am very grateful for the diligent proofreading and moral support of Professors Wallace Goldstein and Frank Salvidio at Westfield State College.

I owe a special thanks to my wife Jane for her careful proofreading of the manuscript. Her patience, as well as that of my son Bill, during this writing project is duly noted.

Fort Ticonderoga and Fort William Henry deserve acknowledgment for instilling a sense of history in the many young visitors to the area. The region has fascinated me since my first visit with my family in 1952 when I was nine years old. During a second excursion, two years later, I witnessed the archaeological excavation of Fort William Henry. My younger brother Richard and I observed history coming alive as relics buried for 197 years were uncovered before our eyes. A decade and a half later, we continued our interest in the history of the region by scrutinizing shipwrecks at the bottom of the lake. Today, shipwrecks are recognized as a part of our heritage, deserving protection for future generations. The efforts of Bateaux Below, under Executive Director Joseph Zarzynski, merit commendation for the sponsorship with the state of New York of the first Submerged Heritage Preserves at Lake George.

Introduction

EVER SINCE THE FIRST RECORDED IMPRESSIONS, Lake George has been regarded as a special place by those who have visited the region. Even during the war periods soldiers couldn't help but notice the towering mountains and crystal-clear water of the lake. As a result of the campaigns during the French and Indian War and the American Revolution, Lake George was one of the best-known places in the United States before the turn of the nineteenth century. Writing in 1802, Timothy Dwight, president of Yale College, set the stage for the influx of visitors that would occur later in the century: "Lake George is universally considered as being in itself...the most beautiful object of the same nature in the United States."[1]

The beauty of Lake George can be traced to a myriad of geological changes extending over a billion years. At one time, a primordial sea covered a large portion of present-day Canada and the northeastern United States. For more than a quarter of a billion years, sediment and sea organisms were deposited into this sea basin and later solidified into sandstone, shale, and limestone layers. At some point thereafter, the unstable crust of the earth was thrust upward, transforming the sea floor into lofty peaks and the sediments into quartzites, marble, and schists. After the mountains were formed, a new inflow of water, called the Cambrian Sea, inundated the area. Further crustal disturbances or faults (fracturing of the earth's crust) caused the depression which formed Lake George. The faults created northern and southern basins, separated at the Narrows. The southern basin was fed by a river flowing into Northwest Bay, with outlets in the south at Dunham, Harris, and Warner bays, while the northern waterway flowed from the Narrows, exiting west of Rogers Rock through the Trout Brook channel (Ticonderoga) into Lake Champlain.

Over a million years ago an immense coating of ice, originating in Labrador, gradually slid over the region, burying all of New England and much of New York.

Thousands of feet thick, the glacier not only covered the mountains surrounding Lake George but also blanketed the highest peaks in the Adirondacks. As the glacier melted, the conglomeration of debris obstructed the preglacial rivers and impounded the water, forming Lake George. As the waters rose in the new lake, the land mass at the Narrows was filled with water, leaving the tips of the higher land as islands. The lake then flowed to the north, finding an outlet to Lake Champlain through the LaChute River. This combination of faults and glaciers created a long water channel with a fjord-like landscape. As the glacier receded, deposits of sediment and large boulders were randomly left behind.[2] The transparency of the water was a result of the limited watershed, small amount of surface drainage into the lake, and an abundance of springs and subterranean infiltration of water. Lake George, encompassing nearly 200 islands along its 32-mile length and surrounded by nine mountains that soar above 2,000 feet, is the largest lake in the Adirondacks.

Although the earliest journals that described the wonders of Lake George were written by Europeans, the first visitors to the lake were Native Americans, thousands of years before. Paleoindians were present as early as 9300 B.C. in the Lake Champlain region, while Native Americans inhabited the areas in the southern part of Lake George during the Vergennes Archaic period, which dated from 3500 B.C.[3] Excavations at Assembly Point in the southern basin of Lake George during 1964-1965 suggest that occupation of the area by native peoples extended over 5,000 years. The most extensive archaeological finds at Assembly Point have been associated with the late Middle Woodland era and are dated at 800 A.D. Occupied during the spring-summer-fall seasons, the site yielded 52 chipped stone artifacts, a clay pipestem, fragments of basket-impressed pottery, netsinkers, mortars (milling stones), and adzes.[4]

By the late seventeenth century the route through Lake George, known as the "Kayaderosseras Trail," was used frequently for raids upon English settlements and Iroquois villages by Native Americans allied with New France. The rivalry between France and England for control of North America escalated thereafter into three wars: King William's War (1689-1697), Queen Anne's War (1702-1713), and King George's War (1744-1748). The struggle finally culminated in a decisive conflict, the French and Indian War (1755-1763), the North American theater of the Seven Years' War. Between wars, however, Native Americans continued to make use of Lake George as a fishing and hunting ground.

Lake George was actually the third name attached to the lake. According to documents associated with Father Isaac Jogues, the most renowned Jesuit missionary in New France, the original Iroquois name for the lake was "Andiatarocté. . .there where the lake is shut in."[5] Captured in Canada by an Iroquois war party in 1642, Father Jogues was tortured and transported south on Lake Champlain to the Hudson River by a route through Wood Creek to Iroquois villages on the south bank of the Mohawk River. Although earlier writers suggested that Jogues was conveyed across Lake George in 1642, his report of the captivity failed to mention entering a second lake.[6] Four years later, despite the cruelty inflicted upon him in 1642, Father Jogues volunteered to serve as an ambassador to the Mohawk. Arriving with his party at the northern end of Lake Andiatarocté on May 30, 1646, the eve of the Feast of Corpus Christi, Father Jogues christened the primitive waterway, Lac du Saint Sacrement.[7] Barely five months later, after insects had destroyed crops at the Iroquois village, the superstitious Mohawk blamed Jogues for the problem

Martyrdom of Father Isaac Jogues in 1646 by A. Diepenbeck.
(National Archives of Canada)

and killed him. Father Isaac Jogues was canonized in 1930. Facing the lake that he named three and a half centuries before is a statue of Jogues erected in 1939 at the Lake George Battlefield Park.

Jogue's name for the lake survived for 109 years until 1755 when General William Johnson changed it to Lake George in honor of King George II of Great Britain. In the nineteenth century James Fenimore Cooper led a campaign to rename the lake, Horicon, but the change did not win acceptance with the public, despite its adoption by a number of writers of the period.

Lake George's history figures prominently at the very beginning of the American experience. As a natural water highway in the eighteenth century, Lake George was immersed in the larger political and military struggle for the continent. The first contest pitted British and provincial armies against the French and their Native American allies; in the second conflict Americans sought to wrest control from the British. As Benjamin F. DeCosta noted in his 1869 tome *Lake George, Its Scenes and Characteristics*, "there is hardly a spot, either on land or water, that has not been the scene of some warlike exploit or heroic adventure."[8] The list of those who have beheld the lucid waters of Lake George and passed before its majestic mountainsides are a microcosm of early American history: William Johnson, Robert Rogers, John Stark, James Abercromby, Jeffery Amherst, the Marquis de Montcalm, Paul Revere, John André, Henry Knox, Philip Schuyler, Benjamin Franklin, Charles Carroll, George Washington, and Thomas Jefferson.

From the earliest days of travel to Lake George, military history has been interwoven with the tourist trade. Travel books written in the nineteenth and early twentieth centuries recounted the fierce battles at the lake and described the remains of the forts and other notable scenes connected with the lake's stormy past. As visitors viewed the relics of the eighteenth-century conflicts, profound feelings stirred their imaginations. The disintegrating remnants of Forts William Henry, George, and Ticonderoga seemed to cast a spell upon visitors. In 1800, 24-year-old Abigail May "paced over the stones [at Fort Ticonderoga] awe struck. . .a cold chill ran through my veins. . .every thing makes this spot teem with melancholy reflections—I knew not how to leave."[9] Although Fort Ticonderoga lies on Lake Champlain at the outlet from Lake George, the campaigns of the French and Indian War and the American Revolution also linked the fort to the latter lake. As Addison Richards noted in his 1853 article in *Harper's New Monthly Magazine*, "Ticonderoga though geographically belonging to Lake Champlain, is essentially, in all its historical associations" bound to Lake George.[10] With the publication of James Fenimore Cooper's *The Last of the Mohicans* in 1826, Lake George's historical legacy was further solidified in the minds of the public. Soon the names of hotels, steamboats, and islands would reflect the words of Cooper. Years later, the writings of Francis Parkman, the distinguished nineteenth-century historian, would bring realism and scholarship to the story of Lake George during the bloody years of the French and Indian War.

Chronicles of Lake George relies primarily on the diaries, journals, and guidebooks of the early travelers to the region. The individuals who were dispatched to the lake during the eighteenth-century wars witnessed history unfolding, while others traveled as tourists during the nineteenth century. The stories told by the journal keepers represent personal glimpses into their lives and the historic occurrences of the day. In reading these diaries, we are sharing the experiences of the chroniclers as they participated in major military campaigns or leisurely enjoyed the region of Lake George in a later era. While the words of the participants may not be as eloquent as those later written by novelists who would attempt to recreate the imagery of historical events, they present the views, ideas, and thoughts of eyewitnesses at that time.

Primary sources allow one to separate myths from facts. In 1940 Wallace E. Lamb, author of *The Lake Champlain and Lake George Valleys*, warned that authors writing about the lakes had a "tendency. . .to accept the word of previous writers without question and to be exceedingly credulous of contemporary legends."[11] Original journals, however, are never foolproof, since the perceptions of individual writers often differ.

Like time travelers, the chroniclers of Lake George have viewed the lake during different epochs. From explorers aboard bateaux who observed virgin forests to vacationers perusing elegant hotels from the decks of steamboats; from soldiers who manned radeaux and armed sloops to today's boatsmen on high-powered craft; from troops shocked by deafening artillery explosions during the 1757 siege at Fort William Henry to tourists who blithely watch radiant bursts of fireworks from the sidewalks along the replica of the fort—all of these visitors have formed indelible impressions of Lake George.

Notes

1. Timothy Dwight, *Travels; in New-England and New-York* (New Haven: S. Converse, 1822), 353.
2. *Lake George: Complete Report of the New York State Joint Legislative Committee on Lake George Water Conditions* (Albany: New York State Legislature, 1945), 1-5, 217-22.
3. William A. Haviland and Marjory W. Power, *The Original Vermonters* (Hanover, N.H.: University Press of New England, 1981), 31, 56, 72.
4. Robert E. Funk, Paul L. Weinman, and Thomas P. Weinman, *Bulletin of the New York State Archaeological Association* 37 (1966): 1-4, 6, 8, 11, 13; For more information on additional Native American archaeological sites in the southern basin see Paul L. Weinman, *Bulletin of the New York State Archaeological Association* 34 (1965): 6-10; See also *Lake George Mirror* 11 July 1914.
5. Reuben Gold Thwaites, ed., *Travels and Explorations of the Jesuit Missionaries in New France* (Cleveland: The Burrows Brothers Company, 1898), Volume 29, 48-49.
6. Isaac Jogues, "Of the Captivity of Father Jogues, of the Society of Jesus, Among the Mohawks, in 1642 and 1643," *Collections of the New-York Historical Society* 3 (2nd Series) (1857): 180; See also Francis Talbot, *Saint Among Savages* (New York: Harper & Brothers Publishers, 1935), 447; Early writers had suggested that Father Jogues had passed through Lake George. See Francis Parkman, *The Jesuits in North America* (Boston: Little, Brown and Company, 1867), 312-13; Nathaniel Bartlett Sylvester, *Historical Sketches of Northern New York and the Adirondack Wilderness* (Troy, N.Y.: William H. Young, 1877), 67; Thomas J. Campbell, "The First Missionaries on Lake Champlain," *Proceedings of the New York State Historical Association* 10 (1911): 134.
7. Talbot, 382; Thwaites, 48-49; John Gilmary Shea, "The Jogues Papers," *Collections of the New-York Historical Society* 3 (2nd Series) (1857): 170.
8. B. F. DeCosta, *Lake George; Its Scenes and Characteristics* (New York: Anson D. F. Randolph & Co., 1869), 16.
9. Abigail May, "The Journal of Abigail May," printed copy, *New York State Historical Association*, No. 1, 71.
10. T. Addison Richards, "Lake George," *Harper's New Monthly Magazine*, July 1853, 170.
11. Wallace E. Lamb, *The Lake Champlain and Lake George Valleys* (New York: The American Historical Company, Inc., 1940), xviii.

Part I
Passage in the Wilderness

Portrait of Peter Kalm by J. G. Geitel (1764).
(National Museum, Helsinki, Finland)

1. Peter Kalm 1749

ALTHOUGH INITIALLY INTERESTED IN THEOLOGY, Peter Kalm became a renowned naturalist who explored New Jersey, Pennsylvania, New York, and Canada at a time when North America was largely wilderness. Born in Sweden in 1716, he completed his undergraduate studies at Turku University in Finland (then part of Sweden) before entering the University of Uppsala (Sweden) in 1740. Recognizing the young man's scientific ability, a number of benefactors promoted his naturalist travels in Finland, Sweden, Russia, and the Ukraine. Under the tutelage of his professors at the University of Uppsala, Kalm became a utilitarian, viewing activities in light of their usefulness to the national welfare.

Following his authorship of a number of technical reports, he was elected to the Swedish Academy of Sciences in 1745 and two years later was appointed the first professor of economics at his old alma mater, Turku University. At the time economics was linked to the natural sciences as a basis for creating national wealth. The appointment of Kalm to a chair in economics was connected to a proposed expedition to North America in search of plants that would be suitable for cultivation in Sweden. The North American expedition had been under discussion by members of the Swedish Academy of Sciences since 1744. The primary motive of the proposed journey was economic, with knowledge as a subordinate goal. Kalm himself was not an unconditional admirer of the pristine wilderness but was more interested in adapting nature to the requirements of man.[1]

After departing from Sweden on November 30, 1747, Kalm and his dedicated servant Lars Jungström were forced to spend two months on the south coast of Norway while their ship underwent repairs following a severe storm.* Arriving in London on February 6, 1748, Kalm was again delayed as ship captains awaited the

*Kalm's dates, based on a calendar that was discontinued in 1752, are earlier than a modern calendar.

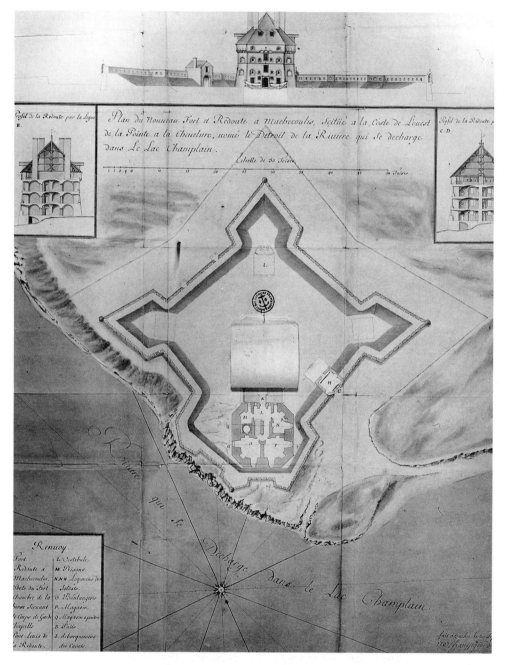

Peter Kalm spent two days at Fort St. Frédéric on
Lake Champlain before entering Lake George.
Plans by Chaussegros de Lery, 1737.
(National Archives of Canada)

end of the Austrian War of Succession and the formation of a convoy to lessen the danger from privateers. Finally, Kalm and Jungström, along with 60 emigrants from southern Germany, embarked for America on August 5, 1748, aboard the ship *Mary Gally*. Ideal weather allowed for a relatively uneventful passage. Although the *Mary Gally* ran aground on a sandbar on September 13, the vessel landed at the port of Philadelphia two days later. Kalm was clearly pleased to reach America in just under six weeks since he noted that it was common for the voyage to last 14 to 19 weeks during the winter. Upon his arrival in Philadelphia, the young professor was befriended by Benjamin Franklin who introduced him to many of his friends. Kalm was quite impressed with the public library in Philadelphia, founded by Franklin in 1742. He spent a considerable period of time with Franklin during the following winter.

Kalm's journey into the wilderness of North America occurred at the end of King George's War (1744-1748) and prior to the French and Indian War (1755-1763). As Kalm departed from New York City* on June 10, 1749, bound for Albany, he observed porpoises and sturgeon in the Hudson River. After a short visit to Albany, Kalm journeyed north on the Hudson River and Lake Champlain, reaching the French fortress of St. Frédéric at Crown Point on July 2. Kalm received a friendly welcome at the fort after presenting his passport, procured in London by the former Swedish minister to France, and issued by "His Most Christian Majesty the King of France."[3]

The French had initially fortified Chimney Point on the Vermont shore in 1731 but had substantially completed Fort St. Frédéric on the western side of the lake by 1737. The stone fortification had four large bastions at each corner with sentry huts and a four-story, medieval-style citadel at the northeast corner armed with 20 cannon. After seventeen days at Crown Point, during which Kalm described the fort and surrounding terrain and vegetation, he re-embarked on his voyage to Canada. Because the expedition was to collect plants that could be adapted to Sweden's climate, Kalm's directives were to concentrate on comparable latitudes in North America.

The thirty-three-year-old bachelor was fastidious in his observations throughout the journey and particularly remarked on the short skirts of Canadian women "which scarcely reach down to the middle of their legs."[4] After visiting St. Jean, Montreal, and Three Rivers, Kalm began a lengthy stay at Quebec City where he noted that the "civility of the inhabitants here is more refined than that of the Dutch and English."[5] By the end of September, Kalm had returned to Montreal. The French authorities denied him permission to travel to Forts Frontenac and Niagara which resulted in his return trip through the Richelieu River and Lake Champlain.

After a two-day stopover at Fort St. Frédéric, Kalm canoed to the outlet of Lake George at Ticonderoga. His journey provides one of the earliest detailed descriptions of the natural wonders of Lake George, then called St. Sacrement by the French. Kalm was the first competent scientist to study colonial America extensively and

---

*On Kalm's first visit to New York City on November 2, 1748, he noted that "I have been told by Englishmen, and not only by such as were born in America but also by those who came from Europe, that the English colonies in North America, in the space of thirty or fifty years, would be able to form a state by themselves entirely independent of Old England. But as the whole country which lies along the seashore is unguarded, and on the land side is harassed by the French, these dangerous neighbors in times of war are sufficient to prevent the connection of the colonies with their mother country from being quite broken off."[2]

have the results published. His first three volumes were printed in Stockholm between 1753 and 1761. In a short period of time, German, English, and Dutch translations were published. The following version of his journal, the first American edition of Kalm's work, was edited by Adolph B. Benson and published in 1937.

Unfortunately, most of the plants that Kalm brought to Finland did not survive. Upon his return to Finland from America, Kalm lectured on his travels and ideas on economic development. He influenced the thinking of many and continued to attract new students to his classes until the end of his career.

Peter Kalm's Travels in North America[6]

October the 21st (1749). In the morning we continued our journey and after rowing one and a half French miles we turned to the right and took the course which led to Lac St. Sacrement [Lake George].* On both sides we were inclosed by rocky hills or mountains, steep on nearly all sides and fairly high. They were valueless for purposes of cultivation, but no matter how rocky and useless they were, like our worst wooded hills, they were everywhere overgrown with the arbor vitae. Such hills must have been its native habitat. The channel from Lac Sacrement became indeed narrow, hardly a gunshot across, and also so shallow that the boat could scarcely proceed. After rowing three miles we came to the portage where we had to carry the canoe and our goods overland for a distance of a mile and a half. Here is a waterfall over a cliff of eighteen to twenty-four feet sloping height, and furthermore, above this same fall, it is so rocky and narrow that no boat can proceed.

Bustards [cranes] and a few ducks lay in large flocks, swimming about at the entrance of the channel where it flows into Lac Sacrement. Hundreds of them rose into the air as we approached. At this time of the year the natives travel along the rivers and inlets killing large numbers of these birds.

We travelled overland a mile and a half carrying our belongings and the canoe. A native and his wife, both Iroquois Indians, followed us with their canoe, which the native without any effort carried on his head the whole distance. The region was slightly elevated, but yet fairly level and everywhere overgrown with woodland, which consisted largely of spruce and pine with no rocks of any considerable size. At 11 o'clock we came to the beginning of Lac St. Sacrement itself where we put our belongings aboard, after we had pushed our boat into the water.

Lac St. Sacrement is a long, narrow lake which extends mostly from northeast to southwest, but with few small bends. To begin with it was so shallow that we could scarcely proceed with our boat, which was somewhat heavily loaded. After rowing a distance of three or four gunshots we came to a place where the water flowed over a cliff and was only about twelve feet wide. We pulled the boat over this however without having to unload it, but we had to pull it six to twelve feet only before the water again became deep and the lake wider. On both sides of the lake are high, quite steep mountains covered with forests which send up into the air one high peak after another. The forests consist partly of pine and partly of leaf-bearing trees. There are a great many small islands scattered about in the lake. Bulrushes grow in many places in the middle of the lake, also near the shore. The islands are tops of small mountains or rocky formations. Some of the mountains are unusually high, especially on the northwestern side where they are more separated and not in a range as on the southeastern side. It was sometimes so shallow where the rushes grew that we could scarcely float along. The common reed also flourished here. The water was clear and had a pleasant taste. In some of the shallow places there were pebbles and sand. The width of the lake is half an English mile, now a little more, now a little less. In some places there were neither islands nor rushes to

*Lake St. Sacrement was renamed Lake George in 1755 by General William Johnson, in command of the English provincial troops at the lake on their first Crown Point expedition during the French and Indian War.

be found. The land on both sides between the mountains seemed to be of such a character that it would not be worth while cultivating, since it would not yield much of an income. He who settled here would doubtless have to live very frugally so far as grain was concerned, but he could have plenty of game, since here is where the natives start their hunt for the roe deer.

Juniper was found here and there on the stony islands and rocks of this lake. They were as large as our ordinary ones and grew in the same way.

The shore is filled with rocks, both large and small. The sides just above are rather steep. In some places are found pines, firs, and arbor vitae. The birch also is found now and then on the sides of this steep, rocky shore. The water is clear, so that it is possible to see the bottom even though the depth is great. The mountains on the edge of the lake are in some places very steep, extending out into the water where it is quite deep.

Toward evening quite a strong wind blew against us. It gained force from the high mountains situated on both sides of the lake and consequently became stronger and the waves grew higher. On much of our course we had many small rocky islands now overgrown with fir and sweet gale, which was especially plentiful on the lowlands. These islets or cliffs sloped gently on all sides. Pines were the trees most frequently found on them and they were not exceptionally tall. We sailed between and in back of the islands so that the wind and waves might not trouble us so much. The water was everywhere quite clear. The shore was sandy in places. We followed the northwest shore.

The red juniper was found now on the mountains and now in the clefts of the mountains. In some of the inlets where the mountains were farther apart, the land was level and it would not have been so hard to cultivate, for it was mostly overgrown by deciduous trees.

There were chestnut trees here and there near the water's edge.

At a certain place the lake was about two English miles in breadth, but it grew narrower again. On the northwest the land for a while remained level and not so high, but on the southeast it was just the opposite, high and steep, one high mountain after the other. The shore was rocky, yet not precipitous. Pines, firs (the perusse) and hardwood trees flourished on the plain. The width of the lake was one English mile.

The reindeer moss flourished on the rocks in the woods.

We encamped for the night back of a point northeast of the high mountains located on the southeast shore of the lake. These are almost the highest of the mountains. The length of the lake was said to be twenty-four miles and we estimated that we still had nine miles to its end.* The neighboring forest consisted mostly of birches which still retained their leaves. Next in number was the waterbeech (Carpinus) and the mountain maple (Acer spicatum), but I could find no seeds of the latter. To be sure I found seeds here and there under the trees, but I am not certain that they were of this particular tree. Yet I gathered them.

October the 22nd. The wind was so strong that we could not proceed in our boat, which now was very heavily loaded with food which the men had taken along to have on their return journey. We had to stop for a considerable time. The wind came in gusts.

---

*Lake George is 32 miles long.

A fog as thick as smoke arose to-day from the high mountains so that at a distance it appeared like the smoke from a burning charcoal kiln.

Tales of Horror. During the evenings my companions were busy telling one another how they had gone forth in the last war to attack the English; how they had had Indians along and how they had beaten to death the enemy and scalped him. They also told how the natives often scalped the enemy while he was still alive; how they did the same thing with prisoners who were too weak to follow them, and of other gruesome deeds which it was horrible for me to listen to in these wildernesses, where the forests were now full of Indians who to-day might be at peace with one another and to-morrow at war, killing and beating to death whomsoever they could steal upon. A little while ago there was a crackling sound in the woods just as if something had walked or approached slowly in order to steal upon us. Almost everyone arose to see what was the matter, but we heard nothing more. It was said that we had just been talking about scalping and that we could suffer the same fate before we were aware of it. The long autumn nights are rather terrifying in these vast wildernesses. May God be with us!

October the 23rd. We continued our journey from this place at dawn, inasmuch as both the weather and wind were less severe.

The lake had at this point about the same appearance as before described; namely, on both sides high, fairly steep and wooded mountains. I do not know on which side they were the higher. There were small rocks here and there in the lake. The shore in some places was covered with a light sand, in other places with stones or bed rock. The water was clear and pleasant to the taste. Here it would have been impossible to paddle a canoe at night because of the many rocks along the shore. The lake extended from northeast to southwest with an occasional short curve. It seemed that the curves bent more toward the west than the east and left side, along which we were now proceeding.

Indians. One of the natives had put up his tent, if I may so call it, on the shore. He was one of those who had set out to hunt. The canoe lay upside down on the shore, as was the custom, and a short distance above in the woods, the Indian had made his hut which was constructed in the following way. He had placed pieces of birch bark and other bark on top of slender rods as a roof over himself where he lay and had hung an old [blanket]. ... to protect himself on the sides from the wind and storms. His companion had done likewise on his side and their fire was between them. The wife and children were also sitting before the fire. The native had killed a great number of roe deer and hung up the flesh on all sides to dry. The skins were also stretched out to dry. At the fire's edge sticks were set into the ground perpendicularly and at the tip of these were pieces of meat for cooking. Indians discarded the horns, yet these were sometimes used for making knife handles and the like. The native men had pulled out the hair from the front part of their heads as far up as the part above their ears, so that the whole of this part of the head was bare, which gave them the appearance of having rather high foreheads. When they sat down they crossed their legs in front of them, one leg in front of the other. After we had bought a little of the meat of the roe deer we continued our journey.

Lac St. Sacrement. The lake had the same appearance as before mentioned with fairly high mountains on both sides, the one mountain piled upon the other so to speak. We followed along the northwest shore and in one place came upon a terribly high and steep mountain, which at the top, on the side toward the lake, was almost perpendicular. Below and next to the water there was a rather steep hill which was composed of large and small stones that had fallen down from the mountain. It was awe-inspiring when we rowed at the foot of the mountain and looked up, for it seemed as if the mountain hung right over our heads as we proceeded.* The lake at the shore was very deep. The shore now for a while consisted of either stones or bed-rock and beyond that point the shore was precipitous. The mountains were everywhere overgrown with forests. The wind began to blow in strong gusts against us and the waves were fairly high, so that it was not especially pleasant to sit here in the heavily loaded boat and write. I should not have wished to have the boat founder here, since it was so fearfully deep that no one of us could have saved his life. Fog was rising from the mountains in many places just like the smoke from a charcoal kiln. There were many islands here and there in the lake.

The trees about this lake had not so generally lost their leaves as those had in the neighborhood of Montreal and Lake Champlain. Many trees still retained their green leaves and the farther south I proceeded the greater was the difference that I perceived. These high mountains surrounding all sides prevented the cold from being felt as early as around Lake Champlain, where the mountains are not as high.

The red juniper grew here and there in the crevices of the rocks and cliffs. Such are natural places for their growth. Some of them doubtless had berries.

The shores for about six miles consisted of bed rock only or large boulders, and was so steep that in case of a storm a birchbark canoe could not make a landing there. It is possible that one might be able to save one's life with difficulty, but hardly the boat, and one's belongings. In many places the rocks were so steep that it would have been impossible to have escaped alive, if the waves had forced one to seek land in this locality. Judging from the moss on the rocks the water in this lake when at its full height is from two to three feet higher than at present. Above this distance the mountains and rocks were covered with lichens and mosses.

The pitch pine was generally found growing about the lake in sandy and poor soil and in the crevices of the mountains. Also the scrub pine flourished in similar places.

The arbor vitae was plentiful in some places and grew much under the same conditions as the red juniper, even among the rocks.

Birch likewise grew in the region about the lake and often in the crevices in the bed-rock. The leaves were yellow, but had not fallen from their branches. The opposite was true at Lake Champlain, where most of the trees had lost their leaves.

The mountains everywhere on both sides were fearfully high, one close to the other and often quite steep, although covered with forests of trees and pines. Here and there in the lake was a small rocky island with a few trees upon it.

The wind was about the same as it had been the days before; it blew in gusts, at times very strong, again more gentle and almost calm. Then it would change.

Juniper (the Swedish) also flourished here and there in the crevices of the rocks. The oak (the white, red and black) was found to grow on both sides of this lake.

There was an island in the lake of some considerable size in proportion to the other small islands. It consisted of a long low rock overgrown with shrubs.

The trees which grew among the stones that had tumbled down from the mountains were, among others, the following:

*Kalm may have been in the area of Deer Leap south of Sabbath Day Point.

Birch in considerable numbers and even flourishing luxuriantly where the soil was the poorest: firs, both perusse and epinette; pines of all kinds; arbor vitae, in natural habitat; and a fair quantity of red juniper.

Note. Nearly all of these were trees which throve in the clefts of the mountains and grew quite rapidly. If anyone should wish to make use of such crevices, he should plant these trees and others which he finds will thrive there. Yet I did not find very many firs in the clefts of the bed-rock, but all varieties of pines, red and ordinary junipers, sometimes also the birch.

There were at this place in the lake several small islands covered with woodland and situated close to one another. All were of bed-rock covered with trees, mostly firs.*

"Lake George." Painting by John Frederick Kensett.
(Metropolitan Museum of Art)

The lake was nearly everywhere about an English mile across, sometimes it grew a little wider and again it became narrower. Just about southwest of these islands it seemed to be quite broad. We rowed down toward the southeastern side and followed it. The lake now became about a couple of English miles broad with small islands here and there and surrounded by high mountains on all sides.

At noon the wind became so strong, augmented no doubt by the greater breadth of the lake here, that we could no longer continue our rowing. We were forced to seek the shore until it calmed down somewhat. We landed in back of a peninsula formed by a mountain. This was a barren place as far as herbs were concerned, as nothing much was to be found on a mountain. The rarer kinds found were these:

*This section of the lake was undoubtedly the Narrows.

Bearberry plants covered the mountains in many places and flourished here in the same kind of places as ours [in Sweden]. The crevices in the mountains were full of them. Sweet fern (Myrica) grew everywhere in this locality. The so-called tea bush (moxie plum) was also common. The white pine (Pinus alba) throve in this region and grew to an unusual height. The Andromeda was found here also. The juniper was everywhere in the crevices. Indian grass, so called in New Sweden, was commonly found here. I do not recall that I have seen it farther north.

At 2:30 o'clock in the afternoon the weather became more calm and we set forth from here.

Flies now began to follow us, since we had received fresh venison which we were carrying along with us. They were the ordinary house flies.

The wind had nearly died down when we set out from the shore. It has not been very windy since. A squall accompanied with rain came, and suddenly there was such commotion in the lake that it looked almost like a boiling kettle. The waves went crisscross and were so large that we were in great danger. Yet it was almost calm. As soon as the squall and rain subsided, the strong agitation of the waters ceased. When the movement of the waters was at its height, we were in such a place that it would have been an impossibility for us to reach the shore, since it consisted of precipitous mountains reaching to the water's edge. The commotion of the waters was greatest about the promontories.

Arbor vitae flourished most where the shore consisted of fairly large rocks covered with a little soil or moss. The red American larch, which is used in making a beverage, grew here as did the perusse, its companion.

Lichen. Reindeer moss was everywhere abundant on the wooded mountains.

The shore on the southeastern side of the lake where we were rowing to-day consisted either of bed-rock, more or less steep, or it was covered with fairly large stones which could hardly be called cobble stones. The lake was very deep at the edge of the shore. We saw scarcely any other trees than varieties of pines and firs with an occasional birch among them.

The lake on which we had travelled this afternoon was nearly everywhere two English miles broad, if not a little more. My companions guessed that it was three miles or more in some places. Near the shore there was occasionally an island, but seldom any in the middle of the lake. There were mountains on both sides, yet they did not seem as high as those we had seen before, although some were as high if not higher: a mountain just now appeared on the southeastern side where we are rowing, and almost in front of it, in the center of the lake, an island is located. The rocks and mountains about the lake are of granite, and nowhere in this region have I found the black limestone. The sunshine about 3:30 P.M. was quite warm, yet the thermometer did not rise higher than fourteen degrees above 0° C. Toward the end of the lake were large islands covered with woodland. The forests were mostly pine or fir, a sign that the seeds had been carried there by the wind, but not so the seeds from hardwood trees. The seeds of the latter which had been carried by the water had either become decayed or had not reached land because of the rocky shore. There was a birch here and there. Perhaps the firs had come here first, grown up and when the leaf-bearing trees had come later, they did not thrive, since the firs had had the upper hand and had stifled them. This theory seems strengthened by the fact that oak and other trees are to be found here, but they are rare and few in number, small, miserable specimens, surrounded and crowded by the firs.

We had now approached the end of the lake. Now again I encountered the same difficulty as last summer when I travelled to Canada through these wastes, namely, that the person who was to be our guide could find neither the way nor the portage a second time. We then had to begin by following along the shore, thus hunting for the road again. If we do not find it, things will go wrong. Thank God, we have enough food, but if bad weather should set in, there is no pleasure in being in these vast wildernesses.

I have seen very few sugar maples in the vicinity of this lake, and in most places none at all.

The lake divides into two branches at its end, one toward the right and the other toward the left, or one toward the W.S.W. and the other S.S.W. We are now following the left, but after we had gone to the end of the bay and found only a small brook which ran out of a swamp or morass, but no trail nor sign of a portage, we had the pleasure of turning back to see if we were to be more successful along the other branch, which flows W.S.W. or toward the right when one comes from Canada.* The land between these two branches or bays is a long peninsula of about a quarter of a mile or so. It is a lowland, mostly overgrown with fir. Arbor vitae is especially plentiful on the shore of this inlet and next to it in number is the perusse. After four o'clock it was extremely calm and the water in the lake very smooth. Once in a while there would come a slight gust of wind.

The wolves were howling fearfully in the bay which we had just left. It was said that they had just torn to bits a roe deer over which they rejoiced, or they had killed one and were calling the others to the feast.

We continued our journey farther in search of the right place where one goes ashore and passes over to the English provinces. We discovered smoke coming from a place on shore, toward which we rowed in order to come in touch with people from whom we could get all information [we wanted].** There were three boats of Abenaquis Indians who had set up camp at this place. The greater part of them were out hunting, so that there were a couple of men only and a few children left with the boats. The men were almost drunk, since the Englishmen who had travelled through here a couple of days before, had given them rum in payment for the meat of the roe deer which they had given them. As soon as we came ashore, they put on the pot to boil meat for us. According to their wishes we must of necessity stay over night and eat with them. But as the natives when they are intoxicated are often very troublesome and even dangerous, we decided that it was wisest to proceed from this place, especially since we learned that the portage was at the end of the bay on which we were now rowing. We continued a little farther on and set up our quarters for the night, as usual, on the shore.

October the 24th. We continued our journey from this place, rowing about a quarter of a Swedish mile before we came to the end of Lake St. Sacrement. Here the shore became sandy and sloping. My companions left their boat and the greater part of their food on the shore, since they had all they could do to take care of my belongings. They had to carry the latter fifteen miles if not more over land from the aforesaid lake to an arm of the Hudson River. The mountains at the end of the lake

*Kalm may have first followed Harris Bay.

**Captain Phineas Stevens, on a 1749 scouting expedition for Massachusetts, observed "on the side of the lake St. Sacrament wigwams of St. Francois Indians, who appeared friendly...Oct. 15, sailed twelve miles on said lake-came to a wigwam of French Mohawks."[7]

did not seem as high as those we had seen before on both sides of the lake. In the beginning, and almost along the whole way, we had mostly pine woods around us, though here and there was a clump of oaks. The pine woods consisted in part of red and white pine and cypress. Both white and red oak grew abundantly among the pines, but they were small.

Notes

1. Martti Kerkkonen, *Peter Kalm's North American Journey* (Helsinki, Finland: The Finnish Historical Society, 1959), 153.
2. Adolph B. Benson, ed., *Peter Kalm's Travels in North America* (New York: Wilson-Erickson, Inc., 1937), Volume 1, 139-40.
3. Kerkkonen, 104.
4. Benson, 417.
5. Ibid., 446.
6. Ibid., 582-99.
7. Phineas Stevens, "Journal of Capt. Phineas Stevens to and from Canada - 1749," *Collections of the New Hampshire Historical Society* 5 (1837):201.

Part II
The French and Indian War

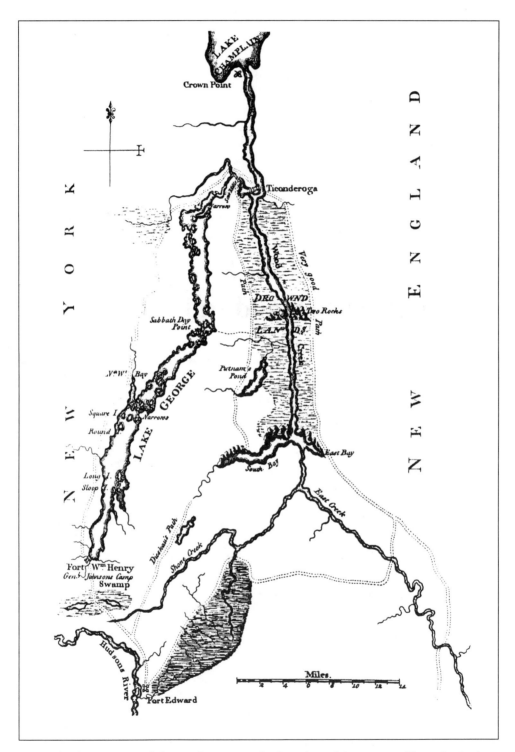

Map of Lake George and the southern part of Lake Champlain, engraved by John Lodge.
From *The History of the Late War in North-America* by Thomas Mante (1772).

2. Thomas Williams 1755

THE UNEASY PEACE following King George's War (1744-1748) began to unravel in 1754 with the surrender of Lieutenant Colonel George Washington's provincial force at Fort Necessity in western Pennsylvania and through subsequent decisions by the British and French to commit several thousand fresh troops to North America. Although a congress of delegates from the colonies, meeting in Albany in 1754, failed to agree on a collective plan for military action, the participants did recommend a "Grand Council" of delegates from each colony which would "raise and pay soldiers and build forts for the defence of any of the colonies, and equip vessels of force to guard the coasts and protect trade on the ocean, lakes, or great rivers."[1] In April 1755 at a conference of English colonial governors, the die was cast for the final confrontation in the struggle for the political and economic control of North America when General Edward Braddock, the British military commander-in-chief, approved plans to forcibly remove the French from four strategic forts in North America.

One expedition, which had been considered during King George's War, finally came to fruition with the commitment of a provincial army to capture the French fortress at Crown Point on Lake Champlain. Fort St. Frédéric had long been a staging area for French and Indian raids into New England and New York. William Johnson, a militia officer in New York and an expert on Indian affairs, was chosen to lead the military expedition to capture the French fort. Given Johnson's earlier experience with Native Americans in New York, the British government had officially appointed him the "Colonel of the Six Nations" in 1755 with direct British financial support. The first British campaign in July 1755 against Fort Duquesne (near modern-day Pittsburgh) ended in disaster and the death of General Edward Braddock. The expedition under General William Johnson, however, would achieve victory during the campaign although its chief objective, the capture of Fort St. Frédéric, would elude the British until 1759.

The Crown Point army of 1755, composed of approximately 3,900 colonial militia, began to gather in Albany in June. After a formal review of the army in mid-July by General William Johnson and Governor William Shirley of Massachusetts,* troops led by General Phineas Lyman of Suffield, Connecticut, began a trek northward to cut a road for the rest of the army. At Saratoga Lyman's troops "dug up about 1,100 Shot [cannonballs]" at the remains of Fort Clinton, according to Lieutenant Colonel Seth Pomeroy from Northampton, Massachusetts.[3] While some of the militia cleared roads for the wagons along the Hudson River, other troops proceeded upstream with supplies in 180 bateaux.**

On August 3 the army reached a sharp bend in the Hudson River called the "Great Carrying Place" because it had been the traditional portage to Lake Champlain and Lake George. The portage area had been both the site of Fort Nicholson, an outpost used in the 1709 campaign against the French, and later the trading post of John Lydius, which had been burned by the French in 1745. The contingent at the carrying place promptly commenced building storehouses and later began work on a fort. William Johnson and the rest of the army arrived at the Hudson River camp on August 14 "with some Indians and 20 cannon, 2 of which were thirty-two pounders, and a great many wagons."[4] Captain William Eyre of the Royal Engineers helped lay out the fort at the portage that would be named Fort Lyman.[5] Johnson renamed the outpost Fort Edward on September 21.

On August 28 General William Johnson and 1,500 troops reached the shores of Lake St. Sacrement, a place that Johnson had viewed on his scouting expedition of 1747 during King George's War. On the night of August 31, approximately 150 wagons arrived at the lake with bateaux, supplies, and artillery; more wagons rolled into the camp over the following three days.

As the English provincial force organized its camp at the southern end of Lake George, a French expedition under the leadership of Baron de Dieskau proceeded from Fort St. Frédéric south on Lake Champlain to attack the new fort at the "Great Carrying Place." Leaving more than half his army at Ticonderoga, General Dieskau moved swiftly to South Bay with 1,500 Canadians, Indians, and regular troops. Fearing the cannon at the fort and arguing that the English outpost was "on territory rightfully belonging to them," the Indians refused to attack Fort Lyman causing Dieskau to divert his expedition to Johnson's Lake George camp.[6]

Among the provincial troops at the Lake George camp was 37-year-old Dr. Thomas Williams of Deerfield, Massachusetts, serving as a regimental surgeon, his older brother, Colonel Ephraim Williams, and his half-brother, Josiah Williams. Another relative, Stephen Williams of Longmeadow, Massachusetts, who had been

---

*Following the death of General Edward Braddock, William Shirley was appointed commander-in-chief of all British and colonial troops in North America. During King George's War, Shirley had organized the successful capture of the French fortress of Louisbourg on Cape Breton Island in 1745 and formulated plans for an assault on Fort St. Frédéric, but nothing materialized of the latter campaign. Shirley was a major force behind the 1755 Crown Point expedition, circulating a letter to colonial governors in February which outlined the campaign and proposed the appointment of William Johnson as commander.[2]

**The bateau was a flat-bottomed, double-ended vessel constructed with oak frames and pine planks. The 25- to 35-foot boats were usually rowed, but sails were often improvised when the wind blew in the right direction.

captured in the 1704 raid on Deerfield, had been appointed chaplain of the regiment. Both Ephraim and Thomas Williams had served during King George's War at Fort Massachusetts (near present-day Williamstown) but were away from the garrison when it surrendered in 1746 after a 28-hour siege by the French. Thomas Williams had studied medicine in Boston with Dr. Samuel Wheat and later received a Master of Arts degree from Yale College. His degree was apparently earned by the delivery of an address to indicate "notable progress in learning" and a nine-pound payment for tuition.[7]

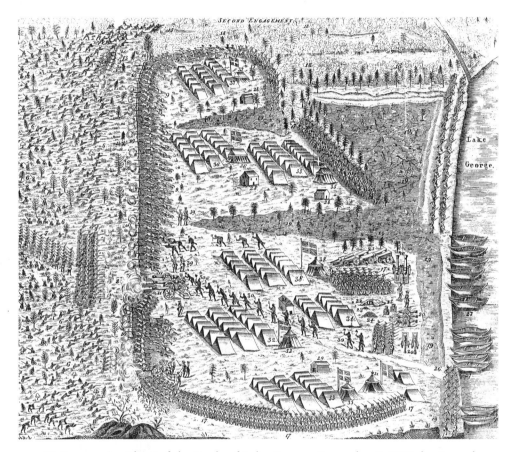

"A Prospective-Plan" of the Battle of Lake George, September 8, 1755, by Samuel Blodget. Blodget was an eyewitness to the battle who first published the "Plan" in Boston in 1755 with the engraving by Thomas Johnston. The "Plan" was republished in London the following year by Thomas Jeffreys. (American Antiquarian Society)

By mid-August 1755 Thomas Williams had become dissatisfied with the slow progress of the army which was then at the "Great Carrying Place" debating the appropriate route to take for the attack on Crown Point: "I must think it is a very grand mistake that the business was not done two months ago, but so it is, & impatience will only add to difficulty."[8] In a letter to his wife Esther, Williams philosophically resolved to remain calm despite the "additional affection of leaving the Dear wife of my bosom, pleasant children, & agreeable relatives & friends, I could not have reconciled myself unto, had I not thought I had a clear call, to serve my God, my King, & country."[9]

The provincial army at Lake George received information late on the day of September 7 of a French advance toward Fort Lyman. The following morning, a council of war agreed to send 1,000 troops, led by Colonel Ephraim Williams, and nearly 200 Indians under King Hendrick, the aging Mohawk chief, to check the anticipated French strike at Fort Lyman. The detachment of provincial troops and Hendrick's Indians were only a few miles from Lake George when they were ambushed by Dieskau's forces, who had been deployed in the shape of a hook on both sides of the military road that connected Fort Lyman to the lake. The provincial contingent, most of whom had never been tested under fire, were nearly annihilated by the French and Indians and retreated panic-stricken to Johnson's camp at the lake. Both Ephraim Williams and King Hendrick were killed at the site of the initial attack.

As the unnerved remnants of Williams' detachment approached the Lake George camp, the provincial recruits were initially seized with panic but ultimately stood their ground behind a crude barricade of logs, bateaux, and wagons. The blast of cannon fire from Johnson's artillery, however, dissuaded the Indians and Canadian troops from a frontal assault. Nevertheless, the French regulars, firing by platoons, made a center attack but were firing at too great a distance for accuracy. Early in the battle, Johnson was wounded; this left the field command to General Lyman. At the end of the afternoon, the French forces had finally been routed and retired from the battlefield, leaving behind their wounded commander, General Dieskau.

The following letter, written three days after the Battle of Lake George, poignantly describes the engagement on September 8, 1755.[10] Although victorious, the provincial army at Lake George became dispirited over the loss of friends and relatives in the battles. For many reasons, the expedition never proceeded beyond the foot of Lake George with the remaining season devoted to the building of Fort William Henry.

Thomas Williams would again serve as a surgeon the next year at Fort Edward. After the war, he pursued a notable career in politics in Deerfield, Massachusetts. Thomas died in 1775 at the age of 57; his wife Esther lived until 1800.

Lake George, Sept. 11, 1755

My Dear Spouse:

Last monday, the 8th instant, was the most awful day that my eyes ever beheld, & may I not say that ever was seen in New England, considering the transactions of it. Having intelligence that an army of French & Indians that were discovered by our Indian scouts, part of our army were detached to intercept their retreat, as it was supposed they were designated for Fort Lyman [later Fort Edward], at the south end of the Carrying-place; about 1000 whites under the command of my dear brother Ephraim who led the van, & Lt. Col. [Nathan] Whiting who brought up the rear & about 150 Mohawks under the Command of King Hendrick, their principal speaker, were attacked by the French Army consisting of 1200 regulars, & about 900 Canadians & Savages, about 3 miles from our encampment.* & the main of our detachment it is said, put to a precipitate flight, but the certainty is not yet known, besure those brave men who stood fighting for our dear country perished in the field of battle. The attack began about half an hour after ten in the morning, & continued till about four in the afternoon before the enemy began their retreat.** The enemy were about an hour & a half driving our people [Ephraim William's detachment] before them, before they reached the [Lake George] camp, where to give them due credit they fought like brave fellows on both sides for near four hours, disputing every inch of ground, in the whole of which time there seemed to be nothing but thunder & lightning & perpetual pillars of smoke. Our Cannon (which under God it appears to me) saved us were heard down as low as near Saratoga, notwithstanding the wind was in the south, & something considerable, & which by the way was a great disadvantage to our troops, as the smoke was drove in our faces.*** The wounded were brought in very fast, & it was with the utmost difficulty that their wounds could be dressed fast enough, even in the most superficial manner, having in about three hours near forty men to be dressed, & Dr. Pynchon, his mate & Billy (one of his students) & myself were all to do it, my mate being at Fort Lyman attending upon divers[e] sick men there. The bullets flew like hail-stones about our ears all the time of dressing, as we had not a place prepared of safety, to dress the wounded in, but through God's goodness we received no hurt any more than the bark of the trees & chips flying in our faces by accidental shots, which were something frequent. Our Tent was shot through in diver[se] places, which we thought best to leave & retire a few rods behind a shelter of a log house, which [was]

---

*According to Pierre André M. de Montreuil, Dieskau's second-in-command, the French force consisted of 680 Canadian troops, 600 Indians, and 220 regulars. One hundred twenty troops remained at South Bay (Lake Champlain) to guard the vessels.[11]

**Williams is apparently referring to the time period of the first two engagements of the day: the ambush of Colonel Ephraim Williams' column and the main attack on General William Johnson's camp at Lake George. Lieutenant Colonel Seth Pomeroy noted that "the Fire begun between 11 & 12 of ye Clock and Continued till 5 afternoon ye most violent Fire Perhaps y[e]t Ever was heard in this Country In any Battle."[12]

***Captain William Eyre, a British engineering officer and director of the artillery, was instrumental in repulsing the French attack with a barrage of cannon fire, mortar rounds, and grapeshot. Eyre later supervised construction of Fort William Henry with William Johnson and served each year of the French and Indian War.

so loose laid as to let the balls through very often. I have not time to give a list of the dead which are many, by reason I have not time to attend the wounded as they ought to be. My necessary food & sleep are almost strangers to me since the fatal day; fatal indeed to my dear brother Ephraim, who was killed in the beginning of the action, by a ball through his head. Great numbers of brave men, & some of the flower of our army died with him on the spot, a list of which I refer you to Capt. Burke's letter to Lt. Hoit, having not time to get a copy of one myself.* Twenty odd wounded in our regiment, amongst whom some, I fear will prove mortal, & poor brother Josiah makes one of the number, having a ball lodged in his intestines,

Battle of Lake George, September 8, 1755. Painting by F. C. Yohn.
(Continental Insurance Company Collection)

which entered towards the upper part of his thigh & passed through his groin. Poor Capt. [Elisha] Hawley is yet alive, though I did not think he would live two hours after bringing him in being shot in at the left pap [chest] (& the ball cut out near his shoulder blade) cutting his pleura, & piercing through the left lobe of his lungs. As the violence of his symptoms are this day somewhat abated, I have some small hopes he may recover.** Our Mohawks suffered considerable in the action, having thirty three killed, with the brave King Hendrick, which has exasperated them much, so that it is with a great deal of difficulty that we can keep them from sacrificing the French General & Aid-de-camp, & the rest of the French prisoners, about 21 in

*The total English provincial casualties amounted to 216 killed and 96 wounded.[13] James Hill, a 20-year-old private from Newbury, Massachusetts, mentioned that 139 had been killed in the ambush of Colonel Williams' detachment.[14]

**Captain Elisha Hawley succumbed from his wounds.[15]

number, which we have taken.* The French General is much wounded, whose name & title is as follows: (as appears by his papers) M. Le Baron des Dieskau, Marshall de Camp et Armies Envoye in Canada pour Commander Tout les Troupes. It seems he was a Lt. Col. under Count Saxe [in the] last war in Flanders; & was sent over with the same power & command from that country that the late Gen. [Edward] Braddock was from England; but must conclude, being interrupted every moment by my patients wanting something or other.

Our recruits begin to come up, which if the remainder soon join, hope we shall yet see Crown Point in a few weeks, & by God Almighty's assistance make it our own.** The remainder of the French army were attacked by 250 of the New Hampshire troops after they left us; & put to a precipitate flight, as they were not

Death of Colonel Ephraim Williams, September 8, 1755. Painting by F. C. Yohn.
(Continental Insurance Company Collection)

apprised of those troops, they left their baggage & most of their provisions, packs, & some guns, & many dead bodies on the spot where the attack began in the morning, when our troops came upon them, as they were sitting down to rest after

*Agitated over the loss of their brothers in the battle, the Mohawk threatened to kill General Dieskau. Daniel Claus protected Dieskau from the Mohawk threats and demands for "his Watch, Buckles & c. as Trophies."[16] Following this altercation, Baron Dieskau was "pestered with the reproaches of Genl. [Phineas] Lyman who charged [French] Troops with firing poisoned [musket] Balls" and "came every day for several days parading" in front of Dieskau's tent.[17] In a September 26, 1755, letter to his wife, Thomas Williams suggested that the French musket balls had been "rolled up with a dissolution of copper & yellow arsenic."[18]

**As a result of the trauma from the September 8 battle, illness among the troops, lack of sufficient boats, inadequate provisions, and other reasons, General Johnson and his officers had little incentive to press forward with the Crown Point expedition. Instead, the army remained at Lake George in the fall of 1755 engaged in the construction of Fort William Henry.

their fatigue with us.* The French General says he lost 600 of his men, & the Aid-de-Camp says more, & that they have lost 1000.** It is certain they were smartly paid, for they left their garments & weapons of war for miles together after the brush with the [New] Hampshire troops like the Assyrians in their flight. If we had had 5[00] or 600 fresh troops to have followed them it is thought very few would have gone back to Crown Point to tell what had become of their brethren.*** It is now 11 oclock at night & I have had scarce any sleep since the action, must therefore wish you a good night, looking to a merciful & gracious God to keep & preserve you with all my dear relatives & friends & in his own due time return me home to you in safety laden with the experience of his salvation, & a grateful sense of his divine mercies to us all. With love to my dear children & proper regards to all, as due, I subscribe myself.

Your affectionate Husband till Death.
THOS. WILLIAMS

*This engagement occurred when a detachment of 120 New Hampshire and 90 New York troops from Fort Lyman surprised a Canadian and Indian party who were busy scalping and looting the dead troops at the scene of the ambush of Ephraim Williams. Historical tradition suggests that many of the Canadian and Indian bodies were dumped into a pond since called "Bloody Pond."

** Montreuil, Dieskau's aide, later recorded 132 French killed and 300 wounded.[19]

***At the end of the afternoon of September 8, some provincial troops initially pursued their French adversaries. General Phineas Lyman of Connecticut recounted the episode in a letter to his wife: "The fight continued as hot as fire until past five, when the enemy slackened and retreated; our men sprang over the breastwork and followed them like lions and made terrible havoc and soon brought arms full of guns, laced hats, cartridge boxes and brought in. . .General [Dieskau] of the army and many other prisoners."[20]

Notes

1. "Journal of the Proceedings of the Congress Held at Albany, in 1754," *Collections of the Massachusetts Historical Society* 5 (3rd Series) (1836): 72.
2. Charles Henry Lincoln, *Manuscript Records of the French and Indian War* (1909; reprint ed., Bowie, MD: Heritage Books, 1992), 9.
3. Seth Pomeroy, *The Journals and Papers of Seth Pomeroy*, ed. by Louis Effingham De Forest (New York: Society of Colonial Wars in the State of New York, 1926), 105; Fort Clinton, built in 1745 near the location of Fort Saratoga (1709), had been burned on October 5, 1747, because it had become impossible to defend against the French. See Peter S. Palmer, *History of Lake Champlain*, 4th ed. (1886; reprint ed., Fleischmanns, N.Y.: Purple Mountain Press, 1992), 145; See also John Burk, "John Burk's Diary," in *History of the Town of Bernardston*, by Lucy Cutler Kellogg (Greenfield, MA.: Press of E. A. Hall & Co., 1902), 42.
4. Burk, 43; Two brass field pieces had been transported earlier to the portage by General Lyman's troops. See Pomeroy, 104.
5. James Sullivan, ed., *The Papers of Sir William Johnson* (Albany: The University of the State of New York, 1921), Volume 1, 861, 883; Some sources indicate that the layout of the fort occurred earlier. Richard Godfrey on August 7 noted "Began to build a fort, Near where General Nicholson Built a fort when formerly they went on an Expedition for Canady. Some called it Liddises Truck House. The fort house was one Hundred foot one way, 18 foot the other, and near Half an Acre Picketed in, and another Guard House 30 foot one way, 14 ye other, this done by the 13 day of August." Richard Godfrey, "A Journal of the March of Captain Richard Godfrey's Company, 1755," in *History of Taunton, Mass.*, by Samuel H. Emery (Syracuse, N.Y.: D. Mason, 1893), 421-22.
6. E. B. O'Callaghan, ed., *Documents Relative to the Colonial History of the State of New York* (Albany: Weed, Parsons and Company, 1858), Volume 10, 342; See also *The London Magazine* (October 1759): 534.
7. Wyllis E. Wright, *Colonel Ephraim Williams, A Documentary Life* (Pittsfield, MA.: Berkshire County Historical Society, 1970), 4.
8. Thomas Williams, "Correspondence of Doctor Thomas Williams, of Deerfield, Mass., A Surgeon in the Army," *The Historical Magazine* 7 (April 1870): 211.
9. Ibid.
10. Ibid., 211-13.
11. O'Callaghan, 10:335; See also Sullivan, 2:26-27, 58, 72.
12. Pomeroy, 114.
13. Wright, 149; See also Frank D. Andrews, *Connecticut Soldiers in the French and Indian War* (Vineland, N.J.: Frank D. Andrews, 1925), 31-34.
14. James Hill, "The Diary of a Private on the First Expedition to Crown Point," ed. by Edna V. Moffett, *The New England Quarterly* 5 (1932): 608.
15. Andrews, 32.
16. Daniel Claus, *Daniel Claus' Narrative of His Relations with Sir William Johnson and Experiences in the Lake George Fight* (New York: Society of Colonial Wars in the State of New York, 1904), 16.
17. Ibid., 17.
18. Thomas, 213.
19. O'Callaghan, 10: 336.
20. Delphina L. H. Clark, *Phineas Lyman----Connecticut's General* (Springfield, MA.: Connecticut Valley Historical Museum, 1964), 19.

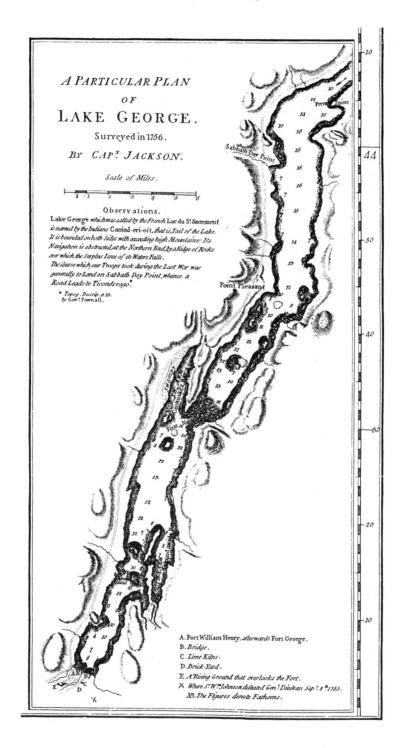

"A Particular Plan of Lake George" from the *American Military Pocket Atlas*
by R. Sayer and J. Bennett, London (1776).
(Library of Congress)

3. Thomas Brown 1757

An ACCOUNT of the French and Indian War period at Lake George would not be complete without a narrative from the exploits of the young provincial Rangers. Many bold episodes have been recorded in human history, but the daring adventures of the Rangers and their feats of bravery are still among the most astonishing tales told. The fame of the Rangers ultimately led to a new field strategy for the British army involving the use of advance units. Robert Rogers' "Rules of Ranging" was undoubtedly the first written guide to warfare in America.

After learning of the call for volunteers in early 1755 to drive the French from the northern frontier, Robert Rogers of New Hampshire quickly began enlisting recruits for the campaign. At the time Rogers was under a legal cloud because of his involvement in passing counterfeit money. With his previous militia experience, Rogers was able to raise 50 men to form a New Hampshire company with himself as captain and John Stark as his lieutenant. As a result of his attempt to stay out of prison, Rogers created the foundation for a scouting company that would have lasting influence during the French and Indian War and beyond.

The value of Rogers' aggressive scouting assignments became apparent during the 1755-1756 campaigns at Lake George. Upon his return from the last scout of the 1755-56 winter, Rogers received a letter at Fort William Henry from William Shirley, commander-in-chief of the British forces in America and the governor of Massachusetts, summoning him to Boston. Rogers was given orders to raise a 60-man independent company, separate from both the provincial and regular units. He was ordered to Lake George "to distress the French and their allies. . .to endeavour to way-lay, attack, and destroy their convoys of provisions by land and water."[1] Rogers' instructions also delineated the pay scales which provided for twice the pay for a Ranger private as for provincial troops, and roughly the same pay for officers

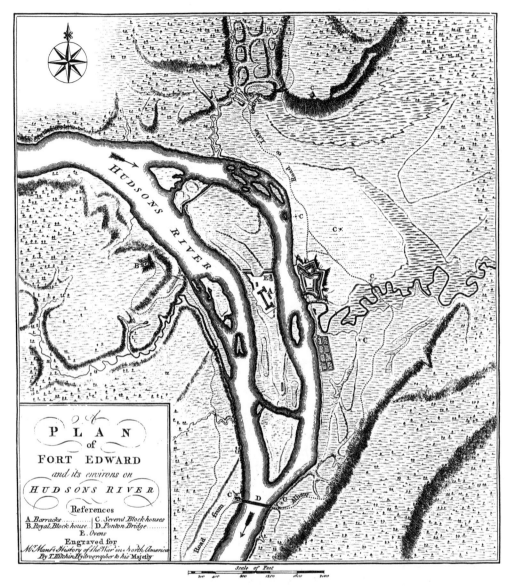

Plan of Fort Edward and Rogers Island, engraved by T. Kitchin.
From *The History of the Late War in North-America* by Thomas Mante (1772).

as then existed in the British army. In addition, Rangers received five pounds for every French or Indian prisoner, or his scalp. Ten Spanish dollars were given to each man for clothes, arms, and blankets. The early Rangers wore a hodgepodge of homemade clothing, including leggings and a leather hunting shirt or short coat. Each carried a musket, hatchet or tomahawk, scalping knife, powder horn, and a leather bag for musket balls. There is conjecture that Rogers tried to instill an "Esprit de Corps" with more uniformity in the Ranger dress. By 1758 Rogers had outfitted the Rangers in green hunting shirts and jackets. However, he might have used green, apparently his favorite color, as early as the 1756 Ranger campaign.[2]

Several additional Ranger companies were authorized during 1756. For the rest of the year the Rangers continued their scouting expeditions into French territory which provided the only real military activity of the 1756 Crown Point campaign. A 70-acre island in the Hudson River adjacent to Fort Edward became the headquarters for the Rangers where "small, peak-roofed, huts" were built as living quarters.[3] Eventually, a blockhouse, hospital, and barracks would be built on the island during the war.

During the winter of 1756-57, two Ranger companies remained at Fort William Henry while two other companies were assigned to Fort Edward. That winter witnessed the first major battle involving the Rangers. On January 15, 1757, Rogers left Fort Edward on a scout with 50 privates, accompanied by Lieutenant John Stark and Ensign Caleb Page. The units initially marched to Fort William Henry where they gathered provisions and constructed snowshoes for the expedition to Ticonderoga and Crown Point. Twenty-eight more Rangers, along with Captain Thomas Speakman, Lieutenant Samuel Kennedy, Ensign James Rogers (Robert's older

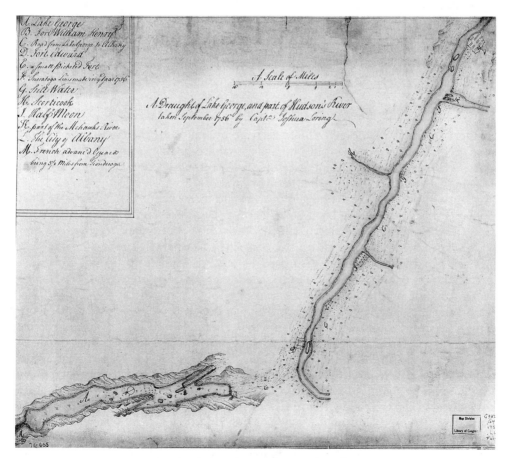

"A Draught of Lake George, and part of Hudson's River"
by Captain Joshua Loring, 1756.
(William Faden Collection, Library of Congress)

"The First Battle on Snowshoes," January 21, 1757.
Painting by Gary S. Zaboly.

brother) and two additional volunteers were drawn from the companies at Fort William Henry. Sixteen-year-old Thomas Brown from Charlestown (Boston), Massachusetts, was a private in Captain Speakman's company who would later write an intriguing account of the First Battle on Snowshoes.

Late on the 17th of January, 86 officers and men silently trudged out of Fort William Henry wrapped in blankets to protect themselves in the freezing temperatures. The party marched northward on snowshoes until they reached the first Narrows, where they camped on the east side of the lake. The next morning a number of the Rangers were dismissed because of injuries (probably frostbite), leaving the expedition with 74 officers and men who were able to cover 12 miles before camping on the west side of the lake on the evening of January 18.

By the 21st, the detachment was midway between Crown Point and Ticonderoga, according to Rogers, when they observed a horsedrawn sleigh on the ice headed toward Fort St. Frédéric. Lieutenant Stark was sent with 20 Rangers along the shoreline to halt the northward journey of the sleigh while Rogers went south to cut off any retreat. To Rogers' astonishment, he soon observed eight to ten more sleighs moving swiftly northward at a distance behind the first sleigh. Rogers immediately tried to send word to Stark to stay off the ice. Stark, however, was not warned in time and could not have seen the additional sleighs from his position north of Five Mile Point in the limited visibility caused by rain. The trap was sprung too soon, and the rearmost sleighs quickly turned around and made a desperate retreat back to Fort Carillon (Ticonderoga). "We pursued them," according to

Rogers, and "took seven prisoners, three sleds [sleighs], and six horses; the remainder made their escape."[4]

From the prisoners the Rangers quickly realized their precarious position. They were deep in enemy territory between two French forts and their position had now been exposed. The prisoners, questioned separately, reported that 200 Canadians and 45 Indians had just arrived at Carillon where 350 men were stationed. Six hundred regular troops were at St. Frédéric and reinforcements were expected at both French fortresses in the near future. Although a council of war advised a retreat by another route, Rogers decided to follow the original route, hoping to escape to the last campsite through the forest southwest of Five Mile Point. Ranger tactics usually called for a different return route, but an overconfident Rogers made a crucial error in assuming the French would not try to cut him off. At the campsite the Rangers were able to relight the campfires to dry out their wet muskets in preparation for a possible attack. With all deliberate speed, the men began their return march single file through the dense, snow-covered forest and broken terrain. By two o'clock in the afternoon, with only a short distance of the journey covered, the Rangers reached the crest of a hill on the west side of a gorge. Rogers and Lieutenant Samuel Kennedy were at the front of the line when suddenly "a volley of about 200 shot, at the distance of about five yards from the nearest, or front, and thirty from the rear of their party" cut through the Rangers.[5] Kennedy and several Rangers were instantly killed while Rogers received a flesh wound across his forehead.

Upon learning of the ambush of the sleighs on Lake Champlain, the French commander at Fort Carillon had hurriedly dispatched 89 regulars and 90 Canadians and Indians under M. de Basserode, captain of the Languedoc Regiment, to intercept

"The March of Rogers' Rangers." Painting by Frederic Remington.
From *Harper's New Monthly Magazine*, November 1897.

the Rangers' retreat.[6] Basserode surmised that the English party might follow the ravine southwest of Carillon. The French had formed themselves in a half circle on the southern edge of the ravine and waited for the Rangers to cross the gorge.* Some of the Rangers heard the French muskets being cocked; then shots abruptly pierced the wilderness. Luckily for the Rangers, many of the French muskets failed to fire in the rain. The Rangers returned the fire and Rogers ordered the men back to the opposite side of the gorge where the end of the Ranger file under Stark had been located when the French originally discharged their muskets. The French, however, pursued the Rangers downhill with bayonets to intercept them before they reached the opposite summit of the ravine. Captain Speakman was severely wounded and Ensign Caleb Page killed in the ensuing melee. The Rangers now faced more than twice their number in seasoned regular troops, Canadians, and Native Americans. Although many of the Rangers had been on scouting expeditions before, most had never experienced a large-scale battle. At the first shot, Thomas Brown was wounded. Following orders, he immediately killed his prisoner from the sleigh ambush by knocking him on the head.

The French force was beaten back from the opposite side of the ravine, but then part of the French detachment attempted a renewed attack on the Rangers' right flank. "Having the advantage of the ground, and being sheltered by large trees, we maintained a continual fire upon them" until they were forced to retreat, Rogers recounted.[7] Nevertheless, Basserode's men soon began another flanking attack. If the French had gotten to the rear of the Rangers, they might have annihilated them with a pincer strategy. The Rangers, however, held back their attackers. During the engagement the French also tried to use psychology on their enemy by threatening the Rangers with severe treatment if they refused to surrender and warned that large reinforcements were momentarily expected that would cut them to pieces. The French officers alternated these threats with flattery and good will, according to Rogers, suggesting "upon our surrender, be treated with the greatest compassion and kindness; calling me by name, they gave me the strongest assurances of their esteem and friendship."[8] Just before darkness, Rogers had a musket ball pass through his hand and wrist which prevented him from loading his musket. According to Samuel (Stilson) Eastman, one of the Rangers from New Hampshire, Rogers contemplated a retreat upon receiving his second wound.[9] John Stark, by then the only officer alive and uninjured, ordered the men to stand their positions until darkness or he would shoot the first man who fled. As he spoke, a bullet smashed the lock on his musket; he sprang forward and seized a firearm from a French soldier who had just fallen and continued the action. At dark the firing ceased on both sides.

In the darkness Rogers ordered a retreat. By the next morning the Rangers had reached Lake George about six miles south of the French position. Stark was dispatched to Fort William Henry with two men to obtain sleighs for the wounded. The following morning, 15 men from the fort met Rogers at the first Narrows. On January 23, 1757, the remains of the expedition, 48 men and 6 wounded, arrived at Fort William Henry. The Ranger losses were approximately 14 killed, 9 wounded, and 7 taken prisoner. The French, on the other hand, estimated that 34-42 Rangers had been left dead on the battlefield. The French lost 19 killed on the field of battle

---

*While Putnam Creek, west of Crown Point, has been suggested as the location of the battle, recent analysis by Ranger historian Gary S. Zaboly points to the northern section of Trout Brook, situated west of Ticonderoga and Lake George, as the site of the First Battle on Snowshoes.

and 27 wounded, of whom 23 died. Rogers' journal, by comparison, inaccurately estimated the French dead from the battle and resulting wounds at 116.[10]

Not all of the wounded men were evacuated in the confusion and darkness on the day of the battle. On the day that Rogers and his men retreated southward on Lake George, they observed someone following them at a distance. The unknown figure was Sergeant Joshua Martin who had been left for dead at the gorge. Despite a shattered hipjoint and stomach wound, Martin survived and was shortly recommended by Rogers to the position of ensign.

Several other wounded men, however, were not as lucky. Captain Thomas Speakman, Robert Baker (a volunteer from the regulars), and Thomas Brown were left behind at the site of the battle. Private Brown's torturous account of his survival was printed in Boston in 1760. Brown's story is one of the best narratives of the treatment of military prisoners during the French and Indian War.

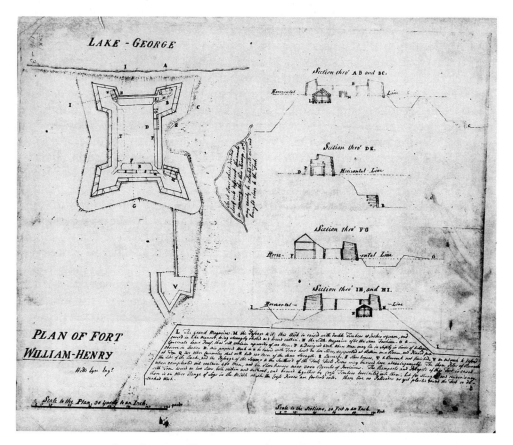

"Plan of Fort William-Henry" by William Eyre, engineer.
(National Archives of Canada)

A Narrativ[e] of Thomas Brown[11]

As I am but a Youth, I shall not make those Remarks on the Difficulties I have met with, or the kind Appearance of a good God for my Preservation, as one of riper Years might do; but shall leave that to the Reader as he goes along, and shall only beg his Prayers, that Mercies and Afflictions may be sanctified to me, and relate Matters of Fact as they occur to my Mind.

I was born in Charlestown, near Boston in New-England, in the Year 1740, and put an Apprentice by my Father to Mr. Mark White of Acton, and in the Year 1756, in the Month of May, I inlisted into Major [Robert] Roger's Corps of Rangers, in the Company commanded by Capt. [Thomas] Spikeman [Speakman].*

We march'd for Albany, where we arriv'd the first of August [1756], and from thence to Fort Edward. I was out on several Scouts, in one of which I kill'd an Indian. On the 18th of Jan. 1757, we march'd on a Scout from Fort William Henry; Major Rogers himself headed us. All were Voluntiers that went on this Scout. We came to the Road leading from Ti[c]onderoga to Crown Point, and on Lake Champlain (which was froze over) we saw about 50 sleys [sleighs];** the Major thought proper to attack them and ordered us all, about 60 in Number, to lay in Ambush, and when they were near enough we were order'd to pursue them. I happened to be near the Major when he took the first Prisoner, a Frenchman: I singled out one and follow'd him: they fled some one Way and some another, but I soon came up with him and took him. We took seven in all, the rest Escaping, some to Crown Point, and some return'd to Ti[c]onderoga: When we had brought the Prisoners to Land the Major examined them, and they inform'd him that there were 35 Indians and 500 Regulars at Ti[c]onderoga.

It being a rainy Day we made a Fire and dry'd our Guns. The Major tho't best to return to Fort William Henry in the same Path we came,*** the Snow being very deep; we march'd in an Indian-File and kept the Prisoners in the Rear, lest we should be attack'd: We proceeded in this Order about a Mile and a half, and as we were ascending a Hill, and the Centre of our Men were at the Top, the French, to the Number of 400, besides 30 or 40 Indians, fir'd on us before we discovered them: The Major ordered us to advance. I receiv'd a Wound from the Enemy (the first Shot they made on us) thro' the Body, upon which I retir'd into the Rear, to the Prisoner I had taken on the Lake, knock'd him on the Head and killed him, lest he should Escape and give Information to the Enemy; and as I was going to place myself behind a large Rock, there started up an Indian from the other Side; I threw myself backward

---

*Captain Thomas Speakman of Boston participated in the capture of Fort Beauséjour (present-day New Brunswick) and the subsequent removal of the Acadians from Nova Scotia. Speakman was commissioned a captain of a Ranger company on September 1, 1756, by John Campbell, Earl of Loudoun, the British commander-in-chief in America.

**Robert Rogers' decision to attack the French party was based on the observation of one sleigh. Subsequently, Rogers discovered eight to ten sleighs on the lake.[12]

***Later that year Rogers' "Rules of Ranging" suggested never returning by the same route: "In your return take a different route from that in which you went out, that you may the better discover any party in your rear."[13] Two Rangers, John Shute and Samuel Eastman, disclosed later that a council of war recommended following a different route on the return to Fort William Henry but the council was overruled by Rogers.[14]

into the Snow, and it being very deep, sunk so low that I broke my Snowshoes (I had Time to pull 'em off, but was obliged to let my Shoes go with them) one Indian threw his Tomahawk at me, and another was just upon seizing me; but I happily escaped and got to the Centre of our Men, and fix'd myself behind a large Pine, where I loaded and fir'd every Opportunity; after I had discharged 6 or 7 Times, there came a Ball and cut off my Gun just at the Lock. About half an Hour after, I receiv'd a Shot in my Knee; I crawled again into the Rear, and as I was turning about receiv'd a Shot in my Shoulder. The Engagement held, as near as I could guess, 5 1/2 Hours, and as I learnt after I was taken, we Killed more of the Enemy than we were in Number.* By this Time it grew dark and the Firing Ceased on both Sides, and as we were so few the Major took the Advantage of the Night and escaped with the well Men, without informing the wounded of his Design, lest they should inform the Enemy and they should pursue him before he had got out of their Reach.**

Capt. Spikeman, one [Robert] Baker and myself, all very badly wounded, made a small Fire and sat about half an Hour, when looking round we could not see any of our Men; Captain Spikeman called to Major Rogers, but received no Answer, except from the Enemy at some Distance; upon this we concluded our People were fled. All hope of Escape now vanish'd; we were so wounded that we could not travel; I could but just walk, the others could scarce move; we therefore concluded to surrender ourselves to the French: Just as we came to this Conclusion, I saw an Indian coming towards us over a small Rivulet that parted us in the Engagement: I crawl'd so far from the Fire that I could not be seen, though I could see what was acted at the Fire; the Indian came to Capt. Spikeman, who was not able to resist, and stripp'd and scalp'd him alive; Baker, who was lying by the Captain, pull'd out his Knife to stab himself, which the Indian prevented and carried him away: Seeing this dreadful Tragedy, I concluded, if possible, to crawl into the Woods and there die of my Wounds: But not being far from Capt. Spikeman, he saw me and beg'd me for God's sake! to give him a Tomahawk, that he might put an End to his Life! I refus'd him, and Exhorted him as well as I could to pray for Mercy, as he could not live many Minutes in that deplorable Condition, being on the frozen Ground, cover'd with Snow. He desir'd me to let his Wife Know (if I lived to get home) the dreadful Death he died. As I was travelling as well as I could, or rather creeping along, I found one of our People dead; I pull'd off his Stockings (he had no Shoes) and put them on my own Legs.

---

*Sergeant William Morris, captured during the battle and taken to Fort Carillon, reported that 30 of the French force had been killed and 32 additional men died from their wounds. Similarly, Sergeant James Henry, another Ranger prisoner, noted 32 of the French and Indians had been killed and 34 had died of wounds suffered in the battle. Morris escaped from his captors at Montreal and returned safely to Fort William Henry on May 18, 1757. Henry fled from a logging detail at Lake Champlain and returned a month after Morris.[15]

**Rogers' official report noted that "I consulted all my Officers who unanimously were of Opinion, that it was more prudent to carry off the wounded of our Party and take Advantage of the Night to return Homeward."[16] According to the *Memoir of John Stark*, the remnants of the Ranger party marched all night to reach Lake George: "The wounded, who, during the night march, had kept up their spirits, were by that time so overcome with cold, fatigue, and loss of blood, that they could march no farther."[17] Stark volunteered to press forward to Fort William Henry to obtain sleighs for the wounded. Lieutenant Charles Buckley and 15 men with sleighs met the remnants of Rogers' party at the first Narrows.

By this Time the Body of the Enemy had made a Fire, and had a large Number of Centries [Sentries] out on our Path, so that I was obliged to creep quite round them before I could get into the Path; but just before I came to it I saw a Frenchman behind a Tree, within two Rods of me, but the Fire shining right on him prevented his seeing me. They cried out about every Quarter of an Hour in French, All is Well! And while he that was so near me was speaking, I took the Opportunity to creep away, that he might not hear me, and by this Means got clear of him and got into our Path. But the Snow and cold put by Feet into such Pain, as I had no Shoes, that I could not go on: I therefore sat down by a Brook, and wrapt my Feet in my Blanket. But my Body being cold by sitting still, I got up, and crawl'd along in this miserable Condition the Remainder of the Night.

The next Day, about 11 o'Clock, I heard the Shouts of Indians behind me, and I suppos'd they saw me; within a few Minutes four came down a Mountain, running towards me: I threw off my Blanket, and Fear and Dread quickened my Pace for a while; but, by Reason of the Loss of so much Blood from my Wounds, I soon fail'd. When they were within a few Rods of me they cock'd their Guns, and told me to stop; but I refus'd, hoping they would fire and kill me on the Spot; which I chose, rather than the dreadful Death Capt. Spikeman died of. They soon came up with me, took me by the Neck and Kiss'd me. On searching my Pockets they found some money, which they were so fond of, that in trying who could get most, they had like to have Kill'd me. They took some dry Leaves and put them into my Wounds, and then turn'd about and ordered me to follow them.

When we came near the main Body of the Enemy, the Indians made a Live-Shout, as they call it when they bring in a Prisoner alive (different from the Shout they make when they bring in Scalps, which they call a Dead-Shout). The Indians ran to meet us, and one of them struck me with a Cutlass across the Side; he cut thro' my Cloaths, but did not touch my Flesh; others ran against me with their Heads: I ask'd if there was no Interpreter, upon which a Frenchman cry'd, I am one: I ask'd him, if this [was the] way they treated their Prisoners, to let them be cut and beat to Pieces by the Indians? He desired me to come to him; but the Indians would not let me, holding me one by one Arm and another by the other: But there arising a Difference between the four Indians that took me, they fell to fighting, which their commanding Officer seeing, he came and took me away and carry'd me to the Interpreter; who drew his Sword, and pointing it to my Breast, charged me to tell the Truth, or he would run me through: He then ask'd me what Number our Scout consisted of?—I told him 50: He ask'd where they were gone? I told him, I supposed as they were so numerous they could best tell. He said I told him wrong; for he Knew of more than 100 that were slain; I told him we had lost but 19 in all*: He said, there were as many Officers. On which he led me to Lieut. [Samuel] Kennedy. I say he was much Tomahawk'd by the Indians. He ask'd me if he was an Officer: I told him, he was a Lieutenant: And then he took me to another [Caleb Page]; who, I told him, was an Ensign: From thence he carried me to Captain Spikeman, who was laying in the Place I left him; they had cut off his Head, and fix'd it on a Pole.

I beg'd for a Pair of Shoes, and something to Eat; the Interpreter told me, I should have Relief when I came to Ti[c]onderoga, which was but one Mile and a 1/4 off,

---

*According to Rogers, 74 Rangers were in the battle, 14 of whom were killed and 6 wounded.[18] Other sources indicated that 13 were killed and 13 wounded.[19]

and then delivered me to the 4 Indians that took me. The Indians gave me a Piece of Bread, and put a Pair of Shoes on my Feet.

About this Time Robert Baker, mentioned above, was brought where I was; we were extremely glad to see each other, tho' we were in such a distress'd Condition: he told me of five Men that were taken.* We were ordered to march on toward Ti[c]onderoga: But Baker replied, he could not walk. An Indian then pushed him forward; but he could not go, and therefore sat down and cried; whereupon an Indian took him by the Hair, and was going to kill him with his Tomahawk: I was moved with Pity for him, and, as weak as I was, I took his Arms over my Shoulders, and was enabled to get him to the Fort.

We were immediately sent to the Guard House, and, about half and Hour after, brought before the Commanding-Officer [Paul-Louis Dazemard de Lusignan], who, by his Interpreter, examined us separately; after which he again sent us to the Guard-House. The Interpreter came and told us, that we were to be hang'd the next Day, because we had kill'd the 7 Prisoners we had taken on the Lake; but was afterwards so kind as to tell us, this was done only to terrify us. About an Hour after came a Doctor, and his Mate, and dressed our Wounds; and the Commanding-officer sent us a Quart of Claret [red wine]. We lay all Night on the Boards, without Blankets. The next Day I was put into the Hospital, (the other Prisoners were carried another Way) here I tarried till the 19th of Feb. and the Indians insisted on having me, to carry to their Homes, and broke into the Hospital; but the Centinel call'd the Guard and turn'd them out; after which the commanding Officer prevailed with them to let me stay 'till the 1st of March, by which Time I was able to walk about the Fort.

As I was one Day in the Interpreter's Lodging, there came in 10 or 12 Indians, with the Scalps they had taken, in order to have a War-Dance: They set me on the Floor, and put 7 of the Scalps on my head while they danc'd; when it was over, they lifted me up in triumph. But as I went and stood by the Door, two Indians began to dance a Live-Dance, and one of them threw a Tomahawk at me, to kill me, but I watch'd his Motion and dodg'd the Weapon.

I lived with the Interpreter 'till the first of March, when General Rigeav [Rigaud] came to the Fort with about 9000 Men, in order, as they said, to make an Attempt on Fort William Henry.** Their Design was to scale the Walls, for which Purpose I saw them making scaling-Ladders. The Day before they marched the General sent for me and said, Young Man, you are a likely Fellow; it's Pity you should live with such an ignorant People as the English; you had better live with me. I told him I was willing to live with him. He answer'd, I should, and go with him where he went. I replied, Perhaps he would have me to go to War with him: He said That was the Thing; he wanted me to direct him to Fort William Henry, and show him where he might scale the Walls. I told him I was sorry that a Gentleman should desire such a Thing of a Youth, or endeavor to draw him away from his Duty. He added, He would give me 7000 Livres on his Return. I replied that I was not to be bought with

*The five other captives included Sergeant James Henry, Sergeant William Morris, Private David Kimble, Private Hugh Morrison, and Private Benjamin Woodall.

**Approximately 1,600 men under de Rigaud de Vaudreuil, brother of the governor of French Canada, had arrived at Carillon for a winter attack on Fort William Henry. Rigaud, the leader of the successful attack on Fort Massachusetts in 1746, spent more than a week in the cold with his troops in a futile attempt to destroy Fort William Henry. The raiders, however, did burn the fort's outer buildings, hundreds of bateaux, and several other vessels.

Money, to be a Traitor to my Country and assist in destroying my Friends. He smiled, and said In War you must not mind even [your] Father nor Mother. When he found that he could not prevail with me, by all the fair Promises he made, he ordered me back to the Fort; and had two other Prisoners brought before him, to whom he made the same proposals as he had to me; to which they [Privates David Kimble and Benjamin Woodall] consented. The next Day I went into the Room where they were, and asked them if they had been with the General; they said they had, and that they were to have 7000 Livres apiece, as a Reward. I asked them if that was the Value of their Fathers and Mothers, and of their Country? They said they were obliged to go. I said the General could not force them; and added, that if they went on such a Design they must never return among their Friends; for if they did, and Baker* and I should live to get Home we would endeavour they should be hang'd. At this Time a Smith came and put Irons on my Feet: But the General gave those two Men who promis'd to go with him, a Blanket, a Pair of Stockings and Shoes. They were taken out of the Guard-House, and marched with the French as Pilots. The General did not succeed; he only burnt our Battoes, &c, and returned to Ti[c]onderoga. The poor Fellows never had their Reward, but instead of that were sent to the Guard-House and put in Irons.

Soon after that I was taken out of Irons, and went to live with the Interpreter till the 27th of March, at which Time the Indians took me with them in order to go to Montreal, and set me to draw a large Sled with Provisions, my Arms being tied with a Rope. By the Time we got to Crown Point, I was so lame that I could not walk. The Indians went ashore and built a Fire, and then told me I must dance; to which I complied rather than be kill'd. When we s[e]t off again I knew how to get rid of my Sled, and I knew I was not able to draw it: but this Fancy came into my Head: I took three Squaws on my Sled and pleasantly told them I wish'd I was able to draw 'em. All this took with the Indians; they freed me of the Sled, and gave it to other Prisoners. They stripp'd off all my Cloaths, and gave me a Blanket. And the next Morning they cut off my Hair and painted me, and with Needles and Indian ink prick'd on the back of my Hand the Form of one of the Scaling-Ladders which the French made to carry to Fort William Henry. I understood they were vex'd with the French for the Disappointment.

We travelled about nine Miles on Lake Champlain, and when the Sun was two Hours high we stop'd; they made a Fire, and took one of the Prisoners that had not been wounded, and were going to cut off his Hair, as they had done mine. He foolishly resisted them, upon which they prepar'd to burn him; but the Commanding Officer prevented it at this Time. But the next Night they made a Fire, stripp'd and ty'd him to a Stake, and the Squaws cut Pieces of Pine, like Scures [skewers], and thrust them into his Flesh, and set them on Fire, and then fell to pow wawing and dancing round him; and ordered me to do the same. Love of Life obliged me to comply, for I could expect no better Treatment if I refus'd. With a bitter and heavy Heart I feigned myself merry. They cut the poor man's Cords and made him run backwards and forwards. I heard the poor Man's Cries to Heaven for Mercy; and at length, thro' extreme Anguish and Pain, he pitched himself into the Flames and expired.

*In August 1757 Robert Baker, a volunteer from the 44th British Regiment, remained a prisoner in Canada but no record of his exchange has been found.

From thence we travelled, without any Thing worthy of Notice happening, 'till we came to an Indian Town, about 20 miles from Montreal. When we were about a gun's shot from the Town, the Indians made as many live Shouts as they had Prisoners, and as many dead Ones as they had Scalps. The Men and Women came out to meet us, and stripp'd me naked; after which they pointed to a Wigwam and told me to run to it, pursuing me all the Way with Sticks and Stones.

Next Day we went to Montreal, where I was carried before Governor [Rigaud de] Vaudreuill and examined. Afterwards I was taken into a French Merchant's House, and there I lived three Days. The third Night two of the Indians that took me came in drunk and asked for me; upon which the Lady called me into the Room, and as I went and stood by the Door, one of them begun to dance the War-Dance about me, designing to kill me; but as he lifted up his Hand to stab me, I catch'd hold of it with one of mine, and with the other knock'd him down, and then ran up [the] Garret [attic] and hid. The Lady sent for some Neighbours to clear the House of her Guests which they did. It was a very cold Night, and one of the Indians being excessive drunk, fell down near the House and was found in the Morning froze to death. The Indians came to the House, and finding their Brother dead, said I had kill'd him; and gathering a number together with their Guns, beset the House and demanded me of the Lady, saying I should die the most cruel Death. The Lady told me of it, and advis'd me to hide myself in the Cellar, under the Pipes [casks] of Wine; which I did. They searched the House and even came down Cellar, but could not find me. The Lady desired a Frenchman to tell the Indians That he saw me without the City, running away: They soon took after me, every Way. The Merchant pitying my condition, cover'd me with a Blanket and carried me in his Conveyance about five Miles, to a Village where his Wife's Father lived, in order to keep me out of the Way of the Indians. When the Indians that pursued me had returned, and could not find me, they concluded that I was concealed by the Merchant; and applied to the Governor that I might be delivered to them in order that they might kill me for killing their Brother; adding, by way of threatening, that if I was not delivered up to them they would turn and be against the French.

The Governor told them he had examined into the Matter, and found that I did not kill the Indian nor know any Thing about it; but that he froze to Death. On this they said they would not kill me, but would have me to live with them. The Governor then informed them where I was, and they came and took me with them to Montreal again, and dressed me in their Habit.

On the 1st of May we set off to go to the Mississippi, where my Indian Master belonged, and two other English Prisoners with them. For several Days the Indians treated me very ill; but it wore off. We went in Bark Canoes, 'till we came to Lake Sacrament, the first Carrying-Place. We continued our Journey till we came to the Ohio, where General Braddock was defeated.* Here they took one of the Prisoners, and with a Knife ript open his Belly, took one End of his Guts and tied to a Tree, and then whipt the miserable Man round and round till he expired; obliging me to dance, while they made their Game [of] the dying Man.

---

*Major General Edward Braddock, the British commander-in-chief, was killed on July 9, 1755, as he led an expeditionary force against Fort Duquesne at the confluence of the Ohio, Allegheny, and Monongahela rivers at the site of present-day Pittsburgh.

From hence we set off to go to an Indian Town about 200 Miles from the Ohio, where we arrived in 15 Days, and tarried there. The third Night one of the Indians had a mind to Kill me; as I was standing by the Fire he ran against me to push me into the Flames, but I jumped over, and Escaped being burnt; he followed me round and round and struck me several Times with his Head and Fist; which so provoked me that as he was Coming at me again I struck him and knock'd him backwards. The other Indians laugh'd, and said I was a good Fellow.

The next day we set off for the Mississippi, where we arrived the 23d of August, having passed over thirty-two Carrying-Places from our leaving Montreal. When we came here I was ordered to live with a Squaw, who was to be my Mother. I liv'd with her during the Winter, and was employed in Hunting, dressing Leather, &c., being cloath'd after the Indian Fashion.

In the Spring a French Merchant came a Trading in Bark Canoes, and on his Return wanted Hands to help him; he prevailed with my Mistress to let me go with him to Montreal. When we came there, and the Canoes were unloaded, I went into the Country and liv'd with his Wife's Father, and worked at the Farming Business for my Victuals [food] and Cloathing; I fared no better than a Slave. The Family often endeavoured to persuade me to be of their Religion, making many fair Promises if I would. Wanting to see what Alteration this would make in their Conduct towards me, one Sunday Morning I came to my Mistress, and said, Mother, will you give me good Cloaths, if I will go to Mass? She answered Yes, Son, as good as any in the House. She did so, and I rode to Church with two of her Daughters; in giving me Directions how to behave they told me I must do as they did. When we came Home I sat at the Table and ate with the Family, and Every Night and Morning was taught my Prayers.

Thus I lived 'till the next Spring, when my Master's Son-in-Law, that bro't me from the Mississippi, came for me to return with him, as he was going again there to trade. I refus'd to go, and applied to the Governor. I was then put into Gaol [jail], where I tarried 5 weeks, living on Bread and Water and Horse-Beef. When some Prisoners were going to be sent to Quebeck, in order to be transported to Old France, I went with them. Here we laid in Gaol 6 Weeks. But happening to see one of my Master's Sons, he prevailed with me to go back with him and work as formerly; I consented, and tarried with him till the 8th of September.

There was at the next House an English Lad, a Prisoner; we agreed to run away together, through the Woods, that so, if possible, we might get home to our Friends. But how to get Provisions for the Way, we Knew not; till I was allowed a Gun to kill Pigeons, which were very plenty here. I shot a number, split and dried them, and concealed [them] in the Woods. We agreed to set off on a Sunday Morning, and were to meet at an appointed Place: which we did, and began our Journey towards Crown-Point. After we had travelled 22 Days, 15 of which we had no Provision except Roots, Worms and such like, we were so weak and faint that we could scarce walk. My Companion gave out, and could go no further; he desired me to leave him, but I would not. I went and found three Frogs, and divided them between us. The next Morning he died. I sat down by him, and at first concluded to make a Fire, as I had my Gun, and eat his Flesh, and if no Relief came, to die with him; but finally came to this Resolution: To cut off of his Bones as much Flesh as I could and tie it up in a Handkerchief, and so proceed as well as I could. Accordingly I did so, and buried my Companion on the Day I left him. I got three Frogs more the next Day.

Being weak and tired, about 9 o'clock I sat down, but could not eat my Friend's Flesh. I expected soon to die myself; and while I was commending my Soul to God I saw a Partridge light just by me, which I thought was sent by Providence. I was so weak that I could not hold out my Gun; but by resting, I brought my Piece to bear, so that I kill'd the Partridge. While I was eating of it, there came two Pigeons, so near, that I kill'd 'em both. As I fired two Guns, I heard a Gun at a Distance: I fired again, and was answered twice. This roused me; I got up and travelled as fast as I could towards the Report of the Guns; and about half a Mile off, I saw three Canadians. I went to 'em, and pretended to be a Dutchman, one of their own Regulars, that was lost in the Woods. They brought me to Crown Point; upon which I desired to see the Commanding Officer. He knew me again, and asked me how I came there. I told him my story and what difficulties I had met with. He ordered me to the Guard-House, and to be put in irons. About an hour after he sent me a Bowl of Rice.

After I had been at Crown Point ten or twelve Days, the Commanding Officer sent me back, under a Guard of 12 Soldiers, to Montreal, in a Battoe, and wrote a Letter (as I afterwards understood) to my Master not to hurt me.

When I came to the House, one of his Daughters met me at the Door, and pushed me back, and went and called her Father. At this House there was a French Captain, of the Regulars, billeted; he was a Protestant. He hearing my Voice, called me to him and asked me where I had been. Upon my telling him he called me a Fool, for attempting a thing so impossible. My Master coming in, took me by the Shoulder, and threatened to kill me for stealing his Gun when I ran away. But the good Captain prevented him from using any Violence. The Captain asked me if I had been before the Governor; I told him I had not; and he then advis'd my Master to send his Son with me (who was an Ensign among the Canadians). When we came to a small Ferry, which we were to pass, I refus'd to go any further; and after a great deal of do, he went without me. On his Return, he said he had got leave of the Governor, that I should go back to his Father and work as formerly. Accordingly I lived with him 'till the 19th of November [1758]; and when Col. Schuyler was coming away, I came with him to Albany.*

Here I was taken Sick, and some of the Light Infantry promised me if I would inlist, that they would provide for me; and having neither Friends nor Money, I was obliged to consent. They ordered me a Bed, and Care to be taken of me. Five Days after, they put me on board a Sloop, and sent me to Kingston [N.Y.], and put me into a Hospital, where I was three Months.

The Regiment remained here till May [1759], when we went to Albany, from thence to Fort William Henry, and then to Ti[c]onderoga and Crown Point; both of which Places surrendered to General [Jeffery] Amherst.

On Sept. 19th [1759], went [as a] Pilot of a Scout to Cachanowaga [Caughnawaga], with Lieutenant McCurdy, and on our Return, as we were on Lake Champlain, turning a Point of Land, and under great Way, we discovered in a large Cove a French Brig,** but it was unhappily too late for us to make our Escape. We were pursued and taken Prisoners (being 7 in Number), and the next Morning sent to Nut Island [Isle-aux-Noix]; where we were stripp'd by the Indians, and dressed

---

*Colonel Peter Schuyler of New York had been active in securing the release of other prisoners in Canada.[20]

**Brown observed the 10-gun schooner *La Vigilante*, commanded by Joseph Payant St. Onge.

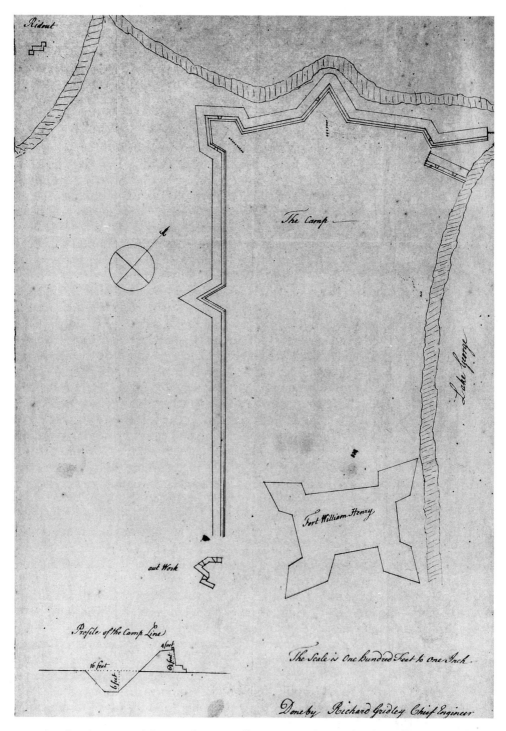

Plan for the outer defenses of Fort William Henry by Richard Gridley, a noted provincial engineer from Boston who designed the successful offensive works in the 1745 Louisbourg campaign and the defensive earthworks at Bunker Hill in 1775.
(National Archives of Canada)

after their manner. From thence we were conducted to Montreal and examined before the Governor; after which we were ordered to Prison. I applied to the Governor, and told him That I had been a Prisoner there two Years, and had liv'd with such a Farmer, and desired Liberty to go to him again; upon which he sent for my Master's Son, and being inform'd of the Truth of what I related, consented.

I tarried with the Farmer till November 25th [1759], when by a Flag of Truce 250 English Prisoners came to Crown Point, where I rejoined my regiment.

After repeated Application to General Amherst I was dismissed, and returned in Peace to my Father's House the Beginning of January, 1760, after having been absent 3 Years and almost 8 Months.

"O! that Men would praise the Lord for his Goodness, and for his wonderful Works to the Children of Men!"

"Bless the Lord, O my Soul!"

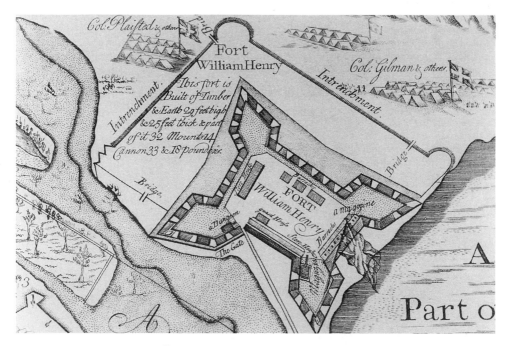

Fort William Henry in 1756, engraved and printed
by Thomas Johnston in Boston, 1756.
(American Antiquarian Society)

Notes

1. Robert Rogers, *Journals of Major Robert Rogers* (1765; reprint ed., Ann Arbor, MI: University Microfilms, Inc., 1966), 15.
2. Burt G. Loescher, *The History of Rogers Rangers* (San Francisco: Burt G. Loescher, 1946), Volume 1, 272, 115.
3. Richard A. Mason, ed., *Exploring Rogers Island* (Fort Edward, N.Y.: The Rogers Island Historical Association, 1969), 17.
4. Rogers, 40.
5. Ibid., 41.
6. Louis Antoine de Bougainville, *Adventure in the Wilderness: The American Journals of Louis Antoine de Bougainville 1756-1760*, trans. and ed. Edward P. Hamilton (Norman, OK: University of Oklahoma Press, 1964), 81; Loescher, 1: 347-48.
7. Rogers, 42.
8. Ibid., 43.
9. Luther Roby, *Reminiscences of the French War; Rogers' Expeditions and Maj. Gen. John Stark* (Concord, N.H.: Luther Roby, 1831), 178.
10. Rogers, 43-44; Loescher, 1: 137, 348.
11. Thomas Brown, *A Plain Narrativ[e] of the Uncommon Sufferings and Remarkable Deliverance of Thomas Brown* (Boston: Fowle and Draper, 1760).
12. Rogers, 40; One of the earliest secondary accounts of the battle was written in 1760, see Samuel Niles, "A Summary Historical Narrative of the Wars in New-England with the French and Indians, in Several Parts of the Country," *Collections of the Massachusetts Historical Society* 5, Fourth Series (1861): 433-36.
13. Rogers, 61.
14. Roby, 36; Loescher, 1: 340.
15. Loescher, 1: 330-36.
16. Ibid., 327.
17. Caleb Stark, *Memoir and Official Correspondence of Gen. John Stark, With Notices of Several Other Offices of the Revolution* (1860; reprint ed., Gregg Press, 1972), 18.
18. Rogers, 39, 45.
19. Loescher, 1: 330.
20. Colin G. Calloway, comp., *North Country Captives* (Hanover, N.H.: University Press of New England, 1992), 96-98.

Detail of a plan of Fort William Henry (1756) with a proposed redoubt on "the Rising Ground to the West." The redoubt (small fort) was built in 1758 and subsequently called Fort Gage. (National Archives of Canada)

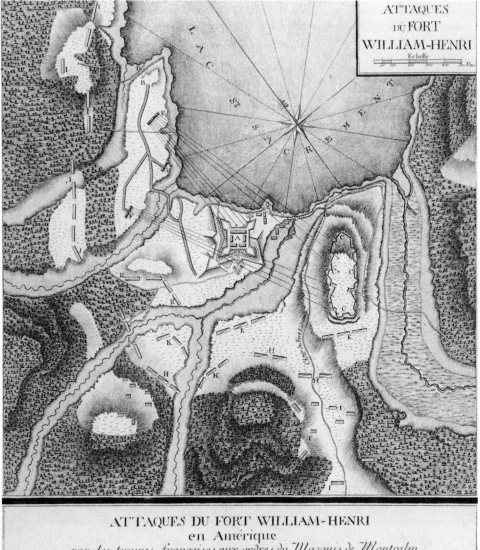

French map of the August 1757 attack on Fort William Henry and the entrenched camp.
(National Archives of Canada)

4. An Anonymous Journal Kept During the Siege of Fort William Henry 1757

The story of the siege and massacre at Fort William Henry in August 1757 quickly spread throughout the colonies and to England. The impact of the defeat would shape the perspective regarding the immediate war effort as well as influence attitudes toward Native Americans into the next century. Newspaper accounts of the massacre and several contemporary books were followed by James Fenimore Cooper's 1826 novel *The Last of the Mohicans* and later by the historical chronicles of Francis Parkman.

Although British plans were formulated in 1756 to attack Fort Carillon at Ticonderoga, the surrender of the Oswego garrisons to the French postponed any operations at Lake George. After a March 1757 raid by French forces on Fort William Henry, the British suspected that another attack on the fort was likely. Nevertheless, a major part of their army was diverted in 1757 to the ill-fated expedition to capture the French fortress of Louisbourg on Cape Breton Island. Aware of the Louisbourg campaign, the governor of New France decided "to take advantage of the absence of the best troops [and]. . .lay siege to Fort William Henry."[1] With that objective, the Marquis de Montcalm, one of the finest French generals of the war, amassed an army at Fort Carillon of 3,081 regulars, 188 artillerymen, 2,946 Canadian militia, and 1,806 Indians representing 40 Indian nations east of the Mississippi River.[2]

Fort William Henry, constructed of huge logs set in cross tiers filled with dirt, formed an irregular square with four bastions, barracks, storehouses, casements, and a magazine. The walls were 12- to 30-feet thick and approximately 17-feet high, surrounded by a dry moat and standing rows of logs with sharpened ends.[3] To the

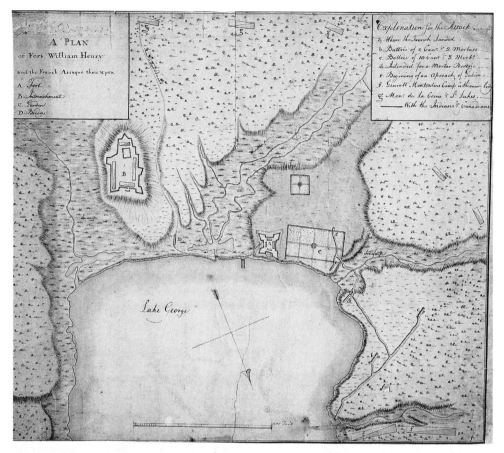

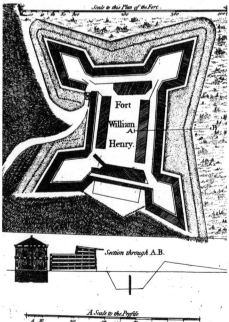

Above: Eighteenth-century map of English and French positions during the 1757 siege of Fort William Henry.

Left: Plan of Fort William Henry from *A Set of Plans and Forts in America* by Ann Rocque (1765).

Below: Detail of "A Draught of Lake George" (ca. 1756). (National Archives of Canada)

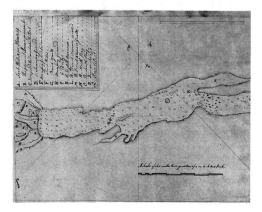

east of the fort was an entrenched camp with rudimentary barricades. Since the fort was designed to garrison about 500 soldiers, the largest number of troops in 1757 was stationed at the entrenched camp near the site of William Johnson's 1755 battle with the French. Lieutenant Colonel George Monro of the 35th Regiment commanded Fort William Henry and the entrenched camp while Major General Daniel Webb was in charge of Fort Edward on the Hudson River as well as being the overall commander in New York during the absence of Lord Loudoun.

Tensions increased ten days before the French attack on Fort William Henry when 350 men in whaleboats from a New Jersey provincial regiment under Colonel John Parker were ambushed on the lake at Sabbath Day Point.[4] A few days later, under pressure from Monro, General Webb transferred 823 Massachusetts troops with Colonel Joseph Frye and more than 100 Royal Americans under Lieutenant Colonel John Young from Fort Edward to Fort William Henry. The total number of troops at the lake before the siege was approximately 2,300, the majority being provincial troops.

Meanwhile, 2,488 French troops and Indians set out on foot from Carillon on July 30 following an old Mohawk trail along the west side of Lake George. Two days later Montcalm and the main army embarked aboard 250 bateaux and 31 artillery rafts that had been constructed by placing a platform over two bateaux. On August 3 the French army had disembarked on the western shore of the lake, several miles north of Fort William Henry. After beginning his entrenchments, Montcalm sent an aide with a letter requesting surrender of the garrison, but Colonel Monro replied that he intended to defend the fort to the last man.

That same day, Monro sent two letters to Webb at Fort Edward seeking additional reinforcements. Webb's first reply promised to assist the garrison "as

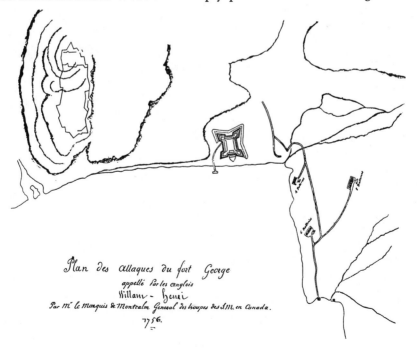

French plans drawn in 1756 for the siege of Fort William Henry.
(National Archives of Canada)

A sketch of a sloop at Fort William Henry carved on a provincial powder horn (ca. 1756). From *History of the Town of Queensbury* by A. W. Holden (1874).

soon as possible with the whole army if require'd."[5] General Webb, ill and dispirited by palsy, sent letters to New England governors for reinforcements. On August 4 Monro sent two more urgent messages for help. Webb's reply that it was "not. . .prudent. . .to assist you" was found in the lining of the messenger's jacket by the French who held it as a ploy for a future surrender offer.

By then, 800 French troops had been assigned to trench digging around the clock in order to bring the artillery closer to the fort. Each day the increasingly desperate troops at the fort poured cannon fire on the French entrenchments. On August 6 Seth Metcalf at Fort Edward recorded that "the cannon Began to fier very Early in the morning at A most terrible manner and so continued all Day by Spels."[6] The cannon heard at Fort Edward came from the first French battery; on August 7 at six in the morning Montcalm opened a second battery. Three hours later the French

Recovery of a French and Indian War grapnel anchor near Fort William Henry in the 1950s. (Fort William Henry Museum)

commander sent his aide, Louis Antoine de Bougainville, under a flag of truce to the British fort. Blindfolded, Bougainville was led to the entrenched camp where he handed Monro a letter from Webb that had been intercepted on August 4. It stated that no reinforcements were to be dispatched. Despite the setback, Monro again refused to consider surrender and the cannonading resumed. Later, a howitzer shell landed on an ammunition box killing or wounding 16, including one "provencial Officer that never was heard of but part of his Coat was found."[7] Early on August 9, the French had completed work on a third battery which could now make virtually all of the fort and nearby entrenched camp vulnerable to shelling.

Many of the cannon and mortars burst inside the fort because of metal fatigue and "very few shott or shells" were left.[8] Early on the morning of August 9, a council of war "were of opinion, nothing further could be done for the defense of Fort William Henry" and urged Monro to seek terms of capitulation.[9] A white flag was observed by the French at seven o'clock. Fort William Henry had survived the assault substantially intact, but the dwindling number of cannon, depleted ammunition, and lack of reinforcements ended the beleaguered garrison's stand against an overwhelming French army.

Following the surrender, the British and provincial troops were to be escorted to Fort Edward. Captain James Furnis, the British Comptroller of Ordinance in America, who was present at Fort William Henry, reported that the English troops, on Montcalm's advice, began to march out of the encampment late at night on August 9, but threats from the Native Americans allied with the French army forced the orders to be rescinded.[10] A contemporary report suggested that "immediately on the surrender, an English officer heard the Indian chief violently accuse the French General with being false and a lyar to them; that he had promised them the plunder of the English and they would have it."[11] At five o'clock in the morning, the Indians began to scalp the wounded and strip the captured officers of their personal belongings. The horrified troops began their march shortly thereafter, but the Indians "fell upon the rear, killing & scalping."[12] The following event, known as the "Massacre," has been the subject of numerous narratives and many interpretations. Jonathan Carver, a private in the Massachusetts regiment, later related the horrible spectacle where "men, women, and children were dispatched in the most wanton and cruel manner, and immediately scalped. Many of these savages drank the blood of their victims, as it flowed warm from the fatal wound."[13] When the provincial officers appealed to the French to end the "horrid scene of blood and slaughter. . .they refus'd & told them they must take to the woods and shift for themselves."[14] Hundreds of terrified men fled into the woods and arrived at Fort Edward over the next several days, disoriented and famished. Others were conducted back to the entrenched camp at the lake and escorted five days later to Fort Edward. Hundreds of prisoners, however, were taken to Canada by the Indians where most were later ransomed to French authorities.

Shortly thereafter, Major Israel Putnam of the Connecticut Rangers viewed the ruins of Fort William Henry. Biographers of Putnam later recounted his scout in hyperbole, embellishing the "Massacre": "The Fort was entirely destroyed: the barracks, outhouses, and buildings were a heap of ruins—the cannon, stores, boats, and vessels were all carried away. The fires were still burning—the smoke and stench offensive and suffocating. Innumerable fragments of human skulls, and bones and

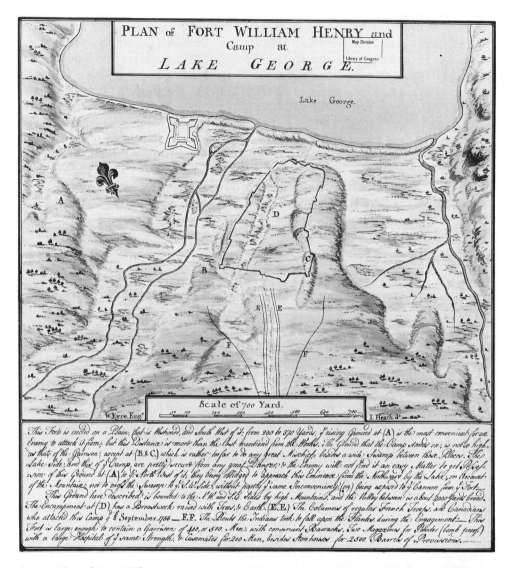

Above: "Plan of Fort William Henry and Camp at Lake George" by William Eyre, engineer (ca. 1756).
(William Faden Collection, Library of Congress)

Right: French attempt to restrain their Indian allies at Fort William Henry prior to British march to Fort Edward. Painting by J. L. G. Ferris.
(Continental Insurance Company Collection).

carcasses half consumed, were still frying and broiling in the decaying fires. Dead bodies mangled with scalping knives and tomahawks, in all the wantonness of Indian barbarity, were everywhere to be seen. More than one hundred women butchered and shockingly mangled, lay upon the ground still weltering in their gore."[15]

Lingering questions remain about the defense of Fort William Henry. By August 12, there were over 4,200 provincials at Fort Edward; William Johnson had arrived as early as August 6 with nearly 1,000 provincial troops and Indians. Why hadn't Webb called for reinforcements in July when scouting reports indicated the threat of a French invasion?* Why weren't the larger vessels including "2 Galliots [galleys],. . .2 Sloops" mentioned by Colonel James Montresor used initially against the French bateaux and rafts on the lake?[16] In reality, the two row galleys were never completed,for as James Furnis noted, the French "on the 14th burnt the Fort** and Breast Work, with two Row Galleys which were ready to launch."[17] The sloops, however, were taken by the French forces. A few weeks later, Israel Putnam with a scouting party observed "one of our Sloops lies out in the Lake, at Anchor, in order to give [the French] the earliest Intelligence."[18]

The following anonymous journal of an officer at Fort William Henry was found among the papers of Colonel James Burd, a contemporary British officer in command of Fort Augusta on the Susquehanna River in Pennsylvania. The journal provides a dramatic inside view of the siege, describing the hope for reinforcements and the emotions of the valiant defenders of Fort William Henry. From the text of the journal, the writer appears to be an artillery officer assigned to duty in the fort rather than the entrenched camp.

---

*Colonel Monro later brought accusations against General Webb for his conduct prior to and during the siege of Fort William Henry. Monro died of apoplexy (stroke) several months after the surrender of the fort.

**The buried ruins of Fort William Henry remained relatively undisturbed until the early 1950s when a thorough excavation of the site began under the direction of senior archaeologist Stanley Gifford prior to the construction of a replica of the fort. An Albany real estate broker, Harold Veeder, had organized the Fort William Henry Corporation in 1952 which acquired the ruins to preserve the site and reconstruct the fort. In 1953 and 1954, tracing the visible outline of the fort and using the 1755 construction plans, Gifford and his team discovered brick-and stone-lined rooms under the east and west barracks, remnants of the bastions, a well, a cemetery, and hundreds of military artifacts. In the first year of work at the Fort William Henry site, 60,000 tourists viewed the excavation.[19] After 40 years on public display, the skeletons uncovered in the early 1950s at Fort William Henry were prepared for reburial. In 1993, prior to their reinterment, physical anthropologists Dr. Maria A. Liston of Adirondack Community College and Dr. Brenda J. Baker of the New York State Museum analyzed the skeletons. Their examination indicated that the skeletons probably belonged to the victims of the 1757 massacre of the sick and wounded by Montcalm's Native American allies. The pathological findings also revealed a multitude of physical problems: herniated discs, torn muscles, amputations, fractured bones, systemic infections, tubercular lesions, and evidence that one victim had been beheaded.[20]

Archaeological work during reconstruction at Fort William Henry in the 1950s.

Clockwise from below left: Discovery of a skull. U.S. Army ordnance experts defuse unexploded mortar bomb discovered in the East Barracks in 1955. Excavated skeletons in the military cemetery. Stanley Gifford, senior archaeologist, inspecting Native American stone artifacts. Excavation in 1954 of the fort's blacksmith shop, East Barracks area. Recovery of a cannon. (Fort William Henry Museum)

Fort William Henry following reconstruction in the 1950s.

(Top and bottom: postcards, author's collection. Middle: photo by author)

A Journal Kept During the Siege of Fort William Henry.[18]

Tuesday
August 2[d] 1757

In the Evening Col. [John] Young of the 3[d] Battalion of the Royal Americans and Col. [Joseph] Fry[e] of the N. England Forces came to the Camp at Lake George with a reinforcement of 1100 men Regulars and Provincials* making with what we had before upwards of 2400 men the whole under command of Col. [George] Monro of the 35[th] Regiment.

Lieut. Forty of the 35[th] Reg[t] and Cap[t]. of one of ye gallies detached 14 of his Sailors to reconitre the lake this Evening who returned about midnight and reported that they saw a large number of the Enemys Boats which gave them cha[s]e and had like to have been taken. During this night the Camp was frequently alarmed by the Enemys firing on our Centurys[sentries].

Wednesday 3[d]. Early this morning our Century discovered a large number of Boats on the lake close under a point of Land on the west shore distance about 5 miles upon which we fired our warning Guns (32 pounders) a Signal agreed on upon the approach of the Enemy. The French fired at the fort from their Boats lying at the point but their Shot did not reach halfway: At this point the Enemy landed their forces and Artillery.** This morning we brought in our live Stock put them into the Picquet[picketed] Store yard but being neglected afterwards strayed and fell into the Enemy's Hands.

Cap[t]. W[m] Arbuthnot was ordered out with a Party of his N. England Forces to burn and destroy some Huts and Hedges on the west of the Fort, which he did with difficulty. Nine o'Clock discovered a number of French Regulars marching S. W. near the foot of a Hill distant about 1000 yds which we apprehended were intended to cut off our Communication with Fort Edward. Lieu[t]. Collins of the Royal Regiment of Artillery gave orders to cannonade them as they marched which was done. Our rangers and a party of Provincials were Smartly engaged with enemy S. W. of the Camp on the Ground w[h]ere S[ir] W[m] Johnson engaged and beat the Enemy in the year 1755 and beat them off several times.***

Twelve o'Clock we could plainly see from the Fort that the Enemy were throwing up an entrenchment and erecting a Battery at the distance of about 7 or 800 yards on a Clear Ground bearing N, B, W, Saw several large Boats coming to the Point w[h]ere the Enemy landed.

---

*The reinforcements sent from Fort Edward by General Daniel Webb included 823 Massachusetts provincial troops under Colonel Joseph Frye and 200 Royal Americans and Independents led by Lieutenant John Young.[21]

**The Marquis de Montcalm landed his forces on the southwestern shore at an inlet later called Artillery Cove (north of Pine Point), only about one mile north of Fort William Henry.

***The entrenched camp, located southeast of Fort William Henry, was protected by a breastwork of logs, stumps, rocks, six cannon and a number of swivel guns. The camp, separated from the fort by a swamp, was situated on an elevated piece of ground adjacent to the 1755 battle site and the subsequent site of Fort George. The majority of troops and officers, including Lieutenant Colonel George Monro, were in the entrenched camp for most of the siege. Captain John Ormsby of the 35th Regiment of Foot was in command at the fort.

Two o'Clock Monsr. MontCalm sent an officer with a Flag to demand the Fort but the brave Col^o. Monro rejected the Summons with Scorn.* The Remainder of this day was spent in Bombarding the Enemys works, Capt. McCloud commanding and cannonading. The Artillery fired Several Shot from the Camp which did great Service in beating back the Indians. One of our Balls fell on an Indian Hutt and killed many.

Tuesday [*sic*] 4th. Early this morning the Enemy's works were in great forwardness with a ten Gun Battery almost finished. Their Entrenchment approached towards the Fort thus. . .Saw several large Boats coming to the Point w[h]ere the Enemy landed from Ticonderoga: this day we had several Skirmishes from all quarters in which our people behaved with great Bravery, a mortar being pointed towards another Indian Hutt fell on it and killed Several. During this day we cannonaded the French Battery and threw a large number of Shells into their Entrenchm^{ts}. The Artillery at the Camp kept a Constant fire on the Enemy as they came to Attack our out Guards and Rangers who drove them off into the woods. The Rangers brought in an Enemy wounded Indian but he soon died.

Friday 5th.** This morning the Enemy began to cannonade our Forts with nine pieces of Cannon 18 & 12 pounders. It was some Time before they could find their mark. At Eleven they tried their Shells, mostly 13 Inches diameter, which fell short but towards the afternoon they got their distance very well, several of their Small Shells falling into the Parade[ground]. One of their Shott carried away the Pully of our Flag Staff and the falling of our flag Much rejoyced the Enemy; but it was soon hoisted tho' one of the men that was doing this had his head Shot off with a Ball, and another wounded. A part of the Enemy and their Indian [allies] advanced near our Camp on which the brave Capt. Waldo of the N. England forces [Joseph Frye's regiment] went out to take Possession of a piece of rising Ground near the wood on which a brisk fire [e]nsued on both sides. Col. Monro sent out a second party to Surround the Enemy, but they were forced back and the Enemy advanced up to our quarter Guard. Capt. M. Cloud brought his Cannon to bear upon them soon dispersed them. Here an unlucky accident happened, as some of our men were returning to Camp were taken for the enemy and fired upon by which Several were killed & wounded. During this Attack poor Capt. Waldo was Shot and Soon Expired. Capt. Cunningham of the 35th. Reg^t. was wounded in the right arm.

Saturday 6th. Last night the enemy carried on their Entrenchm^{ts} and Erected a Battery of 10 Guns mostly 18 Pounders about 6 or 700 yards from us bearing N. W. both of Cannon & Mortars. This was the hotest days action from all quarters; tho' as yet our Garrison remained in high spirits expecting Sir W. Johnson with the Militia and Gen. Liman with the N. England Forces*** to the number of 3 or 4000

---

*General Montcalm sent Sieur Fonvive, one his aides, with a message for the garrison to surrender and warned that "I have it yet in my power to restrain the savages and to oblige them to observe a capitulation, as none of them have been as yet killed."[22]

**The date was actually August 6. Part of the entry on this day is a re-creation of events over more than one day. The diarist's next two dates are also in error.

***Sir William Johnson had arrived at Fort Edward on August 6, with more than 800 New York militia, Mohawk, and Mohican in anticipation of reinforcing Fort William Henry. General Phineas Lyman and his Connecticut regiments had reached Fort Edward on May 26. On August 5 a council of war at Fort Edward presided over by General Daniel Webb decided that it was "Not practicable" to reinforce Fort William Henry, given the forces present at Fort Edward.[23] By August 12, after the surrender of Fort William Henry, there were 4,239 troops at Fort Edward with additional militia on the way.

men which we heard were on their march with some more Cannon. Would to God they were permitted to come as their Good will was not wanting. A party of Indians were seen advancing with great Speed towards the road that leads to Fort Edward which Confirmed us in our Belief of a Relief.

About 11 o'Clock Monsr. Montcalm sent an officer with a Flag with a letter that was intercepted by the above mentioned Indians from Genl. Webb wrote by his Aid-de-Camp M^r. Bartman to Col: Monro acquainting him that his Excellency could not give him his assistance as the Militia had not yet come up to Fort Edward, &c.* The French officer delivered another letter from Montcalm acquainting Col: Monro that he came from Europe and Should Carry on the war as a Gentleman and not as the Savages do but like a true Frenchman, both broke his word and Articles of Capitulation as will appear in the Sequel of this relation. During this interval the Enemy made a Sh[o]w of all their Indians, about 1200, on a rising Ground about 250 yards distance bearing S: W: which [while] their Engineers recon[no]it[e]red our old Camp Ground which was afterwards a great Advantage to them. As soon as their Officer returned they began their fire in good Earnest which we returned with the utmost bravery. This day we Split two of our heaviest Pieces of Cannon (vizt. 32 pounders) and our largest Mortar was rendered useless which was very unlucky for us as we could not be Supplied with others in their place. This day Col^o. Monro published his orders to all in the Fort that if any person proved cowardly or offered to advise giving up the Fort that he should be immediately hanged over the walls of the Fort and he did not doubt but the officers in the Garrison would stand by him to the last and that he was determined to stand it out to the last or as long as [his] two Legs were together.

Sunday 7th. The Enemy continued plying us very hard with their Cannon and Bombs while the Compliment was returned by us with all our Artillery, still hoping for a Reinforcement from Fort Edward. A Shell fell into the South Bastion broke one man's Leg and wounded another; Split one of our 18 Pounders and burst a Mortar. Several of the Enemys Shells fell near the Camp S.SE of our Fort about 400 yards distance and on a line with the fort from the Enemys two Batteries, so that their Shot missing the Fort could Strike the Camp. It appeared that the Enemy could throw their Shells 1300 yards. A Shell fell amongst the officers whilst at dinner, but did no other mischief than Spoil their dinner by the dirt it tore up. Another Shell fell into the east or flag Bastion and wounded two or three men.

Monday 8th. We now began to believe we were much slighted, having received no reinforcement from Fort Edward as was long expected. The Enemy were continuing their Approaches with their Entrenchments from the 2^d Battery towards the Hill on our old Camp Ground, where they were erecting a third Battery, which would have greatly distressed us: There were frequently during these last 2 or 3 days smart skirmishes near our Camp, but we beat them off the Ground. This night we could hear the Enemy at Work in our Garden, on which some Grape Shott was sent

---

*Under a flag of truce, General Montcalm had sent his aide, Louis Antoine de Bougainville, to Fort William Henry with a letter dated August 4 from General Webb (written by Webb's aide, George Bartman). It had been discovered in the coat lining of the messenger who had been killed trying to deliver the note to the fort. The letter informed Colonel Monro that General Webb did "not think it prudent (as you know his strength at this place) to attempt a Junction or to assist you till reinforc'd by the Militia of the Colonies," since a Canadian prisoner suggested that the French army numbered 11,000.[24] This number was an exaggeration, a ploy quite common to deceive enemy captors.

in amongst them, which had good Effect as it drove them off, however they had got their 3^d Battery almost finished by Day Light.*

Tuesday 9th. This Day the Enemies Lines were finished, parallel to our West Curtain in the Garden, Distance about 150 Yards. Col^o. M[o]nro, after a Council of War had been convened, wherein the Officers were of Opinion, that the Loss of our heavy Cannon vizt. 2, 32 pounders, 1, 24 pounders, two 18 pounders, one 9 pounder & 3 Mortars bursting would render it impossible to defend the Fort much longer,** as the Enemies Batteries had increased and our Metal failing us, & no help coming, wherefore it was thought advisable that a white Flag should be hung out in order to capitulate; which was done accordingly, and the firing ceased: The Enemy very readily granted the Capitulation: had Monsieur Montcalm been a Man of Honor, he would have performed his part; but instead of that such a Scene of Barbarity ensued as is scarce to be credited: After the Articles were agreed on & signed, the Officers left the Fort to a Regiment of the French Regulars who were ready at the Gate, thro' which we marched with most of our valuable Effects & Arms to the [entrenched] Camp and in the Evening three Companies of the 35th. Regim^t. had marched out & the other three Companies were on their march out of the Breastwork, when we received Orders to return to our Posts again where we remained till next morning.***

Wednesday 10th. This morning the Marquis [de] Montcalm being desirous of our being eye witnesses of how well he was able to perform his part of the Capitulation (see the 7th. Article), the Indian Doctors began with their Tomhawks to cure the sick and wounded.† They began to seize on all the negroes and Indians whom they unmercifully drag[g]ed over the breast work and scalped. Then began to plunder Col^o. Youngs and some other officers Baggage on which Col^o. Monro applyed to Moncalm to put a Stop to these inhuman Cruelties but to no purpose, for they proceeded without interruption in taking the Officers Swords Hats Watches Fuzees Cloaths and Shirts leaving [them] quite naked and this they did to every one they could lay hands on. By this time the 35th. Reg^t. had almost formed their line of March and the Provincials coming out of the breast work the French officers did all they could to throw them into Confusion alledging as soon as the Indians had done stripping them they would fall on and scalp them which thru them in a panick that rushed on the front and forced them into Confusion, the Indians pursued tearing

---

*A large rectangular garden was located west of the fort near the lake. The French placed their third artillery battery on the west side of the garden.

**Colonel Joseph Frye noted in his journal on August 9 that only two 6-pound cannon, one 9-pound cannon, two 4-pound cannon, one 7-inch mortar, and one 7-inch "hoitt [howitzer]" were still usable.[25]

***Captain James Furnis, an eyewitness to the events at the fort, recorded that "the Marquis de Montcalm thought it adviseable for us to march off by Night. We accordingly began to march about eleven o'clock," but the order was reversed by Montcalm since the "Savages[were] not satisfied with the Plunder they had got in the Morning, intended to attack us on our March."[26] Prior to the aborted march, Montcalm's Native American allies had entered the entrenched camp for plunder.

†Article 7 of the capitulation stated that "all the sick and wounded who are not in a condition to be removed to Fort Edward, shall remain under the protection of the Marquis de Montcalm who will take proper care of them and return them immediately after they are cured."[27] However, Jonathan Carver, a provincial soldier, later disclosed that some of the Indians "began to attack the sick and wounded" the morning after capitulation while Father Roubaud, a Jesuit missionary, had observed the Indians on the previous day butcher some of the wounded that had been left in the fort. One Indian emerged from a casemate of the fort carrying "in his hand a human head, from which trickled streams of blood."[28]

the Children from their Mothers Bosoms and their mothers from their Husbands, then Singling out the men and Carrying them in the woods and killing a great many whom we saw lying on the road side.* The greates[t] part and best of the plunder was brought to the french General. Our officers did all in their power to quiet our Soldiers advising them not to take notice but suffer themselves to be stript without Resistance lest it should be Construed as a Breach of our part of the Capitulation and those that were in the rear Should fall a Sacrifice to their unbounded fury. Those therefore that had been able to perserve their arms carried them club[b]ed. The French it is true had a detachm^t. of their men drawn up as is mentioned in the 1^s & 6th. Article of Capitulation but their only business was to receive the plunder by the Savages.**

Massacre at Fort William Henry from an old print. (Fort William Henry Museum)

*Colonel Samuel Angell, in command of the Rhode Island regiment at Fort William Henry, related the incident in a letter four days later. "When our people began to draw up for a march, the horrible scene of massacre then began by the savages [on] our sick and wounded men; next, by their drawing out all the black men, scalping the Indians, and keeping the negroes for slaves. All this did not satisfy them; but they fell to stripping and scalping without distinction; which put our men to the flight, each man for himself."[29] Captain James Furnis recorded that the officers and soldiers "delivered every thing up to them [Native Americans] except their arms and the clouths on our Backs," but "they took our Hats, and swords from us, and began to strip us...scalping many who were so unlucky to be in the rear or made the least resistance."[30]

**Although the writer twice mentioned that French officers received plunder collected by Native Americans, there is no collaborating evidence that this occurred. The "trophies of war" were retained by the Native Americans.

Notes:

1. Louis Antoine de Bougainville, *Adventure in the Wilderness: The American Journal of Louis Antoine de Bougainville 1756-1760*, trans. and ed. Edward P. Hamilton (Norman, OK: University of Oklahoma Press, 1964), 119.
2. E. B. O'Callaghan, ed., *Documents Relative to the Colonial History of the State of New York* (Albany: Weed, Parsons and Company, 1858), Volume 10, 606-7; See also Bougainville, 153.
3. Nathaniel Dwight, "The Journal of Capt. Nathaniel Dwight of Belchertown, Mass., During the Crown Point Expedition, 1755," *The New York Geneological and Biographical Record* 33 (April 1902): 65; Reuben Gold Thwaites, ed., *Travels and Explorations of the Jesuit Missionaries in New France* (Cleveland: The Burrows Brothers Company, 1900), Volume 70, 153, 155; engraving by Thomas Johnston (American Antiquarian Society).
4. *The London Magazine* (September 1757): p.n.a.
5. George Bartman, "The Siege of Fort William Henry, Letters of George Bartman," *Huntington Library Quarterly* 12 (August 1949): 419.
6. Seth Metcalf, *Diary and Journal of Seth Metcalf* (Boston: The Historical Records Survey, 1939), 9.
7. Stanley McCrory Pargellis, *Lord Loudoun in North America* (New Haven: Yale University Press, 1933), 249; Ian K. Steele, *Betrayals: Fort William Henry & the Massacre*, (New York: Oxford University Press, 1990), 106.
8. Joseph Frye, "A Journal of the Attack of Fort William Henry," Parkman Papers 42: 146, Massachusetts Historical Society, Boston.
9. Ibid., 147.
10. James Furnis, "An Eyewitness Account by James Furnis of the Surrender of Fort William Henry, August 1757," ed. by William S. Ewing, *New York History* 42 (1961): 313.
11. *The Universal Magazine* (October 1757): 183.
12. Frye, 152.
13. Jonathan Carver, *Travels Through the Interior Parts of North America in the Years 1766, 1767, and 1768* (1778; reprint ed., Minneapolis: Ross & Haines, Inc., 1956), 319; See also Thwaites, 179, 181.
14. Frye, 152.
15. William Cutter, *The Life of Israel Putnam*, 4th ed. (1850; reprint ed., Port Washington, N.Y.: Kennikat Press, 1970), 74; See also David Humphreys, *An Essay of the Life of the Honourable Major General Israel Putnam* (1788; reprint ed., Boston: Samuel Avery, 1818), 38.
16. James Montresor, "Journal of Col. James Montresor," *Collections of the New-York Historical Society* 14 (1881): 37.
17. Furnis, 314.
18. *Boston Evening Post*, 12 September 1757.
19. Stanley M Gifford, *Fort William Henry: A History* (Lake George, N.Y.: Fort William Henry Museum, 1955), 57-59; David R. Starbuck, "A Retrospective on Archaeology at Fort William Henry, 1952-1993: Retelling the Tale of *The Last of the Mohicans*," *Northeast Historical Archaeology* 20 (1993): 8-26; David R Starbuck, "Anatomy of a Massacre," *Archaeology*, November/December 1993, 43-46.
20. Maria A. Liston and Brenda J. Baker, "Military Burials at Fort William Henry," in *Archaeology of the French & Indian War: Military Sites of the Hudson River, Lake George, and Lake Champlain Corridor*, ed. David R. Starbuck (Queensbury, N.Y.: Adirondack Community College, 1994), 11-16.
21. Frye, 137.
22. Thomas Mante, *The History of the Late War in North America* (1772; reprint ed., New York: Research Reprints Inc., n.d.), 91.
23. Montresor, 39.
24. Bartman, 420-21.
25. Frye, 146; See also *The London Magazine* (October 1757): 494.
26. Furnis, 313; See also Frye, 151.
27. O'Callaghan, 10: 78.
28. Carver, 316; Thwaites, 70: 179.
29. Samuel Angell to Governor William Greene, August 14, 1757, *The Historical Magazine* 8 (November 1870): 259; See also Frye, 152.
30. Furnis, 313-14; See also Carver, 317.

"Major Robert Rogers and an Indian Chief." Engraving (ca. 1770), artist unknown.
(William L. Clements Library)

5. Robert Rogers 1758

During THE SUMMER OF 1757 Robert Rogers and most of the Rangers were involved in the unsuccessful expedition to capture the French fortress of Louisbourg on Cape Breton Island. After returning to New York in the early fall, Rogers instructed 55 British volunteers in what was essentially the first Ranger school. John Campell, the Earl of Loudoun and the British commander-in-chief, asked Rogers for a written set of rules involving scouting and forest warfare. What he received from Rogers was perhaps the first manual of war tactics produced in North America, one that would have a lasting impact on small unit strategy to the present day. Rogers' 29 "Rules for Ranging" has survived the test of time and place. During World War II his rules were resurrected, and the American Special Forces were given Rogers' original rules as part of their training for Vietnam.

In December 1757, after recovering from a bout of scurvy, Rogers was sent from Fort Edward with 150 Rangers to reconnoiter Carillon and take a prisoner. On the 18th of December, Rogers camped on the southeast shore of Lake George on the spot where Montcalm had landed his troops the summer before. Despite 15 inches of snow, the Rangers discovered cannonballs and shells hidden by the French during the siege of Fort William Henry in August. On December 22 Rogers encamped near present-day Hague Brook on the northwest side of the lake. On Christmas Eve the Rangers prepared an ambush along the road leading to Fort Carillon. After a lengthy wait, one lone sergeant of the French marines finally emerged from the fort and was captured. His interrogation revealed the troop strength at both Carillon and Fort St. Frédéric. Later, a French hunter was also captured and was used as a decoy in the hope of enticing others to venture out of the fort to rescue him. No one, however, appeared. While the French garrison fired their cannon without effect at the Rangers, Rogers and his men killed 17 head of cattle and burned five large piles of firewood.

In a bit of humorous bravado, Rogers wrote a voucher to the French commander of the fort for cattle that he had killed and stuck it on the horns of one of the oxen.[1] At the northern end of Lake George, the Rangers discovered "where the French had hid the boats they had taken at Fort William Henry, with a great number of cannon-balls; but as the boats were under water we could not destroy them."[2]

Meeting with Lord Loudoun on January 9, 1758, in New York City, Rogers proposed a bold plan to capture Fort St. Frédéric with 400 Rangers during the winter.* His scheme involved ensnaring French soldiers in sleighs on Lake Champlain and using the Rangers, disguised as French troops, to gain entry into the fort. When the gates were opened, the rest of the Rangers would storm the fort. The idea, however, was rejected by British officers who had their own plans to capture Forts Carillon and St. Frédéric.

In addition, Rogers' plan was not seriously considered because Loudoun had his own idea for a winter expedition. On February 2 orders were given to Major General James Abercromby, second-in-command, and Brigadier General George Augustus Viscount Howe, the intended field commander for the expedition, to destroy both Carillon and St. Frédéric. The scheme called for 400-500 Rangers to tramp down the snow with snowshoes to create a path for the regulars and the artillery train. When it became obvious that the plan would not succeed because of the severe winter conditions and the impossibility of lugging artillery in the snow, the blame was placed on Rogers for not having assembled enough snowshoes. In November Loudoun had ordered the Rangers to make two pairs of snowshoes for each man, but flooding of the Hudson River destroyed many snowshoe frames, and Rogers was too involved with other problems including his own illness. In addition, the Rangers had been busy building 300 "hand sleys" or toboggans as well as a large order of "ice-creepers."

The day after the cancellation of the expedition, Lieutenant Colonel William Haviland at Fort Edward ordered a scout under Israel Putnam to take a prisoner at Carillon. Unfortunately, Haviland, at the same time that he revealed the Putnam scouting mission, announced that an expedition of 400 Rangers under Rogers would follow. Rogers immediately became concerned that the French might take prisoners or deserters from Putnam's scout who could reveal Rogers' forthcoming expedition. One man, after getting lost, was found by the French. Although Rogers and others thought that he had deserted and would warn the French that the Rangers were coming, the French were apparently unaware of the expedition until the Rangers

---

*The reason for Rogers' meeting with Lord Loudoun in New York City involved an explanation for a Ranger mutiny on Rogers Island in late December 1757. After two Rangers were flogged in early December 1757, a virtual mutiny of the Rangers occurred on Rogers Island, adjacent to Fort Edward. Based on a confusing set of circumstances, the two Rangers had been implicated in the stealing of rum. The following evening, a mob of Rangers cut down the whipping post, a symbol of British regular army discipline, and tried to free the two men from the guardhouse. The resulting melee could be heard on the shore at Fort Edward by the post-commandant, Lieutenant Colonel William Haviland. Haviland, who had no great affinity for Rogers and his men, duped Rogers into sending over the suspects in the mutiny on the pretext of questioning them. They were immediately thrown into Fort Edward's guardhouse while Rogers was ordered to hold a court of inquiry into the affair. Rogers, who left a sick bed for the proceedings, warned of desertions if the suspects in the mutiny were hanged. Haviland, in turn, wrote disparagingly of the Rangers and urged a court-martial for the mutineers. As a result of Rogers' meeting with Lord Loudoun, the mutineers were turned over to Rogers who dismissed them from the service.

were actually in the vicinity of Carillon. However, in another incident, a servant of a sutler attached to the Rangers, had been captured by the Indians south of Fort Edward a few days before Rogers was to depart from the fort. Louis Antoine de Bougainville's journal, on the other hand, suggested that the French only learned of the Ranger advance from Indian scouts: "Sieur de Hébécourt, commanding at this fort, having been warned by the two Abenaki that they had discovered some fresh tracks, sent out scouts whose report was that there was a great English body marching from the direction of St. Frédéric."[3] One Indian at Carillon in a ritual of witchery earlier claimed to have learned "that they would see the English before long."[4] After that revelation, the Indians went forward to discover the tracks of the Rangers. The revelation, of course, could have come from a prisoner who had been tortured.

On March 10, 1758, Colonel Haviland ordered Rogers on the expedition to Carillon, but with only 183 men instead of the 400 previously announced. As his men marched out of Fort Edward, Rogers was uneasy, fearing that the French had advance knowledge of his operation. The expedition stopped at Sabbath Day Point before continuing northward that evening. Lieutenant William Phillips was sent ahead with 15 men on ice skates as an advance guard. After a false alarm of an enemy campfire, the men camped for the night on the west shore in present-day Hague.

The following morning, after a council of war, a decision was made to don snowshoes and advance northward to the west of Bald Mountain (later called Rogers Rock). At noon the Rangers halted two miles west of the small French fort, Contre Coeur, located at the northern tip of Lake George. In order to avoid being discovered, they waited until the day scouts from Carillon had returned to the fort. At three o'clock in the afternoon, the Rangers resumed their march in two divisions between Trout Brook and Bald Mountain. A mile and a half into the march, the advance guard informed Rogers that they had spotted an enemy party of 96, composed mainly of Indians traveling on the ice of the brook. The Rangers promptly laid down their packs, lined the banks of Trout Brook, and prepared to ambush the unsuspecting Indian scouting party. When the Indians and their French comrades were opposite the Rangers, Rogers fired his musket as a signal, whereupon a volley from the Rangers instantly killed about 40 Indians and caused the rest of their party to retreat quickly.

Rogers ordered Ensign Gregory McDonald to pursue the Indians; McDonald was then followed by Captain Charles Bulkeley and his men. In the meantime, some of Rogers' men began scalping the Indians killed in the first fire. The men were soon startled by renewed musketry. The Rangers who had pursued the Indians ran into the muskets of the main force of the French and Indians only 50 yards away. Rogers had ambushed only the advance guard of the enemy force. The main body, led by Sieur de Langy, consisted of another 205 men who had now turned the tables on the Rangers and had become their pursuers. In total the French force consisted of approximately 300 men: 250 Indians and Canadians with 50 officers, cadets, and soldiers from Carillon. As the smoke cleared over the icy landscape, Rogers found 50 of his men dead.

Rogers and his men then moved eastward toward the ridgeline of Bald Mountain, withstanding a renewed French attack. Ensign Joseph Waite's rear guard of 12

Robert Rogers and his Rangers prepare to fire on the advance guard of
French and Indians on Trout Brook. Painting by Gary S. Zaboly.

men was separated from Rogers' main body during the clash. In an attempt to rejoin Rogers, the detachment braved a deluge of flying musket balls. Only two survived.

The Rangers had now taken a position on a small hill or ridge on the west side of Bald Mountain to prepare for a renewed enemy onslaught (near the present Ticonderoga Country Club House on Route 9). Within a short period of time, the Indians with their Canadian and French companions attacked for a third time in a three-pronged assault on the Rangers' center and both flanks. At this point the Rangers began to discard their new green coats which provided a distinct mark against the snow for their adversaries. The badly-mauled Rangers again valiantly fought off their attackers. No sooner had the strike ended when a fourth attack was mounted against the Rangers. After learning from Lieutenant William Phillips that 200 Indians were climbing the mountain on the Rangers' right flank, Rogers sent Phillips to intercept them, and directed Lieutenant Edward Crofton with 15 men to take possession of the hill on the left flank. This last engagement was the most intense attack of the day and nearly annihilated the Ranger detachment. Yet the Rangers endured the onslaught despite an estimated loss of 100 men.

With 20 men Rogers finally scurried up the hill toward Phillips and Crofton. He and his men stopped and fired on their Indian foes. At this point, however, Phillips and his men were encircled by Indians and ready to capitulate. Phillips spoke to Rogers, suggesting that "if they would give him & party good quarters would Surrender to them, other wise would fight whilst one Man was left to fire a gun."[5] When Phillips gave up, with darkness closing in, Rogers decided to retreat to Lake George with his few remaining Rangers. Phillips and his men were tied to trees; many were hacked to pieces. There were only a few documented prisoners who survived.* The remaining Rangers adopted the Ranger rule on retreat and dispersed in many directions. Rogers and his men later reassembled at Lake George in the evening.

One question about the route of retreat has intrigued historians for two centuries. The story which has given "Rogers Rock" its present name suggests that Rogers was pursued by the Indians to the edge of the 500-foot, nearly-perpendicular cliff of Bald Mountain overlooking Lake George. According to the tale, Rogers threw his knapsack over the cliff, reversed his snowshoes and backtracked to an easier descent to the icy lake. When the Indians saw him walking on the frozen surface below, they surmised that he had been endowed with the "Great Spirit" and ended their chase. There is little evidence for the story, including Rogers' own journal, which does not mention the incident. However, a land petition of 1766 called the cliff "Rodgers' Leap," and Lieutenant James Hadden, with the British army in 1777, also referred to the landmark: "We passed Rogers's Rock famous for his descending a part of it with his Detachment (during the last war) where it appears almost perpendicular."[6] In the early nineteenth century, Horatio Gates Spafford, a distinguished member of the New York Historical Society and a newspaper publisher, wrote that "the bones of the victims remain yet unburied on the summit."[7] Rogers didn't write everything in his journal, as was the case of his note to the commandant of Fort Carillon in December 1757 which thanked him for the fresh

---

*William Phillips lived through the ordeal and eventually escaped captivity. Joseph Waite also survived, serving with the Rangers until 1762, and later with the New Hampshire militia during the Revolutionary War at Lake Champlain where he was mortally wounded two weeks before the Battle of Valcour Island in 1776.

Rogers Rock
(Photo by the author)

meat. However, this unusually bold deed surely would have been recorded in his journal if it had occurred. Nonetheless, the story apparently spread shortly after the war.

The survivors of the battle rendezvoused on the shoreline of Lake George where they had earlier hidden their hand sleighs (toboggans). Rogers immediately dispatched a messenger to Fort Edward for help. That night Rogers and the survivors remained at the lake without blankets or a fire. Rogers had no coat that night since he had thrown it down in the heat of the battle. Finding the jacket with Rogers' commission papers in the pocket, the Native American allies of the French thought that they had finally killed the famous scout. The next morning the surviving Rangers trudged southward on the lake where they were met at an island by a relief detachment from Fort Edward under Captain John Stark. They camped on the island that night. The next day, young Jabez Fitch from Connecticut recorded the arrival of the Rangers at Fort Edward in his diary: "About 3 o clock ye Party Began t[o] Com[e] in in Small Numbers—about 5 o clock I Se[e] ye Majr Com[e] in Him Self Being in ye Rear of ye Whol[e]—This was a Vast Cold & Tedious Day. Espacially for ye Wounded Men. . . The Whol[e] Scout consisted of 180 & About 40 Returned 5 of which were wounded."[8]

According to General Marquis de Montcalm, the Indians returned with "one hundred and forty-six scalps; they retained only three prisoners to furnish live letters to their father."[9] A later French report, however, listed only 114 scalps taken after the engagement.[10] Although most French accounts minimized their losses, the commander at Carillon, Captain de Hebecourt, in one letter related that "we had a wonderful result but it cost us dearly through the loss which we suffered."[11] Rogers exaggerated his estimate of the Indian dead at 150 with as many wounded. The Ranger loss, by any calculation, was very high with 124 killed and four men who later died of their wounds at Fort Edward.[12]

Several men became lost in the wilderness of the lake valleys following the battle and were taken prisoner six days after the engagement. Two volunteers from the British 27th Regiment at Fort Edward, Captain-Lieutenant Henry Pringle and Lieutenant Boyle Roche, and an unnamed servant of Rogers, spent a harrowing week in the freezing temperatures without food in search of a route back to Fort Edward. On the sixth night, the men exercised all night

Rogers' Rangers on Lake George from *Our Pioneers* by Augustus Lynch Mason (1904).
(Library of Congress)

to avoid freezing to death. The servant, unfortunately, sat down and died immediately. The following morning on March 20, Pringle and Roche surrendered at Fort Carillon. It was two years before the two officers were exchanged.

When the reports surfaced that the French had suffered only minor casualties in the engagement, Rogers came under some criticism. However, a letter by Henry Pringle from Carillon, dated March 28, 1758, describing the mismatched forces and the severity of the engagement arrived at Fort Edward, the negative assessment of Rogers' role in the engagement ended. On April 6, 1758, Rogers was promoted to the rank of major by General James Abercromby.

Later that year Rogers and his Rangers took part in the disastrous expedition against Carillon under General James Abercromby. In 1759 Rogers and his Ranger units accompanied General Jeffery Amherst on his successful expedition against Carillon and St. Frédéric. Amherst later ordered Rogers on an expedition to destroy the Indian village of St. Francis in Canada. The onerous journey with 190 hand-picked men was the largest Ranger foray of 1759 and one of the most famous. The fame of Robert Rogers was probably at its peak after the St. Francis raid since the story appeared in large type in provincial newspapers throughout the colonies. The account of the St. Francis raid later became the subject of Kenneth Roberts' book *Northwest Passage*. The following year Rogers and his men fought at Point au Fer and Isle-aux-Noix. In September Rogers was ordered by Amherst to the western frontier, where he presided over the French surrender of Detroit in early December.

Rogers' personal life and fortunes, however, took a turn for the worse after the French and Indian War. Financial difficulties, controversy, and imprisonment dogged him for much of his lifetime. To help cover his debts, incurred during the war in part for supplies for his men, Rogers unsuccessfully petitioned for a grant of approximately 25,000 acres on the southwestern shore of Lake George. As a result of seeking a commission with the British army during the American Revolution, Rogers' arrest was ordered by George Washington, but he escaped and served during the war as leader of "Rogers' Queens' Rangers." When hostilities ended, he made his way to England alone (his wife had divorced him in 1778) to a life of drinking and illness. On May 18, 1795, the old Ranger, who had escaped the musket balls and tomahawks of the French and Indians during his years in the Lake George and Champlain valleys, died a broken man at the age of 63 in a cheap boarding house in England. The following account from Robert Rogers' journal describes the Second Battle on Snowshoes (1758).

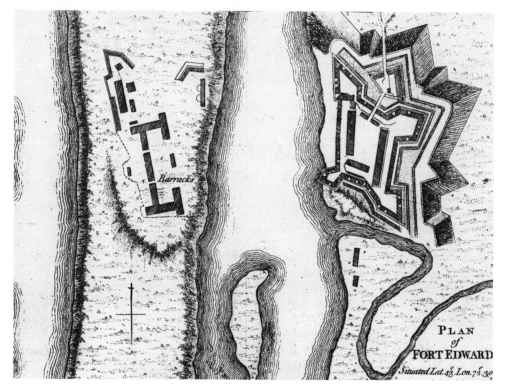

Plan of Fort Edward and Rogers Island (ca. 1765).
(National Archives of Canada)

Journal of Robert Rogers[13]

March 10, 1758. Soon after the said Captain [Israel] Putnam's return, in consequence of positive orders from Col. [William] Haviland, I this day began a march from Fort Edward for the neighbourhood of Carillon, not with a party of 400, as at first given out, but of 180 men only, officers included, one Captain, one Lieutenant, and one Ensign, and three volunteers, viz. Mess. Creed, Kent and Wrightson, one serjeant, and one private, all volunteers of the 27th regiment; and a detachment from the four companies of Rangers, quartered on the island near Fort Edward,* viz. Capt. Bulkley, Lieutenants Philips, Moore, Crafton, Campbell, and Pottinger; Ensigns Ross, Wait, McDonald, and White, and 162 private men. I acknowledge I entered upon this service, and viewed this small detachment of brave men march out, with no little concern and uneasiness of mind; for as there was the greatest reason to suspect, that the French were, by the prisoner and deserter above mentioned, fully informed of the design of sending me out upon Putnam's return: what could I think! to see my party, instead of being strengthened and augmented, reduced to less than one half of the number at first proposed. I must confess it appeared to me (ignorant and unskilled as I then was in politicks and the arts of war) incomprehensible; but my commander [Colonel William Haviland] doubtless had his reasons, and is able to vindicate his own conduct. We marched to the half-way brook, in the road leading to Lake George, and there encamped the first night.**

The 11th we proceeded as far as the first Narrows on Lake George, and encamped that evening on the east-side of the lake; and after dark, I sent a party three miles further down, to see if the enemy might be coming towards our forts, but they returned without discovering any. We were however on our guard, and kept parties walking on the lake all night, besides centries [sentries] at all necessary places on the land.

The 12th we marched from our encampment at sun-rise, and having distanced it about three miles, I saw a dog running across the lake, whereupon I sent a detachment to reconnoitre the island, thinking the Indians might have laid in ambush there for us; but no such could be discovered; upon which I thought it expedient to put to shore, and lay by till night, to prevent any party from descrying [discovering] us on the lake, from hills, or otherwise. We halted at a place called Sabbath-day Point, on the west-side of the lake, and sent out parties to look down the lake with perspective glasses, which we had for that purpose. As soon as it was dark we proceeded down the lake. I sent Lieutenant [William] Philips*** with fifteen

---

*Rogers is referring to Rogers Island in the Hudson River, adjacent to Fort Edward. Thousands of provincial soldiers, British regulars, and Rangers lived on the island. While the Rangers lived in rows of small huts, the British soldiers were housed in a large complex of wooden barracks. Beginning in 1991, a long-term professional excavation of the island commenced under the direction of archaeologist Dr. David R. Starbuck.[14] The archaeological dig uncovered the remains of tent sites, latrines, hut sites, fireplaces, a smallpox hospital, and thousands of artifacts, including musket balls, gun flints, nails, a large bush knife, a spade, a wine bottle, knives, forks, spoons, axes, and pottery fragments.

**Halfway Brook was an abandoned post between Fort Edward and Lake George on the military road.

***William Phillips, of Dutch-French-Indian ancestry, served with distinction at the First Battle on Snowshoes in 1757. From the rank of private in 1756, Phillips rose to first lieutenant before the March 1758 expedition. Phillips was forced to surrender in the Second Battle on Snowshoes but escaped late in 1758 while a prisoner in Canada and died in 1819 at the age of 100.

men, as an advanced guard, some of whom went before him on scates[skates], while Ensign [Andrew] Ross flanked us on the left under the west-shore, near which we kept the main body, marching as close as possible, to prevent separation, it being a very dark night. In this manner we continued our march till within eight miles of the French advanced guards, when Lieutenant Philips sent a man on scates back to me, to desire me to halt; upon which I ordered my men to squat down upon the ice. Mr. Philips soon came to me himself, leaving his party to look out, and said, he imagined he had discovered a fire* on the east-shore, but was not certain; upon which I sent with him Ensign [James] White, to make further discovery. In about an hour they returned, fully persuaded that a party of the enemy was encamped there. I then called in the advanced guard, and flanking party, and marched on to the west-shore, where, in a thicket, we hid our sleys and packs, leaving a small guard with them, and with the remainder I marched to attack the enemy's encampment, if there was any; but when we came near the place, no fires were to be seen, which made us conclude that we had mistaken some bleach patches of snow, or pieces of rotten wood, for fire (which in the night, at a distance, resembles it) whereupon we returned to our packs, and there lay the remainder of the night without [a] fire.

The 13th, in the morning, I deliberated with the officers how to proceed, who were unanimously of opinion, that it was best to go by land in snow-shoes, lest the enemy should discover us on the lake; we accordingly continued our march on the west-side, keeping on the back of the mountains that overlooked the French advanced guards. At twelve of the clock we halted two miles west of those guards, and there refreshed ourselves till three, that the day-scout from the fort might be returned home before we advanced; intending at night to ambuscade some of their roads, in order to trepan [entrap] them in the morning. We then marched in two divisions, the one headed by Captain [Charles] Bulkley, the other by myself: Ensigns [James] White and [Joseph] Wait[e] had the rear-guard, the other officers were posted properly in each division, having a rivulet [present-day Trout Brook] at a small distance on our left, and a steep mountain on our right. We kept close to the mountain, that the advanced guard might better observe the rivulet, on the ice of which I imagined they would travel if out, as the snow was four feet deep, and very bad travelling on snow-shoes. In this manner we marched a mile and an half, when our advanced guard informed me of the enemy being in their view; and soon after, that they had ascertained their number to be ninety-six, chiefly Indians.** We immediately laid down our packs, and prepared for battle, supposing these to be the whole number or main body of the enemy, who were marching on our left up the rivulet, upon the ice. I ordered Ensign [Gregory] McDonald to the command of the advanced guard, which, as we faced to the left, made a flanking party to our right. We marched to within a few yards of the bank, which was higher than the ground we occupied; and observing the ground gradually to descend from the bank of the rivulet to the foot of the mountain, we extended our party along the bank, far enough to command the whole of the enemy's at once; we waited till their front

*Rogers' original note: "A small party of the French, as we have since heard, had a fire here at this time; but, discovering my advanced party, extinguished their fire, and carried the news of our approach to the French fort."[15]

**Marquis de Montcalm reported Iroquois, Nipissing and Abenaki Indians had operated with his forces at Carillon.[16] The Native Americans in the advanced party were led by Ensign Sieur de la Durantaye.

was nearly opposite to our left wing, when I fired a gun, as a signal for a general discharge upon them; whereupon we gave them the first fire, which killed [about] forty Indians; the rest retreated, and were pursued by about one half of our people. I now imagined the enemy totally defeated, and ordered Ensign McDonald to head the flying remains of them, that none might escape; but we soon found our mistake, and that the party we had attacked were only their advanced guard, their main body coming up, consisting of 600 more, Canadians and Indians; upon which I ordered our people to retreat to their own ground, which we gained at the expence of fifty men killed; the remainder I rallied, and drew up in pretty good order, where they fought with such intrepidity and bravery as obliged the enemy (tho' seven to one in number) to retreat a second time; but we not being in a condition to pursue them, they rallied again, and recovered their ground, and warmly pushed us in front and both wings, while the mountain defended our rear; but they were so warmly received, that their flanking parties soon retreated to their main body with considerable loss. This threw the whole again into disorder, and they retreated a third time; but our number being now too far reduced to take advantage of their disorder, they rallied again, and made a fresh attack upon us. About this time we discovered 200 Indians going up the mountain on our right, as we supposed, to get possession of the rising ground, and attack our rear; to prevent which I sent Lieutenant Philips, with eighteen men, to gain the first possession, and beat them back; which he did: and being suspicious that the enemy would go round on our left, and take possession of the other part of the hill, I sent Lieutenant [Edward] Crafton,* with fifteen men, to prevent them there; and soon after desired two Gentlemen, who were volunteers in the party,** with a few men, to go and support him, which they did with great bravery.

The enemy pushed us so close in front, that the parties were not more than twenty yards asunder in general, and sometimes intermixed with each other. The fire continued almost constant for an hour and half from the beginning of the attack, in which time we lost eight officers, and more than 100 private men killed on the spot. We were at last obliged to break, and I with about twenty men ran up the hill to Philips and Crafton, where we stopped and fired on the Indians, who were eagerly pushing us, with numbers that we could not withstand. Lieutenant Philips being surrounded by 300 Indians, was at this time capitulating for himself and party, on the other part of the hill. He spoke to me, and said if the enemy would give them

---

*Edward Crofton was a British volunteer who had been assigned to the Rangers by Lord Loudoun after he had requested Loudoun's permission to engage in a duel with another British officer. Crofton later served with notable courage at the battles of Louisbourg and Quebec. In 1761 Crofton was killed by a fellow officer in a duel in Boston.

**Rogers' original note: "I had before this desired these Gentlemen [Captain-Lieutenant Henry Pringle and Lieutenant Boyle Roche] to retire, offering them a Serjeant to conduct them; that as they were not used to snow-shoes, and were quite unacquainted with the woods, they wou'd have no chance of escaping the enemy, in case we should be broke and put to flight, which I very much suspected. They at first seemed to accept the offer, and began to retire; but seeing us so closely beset, they undauntedly returned to our assistance. What befel[l] them after our flight, may be seen by a letter from one of the gentlemen to the commanding officer, which I have inserted next to this account of our scout"[17] Captain-Lieutenant Pringles' letter of March 28, 1758, to Colonel Haviland noted the overwhelming odds facing the Rangers: "it was impossible for a party so weak as ours to hope even a retreat."[18]

good quarters, he thought it best to surrender, otherwise that he would fight while he had one man left to fire a gun.*

I now thought it most prudent to retreat, and bring off with me as many of my party as I possibly could, which I immediately did; the Indians closely pursuing us at the same time, took several prisoners. We came to Lake George in the evening, where we found several wounded men, whom we took with us to the place where we had left our sleds, from whence I sent an express to Fort Edward, desiring Mr. Haviland to send a party to meet us, and assist in bringing in the wounded; with the remainder I tarried there the whole night, without fire or blankets, and in the morning we proceeded up the lake, and met with Captain [John] Stark at Hoop [Sloop] Island, six miles north from Fort William-Henry, and encamped there that night; the next day being the 15th, in the evening, we arrived at Fort Edward.

The number of the enemy was about 700, 600 of which were Indians. By the best accounts we could get, we killed 150 of them, and wounded as many more.**
I will not pretend to determine what we should have done had we been 400 or more strong; but this I am obliged to say of those brave men who attended me (most of whom are now no more) both officers and soldiers in their respective stations behaved with uncommon resolution and courage; nor do I know an instance during the whole action in which I can justly impeach the prudence or good conduct of any one of them.

Notes

1. E. B. O'Callaghan, ed., *Documents Relative to the Colonial History of the State of New York* (Albany: Weed, Parsons and Company, Printers, 1858), Volume 10, 703.
2. Robert Rogers, *Journals of Major Robert Rogers* (London, 1765), 74-75; Israel Putnam had observed one of the sloops on the lake in September. "From Albany we learn, that Capt. Putnam, and a Lieutenant of Otway's Regiment, are gone out upon a Scout to discover the Enemy's Motions: That Fort William Henry was entirely demolished: That one of our Sloops lies out in the Lake, at Anchor, in order to give the earliest Intelligence 'tis thought, in Case an Attempt should be by our People to take Possession of the Ground the Fort was built upon." *Boston Evening Post*, 12 September 1757.
3. Louis Antoine de Bougainville, *Adventure in the Wilderness: The American Journals of Louis Antoine de Bougainville 1756-1760*, trans. and ed. Edward P. Hamilton (Norman, OK: University of Oklahoma Press, 1965), 198.
4. M. Pouchot, *Memoir Upon the Late War in North America Between the French and English, 1755-60*, trans. and ed. Franklin B. Hough (Roxbury, MA.: W. Elliot Woodward, 1866), 100. See also O'Callaghan, 10: 837-38.
5. Burt Garfield Loescher, *The History of Rogers Rangers* (San Francisco: Burt Garfield Loescher, 1946), Volume 1, 367.

*Rogers' original note: "This unfortunate officer, and his whole party, after they surrendered, upon the strongest assurances of good treatment from the enemy, were inhumanly tied up to trees, and hewn to pieces, in a most barbarous and shocking manner."[19] While many in this party were killed, Lieutenant William Phillips survived.

**The Marquis de Montcalm noted only 8 Indians killed and 17 wounded with one Canadian and two cadets wounded. Captain de Hebecourt at Carillon, however, reported that the victory "cost us dearly" in losses.[20]

6. Horatio Rogers, ed., *Hadden's Journal and Orderly Books: A Journal Kept in Canada and Upon Burgoyne's Campaign in 1776 and 1777* (1844; reprint ed., Boston: Gregg Press, 1972), 104.

7. Barney Fowler, *Adirondack Album* (Schenectady, N.Y.: Outdoor Associates, 1974), 7. (original quote from Horatio Gates Spafford, *Gazetteer of the State of New York*, 1813).

8. Jabez Fitch, Jr., *The Diary of Jabez Fitch, Jr. in the French and Indian War 1757*, 3rd ed. (Fort Edward, N.Y.: Rogers Island Historical Association, 1986), 53.

9. Bougainville, 198; O'Callaghan, 10: 693.

10. O'Callaghan, 10: 838.

11. Loescher, 1: 387.

12. Ibid., 370.

13. Rogers, 79-88.

14. David R. Starbuck, *Rogers Island Archeological Site* (Fort Edward, N.Y.: Rogers Island Yacht Club, 1992), 6-15.

15. Rogers, 82.

16. O'Callaghan, 10: 693; See also Gary Zaboly, "The Battle on Snowshoes," *American History Illustrated*, December 1979, 19.

17. Rogers, 86.

18. Ibid., 91.

19. Ibid., 87.

20. O'Callaghan, 10: 693; Loescher: 1, 387.

Second "Battle on Snowshoes 1758." Painting by J. L. G. Ferris.
(Continental Insurance Company Collection)

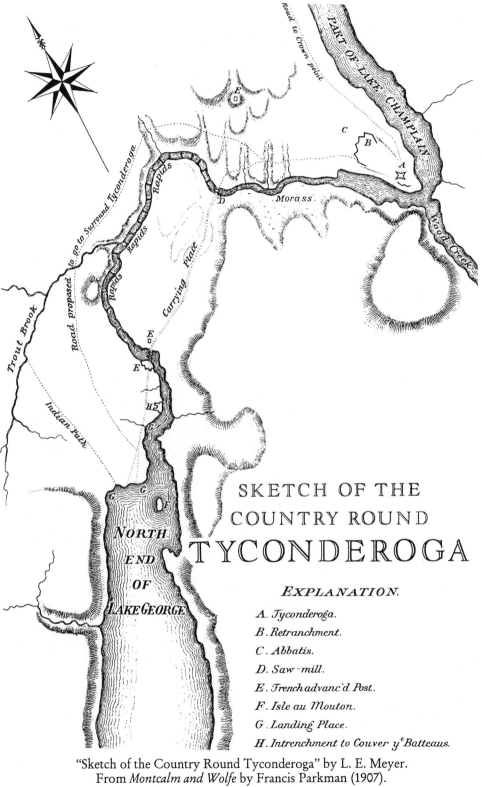

SKETCH OF THE
COUNTRY ROUND
TYCONDEROGA

EXPLANATION.

A. *Tyconderoga.*

B. *Retranchment.*

C. *Abbatis.*

D. *Saw-mill.*

E. *French advanc'd Post.*

F. *Isle au Mouton.*

G. *Landing Place.*

H. *Intrenchment to Couver ye Batteaus.*

"Sketch of the Country Round Tyconderoga" by L. E. Meyer.
From *Montcalm and Wolfe* by Francis Parkman (1907).

6. Abel Spicer 1758

THE SPRING AND SUMMER OF 1758 brought renewed military activity to Lake George as the struggle for the continent resulted in ever larger campaigns. The largest military expedition assembled to date in North America gathered at the southern end of Lake George under the leadership of Major General James Abercromby, the 52-year-old British commander-in-chief. An army of 6,367 British regulars and 9,024 colonial troops massed at the ruins of Fort William Henry in early July of 1758. The objective of the 1758 operation was to capture Fort Carillon first, which had by then supplanted Fort St. Frédéric as the most important French fortress on Lake Champlain. Among the provincial troops was Abel Spicer, a young recruit from Groton, Connecticut, who would write a highly interesting account of the battle at Ticonderoga.

In early July the immense army was transported to the northern end of Lake George in approximately 900 bateaux, 135 whaleboats, a number of rafts, and three small radeaux or floating batteries.[1] Samuel Fisher, an eyewitness, described the army's departure as "a fine Sight, it was very beautiful to See as all Set Sail for Tionterogae. . .fine Musick we had Such as french horns & c."[2] The optimism, however, was short-lived. After stopping at Sabbath Day Point on the western shore (present-day Hague), the armada renewed its voyage northward reaching the northern end of the lake early on the morning of July 6. Upon landing, Brigadier General Viscount Howe, the intended field commander of the campaign, set out with regulars and advance units of provincial troops and Rangers led by Majors Robert Rogers and Israel Putnam in an effort to outflank French defenders at the bridge over the outlet to Lake George. Late in the afternoon the British contingent encountered a 350-man French detachment that was attempting to return to Carillon through the dense forest. Although the British and provincial troops were victorious

in the ensuing battle and captured 148 French soldiers, Lord Howe was killed by the first shots of the engagement. With the death of Howe, Abercromby equivocated before committing his army against the French position.

This first engagement turned out to be a bloody clash that would critically delay the advance against Carillon. Garrett Albertson, a 23-year-old soldier in the "Jersey Blues" regiment, had accompanied the advance party and later related the mistaken fire upon their own troops which greatly distressed the young recruits. According to Albertson, orders were issued to return to the landing site, but

> the army got bewildered or lost, and parted in two divisions; one part on an eminence of rising ground, the other in a valley. Through some unhappy mistake they commenced firing on each other, which continued near a minute, and at length was stopped by a universal cry through the army, - "All is well! All is well!" I can not ascertain how many were killed or wounded; one poor fellow fell near my side, he was shot across his face, his nose shot away, he rose again by taking hold of a bush. "Poor fellow," said I, "you are badly wounded." He cried, "O, pray help me!" I replied, "I cannot, the army is now on the march"; then [I] moved a small distance, when the two divisions of the army joined together and ordered to halt, and lay on our arms all night—no tents. I do not remember ever to have felt greater distress of mind, than I did that night. I thought the hand of Providence was turned against us, in a lonely wilderness. "Oh!" I thought, "if I could but return again to my father's house! I would

Above: Attack by the Scottish Highland soldiers on Montcalm's breastworks, July 8, 1758. Painting by Robert L. Dowling. (Fort Ticonderoga Museum)
Left, above: Fort Ticonderoga today. (Photo by the author)
Left, below: French map showing Fort Carillon and Montcalm's breastworks on July 8, 1758. (National Archives of Canada)

never expose myself again to another campaign." However, the night passed with very little sleep, and at length morning came, the sun arose, and we received orders to march down to our batteaux on the lake, which we soon accomplished, refreshed ourselves, and lay there [a] great part of the day, then received orders to march for fort Ticonderoga, which we did, and lay that night in a place called the Old Saw Mill, about half way to the fort, and heard the French all night chopping and felling timber to fortify their breastwork, and they plainly saw our fires.[3]

The French army of 3,526 men entrenched themselves behind a long defensive breastwork of logs about a quarter-mile west of Fort Carillon. Relying on a faulty assessment of the strength of the log wall, Abercromby sent wave after wave of British regulars and provincials without the aid of artillery against the French lines. Abercromby's precipitous decision to attack the French breastwork was based not only on poor engineering advice but also on information from French prisoners who disclosed the expectation of reinforcements at Carillon.

Shortly after noontime on July 8, the British began their attack in earnest on the breastwork. Without an overall commander on the field of battle, the resolute troops tried to fight their way to the French breastwork, only to be shot or impaled on the spiked branches of an abatis of felled trees before the log wall. Most of the British soldiers never reached the log wall, but were killed by the careful aim of the French defenders. As the provincial regiments approached the battlefield, Garrett Albertson recounted that

The Black Watch at the French lines, July 8, 1758. Painting by J. L. G. Ferris.
(Continental Insurance Company Collection)

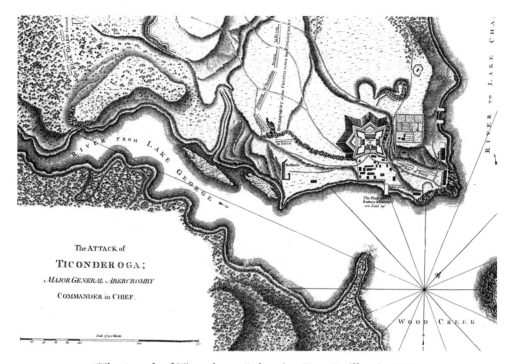

"The Attack of Ticonderoga" showing Fort Carillon in 1758.
From *The History of the Late War in North-America* by Thomas Mante (1772).

the bullets began to whistle round us, I felt a tremor or panic of fear, and I strove to conquer it but in vain; at length, I really thought my hat was rising off my head, I slapped my hand on my head to keep it down—I reflected hard on myself for my timidity—determined to march on, come life or death. When I came to this resolution, I cast my eyes and heart to heaven, and petitioning said, "Lord, if it be thy will, that I come off the field of action this day, thy will be done—if I fall, thy will be done—but receive my soul!" From that moment, I cast up my eyes and smiled—my panic left me—my hat settled on my head, and I felt calm and composed; such is the effect of resignation to the will of Heaven. Our orders were then to march on within gunshot of the breast-work, and every man to shift and cover himself as well as he could, behind trees, stumps or logs, which they did.[4]

Sixteen-year-old David Perry, who had marched from eastern Massachusetts with his provincial unit, experienced his first taste of battle at Ticonderoga: "The ground was strewed with the dead and dying. . .I could hear the men screaming, and see them dying all around me."[5] By seven in the evening, orders were given to stop the reckless bloodbath, but nearly 2,000 of the British and provincial troops had been killed or wounded. Panic-stricken by the defeat, some of the army left for the southern end of Lake George in bateaux during the night. Abercromby and his main force, however, did not depart until the next morning. Even then, as the men rushed to the shore, troops in bateaux were terror-stricken when they mistook their own troops for the French. By sunset most of the soldiers reached their original camp at the ruins of Fort William Henry. Three days after the battle, 3,143 French reinforcements arrived at Carillon. Montcalm's total strength, however, was still less than half the size of Abercromby's army.

The British and provincial troops remained at the southern end of Lake George for the rest of the year engaged in building vessels for use in future campaigns against the French. The troops built a sloop, two radeaux, and several row galleys at a "shipyard at ye southeast corner" of Lake George.[6] Ten days after returning from Ticonderoga, Captain Samuel Cobb, an experienced shipwright and officer in a Massachusetts provincial regiment, noted the beginning of construction of a sloop. The sloop *Earl of Halifax*, "51 Feet Keel, about 100 Tons," was successfully launched on August 10.[7] The vessel sailed on August 25 to the Narrows on her first of six cruises during the remaining season of 1758. Several row galleys and two radeaux or floating batteries were also completed. The largest radeau, named *Land Tortoise* in Colonel Henry Champion's wartime journal, exhibited a seven-sided configuration with bulwarks, or upper sides, curving inward over the crew to protect them from musket fire and boarding by enemy troops. The *Land Tortoise* was designed to be used with seven cannon, 26 oars, and sails. Since Fort William Henry had been burned by the French the previous year, the newly-constructed vessels were purposely sunk in late October by provincial troops for safekeeping over the winter. The vessels were raised for the 1759 campaign but, the *Land Tortoise* was not seen again until 1990 when the radeau was discovered intact in 107 feet of water.

The sinking of the radeau *Land Tortoise* on October 22, 1758, about which William Sweat recorded, "we sunk her once; but one side rise again, so that we were forced to work the chief of the night, before we could keep her down." Painting by Tim Cordell. (Lake George Historical Association)

Although plans were considered and rumors for a renewed expedition to Carillon circulated among the troops in the fall of 1758, the only military action during the remaining season involved several bloody skirmishes and battles with the French and Indians. One French attack occurred on July 20 at Halfway Brook, located between Fort Edward and Lake George, where a stockaded fort was garrisoned by Massachusetts troops. After a detachment of ten provincial soldiers was attacked near the Halfway Brook post, a deadly battle occurred when more than 100 of the troops who had left the fort to investigate the attack were themselves assaulted by a large force of Canadians and Indians. A second attack by 400-500 Canadians and Indians, under the leadership of St. Luc de la Corne, destroyed approximately 40 wagons and killed 116 men, according to Major Robert Rogers.[8] Rogers and Major Israel Putnam were sent by General Abercromby with 700 provincial troops and Rangers to intercept the raiders near Lake Champlain. The flying column left its bateaux on the east side of Lake George at present-day Huletts Landing and crossed the mountainside to reach Lake Champlain. Later a somewhat larger provincial detachment was sent in bateaux to the area around Sabbath Day Point and the eastern shore. Rogers and Putnam did not encounter the French forces and returned shortly to Lake George.

However, a few days later, Rogers and Putnam and a detachment of regulars under Captain James Dalyell were sent to South and East bays on Lake Champlain to locate and attack the French. In a line of march on August 8, the contingent of 530 troops consisting of provincials under Major Putnam at the front, regulars with Captain Dalyell in the middle, and Rangers under Major Rogers at the rear, was assaulted near Fort Anne (Wood Creek) by 500 Canadians and Indians under M. Marin, a Canadian captain. Rogers was able to vanquish the French war party in a battle that lasted nearly two hours, despite the initial advantage of surprise that his adversaries had. Thirty-three of the English party were killed and Major Putnam was captured but survived a harrowing brush with death at the hands of his Indian captives. There were immediate reports of "52 scalps and 2 prisoners" taken by Rogers' men and another 25 bodies of the French force were discovered a week later.[9]

Twenty-two-year-old Abel Spicer enlisted in a provincial company in southern Connecticut in late March of 1758 and sailed from New London on June 11 bound for New York City. He re-embarked from New York City on June 17, arriving in the Albany area early on the morning of the 19th. Spicer describes camp life at Lake George and the surrounding posts in his diary and recounts in some detail in two separate entries the extraordinary battle of July 8, 1758, between the armies of Generals Abercromby and Montcalm. He also relates other engagements that occurred in July and August, including a firsthand account of the French attack on Majors Rogers and Putnam near Wood Creek on August 8. In addition, Spicer's notations include references to the shipbuilding and other maritime activity occurring in 1758 at Lake George. A few of the more routine entries have been deleted in the following version of his diary.

Married in 1762, Abel Spicer raised a family of six children in Connecticut. He was commissioned a captain in the Connecticut militia on May 1, 1775, and commanded a Connecticut company at the Battle of Bunker Hill and during the siege of Boston. In Boston the British now faced American officers who had accompanied them as young provincial soldiers in the 1758 Abercromby expedition against Fort Carillon. Spicer died in 1784 at the age of 48, but his widow, five years his junior, lived until 1812.

While training in Ranger techniques, three British regulars replenish their canteens. Drawing by Gary S. Zaboly.

Diary of Abel Spicer[10] *1758*

Thursday, [June] 29. - We marched from Fort Edward at 6 o'clock in the morning and we had wagons to carry our provisions, and the rangers, part of them, marched before for a front guard and the remainder behind for a rear guard. And we had not marched exceeding 3/4 of a mile beyond the fort before we overtook a number of our wagons with whale boats and bateaux, which waited to be guarded up to the lake, and the front guard marched by them and they came after with our wagons. And here is great numbers of whale boats and bateaux along by the road where the wagons break and drop them.

10 o'clock we came to the Half Way brook, which is supposed to be half way from Fort Edward to the lake, where is a small picket fort which contains an acre and a half or two acres of ground, and here we made a halt and refreshed ourselves. And 11 o'clock we marched again and came to the rock called the Indian bounds, where they used to have their dances. 12 o'clock we came to the place where the English begun to retreat when the enemy first fired on them in the year 1755, and made a small halt and rested ourselves and marched again, and we came to Fort George at 4 o'clock in the afternoon and we marched round the end of the lake on the east side and encamped. And there was sentries set all around the regiment.

Friday, 30th. - We was ordered to clear a place of ground and to fling up a small breast work and to pitch our tents within it. This day Captain [John] Stanton's orders was broke about being a ranger for it was thought that he was acquainted with the woods enough, and all the Indians that belonged to his Company enlisted under Lieutenant DeQuipes for rangers, and four this day was taken out of his Company to go with Ensign Avery a bateauing to carry cannons and mortars and bomb shell and such like things.

Here is two thousand bateaux to carry such stores and provisions, and Colonel Broadstreet hath the chief command of the bateaux.*

This night after prayers the colonel read all the articles of the martial law to all the regiment and made a small speech upon it which was very well pleasing to the soldiers.

This day a man was killed by one of the company which he belonged to by an accident, flashing his gun not knowing it to be charged, but it was with a brace of balls which went through the man's body.**

This night the guard was alarmed by one of the men that stood sentry named Daniel Williams which was frightened and fired at a horse supposing it to be an enemy, which made a great deal of laugh for the rest of the sentry the next day.

Saturday, [July] 1st. - This day we heard that Louisburg was taken but with the loss of a great number of men. The news was something credited. There was such a flying story a few days ago but was not credited.

This day Colonel Wooster's regiment came to Lake George and encamped on the east side of the lake adjoining on our encampment.***

*Colonel John Bradstreet, an American-born regular officer, was in command of the "Battoe Service."

**Because of limited training, accidents involving firearms in the provincial regiments were quite common.

***Colonel David Wooster of Connecticut had served in the 1745 Louisbourg expedition and later became a general in the American Revolution, participating in the siege of St. Jean, Canada, in 1775.

This evening our sutler came in and sold rum for 6 pence one gill, and we was forced to give the Rhode Island sutler one shilling a gill, or go without any, for no other would sell to any but their own regiment. And this evening it was a general talk that the French had sent word that they would come and go to breakfast with us a Sabbath day morning.

And after prayers the orders was for every man to have 30 rounds of ammunition dealt off to him with what he had already got.

Sunday, 2. - Our chaplain preached to us, which is the first time that he hath preached to the regiment, and he took his text in James 5th Chapter and 16th verse. And we had a proclamation read to us this day that came from Governor [Thomas] Fitch which was to put both officers and soldiers in mind of the strictness of the martial law and begging of them to refrain from all the appearances of evil and keep God's holy Sabbath and behave themselves like men in the employment that they are now in and put their trust in the Lord, etc. And in the afternoon Colonel [Eleazer] Fitch's chaplain preached to us.

Monday, 3rd. - This morning was all the Connecticut regiments embodied and exercised and General Abercrombie* came out to see them.

Tuesday, 4th. - Had orders to march the next day by 6 o'clock in the morning, and we had three days provision gave to us, which was one pound of pork a day and one pound of flour. And we had two days provision by us which was dealt out to us before and we was not to have any more till the ninth day of July.

Here is supposed to be 20 thousand men at the lake now. About 6 thousand of them are regulars.

This night came in a number of Mohawks which had a great frolic of hollering, singing and dancing the chief of the night.

This evening Major [Robert] Rogers sent out a large scout to go before the army.

Wednesday, 5th. - We was all rallied by the beat of the drum and ordered to pack up our things and strike our tents and carry them aboard the bateaux. And we was ordered to prayers by sunrise and then to the bateaux. And about 9 o'clock we all got agoing. We carried two floating batteries and the men in general seemed to go on very cheerfully.**

Yesterday here was 20 Frenchman that had been in a flag of truce to Fort Edward and desired that General Abercrombie would guard them. And he told them that tomorrow he would guard them with twenty thousand men, and they was taken along with the army.

And we came on with all speed and made no halt but rode [rowed] all night.

Thursday, 6th. - About 10 o'clock we landed on the west shore and just as we landed here was 3 Frenchmen and a woman taken by the regulars and one Frenchman and an Indian taken by our Provincials. And the French that were encamped there struck their tents and put off as fast as possible. And we marched on as fast as we could towards the fort and before we had got a third part of the way we heard a firing at a distance, for the regulars, some of them, were before us, and Lord [George Viscount] Howe was before, who was killed at the first shot from the enemy, and

---

*Although Spicer and others often used the spelling Abercrombie, actual letters in the Public Records Office of London clearly show a signature spelled Abercromby.

**James Searing, a New York regimental surgeon, noted "three redeaus or floating batteries were prepared, two upon batteaux and one made of timber"; a newspaper report noted "two floating Castles with two Pieces of Cannon mounted on each, of four Pounders."[11]

the skirmish lasted about three hours and the fire ceased. And there was a great number of prisoners brought in and guns and lashed hats, but how many killed it was not known, but there was a great many seen to lie in the woods killed and wounded. The regiment was very much broken to pieces and some came in and some was lost in the woods, and came in the next morning.

Friday, 7th. - After the men had generally got in, we marched again and marched about a mile and was ordered in again. There is prisoners brought in every hour, almost, but how many of our men was killed or taken is not known, but it was supposed there was not many.

The chief that was killed was regulars and Jersey Blues.

About sunset we marched again and the regulars marched about two hours before and we took two brass cannon with us and we marched as far as the Ticonderoga Mills about two miles from the fort and there encamped.

Saturday, 8th. - In the morning there was a number of men sent after some more of the cannon and the whale boats and artillery stores and provisions and such stores and at the same time the engineer went with a guard upon a mountain against the fort to look and see if he could spy a good place to plant the artillery and he came back again about 8 o'clock. And when we came in we was ordered to stay there awhile and rest ourselves and the chief of Colonel [Nathan] Whiting's regiment was sent about 3 miles back after the artillery stores and provisions. And while they was gone Major Rogers fired on the French sentry and then our regulars was marching to the fort and they had two brass cannon on a floating battery and the rest was not got to the lake but came very soon.* But the regulars pushed on as fast as possible and marched up to the breast works ten deep and fired volleys at the breast works, which was as high as the enemies heads, and they had holes between the logs to fire through, and the regulars ventured very near the breast works and they fell like pigeons. And the highlanders fired a few volleys and rushed on upon the breast works with their swords and bayonets and killed some of the French in the trench, and the French fired upon them with grape shot from the fort, which killed almost all that had got into the trench, and them that was left of them was forced to retreat. And before that they had done this the chief of the other forces came up and fired and the French set up their hats just above the top of the breast work for to deceive the soldiers and hoisted English colors for a deception and the regulars marched up to go in and take possession and they fired on them and killed a great number of them. And them that was left behind and had not been in the fight was ordered to build a breast work and after it was built they was ordered to carry back their cannon.** And after all the men had got within the breast work, about midnight, we was ordered to take our packs and go down to the bateaux and we rallied all and marched off and it was very dark and the way miry which made a very tedious march but we arrived to our bateaux just as the day broke.

July 8th A. Dom. 1758.*** Saturday. - This morning after a tedious nights march Captain John Stanton with about half of his men and as many more from other companies that was a mind to go with him went with the engineer to the top

*Two hastily constructed floating batteries were built for the LaChute River but were later repulsed by artillery from the fort.[12]

**Some of the provincial troops had been assigned to the construction of a defensive breastwork adjacent to the outlet from Lake George.

***Spicer later wrote this second account of the battle of July 8.

of a mountain [Sugarloaf Hill, later called Mount Defiance] against the fort to view it and to see if he could find any place to plant their artillery to advantage.* And we went and stayed on the side of the mountain next to the fort where we had a fair prospect at the fort and the men at work. And we [could] see them drum off their guard and while we was there the Mohawks [with Sir William Johnson] fired upon them and we see them run into the fort and within their breast work. And after a small space of time they ventured out to work again and after the engineer had viewed the fort he ordered them all to return back again. And we got to our encampment at 9 o'clock in the morning and at the same time there was a number of men sent to the place where we landed our stores after cannon and artillery stores and whale boats. And they came back before that the engineer [was ready] and was sent back again for more stores. And when he got back the guard that went with him was ordered to tarry there till further orders. And the chief of Colonel Whiting's regiment was sent after stores and the Mohawks went upon the same mountain after we came down and fired and shouted to alarm the French and then came down and went to the fort and fired on the enemy. And the rangers fired on them which alarmed the French and this was before our artillery had got up except six small brass cannon and 3 cohorns which was brought up the night before and they had them on a floating battery. And then the rangers began to fire and then the regulars and Jersey Blues marched on as fast as possible and they had not [gone] above a mile and a half to go before they came to the breast work. And while they was going the French fired on the floating battery from the fort but did no harm to it. The regulars marched on and was ordered not to fire till they had orders and the French fired on them and killed a great many of them, but the regulars was not yet ordered to fire and the French loaded and fired on them again before they had orders which killed the chief of the officers belonging to the regiment that was in the front for they had nothing to shelter them but the open air. And they was ordered to march ten deep and the enemy had a breast work to defend them. And in the height of action the rest of the artillery stores was brought up to the place where we encamped and there was a guard set over it.

And the provincials marched after them but did not venture so near and they had a small wood to cover them and there was but a few of them killed. Some regiments did not go to the field of battle but was ordered to build breast works for fear the enemy would drive them back again and they should have no place to defend themselves. But the battle continued with a continual fire from 1 o'clock in the afternoon till night and the wounded was carried along, them that could not travel, and them that could travel went along back again, to the place where we landed. The streets was almost full all the time of the fight. And in the evening after the battle here there lay men, some dead, some wounded that could not go. The roads was so full that a man could hardly walk without treading on them. And after the fire ceased the men that was left came within the breast works that we had built, but I left before they came in. There was orders to carry back the stores and artillery and put them aboard the bateaux. And after they had got all within the breastwork we was all rallied and ordered to march off as fast as possible and we had but very little sleep for two nights before. The night being cloudy and in the woods which made it very dark so that a man could not see by the man that was before him and

*The artillery was never brought to the field of battle.

the path was very miry so that it would take a man in half leg. And every regiment was scattered amongst other[s] they being rallied in the night, but they got down to the place where they was ordered next morning. The number of the killed and wounded was about 4065 and wounded about 1730, and a great many of them was mortally wounded.*

Sunday, 9th. - We was rallied before we could get any refreshment, for we was exceedingly beat out, and when we had got off we was ordered to wait for the captain of the artillery and he waited for the regulars, and it was ten o'clock before they could get off, for they had their wounded men to take care of. And while they was waiting they was gathered in a large body they was alarmed by the rangers which wanted to get into some of the bateaux to come with us, but they did suppose it to be enemies, and if it had been undoubtedly they would have killed a great number of men. But it was not three minutes before that it was known that it was friends and they cried "All is well," and they took them in and we came to the head of the lake about sunset and unloaded the artillery the same night.

Monday, 10th. - There was almost as many sorts of news as there was men. Some said that they heard some of the officers say that we should go back again. Some said that we should go to Fort Edward and some said that we should go home again, and a great deal of such news. Some officers said they would never go back again, some said that they would be willing to if the regulars did not go. And the chief of the soldiers was very loath to go again and the chief of the officers held a council of war, but what was concluded upon was not divulged. This day was two men killed by men being careless in flashing their guns, but the law is very strict now against firing of guns or flashing.

Tuesday, 11th. - It was generally supposed that we should not go to Ticonderoga again, for it was said that the French had got to the place where we landed and entrenched and planted two cannon. This day was twenty men put under guard for their talk about their going again and about their officers. This day they carried their wounded men out of their tents into the hospital. A great many of them was almost dead with their wounds. This afternoon came orders from the colonel to the officers of the regiment to keep their men in some sort of exercise. Them that was not on duty to be embodied and to exercise the firelock twice a day and to sweep their tents and to keep clean and not to sleep in their tents in the day time.

Wednesday, 12th. - This morning there was a man in our regiment taken with the small pox and was immediately taken to the hospital at Fort Edward. And before night there was three or four of them sick with the same distemper and was immediately sent off to the same hospital. And the orders this day for tomorrow was for the men that was on the east side of the lake to spring their tents and encamp on the south end of the lake and them that was sick to be carried to the hospital.

Friday, 14th. - This morning we sprung our tents and took our packs and moved to the south end of the lake and encamped there. The men now grow sick very fast. There is not less than 9 or 10 that is not fit for duty. This day there came from Fort Edward a great number of wagons and teams to carry back cannon and mortars and shells, etc.

Saturday, 15th. - This morning I wrote a letter to Brother Oliver. The orders this day was for 2 men to go upon guard to go to work where they had talk of

*The actual losses according to Abercromby's official report were 1,944 killed or wounded, whereas the French had 374-444 casualties.[13]

building a fort and 4 men to get stuff to build a hospital, so many from our company. And this day here was three French prisoners taken and brought in which was supposed to be spies. This night orders came out for no man to sell liquor but the sutlers, which was customary before, and that all, both officers and soldiers, should strictly observe the Sabbath, them that was not on duty, and that they should dress themselves in clean clothes before they did appear on parade for the exercise of the day. This evening there came in an English prisoner that was taken at Ticonderoga and said there was 100 prisoners taken in the fight and they was well used by the French.

Tuesday, 18th. - This morning the men that was ordered for work was paraded at 6 o'clock in the morning and some of them was ordered to build a breast work and some of them to get timber to build a store. And we worked in the forenoon and it rained in the afternoon and beat us off from work. This day we had some peas dealt out to us, which was the first sauce that we had in all our campaign.

Wednesday, 19th.* - This day all the men was on duty that was not sick. Some building a breastwork and some hewing timber; some on guard and some [sent] to Albany to guard doctors' stores up to the lake. This day Colonel Whiting being not well and had been so for some days, he went with a guard down to Albany. And about an hour before that the guard had got to Half Way Brook they heard a firing that was a party of Indians that fired on a guard of ten men that went from the fort at Half Way Brook to guard a spot up to the lake and was returning and had got back within fifty or sixty rods of the fort. And the Indians shouted and fired on them and killed eight of them the first shot and they flung their tomahawks at the two that was left and killed one of them and the other got into the fort. And they sailled out of the fort, about 200 of them, and the Indians fired on them and killed the officers that was in the front and then the English fired on them and the fire lasted on both sides about an hour and then the Indians ran off as fast as they could and carried their dead and wounded, so that it was not known how many of them was killed, but they saw them carry off a considerable many. The number of the English that was missing was thirty, but there was but eighteen of them found dead and six of them was commissioned officers, and the men was all scalped except one that was killed close by the fort, and very much cut to pieces. This evening here was a man died which was the second which died out of the regiment.

Thursday, 20th. - This day there was another man died out of the regiment, which was the third. Our duty is very hard now. Every man is on duty that is not so sick as to be cleared by the doctors; some to build hospitals, some to build breastworks and trench, some to mount quarter guard and some to mount picket guard; so many detachments from every company every day.

Monday, 24th. - This day our duty was not so hard as it was for several days before. This evening after prayers General Lyman** and Colonel Fitch came to Colonel Whiting's regiment, he being absent, and Colonel Fitch read to them the martial law and General Lyman made a speech upon it which was very well to the purpose and he told them that he had two men desert from his regiment the night before and he said that he had sent after them and if it was possible to catch them they should be tried for their lives.

---

*The date was actually July 20. A number of provincial diaries also describe this attack.[14]

**General Phineas Lyman of the Connecticut militia served in each campaign in the northern theater during the French and Indian War.

Tuesday, 25th. - This morning at nine o'clock the man that was condemned was hanged and was to hang till sunset. And the man that did hang him was a regular and he was to be guarded down to Albany and to have five guineas gave him and to be freed from the regular service until he had aimed to enlist again. And he that was hanged did hang till sunset according to order and then was taken down and buried with all the clothes on that he had on when he was hanged, and that was a white Holland shirt and breeches of the same, black worsted stockings and a pair of turned pumps and brass buckles in them, and a white cap. A regular never wears a white cap only when he is going to the gallows.

Wednesday, 26th. - The chief of the men that was ordered for work from Colonel Whiting's regiment was to go to clearing a place to build a breast work on a small hill [Fort Gage] which lieth about 100 rods south from the southwest corner of the breast work that is round the encampment.

Thursday, 27th. - This day there was orders immediately to draft two men from each company to go [on] a short scout and after they had got them and paraded them they flung up about going this day but for to draft out some more.

Friday, 28th. - This day here was 93 men drafted from Colonel Whitings regiment for rangers and was paraded about four o'clock in the afternoon and they was ordered to keep in readiness so that if there should be any alarm they might turn out immediately. And in the night we was alarmed, for the French and Indians had cut off about 40 teams and killed 10 or 12 men and several women.* The chief of the teams had sutlers stores and 3 of the men that was killed was sutlers. And as soon as the news came the rangers and some more was drafted out of the other regiments and some of the light infantry and Major [Israel] Putnam and [Robert] Rogers went [as] chief commanders and in less than one hour from the time that we was first rallied we got our provisions and put aboard the bateaux, and got on our way.

Saturday, 29th. - In the morning, sun about two hours high, we landed on the east side of the lake [at Huletts Landing] and there we had our provisions and rum dealt out to us and marched off immediately to go to the South Bay. Sun about two hours high at night, we got so near to the bay that we could hear them fire and halloo as they was going up the bay and then we shifted our course to try to get ahead of them, and we travelled till night and then lay down on the side of a mountain, the ground being very wet by reason of the great amount of rain that we had before, which made bad lodging.

Sunday, 30th. - This morning about sunrise we marched on again, and just as we got on our march we heard the Indians halloo again and we marched on towards the noise, and about 8 o'clock we came to the place where they encamped and the shouting that we heard in the morning was supposed to be the time when they marched off, and they wrote on the trees that they had got seven prisoners and 2 of them was women. And they wrote that their scout was 1800 strong. And after we had been there a little while there was a man hallooed several times on the other side of the bay and Major Rogers answered him, and continued hallooing and two men swam over the bay to see if they could find what was the matter. But Major Rogers did keep hallooing to him and asked him why he did not come to the water side, and he said he was so weak he could not. And these men that swam over came back

*The raid occurred between Fort Edward and the Halfway Brook fort.[15]

again for fear that he was sent to lead them into some snare. And Major Rogers still hallooed to him to come to the water side and at last he got there and Major Rogers did climb into the top of a large tree and then he examined him from where he came, and he said that he was taken by three Indians at the Bloody Pond, which was between Lake George and Half Way Brook, and the Indians carried him away by the South Bay almost to Ticonderoga, and they all lay down and went to sleep and while they was asleep he run away from them, and they did not take his provisions from him and he had five days allowance when he was taken, and he had been five weeks in the woods and nothing else to eat but what he could find in the woods, sometimes goose berries and huckle berries and some sort of roots, but he was almost

British troops being instructed in Ranger tactics. Painting by Frederic Remington.
From *Harper's New Monthly Magazine*, November 1897.

dead and begged for help. And then they made a raft and brought him over and he was so weak that he could not travel and then they made a bier [stretcher] and we brought him about 11 miles and then we came to our bateaux [at Lake George]. And while we was gone the men that was left to take care of the bateaux was surprised in the night and thought that they spied some French bateaux and put back to the camps. And they immediately sent out one thousand regulars and as many provincials to the same place where we left our bateaux and we came to them at night, and we all encamped on a small island a small distance from the shore. And it blew very hard and it rained almost all night and in the morning there was several of the bateaux stove in by the seas tossing them one against another.

Monday, 31st. - This hath been a very wet month. We lay here this day till almost night and then we pushed off and came down to the island where the advance guard was kept and there was stopped about midnight. Some lay in their bateaux for the island would not contain them all. But what it was for was not known, but in the morning we heard that there was a number of Indians and French seen between Fort Edward and Half Way Brook and there was a large scout sent after them.

Tuesday, August 1st. - This morning by sunrise we all pushed off and landed on an island about 10 or 12 miles down the lake and lay there till about noon. And Major Rogers landed on another island about 100 rods from the island where Major Putnam landed, and they had their provision dealt out to them for four days scout and then they pushed off to the shore and the Major Putnam went on the same island and there was not provisions enough for them and they [were] sent back after more provisions. And they was not to go till the next day.

Wednesday, 2d. - This morning Major Putnam's men had ten days rations dealt out to them and Major Rogers had as much for his men. And there was about 100 of the regulars and about 150 of the light infantry and about 400 of the rangers and they got their men served with provisions and landed them on the shore and marched off about 9 o'clock. And they was drawed up in three columns when they marched and Major Rogers marched in the front and Major Putnam on the rear. And the counter sign for the scout was Boston. That was, if any man should hail you, you must answer Boston, and if you hailed anybody and they did not answer Boston, you must take them to be an enemy. And we marched till we came to a place where Rogers encamped with a scout about a month before, which was about half way from the lake to South Bay.

Thursday, 3d. - This morning they sent out two small scouts a little ways round to [see] if they could discover any enemy and to return in two hours. And after they had returned we marched again about South Point as we did the day before. And about 3 o'clock we came within about half a mile of the head of South Bay and made a halt. And Major Putnam went to the bay to see if he could spy any enemy and returned again before night. And then we came to the head of the Bay and encamped there that night, and there was sheds made of bark that looked as though they had been made four or five days.

Friday, 4th. - This morning it rained and had rained all the latter part of the night. And about 8 o'clock in the morning it cleared off and they sent a small scout round and one scout back in the path where we came but they came back and discovered nothing. And then we went upon a small hill which was close by the head of the bay and made a small breast work with old logs that we could pick up without chopping so that it might be done without making much noise. And Major Rogers went with his men and the regulars and the light infantry to Wood Creek and encamped there, which was about 4 or 5 miles from the head of the bay. This night here was one of the light infantry died that was left with Major Putnam when Rogers went to Wood Creek.

Saturday, 5th. - This morning Major Putnam gave liberty for some of them to go away some distance from the bay and build some fires but they had no liberty before. Here was some men sick that was sent back to the camps today and a few well ones sent to take care of them.

Sunday, 6th. - This morning Major Putnam sent off ten more men that was not well. And about noon there was a bateau came up the bay and was discovered and they put back again as fast as they could. And then Major Putnam ordered all his men to pack up and go to Major Rogers at Wood Creek, and we marched off and joined Major Rogers about 5 o'clock in the afternoon. And Roger's men spyed a

Israel Putnam and his Connecticut Rangers were involved in many battles in the Lake George area during the French and Indian War. In 1775 Putnam commanded the Connecticut troops at the Battle of Bunker Hill. (Library of Congress)

bateau in the creek. A regular spyed it first and hailed it and then they made off as fast as they could.

Tuesday, 8th. - Our officers shot at a mark thinking there was no danger.* And about 7 o'clock we marched off in a single file [this portion was so torn as to be illegible] and the reserves were near a mile behind but the rear wheeled to the right which brought us into a half circle and then we began to drive them. And Major Rogers sent a party of a hundred men for a small hill and the right flank to take advantage of the ground and the rest of them was in a half circle. And then Major Rogers sent off to Fort Edward for a recruit of men and then he hallooed to the French and said, "Come up you French dogs like men." And then he hallooed to the officer on the hill and asked him if he wanted more men, if he did he should have 500, which was to frighten the French. And they did not stand it but a little while longer but hallooed to get together and run off as fast as they could. The fight lasted about two hours but after they had gone off we buried the dead and brought off the wounded.** And about sunset the party from Fort Edward met us about half way from Fort Edward to Fort Ann and then the recruits carried the wounded and we traveled till 9 or 10 o'clock and then we halted and built fires. And they brought out doctors in the recruits and they dressed some of the wounds in the night. And two men died of their wounds before morning.

Wednesday, 9th. - This morning about sunrise we marched off and came to Fort Edward about 8 o'clock in the morning and carried the wounded men to the hospital. And Colonel Fitch took an account of all [those] wounded and missing to send by the post to be put in the prints [newspapers]. Out of Colonel Whitings there was almost half wounded and missing, they being in the front. There was not but one commissioner [commissioned officer] went from the regiment, and he was an ensign, and he was shot in the body with five bullets and one in the arm, and he was scalped and stripped, and but one sargeant from the regiment, and he was killed, and but two corporals and they was both wounded, one shot through the thigh and one through the hand, so that we had no officer left.

Thursday, 10th. - This day we intended to go to the lake but there was no guard going and Major Rogers was going the next day and we concluded to stay until he went.

Friday, 11th. - This morning here was 30 teams going to the lake and a guard of about 400 men to guard them but Major Rogers did not go with them as he did intend, for there was Indians seen between Fort Edward and Fort Miller*** the day before and he went out with about 4 or 500 men and returned the next day and discovered no enemy. But the men that belonged to Major Putnam went up with the teams to the lake and then the officers of each regiment took an account of the men that was missing and wounded and they amounted to about 40 missing and as

*Joseph Smith of Groton, Connecticut, recorded that "maj[o]r Rogers and another offi[c]or shot at a mark for a wager upon which the Enemy Discovered them and. ..ambushed them."[16]

**Robert Rogers reported "four different attacks; in short, officers and soldiers throughout the detachment behaved with such vigour and resolution, as in one hour's time broke the enemy, and obliged them to retreat, which they did with such caution in small scattering parties, as gave us no great opportunity to distress them by a pursuit; we kept the field and buried our dead. When the action was over, we had missing fifty-four men, twenty-one of which afterwards came in, being separated from us while the action continued."[17]

***Fort Miller was a post on the west bank of the Hudson River south of Fort Edward.

many wounded. All that went from Captain Stanton's company was Elkanah Morgan, Ralph Hurlbut and myself, and Hurlbut was killed in the fight.

Saturday, 12th. - This day here came a flag of truce from Ticonderoga and brought a letter from Major Putnam, and he gave an account that he was in Ticonderoga and one more commissioner and 4 privates that was taken with him in the beginning of the fight.*

Sunday, 13th. - This day we had a Boston minister preach to us for our minister was sick. And he that preached took his text in the 60th Psalm and 11th verse.

Monday, 14th. - This day here came in another flag of truce from Ticonderoga and demanded the ground that we was on, but he told the general if he would go to winter quarters he would, and he would try it out with him in the spring. This day David Crouch died, which was the first man that died from Captain [John] Stanton's company except Hurlbut that was killed. Here was today another draft of 1000 men from Connecticut forces for 7 day scout and General Lyman to go [as] chief commander.

Tuesday, 15th. - This morning there was a sargeant and 10 men sent from Colonel Whiting's regiment for 7 days scout, and this morning the flag of truce went back again.

Wednesday, 16th. - This morning the gunners begun to build a target to fire their cannon at.

Friday, 18th. - There was a Frenchman brought into our camp that was taken near Ticonderoga by a scout of five or six men.

Saturday, 19th. - This day in the forenoon Major Rogers took his men without the camp beyond the advance guard to exercise them in the woods to skulk and fire as tho engaged by the enemy. The General went to see them and several of the chief officers.

Monday, 21st. - This day the sloop was hauled off from the wharf and laid at anchor and ten four pounders carried aboard, and there was two more for to be carried and twelve swivels.**

Tuesday, 22d. - This day the gunners shot at [a] mark with their cannon. They fired five twelve pounders and five six pounders. About sunset the scout came to our camp with General Lyman, and they came from Fort Edward and they came there two days before, and they had a tedious time in the scout for they had rain half the time.

Thursday, 24th. - This day there was five men of the light infantry tried by a court martial for deserting and was condemned to be put to death, the 26 instant at 9 o'clock in the morning.

Friday, 25th. - This day all the tools that belonged to the King's stores was ordered to be returned to the stores, which made some think they was going to Ticonderoga again. And this morning Captain Stanton and Lieutenant [Robert] Miles [Niles] went to Half Way Brook to relieve the officers there. In the afternoon

---

*Israel Putnam had been taken prisoner by the French and Indians in the August 8 battle. Before reaching Ticonderoga, he survived repeated torture, including an attempted burning while lashed to a tree. He was later exchanged and served to the end of the Seven Years' War. During the ill-fated Havana expedition in 1762, Putnam was one of the few survivors of a shipwreck near Cuba. In 1775 at the age of 57, Putnam commanded Connecticut troops at the Battle of Bunker Hill.

**This was the sloop *Earl of Halifax* launched on August 10.[18]

the sloop [*Halifax*] sailed down the lake to the second island, called Long Island. And the wind died away and they dropped anchor there and came in the next day.

Saturday, 26th. - This morning at nine o'clock the criminals [deserters] that was condemned to be put to death was guarded to the gallows with their hands pinioned and the halter [noose] about their necks. And the minister prayed with them at the gallows and the hangman was a going to climb the ladder to tie the halter round the gallows and they read off their reprieve and they was let at liberty.

In the afternoon here come out orders to draft out of Colonel Whiting's regiment for Rangers one captain, three subalterns, four sargeants, four corporals and a hundred and ten privates.

Monday, 28th. - This morning it came out in general orders that Louisburg was certainly taken, and that every man in the camp should fire three rounds and the cannon should be fired.* And at five o'clock in the afternoon the sloop [*Halifax*] fired 16 four pounders. And then they was all passed, each regiment by themselves, all round the breastwork and fired three rounds, and they fired 63 cannon.

Tuesday, 29th. - This day they began to build the row gallies.**

Wednesday, 30th. - This day here came in a small scout that went from General Lyman's regiment and said that the day after we fired for the rejoicing of Cape Breton being taken that they was within a few miles of Ticonderoga and they heard fifty odd cannon that the French fired. And in the afternoon here came a French man to our camp and resigned himself.

Thursday, 31st. - This day here came a Frenchman to the camp and resigned himself in English.

Friday, September 1st. - This day went out a scout from the camp of 700 men and Captain Dill and the command and they was to be out seven days.

Detail of a "Line of Vessels on Lake George" showing the sloop *Halifax*.
(Public Record Office, London)

Saturday, 2nd. - This morning went out another scout of 60 men in whale boats down the lake. Here was a great talk in the camp that the enemy was coming upon us. And in the night a flag of truce came into our camp from the French and went off before morning.

Sunday, 3d. - This day Mr. Becket of Boston preached to us and after the forenoon service there came out orders for one man from each company to go with all speed to trenching and building a breastwork, for the talk was that there was a large party of French and Indians discovered.

---

*On July 26, the French forces at Louisbourg capitulated to General Jeffery Amherst.

**Samuel Cobb recorded that he had cut "timber for a Row Gally of 40 feet long 15 feet wide 5 feet deep to Carry 12 pounders in the Stern and 5 Swivels in a Side to go with 24 Oars."[19]

Monday, 4th. - This morning several of the cannon was carried to the breast work where the most danger was. And some to digging a trench and building a breastwork by the west corner of the lake. And all the men that was not on duty was all ordered under arms and exercised.

Tuesday, 5th. - This day they began to build a battery and to clear a swamp that was near the breastwork on the east side.

Wednesday, 6th. - This day they went to building the breastwork stronger and one log higher to fire under, for there was great talk of the enemy's coming upon us.

Thursday, 7th. - This day the regiment was all under arms to man the works.

Friday, 8th. - This day the sick was sent to Albany.

Saturday, 9th. - This day a party was going to Fort Edward and a sargeant advanced forward and was fired upon by a party of Indians. The sargeant was killed and one wounded and one supposed to be taken but he came into the camp in the evening.

Sunday, 10th. - This day a minister that belonged to the regulars preached to us.

Monday, 11th. - This day we was all under arms and fired three rounds with the cannon and small arms and built large fires on the mountains that was round the encampment for the rejoicing of the taking of [Fort] Frontenac [at Lake Ontario] and Cattaraugus [Cataraqui].

Tuesday, 12th. - This day the teams came in laden with provisions and swivel guns.

Wednesday, 13th. - This day the teams returned and carried off some of the sick.

Thursday, 14th. - Now 'tis a very healthy time for a campaign although there is a great many sick.

Friday, 15th. - This day they began to draw timber off the mountains to build a large row galley 50 foot long and 20 foot wide.*

Saturday, 16th. - These days here is great talk of our going to Ticonderoga again, as here is such talk very often, but 'tis little regarded and sometime before here is as big talk of the enemies coming on us.

Wednesday, 20th. - This day they went to turning the water out of the bateaux to ca[u]lk them. They was filled with water a few days before.

Thursday, 21st. - This day the details was for more men than there was in the regiment that was well and off from duty.

Friday, 22d. - This day they relieved the men at the Half Way Brook, which they do once a fortnight. And in the afternoon there was a man killed by a tree falling on him.

Saturday, 23d. - This day there was a small scout of men sent out for seven days from our regiment.

Sunday, 24th. - This day we went to Colonel [Ebenezer] Nichols' regiment to [a] meeting, for our minister was gone home. And in the afternoon Major Rogers went with 200 men up the lake. And in the afternoon here was a Frenchman came to our camp and resigned himself to the English, and he said that he run away from a small scout.

*This vessel was actually the radeau *Land Tortoise* which Samuel Cobb recorded as "50 foot Long 19 Wide 6 Deep....with 26 Oars."[20]

Monday, 25th. - This day there was a small scout went after Rogers, and the Frenchman that came in the day before went with them.

Tuesday, 26th. - This day the sick was viewed to see which the doctor thought unfit for duty.

Wednesday, 27th. - This day it came out in general orders for no fires to be made in the camps from 8 o'clock in the morning till sunset, and regimental orders that every man that was well should turn out at the beating of the reveille and wash their face and hands and then exercise till prayers.

Thursday, 28th. - This day the sick was reviewed by the regular doctor to send some of them home, but there was but two out of the whole regiment that was released and there was a hundred odd that was reviewed.

Friday, 29th. - This day Roger's scout came in and brought two bark canoes that the Frenchman that was with them told them of. And this day Elkanah Morgan died.

Saturday, 30th. - This day Major Hall came to the camps to see what was the reason the sick was not sent off faster.

Sunday, October 1st. - This day here came in several of the old militia to see their friends.

Monday, 2d. - This day there was a great many more of the sick sent off than ever there had been at once before.

Tuesday, 3rd. - This day they cut poles to carry the bateaux and drew one of the row gallies out of the lake and loaded it on a pair of wheels.

Wednesday, 4th. - This day Colonel Broadstreet's [Bradstreet's] regiment came to the camps.

Thursday, 5th. - This day the island guard was called in and the men for work was ordered to mending the highway between Half Way Brook and the lake. And in the evening General [Jeffery] Amherst came to the camps and several of his officers.

Friday, 6th. - This day all the whole army that was not on duty was drawn up for the general to view.*

Saturday, 7th. - This day the Half Way Brook was relieved and the general went off with the party that was going to relieve Half Way Brook.

Sunday, 8th. - This day they carried back the row galley that they had mounted on wheels and put it into the lake again.

Monday, 9th. - This day all the sick was viewed by the regular doctor, and by his order they was to be carried off as fast as they could get carriage for them.

Tuesday, 10th. - This day there was several wagon loads of the sick went off.

Wednesday, 11th. - This day the general's order was for every man that was cleared by the doctor might go home if they could travel and if not they should go [in] the first carriage that could be had for them.

Thursday, 12th. - This day Colonel [Samuel] Coit's son came to our camp to bring a horse for his father to ride home, and the Hampshire regiment went off.

Friday, 13th. - This day the cannon balls and shells was carried up from the lake and laid in heaps for the teams to carry off.

Saturday, 14th. - This day they moved the cannon so that the teams might come at them handy.

*General Jeffery Amherst, fresh from his victory at Louisbourg on Cape Breton Island (Nova Scotia), reviewed the troops with Abercromby and decided with other officers that an attempt against Carillon was not possible at that time.

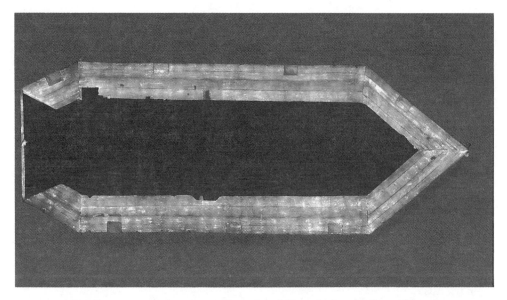

The discovery of the 1758 radeau *Land Tortoise* in 107 feet of water.

Above: Partially funded by a grant from the Lake Champlain Basin Program, Bateaux Below completed the first seamless photomosaic of a shipwreck. The photomosaic, made from 200 color photographic images, shows an overhead view of the upper bulwarks of the vessel. Photographer, Robert Benway; computer assembler, Kendrick McMahan; project director, Joseph Zarzynski. (Bateaux Below, Inc.)

Below: Starboard bow. The vessel is presently protected in a New York State Submerged Heritage Preserve. (Photo by the author)

Right: Port stern section. (Photo by the author)

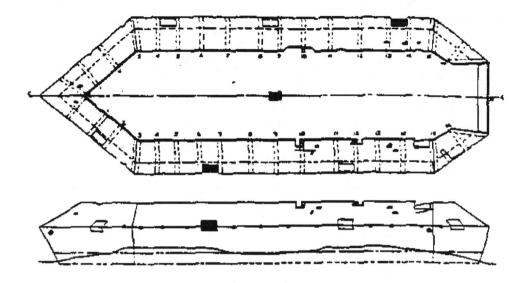

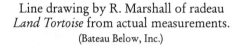

Line drawing by R. Marshall of radeau
Land Tortoise from actual measurements.
(Bateau Below, Inc.)

Sunday, 15th. - This day Colonel Broadstreet's [Bradstreet's] men began to haul the bateaux out of the lake for the wagons to carry off. And in the evening here came 100 ox teams and several wagons.

Monday, 16th. - This day they carried off some of the cannon and hoyts [howitzers] and mortars and artillery stores, and Colonel Hart's regiment marched off with them. And in the evening there came in 1020 wagons.

Tuesday, 17th. - This day the wagons carried off bateaux and they left them at Half Way Brook and Colonel Broadstreet's [Bradstreet's] men went off with them to get them into the river. And Colonel Wooster's [regiment] marched off in the afternoon. And in the evening the same wagons came in and several more and several ox teams.

Wednesday, 18th. - This day they carried off more bateaux and cannon.

Thursday, 19th. - This day Colonel [Jonathan] Bagley's regiment was ordered to be at a minutes warning to load the teams and wagons and to do no other duty.

Friday, 20th. - This day they stripped the sloop [*Halifax*]. And in the evening Major Rogers with sixty men took a number of whale boats and went down the lake.

Saturday, 21. - This morning he took all the whale boats but one and run up into a creek and hauled them up ashore and he lay there and sent back for the rest of them and they was brought in the evening.

Sunday, 22d. - This day they hid all the whale boats and came home by land.

Monday, 23d. - This day they finished carrying off the bateaux, all that was not to be sunk, and buried the sloops guns and rigging.

Tuesday, 24th. - This day they finished sinking the bateaux and sank the sloop and the row gallies and buried the bateau oars and a great deal of their treasure [equipment].*

Wednesday, 25th. - This day all the army was to leave the lake and all got in readiness to march off, but there was not carriage[s] enough to carry their baggage and provision, and by that means there was not but half of them went off.

Thursday, 26th. - This morning they buried some of the provision and carried off the rest and one regular regiment marched off. And in the afternoon there came a flag of truce from Ticonderoga and they went off in the night back again.

Friday, 27th. - This day every man left the lake and some of the regulars was stopped at Half Way Brook and the rest of them at the falls which is half way between Half Way Brook and Fort Edward. and Colonel Whiting and Lyman encamped about half way between the regulars.

Sunken French and Indian War bateau on the southeastern shore of Lake George. One of seven bateaux protected in a New York State Submerged Heritage Preserve.
(Photo by the author)

*Without a garrisoned fort at the southern end of the lake to protect the vessels during the winter, the *Land Tortoise*, *Halifax*, row galleys, whaleboats, and 260 bateaux were sunk with retrieval planned for the 1759 campaign.[21]

Notes

1. *Boston Gazette and Country Journal*, 20 November 1758; See also William Sweat, "Captain William Sweat's Personal Diary of the Expedition Against Ticonderoga," *The Essex Institute Historical Collections* 93 (1957): 42; James Searing, "The Battle of Ticonderoga, 1758," *Proceedings of the New York Historical Society* 5 (1847): 113; Melancthon Taylor Woolsey, *Letters of Melancthon Taylor Woolsey* (Champlain, N.Y.: Moorsfield Press, 1927), 12; *New-York Mercury*, 24 July 1758; For an excellent discussion of the logistical and political problems that plagued the Abercromby expedition see M. John Cardwell, "Mismanagement: The 1758 British Expedition Against Carillon," *The Bulletin of the Fort Ticonderoga Museum* 15 (1992): 237-91.
2. Samuel Fisher, "Diary of Operations Around Lake George 1758," MS, Library of Congress.
3. Garrett Albertson, "A Short Account of the Life and Travels and Adventures of Garrett Albertson, Sr.," *The Bulletin of the Fort Ticonderoga Museum* 4 (July 1936): 44-45.
4. Albertson, 45-46.
5. David Perry, "Recollections of an Old Soldier," *The Bulletin of the Fort Ticonderoga Museum* 14 (Summer 1981): 6.
6. Henry Champion, "The Journal of Colonel Henry Champion," in *Champion Genealogy*, by Francis Bacon Trowbridge (New Haven, CT.: F. B. Trowbridge, 1891), 420; See original "Accounts & Journal of Captain Henry Champion of Colchester, Campaign of 1758," Connecticut State Library, Hartford, CT.
7. *Boston Gazette and Country Journal*, 28 August 1758; *New-York Mercury* 11 September 1758; Samuel Cobb, "The Journal of Captain Samuel Cobb," *The Bulletin of the Fort Ticonderoga Museum* 14 (Summer 1981): 23; Cobb's journal was first published in 1871 with a notation that the author was unknown, see "Journal of a Provincial Officer, in the Campaign, in Northern New York, in 1758," *The Historical Magazine* 10 (July 1871): 113-22.
8. Robert Rogers, *Journals of Major Robert Rogers* (1765; reprint ed., Ann Arbor, MI.: University Microfilms, Inc., 1966), 117; Other sources indicate that 80 scalps and 64 prisoners were taken; See Koert DuBois Burnham and David Kendall Martin, *La Corne St. Luc - His Flame* (Keeseville, N.Y.: The Northern New York American-Canadian Genealogical Society, 1991), 57.
9. Thomas Alexander, "Ens. Alexander's Diary," in *History of Northfield, Massachusetts*, by J. H. Temple and George Sheldon (Albany: Joel Munsell, 1875), 304; Leonard Spaulding, "French and Indian War Record," in *The Vermont Historical Gazetteer*, Volume 5, ed. by Abby Maria Hemenway (Brandon, VT.: Carrie E. H. Page, 1891), 28; Caleb Rea, "The Journal of Dr. Caleb Rea, Written During the Expedition Against Ticonderoga in 1758," *The Essex Institute Historical Collections* 18 (1881): 180.
10. Abel Spicer, "Diary of Abel Spicer," in *History of the Descendants of Peter Spicer*, comp. by Susan Spicer Meech and Susan Billings Meech (Boston: F. H. Gilson, 1911), 390-406.
11. Searing, 113; *New-York Mercury*, 24 July 1758.
12. E. C. Dawes, ed., *Journal of Gen. Rufus Putnam 1757-1760* (Albany: Joel Munsell's Sons, 1886), 69.
13. Gertrude Selwyn Kimball, ed., *Correspondence of William Pitt* (New York: The Macmillan Company, 1906), Volume 1, 300; See also Public Records Office, London, 272, 34/30, fol. 23; *The London Magazine* (August 1758): 427; *The Scots Magazine* (August 1758): 437; *The Universal Magazine* (August 1758): 97; E. B. O'Callaghan, ed., *Documents Relative to the Colonial History of the State of New York* (Albany: Weed, Parsons and Company, 1858), Volume 10, 744; Louis Antoine de Bougainville, *Adventure in the Wilderness: The American Journal of Louis Antoine de Bougainville 1756-1760*, trans. and ed. Edward P. Hamilton (Norman, OK.: University of Oklahoma Press, 1964), 236.
14. Asa Foster, "Diary of Capt. Asa Foster of Andover, Mass," *New-England Historical and Genealogical Register* 213 (1900): 185; Lemuel Lyon, "Military Journal for 1758," in *The Military Journals of Two Private Soldiers, 1758-1775*, by Abraham Tomlinson (1854; reprint ed., New York: Books for Libraries Press, 1970), 25; Joseph Holt, "Journals of Joseph Holt, of Wilton, N.H.," *New-England Historical and Genealogical Register* 10 (January 1856): 308; Archelaus Fuller, "Journal of Col. Archelaus Fuller of Middleton, Mass., in the Expedition Against Ticonderoga in 1758," *The Essex Institute Historical Collections* 46 (1910): 216; Joseph Smith, "Journal of Joseph Smith, of Groton," *Connecticut Society of Colonial Wars Proceedings* 1 (1896): 307; Alexander, 304; Sweat, 45; Bougainville, 245.

15. See also Sweat, 45; Samuel Thompson, *Diary of Lieut. Samuel Thompson*, ed. by William R. Cutter (Boston: Press of David Clapp & Son, 1896), 13; Fuller, 216; Holt 308; Lyon, 26; Smith, 307-8; Foster, 185; Bougainville, 253; Champion, 422.

16. Smith, 308; See also a French report in O'Callaghan, 10: 851.

17. Rogers, 118-19; See also Smith 308; Alexander, 304; Lyon 26-27.

18. *Boston Gazette and Country Journal*, 28 August 1758; See also Benjamin Glasier, "French and Indian War Diary of Benjamin Glasier of Ipswich 1758-1760," *The Essex Institute of Historical Collections* 86 (1950): 80; Cobb, 23; Rea 178; Holt, 309; Sweat, 46.

19. Cobb, 24; See also Glasier, 81; Rea 184, 186; Joseph Nichols, "Joseph Nichols Military Journal 1758-59," MS, Henry E. Huntington Library, HM 89, 74.

20. Cobb, 30; See also Rea 199; Champion, 431; Christopher Comstock, "Diary of Christopher Comstock 1758-59," MS, Connecticut Historical Society.

21. Cobb, 30; Rea, 204; Sweat, 54; Thompson, 18; Champion, 433; John Noyes, "Journal of John Noyes of Newbury in the Expedition Against Ticonderoga, 1758," *The Essex Institute Historical Collections* 45 (1909): 76; Public Records Office, London, 160, 34/57-58, fol. 17.

One of three French and Indian War bateaux raised in 1960.
(Photo by Richard K. Dean)

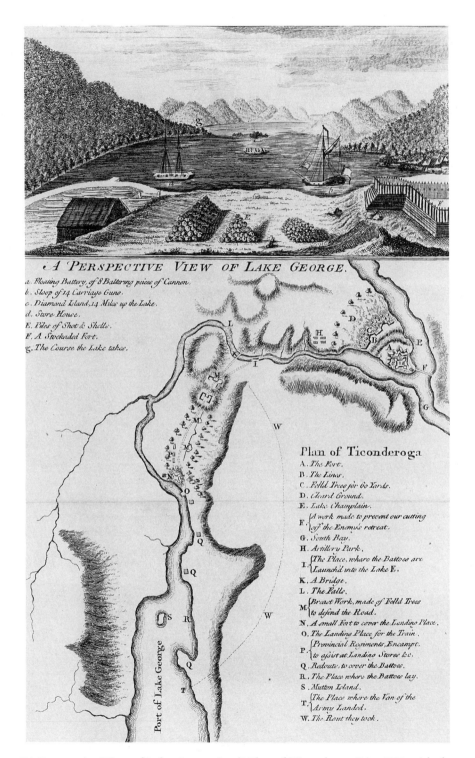

"A Perspective View of Lake George [and] Plan of Ticonderoga" in 1759 with the radeau *Invincible* and sloop *Halifax*. Drawing by Captain-Lieutenant Henry Skinner, published in the November 1759 issue of *The Universal Magazine*. (Library of Congress)

7. Lemuel Wood 1759

FOLLOWING a second year's formidable task of raising and equipping a large army for the Lake George - Lake Champlain campaign, over 10,000 soldiers gathered at the southern end of Lake George in preparation for a renewed expedition against Fort Carillon. Under the competent leadership of the new British commander-in-chief, Major General Jeffery Amherst, assaults were methodically planned on Forts Carillon and St. Frédéric and from there a push onward to Canada during the 1759 season. The Massachusetts contingent at Lake George included seventeen-year-old Lemuel Wood, a keen observer of the day-to-day activities of the Amherst expedition.

While Quebec City was under siege by British forces led by Brigadier General James Wolfe, the undermanned garrisons at Carillon and St. Frédéric anxiously awaited Amherst's offensive. After the assembly of 6,537 British regulars and 4,839 provincial troops at Fort Edward, Amherst departed with his army for Lake George on June 21. Marching in two formal columns of regulars and provincials with the Rangers and light infantry as the advance guard, the army employed elaborate precautions against a possible French ambush.

At Lake George, Amherst met with his chief engineer on June 22 to decide on the site for a new fort at the lake. During the 1759 campaign a series of stockaded forts and outposts were also constructed between Fort Edward and Lake George to deter French ambushes and provide way stations for transporting provisions: Four-Mile Post was the closest to Fort Edward; Fort Amherst was south of Halfway Brook (in present-day Glens Falls); Halfway Brook Post, built in 1758 and rebuilt in 1759, was positioned just north of Halfway Brook; Fort Williams was approximately three miles south of Lake George; and Fort Gage (1758) was located only one mile south of the lake.[1] Although Amherst is remembered primarily for his

Fortifications along the military road between Fort George and Fort Edward in 1759.
Detail of painting by Gary S. Zaboly.

military successes in North America, he was also associated with a large number of
forts constructed during the 1759 campaign.

At Lake George the army was busy unearthing the cannon, ammunition, and
other hardware that had been buried in large pits at the close of the previous year's
campaign. The larger task of retrieval involved raising the vessels that had been
purposely sunk for winter storage. The sloop *Earl of Halifax*, measuring "51 Feet
Keel," was "Drag[d] to Shore" on July 4, according to Salah Barnard, an officer in a
Massachusetts regiment.[3] The effort to raise and drain the *Halifax*, supervised by
Captain Joshua Loring, took over two weeks. On July 16, only five days before the
expedition departed for Ticonderoga, a row galley built in 1758 was raised from "40
feet water."[4] Later in the 1759 campaign the row galleys were moved to Lake
Champlain. At that time these vessels were described as mounting "18 Pounders,
each of them one; the Gun is placed fore and aft, and fires out of the Head, they row
with 14 Oars on each side, carry 30 Men each."[5]

Since the radeau *Land Tortoise*, constructed in 1758, could not be recovered from
the lake, another seven-sided radeau was built under the direction of Major Thomas
Ord, a British officer in charge of the artillery. The radeau *Invincible* was launched
on July 16 and was soon fitted with two masts and armed with "four 24 pounders,
and four 12 pounders."[6] "The Snowshoe launch[d] to Day [July 5]," recorded by Salah

Facing page, above: Detail of a "View of the Lines at Lake George, 1759" showing
the radeau *Invincible* and sloop *Halifax*. Painting by Captain Thomas Davies. (Fort
Ticonderoga Museum)
Below: "Plan of Fort George...1759" shows a stockaded fort and barracks close to
the lake with only one bastion of Fort George completed. (National Archives of Canada)

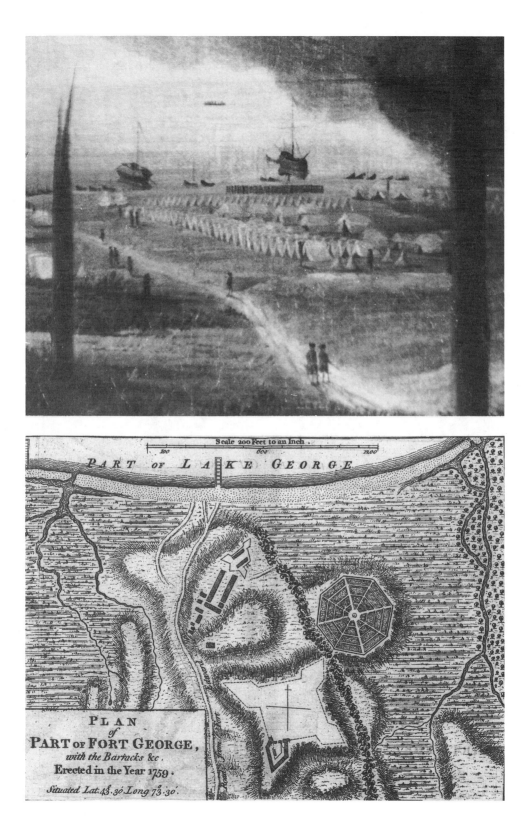

Scale 200 Feet to an Inch.

PART OF LAKE GEORGE

PLAN
of
PART OF FORT GEORGE,
with the Barracks &c.
Erected in the Year 1759.

Situated Lat.43.30 Long 73.30.

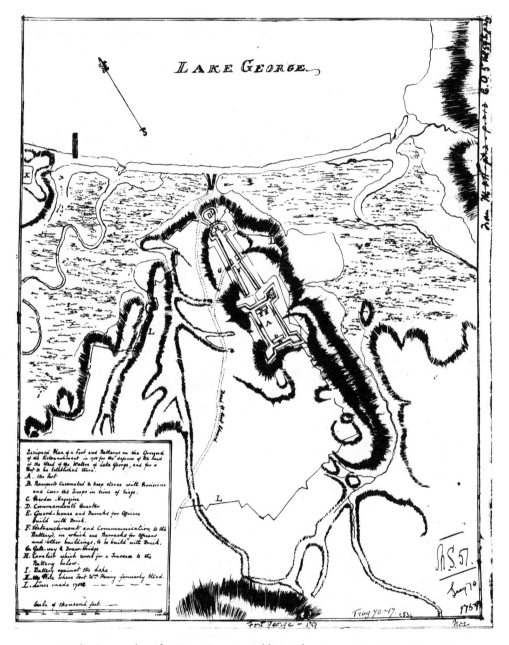

Preliminary plans for Fort George and barracks. (National Archives of Canada)

Barnard, was perhaps the most extensively employed vessel in the naval service at Lake George with documented usage as late as 1765.[7] The provision boat *Snow Shoe*, conceivably named for of its elliptical shape, was also called "the great Scow" and carried 27 soldiers, ammunition, and "Waggoners. . .with 70 horses" on one trip in late July.[8] Another vessel in use was a "Flat bottomed English boat with a three-

ERRATA

Page 125:   third paragraph should read July 21, 1759
Page 127:   line 12 from top should read July 26.

Pounder mounted as a swivel" in her bow which had been transported via the Hudson River and overland to the lake.[9] The artillery was to be carried on improvised rafts,as in the 1758 operation. "The cannon, mortars, and howitzers were not dismounted, but carried over the Lake on rafts which were made by building a stage on three battoes."[10]

Nine days before Amherst departed on his expedition to Ticonderoga, a battle on the lake involving one of the row galleys proved their effectiveness under fire. A force of 400-500 Highlanders, provincials, and Rangers under Major Robert Rogers and Major John Campbell was sent to the first Narrows in bateaux, whaleboats, and a row galley with an 18-pound cannon. As two whaleboats of Rangers approached an island, the French fired upon the intruders, whereupon the rest of the contingent with the row galley came forward and "the 18 Pounder set to work; and in less than a Quarter of an Hour they were all running away. . .the Enemy loss 3 of their Battoes, and all the Hands Kill'd or drowned. This was the first Experiment ever try'd with a Row Galley, and prov'd effectual."[11] On the island the French "had made a breastwork & set up Some Stockades. . . which our people set fire to & burned it down—then return[e]d to Camp."[12]

Meanwhile at the Lake George camp, progress was made on the construction of Fort George, situated east of the ruins of Fort William Henry. The foundation, laid on July 2, encompassed two or three acres. Fort George was to be built of stone and included a hospital with a "Length about 8 Roods [rods] the width about Eighteen feet."[13] Only one stone bastion with 15 guns was completed in 1759, although three wooden stockaded bastions with barracks were finished closer to the shoreline of Lake George. After the capture of Forts Carillon and St. Frédéric, Amherst issued orders on September 8 to transfer workers from Fort George to the new fortification under construction at Crown Point.[14]

On June 21, 1759, at two o'clock in the morning the army began preparations for the departure of the expedition against Carillon. By six o'clock the van of the huge armada was set in motion; by nine the rearmost vessels were on their way. The flotilla was organized in four double columns, led by the English flat-bottomed boat and 43 whaleboats. The column of whaleboats on the right held Rangers, light infantry, and grenadiers and was accompanied by a row galley mounting one 12-pound cannon; the second column was composed of bateaux with regulars and Highlanders; the third column was led by the radeau *Invincible*, followed by 13 rafts with artillery and bateaux with carpenters, engineers, sutlers, baggage, the hospital, the *Snow Shoe*, and two additional rafts with horses; the fourth column of bateaux (on the left) transported provincial troops and was accompanied by a row galley with an 18-pound cannon. The rear was covered by a wide line of bateaux and the sloop *Halifax*.[15] The men rowed in turns to allow sleep between rowing duties, and blanket sails were employed on the whaleboats and bateaux. Fighting high winds and rain, the expedition landed in the evening "at the second Narrows on each side of the Lake,* and a little below the old landing place."[16] Since the rafts were in danger of capsizing in the heavy seas, they were lashed to the radeau *Invincible* overnight.[20]

---

*There is some question regarding the actual landing site. Henry True recorded the area as "about 2 miles out of the sigh[t] of the landing" and Constantine Hardy noted a distance of "three or four miles of the Landing Place."[17] Samuel Merriman further recounted that the flotilla had sailed "as far as ye second Narrows by ye great smooth rock."[18] Although the eighteenth-century secondary account of Captain John Knox placed the landing site "a few hours" from the "second Narrows," it may have been in the area of the Waltonian Islands in Hague which has a view of Rogers Rock.[19]

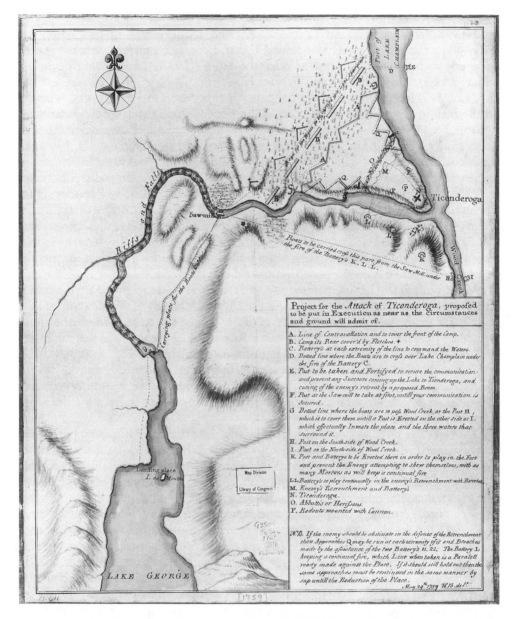

Proposed plan of attack on Ticonderoga, May 29, 1759. Pen and ink and watercolor by
William Brassier. (William Faden Collection, Library of Congress)

The next morning the army landed in Ticonderoga on the east side of Lake
George. The Rangers and light infantry marched immediately northward to the
sawmills on the LaChute River (outlet from Lake George to Lake Champlain).
Brigadier General Chevalier de Bourlamaque, commander at Fort Carillon, with a
party of 300 Indians and some grenadiers engaged the British advance party in a brief
skirmish but quickly returned to the fort. On the same day provincial troops with

Amherst were dispatched to clear the road to Ticonderoga which had been cluttered with trees cut by the French to impede the invaders. The trees were cleared and used to build a defensive breastwork to secure the road. The following morning Amherst heard news that the French had struck their tents, burned their huts, and embarked on their sloops and bateaux. According to a prearranged scheme, Bourlamaque had departed for Fort St. Frédéric with 2,600 regulars and Canadian militia and several hundred Indians, leaving only a token force at Carillon. At the same time, provincial and regular troops took possession of the undefended French breastworks that had turned back Abercromby's army in 1758. Efforts to bring the artillery forward continued on July 23rd and the following two days as the remaining French garrison under Captain de Hebecourt at Carillon bombarded the British and provincial forces with cannon and mortar fire. Late in the evening on June 26, before Amherst could open his batteries on the fort, the French set delayed fuses on the cannon and magazine, set fire to the fort, and evacuated to Crown Point aboard bateaux. Major Robert Rogers with his Rangers and Colonel William Haviland with the light infantry were sent in whaleboats and the English flat-bottomed boat to pursue the French.

With only two walls and one bastion destroyed, Amherst instructed Colonel William Eyre, the engineer who had designed Fort William Henry in 1755, to rebuild the fort. The day following the French departure from Ticonderoga, Amherst ordered Captain Joshua Loring to place the sawmill back in operation in order to build a fleet capable of challenging the French vessels on Lake Champlain: the schooner *La Vigilante* and three sloops or "xebecs", *La Musquelongy*, *La Brochette*, and *L'Esturgeon*.

Amherst's main army departed for Crown Point on August 4, four days after the French had destroyed Fort St. Frédéric and fled to Isle-aux-Noix in the Richelieu River. To gain naval control of Lake Champlain, Amherst subsequently ordered the building of the brig *Duke of Cumberland*, the sloop *Boscawen*, and the radeau *Ligonier*. Two smaller radeaux and several other vessels were also built for Lake Champlain. The row galleys and most of the bateaux and whaleboats had been transferred from Lake George to Lake Champlain. The British and provincial army embarked on the long-planned Canadian invasion on October 11 but was hampered by adverse weather and returned to Crown Point ten days later. The naval fleet under the direction of Joshua Loring, however, was successful in forcing the French to scuttle their three sloops. The sloops were later raised and used by the British in the 1760 campaign. The last major campaign of the French and Indian War involved the convergence in 1760 of three British armies against the French position in Montreal. The Champlain fleet was employed in one prong of the three-pronged advance on Montreal when British and provincial troops captured the French stronghold on Isle-aux-Noix.

Lemuel Wood, born in Boxford, Massachusetts, in October 1741, was a fourth generation descendent of Daniel Wood, who had settled in the Boxford area about 1675. Lemuel Wood served in a company under Captain Francis Peabody of Boxford in the Massachusetts regiment of Colonel Abijah Willard. His journal begins on May 24, 1759, with notations on the march to New York. Wood and his fellow soldiers marched through Worcester, Springfield, Westfield, and Stockbridge, Massachusetts, reaching Greenbush, New York, on the Hudson River on June 11. Eight days later, his regiment reached Fort Miller, south of Fort Edward, just before Amherst began his march to Lake George. Despite the original phonetic spelling and lack of punctuation, the journal is an excellent source of information on the 1759 campaign. The following journal has been converted into a more readable text. Wood was a diligent recorder of eighteenth-century military life including accounts of its brutal discipline. His notes also refer to the maritime activity on the lakes and the siege of Fort Carillon and provide one of the first detailed descriptions by a provincial soldier of the fort at Ticonderoga. He traveled the same route the following year and participated in the siege of Isle-aux-Noix. Wood married in 1782 and had seven children; his last child was born when he was 56 years old. He died in 1819 at the age of 77.

Southern shoreline of Lake George, site of construction of naval vessels in 1758 and 1759.
(Photo by author)

A Journal of the Canada Expedition in the Year 1759[21]

Tuesday June the 19 Day. We traveled to Fort Miller and there we made a halt and marched about 9 miles that day and we camped there above the fort on the plain and set a guard there.*

Wednesday June the 20 Day. We marched 4 miles to Fort Edward where we arrived about noon. The whole army that lay at Fort Edward except we that came up last received orders to get ready to march tomorrow morning to go to the lake. We pitched our tents on the north side of the fort near the hill some distance from the fort.

Thursday June the 21 Day. This morning General [Jeffery] Amherst marched from Fort Edward for the lake with about 3000 regulars, between 3[000] and 4000 of the Connecticut troops and Colonel [Timothy] Ruggles' [Massachusetts] regiment. There followed a large quantity of powder and other artillery stores besides nearly 500 carts and wagons loaded with baggage and stores. We had orders to strike our tents & accordingly we did and removed and pitched near the fort just by the train of artillery. This afternoon Major [Caleb] Willard came up to Fort Edward with two companies belonging to our regiment. We took provision this afternoon for six days.

22. Last night a great number of carts and wagons returned from the lake. This morning they went back again loaded with cannonball, bomb shells and bateaux, provisions &c.

23. This day a considerable number of carts and wagons went from Fort Edward to the lake loaded with stores.

24. This morning we had news by a Ranger that came into Fort Edward who was last Friday near Ticonderoga [where] the enemy were very numerous. They encamped almost from lake to lake. He says they were entrenched at the landing place very strong. P.M. Colonel [Abijah] Willard came up to Fort Edward. There came up with him the chief doctor, the chaplain and 5 companies belonging to his regiment. Abel Dodge belonging to our company who was left sick at Worcester [MA.] came up this afternoon.

26. This day there came orders that all the ship carpenters and house carpenters that belong to Colonel Willard's regiment should go immediately to the lake to work at the King's work. Accordingly Captain [Jacob] Bayley went with 35 men that were carpenters to the lake. We had news by [a] captain belonging to the Rangers who was down the lake Saturday that the Indians were very thick about the lake, that there had been 30 bateaux of the enemy discovered upon the lake not far from our encampment, that the French are very busy in strengthening themselves at the landing place at Ticonderoga.

---

*James Henderson, also from Massachusetts, had an intriguing journal entry on June 5, 1759, which described a mechanism that carried bateaux around the falls at Fort Miller. "The Bateaus is carried on Wheels with great celerity by means of two Ingines the one to load the other to unload the form is thus there is two large crotches Sett up like Well crotches with a large Sweep in each crotch the Bateaux are drawn out of the River by men on Rollers along side the Engine having Slings at each pully hoists up the Bateaux than put[t]ing the Wheels under the Bateau is lowered in a Moment and Drove away Where it is unloaded after the Same Manner and put into the River."[22]

27. Last night Colonel Miller of our regiment came up to Fort Edward: it came out an order this day that no officer in the regiment should wear a Scotch bon[n]et. We take provision for 5 days.

28. This morning there was a party of 100 of [our] regiment and 100 of [the] Hampshires [New Hampshire regiment] and as many of [the] Highlanders went to the Halfway Brook to guard wagons: there were 170 wagons went from Fort Edward to the lake loaded with stores for the army.

29. This morning we heard the report of a number of cannon at Halfway Brook or at the lake supposing the enemy had beset our camps but when they came to the 4 Mile Post* they understood that they were clearing cannon at the lake which occasioned [the] uproar. Our men then returned home.

30. This morning there were ten men came to the 4 Mile Post that came from Canada. One was taken at Oswego, the other at Lake George. They went directly up to the lake but what news they brought we could not tell. In the afternoon there came in about 100 carts from the lake to Fort Edward.

July Sunday the 1st Day. This morning there were between 2[00] and 300 carts and wagons [that] went from Fort Edward to the lake loaded with stores for the army. Our picket guards went to guard them to the Halfway Brook. In the afternoon Captain Barnes' company of our regiment came up to Fort Edward.

2. This day there were a great number of oxen and horses [that] came from the lake to Fort Edward in order to carry the artillery to the lake. In the afternoon we had orders to march tomorrow morning by 7 o'clock.

3. This morning we mustered and struck our tents and marched off for the lake where we arrived about an hour after sunset. There were 10 pieces of cannon went to the lake that were 24 pounders besides small pieces and a number of mortars. We were informed at the lake that yesterday about 20 of the [New] Jersey Blues went out of the encampment a little way into the woods to get bark. They lay down their guns and went to getting bark in sight of the encampment and a party of Indians came upon them, killed and took 13 of them. The Indians put off immediately before the Jersey Blues could [get] there and help.

4. We pitched our tents within the old breastwork in the place where Blakeny's regiment camped last year. P. M. There was a party of 55 men taken out of our regiment to go into the train of the artillery. The officers that went with this party were Captain Hall, Lieutenant Beaman and Ensign Brown. There were 4 sergeants and 48 rank and file. There were 3 of the above party taken out of our company.

5. This morning our regiment and the Hampshires were drawn up and marched over near to where the old fort [Fort William Henry] stood and fired 3 rounds [by] platoons through both regiments. This night a sentry belonging to the Connecticut troops thought he saw an Indian outside of the breastwork. He hailed but had no answer. He then fired upon him. The next morning they saw blood at the place and tracked it some way.

6. This day we had orders [that] every company should prepare a sufficient number of scoops for bailing the bateaux; also all should be in a readiness to cross the lake as soon as orders shall be given. This afternoon all our men that were left sick at Sheffield [MA.] came up to the lake. We had regimental orders that all the

*Four-Mile Post was a stockaded fort on the Hudson River approximately four miles north of Fort Edward.

officers in the regiment should turn out and be exercised twice a day by Captain Sacks.

7. This day we draw fresh provision for 3 days but we could not get a morsel of salt in all the camps.

Monday the 9. Part of Captain Jacobs' men that had been out [on] a scout came in and they said that [they] had been chased by the Indians and the captain and about 20 men were either killed or taken. Joseph Fisk [that] was out in the above scout was killed or taken.

The 10. This day one Abraham Astin, who was late captain of the wagons had stolen some of the King's arms and working tools, was sentenced by a court-martial to receive 400 lashes—accordingly was brought forth and was striped 36 lashes at the head of each regiment [in] the army beginning at Forbes'* [regiment] and ending at [Peter] Schuyler's [New Jersey regiment] through 11 regiments in the whole. There were 11 men who were partners in the theft with the above Abraham Astin. They were sentenced by a court-martial to receive 300 lashes apiece but as their crime did not appear so notorious the general was pleased to pardon them only that they should march round the encampment underguard and see the said Astin receive his punishment. Accordingly they did. We draw four days salt provision.

The 11. This day another man of Captain Jacobs' company came in almost starved. He said [that] they had a brush with the French and Indians but could not tell what [had] become of Captain Jacobs or his men. We heard the French had come up [to] the first Narrows, a considerable number of them and that they lay there beating up or above the Narrows. This day we had orders that all the regiment should take their bateaux in order to cross the lake that they should moor the bateaux out in the lake and set a guard over them and be ready to go over the lake as soon as orders may be given. It was ordered also how every regiment should be placed where they cross the lake.

The 12. This morning Major [Robert] Rogers went down the lake with a party of the Rangers, some Indians, light infantry, Royal Scots and regulars, about 400 in all. [They] carried down with them a row galley with a field piece in it. About 8 o'clock in the morning we heard the report of several cannon down the lake and saw the smoke at the mouth of the Narrows. All the pickets of the lines were ordered out and down the lake to their aid, some by land and some by water. About 12 o'clock there was a whaleboat came in from the party and said that there was a large number of French and Indians down at the first Narrows that our men had driven them off and killed some of them. The French [had] run off [and] left their bateaux and what little they had. A little after sunset Major Rogers came in with the party [that] he had left [with]. A sergeant of the Rangers & a regular were killed, an Indian wounded. He destroyed some of the enemy but how many he could not tell. This afternoon there was a regular soldier named Richard Studs belonging to Blakeney's or the Irish kiliny [Inniskilling] regiment brought to the lake from Fort Edward and he deserted from the lake about 10 days ago and was taken up at Saratoga and about 3 o'clock he [was] brought to the lake. We draw provision for 3 days.

---

*Wood was referring to the regiment of the late Brigadier General John Forbes. Although plagued by illness, Forbes carved out an exhausting route through the Allegheny Mountains of Pennsylvania to capture Fort Duquesne in late 1758. In March 1759 the dedicated officer died in Philadelphia. Both officers and ordinary soldiers continued to refer to the regiment as Forbes'.

The 13. This morning at 6 o'clock a court-martial set for the trial of the deserter that was brought in yesterday. He was sentenced by the court-martial to be shot today at 12 o'clock in the front of the quarter guard of Forbes' regiment. Accordingly all the pickets of the lines were drawn up for the execution of the above prisoner. The provost guard brought forth the prisoner and marched him round before all the regular regiments to which the prisoner was brought and set before one of the platoons and [he] kneeled down upon his knees. He clinched his hands. The platoon of 6 men each of them fired [at] him through the body. The other platoon then came up instantly and fired [at] him through the head and blowed his head all to pieces. They then dug a grave by his side and tumbled him in and covered him up & that was an end of the wool [fool].

The 14. There was delivered out to each regiment a proportion of flour for 5 days which they were ordered to get baked and keep by them ready for [a] sudden push. This afternoon there was a number of regulars came to the lake and also Colonel [Timothy] Ruggles' 2ᵈ Battalion and General [Phineas] Lyman's [Connecticut] regiment.

The 15. This morning the men that came up yesterday were sent to fire [by] platoons and they fired 3 rounds apiece and then came in. The Rangers were ordered to clear their pieces this morning which they did. In the afternoon there were better than 100 men came in that belonged to our regiment [that] came up to the lake.

The 16. Last night there was a large party of regulars, Rangers and light infantry [that] went down the lake in bateaux to see what they could discover. They went down as far as the first Narrows but found no enemy so they returned home again. Likewise also the pickets upon the lines were sent out today on the west side of the lake. They went about 10 miles down the lake but found nothing of the enemy so they returned this afternoon. A party was sent to cut fascines [sticks] to lay in the bottom of the bateaux before they were loaded. This day there was a row galley that had been sunk last fall was found and got up to shore.* Likewise an ark that was built within about 12 days was launched into the lake.** This night we drew 3 days' provision.

The 17. This day there was a draft out of each provincial regiment to go into the Rangers to fill up Major Rogers' company. The men to draw Rangers pay and be dismissed at the time the other provincials are. This afternoon there was a flag of truce [that] came in from Ticonderoga.

The 18. This morning the French flag of truce [that] came in last night returned to Ticonderoga again. We hear that the said flag of truce came to demand the ground here and to give General [Jeffery] Amherst leave to march off peacefully if he pleased but if not.*** This day Thomas Burk, a wagoner was tried by a court-martial of the

Facing page: Detail of "Line of Vessels on Lake George under General Amherst, 1759" showing the English flat-bottomed boat, radeau *Invincible*, row galleys, rafts with cannon, and columns of bateaux. (Public Record Office, London)

*This was a row galley with a length of 40 feet and a beam of 15 feet that had been raised from 40-foot depths. (See note 4)

**Wood is referring to the seven-sided radeau *Invincible*, later armed with eight cannon. (See note 6)

***Actually, the French flag of truce was an attempt to gain intelligence regarding the size of the British forces.

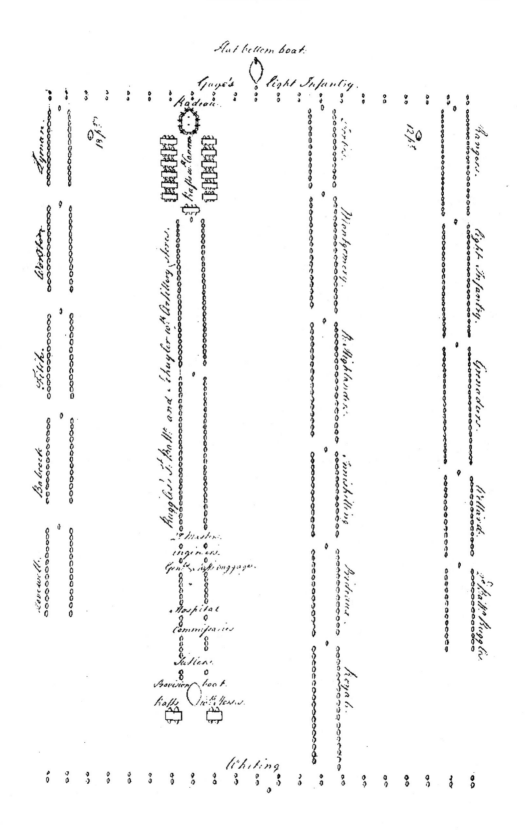

line for abusing and threatening to strike his officer. He was sentenced by the court-martial to receive 400 lashes. General Amherst approved of the above sentence and ordered that he go round the encampment and receive 30 lashes at [the] head of each regiment.

The 19. This morning at 4 o'clock the wagoner that was tried by the court-martial yesterday was brought forth by the provost guard and whipped round the camp beginning at Forbes' [regiment] and so on to the right. He received 30 lashes at the head of the 4 regiments. One tried for desertion was found guilty and sentenced to receive 1000 lashes. The other tried for robbery and being a notorious offender was sentenced to suffer death.

The 20. This morning the criminal [that] was condemned yesterday was brought forth [for] execution. He was marched by the provost guard in the same manner as the last criminal was. He was then brought to the place where the above mentioned criminal was executed, to be shot in the manner as he loves [wishes]. When he came to the place of execution he was very loathe to die. They could not persuade him to kneel down to be shot. They then tied him hand and foot but could not make him stand still. They then took and tied [him] to an old log and he hung down under [the] side [of] the log. They then fired and killed him. This day we draw fresh provision for 3 days. And salt for 2 expecting to go off tomorrow but had no time to cook.

The 21. This morning the army embarked for Ticonderoga and rowed down the lake. The row galleys and the ark [radeau *Invincible*] in the front of the army and the Sloop [*Halifax*] in the rear. The wind blew fresh at southeast. The weather was cool and cloudy. About 2 o'clock we got to the first Narrows, about 3 or 4 o'clock it began to rain and rained most of the afternoon. We rowed on down the lake and [with the] sun about an hour high we passed by Sabbath Day Point and rowed down within a mile or 2 of the second Narrows where we lay in our boats all night.

The 22. This morning we went on and passed through the Narrows and came in sight of the landing place but saw no men there. We went on & landed the Rangers, light infantry and grenadiers together with Ruggles' and Willard's regiments. Landed about 8 o'clock on the east side of the lake and went round in the woods to the top of a high rise where we had a view of Crown Point, South Bay, and part of Lake Champlain & the regulars went and landed without any opposition. We landed on the east side of the lake. . .went on through the woods till we came near the fort. The enemy fired at our men across the river but hurt not a man. We then turned our course and went to the mills where we expected to find a strong fortress but when we came there we found no encampment, no fort, not a man there. The mills were in the same position that we left them last year after Major Rogers burned them down. Major Rogers with his men went over the flats at the mills to the west side of the lake. The enemy met them there and they had a little engagement. Major Rogers soon drove them back, killed some, and took 2 or 3 prisoners. The regiment[s] of Ruggles' and Willard's marched down on the east side of the river till we came down within about half a mile of the fort. There we [began] building a breastwork with all expedition. The regulars and Rangers went over the river at the mills and went to clearing a road for the cannon as fast as possible. The French and Indians came out and kept firing and yelling most part of the afternoon. We went down against the fort very near to it where we had a fair view of it. We [have] near

200 tents pitched. There were 3 sloops in the lake near the fort and a great number of bateaux.* About 3 or 4 o'clock in the afternoon the French sent one sloop and about 30 bateaux loaded. By sunset we got our breastwork in good order and came into it. All but [a] single sentry all around it. We kept in the breastwork this night. One half of us stood up by the breastwork all night and the other half slept. This night all was very still. There was no firing till toward day[break] when our men at the mills were alarmed and a number of guns were fired and one of our sentries fired at the same time but we knew not whether there [were] any enemy or not.

The 23. This morning we finished the breastwork and cleared up the bushes around it. Last night there was a man that was taken by the French when Fort William Henry was taken [in 1757] & had been with them ever since. He ran away from the fort and came to our men. He informed [us] that there were but about 2000 men at the fort [and] that they had got there valuable effects on board [sloops] in order to go off if need. This morning when we came to view the fort again we saw that all their tents were struck and gone and there arose a great smoke from the fort. It was soon noticed that the fort was on fire but afterwards we found it was not the fort but they [had] set their huts on fire and houses near the fort. They came out in small parties and fired [on] our regulars but it did not continue long. Our men kept getting up the cannon and getting it over the falls as fast as possible. Our regulars drove out toward the fort and about 9 o'clock they came before the French breastwork but saw no man there. They supposed the enemy lay close that they might not be discovered. Our men sent 3 or 4 men to the breastwork to see what was there. When they came to the trenches they found not a man there. Our army rushed on and took possession of their breastwork. The French fired with their cannon from the fort on our men very smart but did little or no damage. Our people set to trenching within their breastwork. The French continued firing with their cannon and throwing bombs at our men but could not drive them off. We [were] on the east side of the river, lay in open view of the fort. About noon the French fired 2 cannon across the river at us but [the cannonballs] did not come near us. About 2 o'clock our regiment was ordered back to the mills from thence we went back to our bateaux weary and very hungry having had nothing to eat since we first landed. We no sooner got to the landing place but we were put to drawing cannon to the mills which we did and got back again some time in the night and lay down. The French kept firing with their cannon all night by times and our people were busy all night getting up cannon and artillery stores. The man that came in last night from the French informed [us] that General [Marquis de] Montcalm had been at Ticonderoga not long ago with a strong army but there came a messenger to him from Canada that informed him that General [James] Wolfe with the English fleet had got within 3 leagues of Quebec & landed his army upon which General Montcalm drew off all his forces for the relief of Old Canada.**

The 24. This morning Colonel [Timothy] Ruggles' regiment was ordered away from their post on the side of the river. They threw down their breastwork and

---

*The three French sloops, *La Musquelongy* (The Muskellunge), *La Brochette* (The Pike), and *L'Esturgeon* (The Sturgeon) were constructed by Nicolas-René Levasseur at St. Jean in 1758-59 and carried eight cannon each with a crew of 40-50.

**An army of 9,000 men under General James Wolfe had arrived at Quebec in June. On September 13 the British and French armies met in a bloody battle on the Heights of Abraham, in which the British were victorious, but Wolfe, as well as Montcalm, was killed.

went back to the mills to stay there for the present and our regiment and Colonel [Nathan] Whiting's [Connecticut regiment] were to stay at the landing place, we [were] to transport the stores to the mills and Colonel Ruggles' [regiment] from there to the trenches which we were very busy in doing all day. Our men got up their cannon and mortars and ammunition as fast as possible but fired not a gun at the fort yet all day the enemy kept firing at our men at the trenches but as we heard they did little or no damage. Our men got some pieces of cannon down to the lake side on the north or northwest side of the fort to cut off their communication to Crown Point which it could not fail to do, the lake being not very wide at that place. This morning the general's barge was taken out of Lake George and drawn across the carrying place and put into Lake Champlain just below the mills.* Last night we had one man killed at the trenches and another had his arm shot off with a cannonball and 10 or 12 more wounded by our own men.** This afternoon there [was] a great quantity of ball and shell sent up to the trenches & some mortars.

The 25. This morning the great [13-inch] mortar was sent up to the trenches and some large cannon. We were informed that last night the French sallied out of the fort and set upon our men but did them no damage. Last night the New Hampshire regiment was sent up to the lake to go to Oswego. This morning we had 6 men killed in the trench with a bomb and some more hurt. The French kept firing day and night at our men in the trench while they offered them no abuse at all as this afternoon Colonel [Roger] Townshend who was aid-de-camp to General Amherst who was cut off in two parts with a cannonball as he was a riding at the general's side near the trenches. We heard that there was a great number of bateaux coming from Crown Point to Ticonderoga, supposed to be 4000 men at least.

The 26. Last night the French fired with their cannon very briskly all night at our men in the trenches but did them little damage. This morning there were 3 row galleys drawn out of Lake George across to the mills and put into Lake Champlain and some bateaux and whaleboats drawn at the same time. We drew up [the] chief of the cannon, all but a few pieces of small cannon and a great quantity of powder, ball & shell. This day about noon the flat bottomed boat came down from Fort William Henry with 60 horses on board her*** & wagons on board bateaux. They were immediately set to work carrying up stores and ammunition up to the trenches. The carpenters were sent up this afternoon to lay platforms for the cannon and getting all things ready to open the batteries tomorrow morning at [the] break of day and show the French what they could do. This day we had 8 men killed in the trenches and about 20 wounded. The Indians killed 2 men of [Colonel David] Wooster's regiment near the fort as they were cutting fascines. The enemy kept a pretty steady firing all this day and in the evening till about 8 or 9 o'clock when they [stopped] firing and took what they could carry off with them and pushed off leaving a match to their magazine. About 11 o'clock at night the magazine took fire and blew up. The noise of it was heard by our men at the landing place. It was very loud and shaking. Our men did not march to the fort till morning. The French set fire to their barracks [which] burned down and some part of the fort was hurt but

*This was the 36-foot English flat-bottomed boat that carried a three-pound swivel cannon.[23]

**When some of the British troops became alarmed that the French were making a raid on their entrenchment, the British soldiers accidently fired on one another, leaving two dead and 12 wounded.

***The provision vessel *Snow Shoe*.

the fort being chiefly stone & lime.* Major Rogers with his men pursued after them in whaleboats toward Crown Point and overtook some of them and took a good quantity of powder from them and about 20 prisoners. It is generally thought in the army that the French, when they left the fort, bound their English prisoners to the magazine and left them to be blown up.

The 27. This morning our people went into the fort, struck the flag [and] hoisted the English in its place. They found in the fort 15 pieces of cannon great and small and 2-13 inch mortars and several other small mortars. They also found about 200 barrels of gunpowder but no provision worth anything nor. . .very little plunder of any sort.** In the whole of this siege we had not more than 20 men killed and 70 wounded.***

The 28. The 4 regiments: Lyman's, Fitch's Wooster's, and Schuyler's were set to work to repair the fort. [Colonel Timothy] Ruggles' regiment with the carpenters [were assigned] to build a sawmill on the spot where the French mill was. Whiting's, Willard's, and [Colonel Henry] Babcock's [Rhode Island] regiments were stationed at the landing place to guard and transport provisions and whaleboats and bateaux across the carrying place to Lake Champlain. Our duty very hard at work [during] days and on guard [during] nights and our provision only pork and bread.

The 31. This day we heard from Crown Point that the fort [had been] blown up and all the French [had] gone but we [did] not give much heed to this news. We heard also that General [James] Wolfe with the English fleet had got possession of the island of Orleans and thrown bombs into the city of Quebec till he had leveled it to the ground but we credited this news about as much as the other.† This day a sentry of Colonel [Timothy] Ruggles' 2nd Battalion shot a Highlander that was going to carry off a boat that the sentry had charge of. The sentry was confined and tried by a general court-martial and was judged to have done his duty and was therefore acquitted.‡

Wednesday August the 1. We had news by some Rangers that came from Crown Point this morning that the fort was actually on fire [and] that they went into it and walked round on the walls [and] that the French were all gone. Lieutenant Flatcher who was out with [a] party declared that he set his name on the flag staff this morning. At a general court-martial this day one Thomas Bradley of the late Forbes' regiment, accused of theft, was found guilty and sentenced to receive 1500 lashes. William Ray of Gage's light infantry [was] tried for insolence [and] found guilty. Thomas Read sentenced to suffer death and John Rease to receive 500 lashes. We draw 4 days provision and [a] quart of peas per man.

The 2. This day we had certain news that Crown Point was deserted. Major Rogers went with 150 Rangers to take possession of it. The regular regiments were ordered to be in readiness for marching as soon as ordered as also the regiments of

---

*The terrific explosion which killed 50 horses above the magazine was recorded in the journals of other eyewitnesses.[24]

**Plunder or looting of the enemy occurred often in eighteenth-century military service in North America.

***Amherst reported 16 killed, 51 wounded and one missing.[25]

†Rumors were rampant in military campaigns.

‡Samuel Merriman, a sergeant from Northfield, Massachusetts, in Timothy Ruggles' regiment, was court-martialed for killing a "Desarter" but acquitted.[26]

Watercolors by Thomas Davies.

Top: "A South West View of the Lines and Fort of Tyconderoga." (National Archives of Canada)

Middle: "A South View of Crown Point," 1759. (National Archives of Canada)

Bottom: "A North View of Crown Point." Radeau *Ligonier* is in the foreground. (Library of Congress)

Schuyler's, Fitch's, Babcock's, & Willard's. The other regiments to stay behind but afterwards our regiment was ordered to remain at the landing place and Ruggles' 2nd Battalion to march in their place. As the army was now all in arms for marching for the reduction of all Canada the general was pleased to wipe off the crime of the prisoners now under the sentence of a court-martial and pardoned offenses for their future good behavior.

The 3. Camp news that General Montcalm is fallen into the hands of General Wolfe. That Wolfe has almost if not quite destroyed Quebec. He had run upon them in their trenches 5 or 6 times and drove them out by the point of the bayonet [although] the enemy was greatly superior to him in number. This day a soldier belonging to Forbes' regiment was hanged for desertion on one of the batteries near the fort with a plate hung upon his breast written thereon hanged for deserting to the French. He was to hang on the gallows till retreat beating and then buried under the gallows with his French clothes with him.

The 4. We had news that General [William] Johnson had taken Niagara and that he had taken 500 prisoners and that 6[000] or 7000 of the French Indians had joined him. He had 2 colonels killed in taking it and Colonel Johnson of the New York forces.* Yesterday General Amherst with [the] great[er] part of the army went from Ticonderoga to Crown Point. Last night about midnight there was a post [messenger] came in here, said to be an express from General Wolfe. A sergeant and 12 men

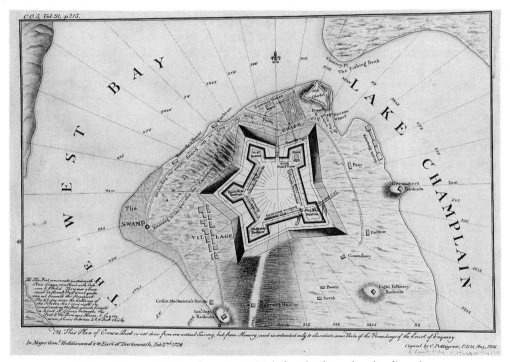

Map of Crown Point showing British fort built under the direction of General Jeffery Amherst. (National Archives of Canada)

*On July 25, 1759, Sir William Johnson with 2,000 troops and 900 Indians captured Fort Niagara on Lake Ontario. Johnson shared the command with Brigadier General John Prideaux, who was accidently killed before the fort surrendered.

were immediately mustered & sent to guard him to the fort but what news he brought we know not.

The 8. This day we heard that our people were going to build a large fort on a hill near to where Crown Point fort stands, so large as to cover 8 acres. Camp news: General Wolfe has deserted and [been] driven off from Quebec and left a great part of his army.

The 9. We heard there was to be a road cleared from Crown Point to Number 4 which was said to be about 50 miles and that a party of men was certainly gone to lay it out.*

Saturday the 11. We had news that a party was set out to work at Crown Point clearing a road to Number 4 and that they got 14 miles already. We drew fresh provisions for 3 days.

Monday the 13. A party of the regiment was set to work to build a hospital for the sick of the regiment. There was one officer out [of] each company and one soldier. These to keep to work at the hospital till it be finished and do no other duty.

Tuesday the 14. We drew provision for 4 days and a quart of peas per man.

Wednesday the 15. This day Lieutenant Granger & Ensign Peabody obtained liberty of the colonel to go up to Ticonderoga. I accidentally went up with them and viewed the fort and went into every hole and corner of it and saw the strength of it and was convinced [that] Fort Edward was [in] no way to be compared with it for strength or beauty. The fort stands on a high ridge upon a point of land just where the streams that come from Lake George and that from South Bay meet together and make Lake Champlain. The ridge on which the fort stands is nearest to the stream that comes from Lake George. The fort is about 30 rods from the end of the point. In the east corner of the fort toward the point was the grand magazine. In the west end were 2 other magazines [both of] which were blown up by which the walls of the fort were so much damaged that 2 regiments would not repair it in a year. Before it was hurt I believe that North America had not a stronger one of its bigness—the walls are chiefly stone and lime about 24 feet high on the west and northwest side. There is a trench without [outside] the walls about 10 feet deep. Five or 6 of it is blown into [filled with] scaled stone. Under the walls of the fort there are large rooms for soldiers to live in and dark prisons arched all around with stone and lime very strong. In the northeast corner of the fort there is a large room under the walls arched very neatly with brick. At one end of it there are 2 very large ovens and conveniences for baking with a chimney. The way into it was very private and hard for a stranger to find. The timber and earth over it is 10 feet thick with a platform for cannon to play on right over the room on the east of the fort there. A road goes down to the end of the point, the road picketed all the way on both sides. At the end of the point there is a small fort [which is] very strongly formed, partly by nature. The walls [are] not very high but rounded next [to] the water. It is at least 60 feet from the top of the walls to the water and of firm stone almost right up and down. At the bottom of which by the water side there is a battery with some cannon to level on the water with a winding way up the rocks to the fort.** Within the

---

*Number Four refers to a fort built to guard against marauding French and Indian war parties at a settlement along the Connecticut River which was incorporated as Charlestown, New Hampshire, in 1753.

**The Lotbinière Battery, a redoubt or small fort, was added closer to the narrows of the lake because the original site of the fort was too far away from the end of the peninsula.

great fort there are large barracks built the whole length of the fort with stone and lime 2 stories high and wide enough for 2 rooms well finished but the roof [is] destroyed by the fire on the west side of the fort.* Without the trench, there is a battery for cannon to play on. Outside of it, a trench. Without the trench, a glacis [sloping bank] of 15 feet high [is] next [to] the fort, artificially built with earth which they have taken of the ridge to the firm stone for 20 rods from this glacis to the lake. On the north is a breastwork with some batteries for cannon [Germain Redoubt]. Within this breastwork toward the point is [a] fine garden with all sorts of varieties. About 60 rods from the fort on the west is the grand breastwork from lake to lake built with logs and earth 8 or 10 feet high, some of the top logs 3 feet through [thick]. It is built full of short crooks and angles so that it may be cleared every way with places for cannon to play on. On the outside a large row of brush about 41 rods off [and] under the breastwork a magazine.

Thursday the 16. Last night 2 sergeants of Captain Walker's company were confined for not going to hear prayers this morning. A court-martial was called for their trial. They were brought to the court-martial and pled guilty and sentenced to [a] reduction in rank. The colonel approved of the sentence.** We heard that last night a flag of truce came into Crown Point from Canada but what they came for we have not yet heard.

Saturday the 18. This morning early Colonel Whiting's Regiment struck their tents and marched off for Crown Point. In the afternoon one half of our regiment struck their tents and marched off to the mills. It fell to our company to remain at the landing place [Lake George]—we drew provision for three days and a pint & a half of peas per man.

Wednesday the 22. By a man that came from Crown Point this day we were informed that the building [of] the new fort went on [so] fast that they kept 1600 men daily at work at it besides those that were cutting timber. He also said that they were going to build a radeau at Crown Point of 80 foot in length.*** Yesterday the Indians took 2 men of [the] late Lord Howes' regiment near Crown Point as they were a picking green peas. The express boat came back from the head of the lake with letters for the general.

Sunday the 26. This day we had a regiment court-martial upon a bateauman belonging to Colonel Bradstreet. He was tried for abusing his officer on board the scow [Snow Shoe]. The said court-martial sentenced him to the [whipping] post and then the colonel forgave him. Captain Peabody president of the court martial. —This day there were about 50 Rangers [that] came over the lake and went up to the fort. About 6 weeks ago they came from Guadeloupe.† Four of the said regulars raised a meeting on board the sloop [Halifax] and were put under guard as soon as

*Amherst and his officers had a good idea of the layout of the fort from a report by Lieutenant Diedrick Brehm, an engineering officer in the Royal American Regiment. Brehm, accompanied by Robert Rogers and his Rangers, had been sent in March to reconnoiter the fort and surrounding area, including the north end of Lake George.[27]

**Encouraged by chaplains, the provincial regiments embraced spiritual help in their military campaigns. The Seven Years' War in America had some aspects of a "holy war" which pitted Protestant provincial soldiers against French Catholics and their Native American allies.

***The 84-foot radeau Ligonier, built under the supervision of Major Thomas Ord, would later be equipped with two masts and six 24-pound cannon.

†Guadeloupe in the French West Indies was captured by British forces in 1759.

they came ashore and our regiment was sent to carry them up to the fort.* We had no preaching from the chaplain [who] was so terribly horrible last Sunday that he has neither preached nor prayed since that we know of.—and I hope he never will again.—Lieutenant Granger came back from Crown Point and I with him by land.

The 27. We had nothing very remarkable. Last Wednesday night the valiant Lieutenant B—was on the picket and as he was going the rounds in the night he was very terribly surprised by a mighty rushing noise in the bushes. He immediately cried Indians, Indians, for he was sure he heard them hammer their flints. The guards were turned out immediately and [the] camp was all alarmed.—The said champion had a brother in camp, a noble warrior. He ran immediately to the colonel and begged a favor of him that he would fire and alarm that they might have help from the fort. But the colonel thought it proper to examine into the affair first and upon a strict examination they found it was oxen that were feeding in the bushes and clashing their horns against the trees [that] was the hammering [of] the flints. The two aforementioned heros have both left the regiment.

The 2. The chaplain ventured to preach a sermon at the mills but we did not hear him. The great flat bottomed boat [*Snow Shoe*] that has kept going backwards and forwards ever since the army crossed the Lake came in this morning bringing some oxen and cows and stores. It brought three 18 pounders and five 12 pounders besides a quantity of ammunition. About 9 o'clock at night there was an express [that] came from the mills informing that there had been Indians discovered near the fort. Our guards were doubled. The story soon got to be that there were 600 Indians and that they had fired upon our men twice but in the morning it all died away.

Tuesday the 11. Last night a very bright light appeared in the north and northwest part of the horizon [and] continued most of the night.—We drew fresh provision for seven days.

Thursday the 13. Today our people got up two large flat bottomed boats that were taken when Fort William Henry was [captured] and sunk at the landing [on Lake George].**—Camp news that Colonel Ruggles' and Colonel Willard's and Colonel Whiting's regiments were to go down to mend the roads between Lake George and Albany by the latter end of this month.

Sunday the 16. News from Crown Point that the army or [a] great part of them are to go forward to Saint Johns [St. Jean, Quebec] as soon as they get the great radeau [*Ligonier*] finished which is building at Crown Point and the brig [*Duke of Cumberland*]. . .ready to sail from Ticonderoga which is of 200 tons burden built there.

Wednesday the 26. The weather continues very warm and pleasant. Last night in the evening we saw a star as we call them shoot in the air. The appearance was very bright and sparkling and the motion slow. Its course was from north to south

---

*Colonel James Montresor at Fort George noted that "the draughts put on board the sloop mutinied which occasioned my sending a Captain & 20 men to take the ring leaders & put them in a Batoe to keep with the sloop and deliver to the commanding officer at the landing place."[28]

**On September 24 Amherst referred to the sunken vessels as scows which were to be raised and used to carry firewood for the winter garrison at the fort.[29] Earlier on July 23, Captain-Lieutenant Henry Skinner noted that "a sloop with eight guns" had been discovered in Lake George.[30] As late as 1761, Captain John Wrightson reported "a large French Boat at the Landing which could be Easily repaired."[31]

about 2 minutes. After it was out of sight we heard a noise as loud as the report of a cannon. We supposed it to be a cannon fired at the head of the lake but upon inquiry we hear there were no cannon fired at the head of the lake or that way—therefore it is generally thought that it was the report of the star we saw.

Thursday the 27. By a Boston newspaper of the 17th instant we have the agreeable news that General Wolfe with the army at Quebec were in high spirits as late as the 19th*.

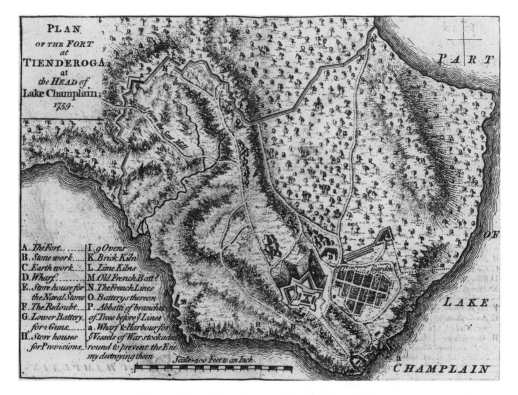

Plan of Fort Ticonderoga (Carillon) in 1759.
(National Archives of Canada)

*Wood's 1759 journal ended on September 27. Some entries involving perpetual rumors about operations in Canada and court-martials in September were omitted.

Notes:

1. For an excellent graphic depiction of these forts and posts see Gary S. Zaboly, ed., "A Royal Artillery Officer with Amherst: The Journal of Captain-Lieutenant Henry Skinner 1 May - 28 July 1759," *The Bulletin of the Fort Ticonderoga Museum* 15 (1993): 362.
2. Samuel Warner, "Extracts from Samuel Warner's Journal, Kept on the Expedition to Crown Point, 1759" in *An Historical Address - Town of Wilbraham*, by Rufus P. Stebbins (Boston: George C. Rand & Avery, 1964), 208; See also Henry True, *Journal and Letters of Rev. Henry True* (Marion, OH.: Star Press, 1900), 18; Henry Skinner, "Proceedings of the Army Under the Command of General Amherst, for the Year 1759," *The Universal Magazine* (November 1759): 268; Zaboly, 373.
3. Salah Barnard, "Journal of Major Salah Barnard," MS, Fort Ticonderoga Museum Library, Ticonderoga, N.Y.; For the dimensions of the *Halifax* see *Boston Gazette and Country Journal*, 28 August 1758; See also J. Clarence Webster, ed., *The Journal of Jeffery Amherst* (Toronto: The Ryerson Press, 1931), 127-29, 131; Skinner, 267-68.
4. Skinner (December 1759): 285; See also Webster, 138; Captain John Knox, *An Historical Journal of the Campaigns in North America*, Volume 1, (1769; edited by Arthur G. Doughty, 1914-1916; reprint ed., Freeport, N.Y.: Books for Libraries Press, 1970), 492.
5. *Boston Gazette and Country Journal*, 8 October 1759; Other witnesses mention smaller cannon on the row galleys in addition to the one 18-pounder. See Samuel Merriman, "Journal of Samuel Merriman," in *A History of Deerfield*, by George Sheldon (1895-96; reprint ed., Somersworth, N.H.: New Hampshire Publishing Company, 1972), 666.
6. Skinner (December 1759): 286; See also Webster, 132-33, 138, 141; James Henderson referred to the vessel as "an Ark of Redoubt," James Henderson, "James Henderson's Journal," in *The First Century of the Colonial Wars in the Commonwealth of Massachusetts* (Boston: Society of Colonial Wars, Mass., 1944), 204.
7. Barnard, p.n.a.; Winslow C. Watson, ed., *Pioneer History of the Champlain Valley* (Albany: J. Munsell, 1863), 95.
8. "Diary of a Soldier at Crown Point, etc., 1759," French and Indian War Collections, Octavo 2, American Antiquarian Society, Worcester, Ma.; James Montresor, "Journals of Col. James Montresor," *Collections of the New-York Historical Society* 14 (1881): 83; See also John Woods, "John Woods His Book," French and Indian War Collections, Octavo 1, American Antiquarian Society; A contemporary newspaper may also be referring to this vessel or the *Invincible*: "a very large Boat, well-arm'd, which carries near a Thousand Barrels of Provisions, and is to be used for any other Luggs." *Boston Gazette and Country Journal*, 30 July 1759.
9. Webster, 137; Zaboly, 378.
10. Skinner (December 1759): 286.
11. *Boston Gazette and Country Journal*, 8 October 1759; See also Warner, 210; Montresor, 81.
12. Barnard, p.n.a.; See also Constantine Hardy, "Extracts from the Journal of Constantine Hardy," *New-England Historical and Genealogical Register* 60 (1906): 237; Knox, 490-91.
13. Warner, 210; See also Skinner (November 1759), 267-68; True, 18; William Henshaw, "William Henshaw's Journal," *Proceedings of the Worcester Society of Antiquity* 25 (1909): 56.
14. Public Record Office, London, 293/2, 34/80, fol. 114.
15. John Hawks, *Orderly Book and Journal of Major John Hawks 1759-1760* (n.a., N.Y.: Society of Colonial Wars, 1911), 41-44; Commissary Wilson, *Commissary Wilson's Orderly Book, 1759* (Albany: J. Munsell, 1857): 87-90.
16. Skinner (December 1759): 286.
17. True, 10; Hardy, 237.
18. Merriman, 664.
19. Knox, 502.
20. Skinner (December 1759), 286: See also Webster, 142; True, 10.
21. Lemuel Wood, "Diaries Kept by Lemuel Wood, of Boxford," *The Essex Institute Historical Collections* 19 (1882): 61-80, 143-92; 20 (1883): 156-60.
22. Henderson, 203.
23. Zaboly, 378; Skinner (December 1759): 284-85.
24. Skinner (December 1759): 288; Webster, 146; Merriam, 665.
25. Webster, 146.

26. Merriman, 665.
27. Diedrick Brehm, "A New Description of Fort Ticonderoga," *The Bulletin of the Fort Ticonderoga Museum* 11 (December 1962): 38-42.
28. Montresor, 92.
29. Public Record Office, London, 293/3, 34/81, fol. 37.
30. Skinner (December 1759): 287.
31. Public Record Office, London, 283, 30/50, vol. 58.

Part III
Between Two Wars

Fort Ticonderoga.
(Photo by the author)

8. Francis Grant 1767

WITH THE END of the French and Indian War, Lake George became a highway for enterprising settlers on their way to the Lake Champlain Valley. During the 1760s, extensive land grants were conveyed by the British Crown to army officers and others at the northern end of the lake.* In 1765 Fort George at the southeast corner of the lake and Samuel Adams' tavern at Sabbath Day Point were both stopping points for travelers. Adams had settled on the point of land at the foot of Tongue Mountain in 1762 before applying for a land grant which he received in 1766.

William Gilliland, one of the early settlers of Lake Champlain, journeyed through Lake George in 1765, staying at Fort George and Adams' tavern. Gilliland, a veteran of the French and Indian War, had acquired a 15,000-acre tract of land near the Boquet River (present-day Willsboro, N.Y.) through a series of land purchases from the original grant recipients. On May 29, 1765, the future colonizer of Willsboro "arrived at Fort George, with all the people, cattle, Bateaux and goods."[1] Two days later Gilliland and his party "embarked at Fort George, for Ticonderoga with all the people and goods in the four bateaux, and all the cattle in the vessel called the Snow shoe,** and arrived at Saml Adams, at Sabbath day point, where we got the cattle on shore and lodged all night."[2]

Land adjacent to the outlet of Lake George in Ticonderoga was granted to John Stoughton, Richard Kellet, and John Kennedy in 1764. The first settlement at the northern end of Lake George was established in 1765 when John Stoughton from East Windsor, Connecticut, along with his two brothers Joseph and Nathaniel,

---

*The land grants were not only rewards for service to veterans but perhaps a method of defending the frontier.

**The *Snow Shoe* was a large provision vessel built by Amherst's army in 1759.

migrated to Ticonderoga. A veteran of the French and Indian War, John Stoughton had served from 1756 to 1760, including three years as an officer under Major General Phineas Lyman of Connecticut. John Stoughton and his family occupied a blockhouse, built during the French and Indian War, at the site of the Lake George landing. Stoughton formed a business partnership with Samuel Deall, a prosperous New York City merchant, to develop a trading and lumbering business in Ticonderoga at the Lake George outlet. By late 1767 Deall had acquired 5,000 acres including the John Kennedy tract in the area between Lake George and Lake Champlain. The partnership with Deall, however, was short-lived due to the death of John Stoughton who drowned when his schooner sank in Lake George.* The following letter to a fourth brother, Lemuel, was written by John's younger brother Nathaniel at Ticonderoga on December 6, 1767.

> Dear Brother;-
>   I must inform you of the melancholy death of my Brother John. He was crossing from Fort George the 25th of November with Hall. They set out from Fort George at 12 o'clock and encountered a fierce wind until they got above the narrows when they perceived a squall arising. My brother ordered Hall to down sail which he did and then turned for an island which was at a short distance but before they could reach it the boat filled with water and perceiving that they were sinking they endeavored to make their escape but my Brother was entangled with a rope about his body with the sheep, as we suppose and was drowned. Hall made his escape to the island. We set out after them Saturday night and found them on Sunday and brought them to the Landing. He was interred on Monday at 4 o'clock in the afternoon. Hall had been upon the island three days and four nights. One horse, six cows and five sheep were saved. He had three wagon loads of goods on board which he had brought from Albany which are most of them lost as far as we can find out.[4]

Samuel Deall, however, continued with his enterprises at Ticonderoga which included the building of a vessel for Lake George in 1769, a sawmill in 1771, and a gristmill the following year. In early 1773, Samuel Deall unsuccessfully petitioned for monopoly rights for a Lake George ferry. Deall died shortly thereafter and his possessions at Ticonderoga were abandoned when his family returned to Britain during the Revolutionary War.

At the time of the Stoughton presence at Ticonderoga in 1767, Francis Grant visited the region during a grand tour of upper New York State and lower Canada. Grant was the third son of Sir Francis Grant Bt.(Lord Cullen) of Monymusk, Aberdeenshire, in northeast Scotland. Grant's journey began in New York City on April 27, 1767, with a three-day passage aboard the sloop *Sally*. His journey proceeded along the Mohawk River to Schenectady, Fort Johnson, and Johnson Hall, where he met with Sir William Johnson. Grant then traveled to Fort Herkimer, Fort Niagara, Niagara Falls, the Thousand Islands, Montreal, Three Rivers, Quebec City, the Richelieu River, and Lake Champlain before reaching Lake George. Grant's entries include notes on the "mothballed" French and Indian War fleet at Ticonderoga, Montcalm's 1758 breastworks, John Stoughton's blockhouse at the Lake George landing, the tavern at Sabbath Day Point, Fort George, Fort Edward, and Rogers Island.

*William Gilliland called the vessel a schooner, which carried his family and stores on June 11, 1766.[3]

Journal From New York to Canada, 1767[5]

Saturday, July 18th, 1767. Proceeded about 11 A.M. for Ticonderoga, 15 miles from Crown Point to the Southward. The Lake continues narrow this distance. Ticonderoga, called by the French Carrillon, is a point formed by the Lake on the East, and a river running from Lake George on the West. There is here the remains of the French Fort, which was a square, defended by two ravellins [V-shaped outworks between two bastions] to the land side. The Fort is reckoned too small for the place, and from the Westward it is commanded by a rising ground the greatest height of which is 1/4 of a mile from the Fort. It is distant from the Point about 300 yards, ascending all the way. At the Point there is a strong redoubt* for the defence of the shipping, which are laid up here, consisting of a large Brigantine which mounted 20 guns, two Schooners, two Sloops, and some small craft; also a Sloop constantly employed in the summer season between this place and St. John's.** At the top of the rising ground to the Westward of the Fort, are Mr. [Marquis de] Montcalm's breast work or lines, at which General [James] Abercromby was defeated in [1758]. These lines still remain entire, and are very strong. They extend all the way from the river to the Lake, about 2 miles in length, flanked at every place, they are built of large round logs of wood, and are about 8 feet thick at [the] bottom, narrowing to the breadth of one log at [the] top. These logs are very large, and at the angles are morticed into one another; the lines are about man height. At the top of the hill there was a battery piquetted [picketed] and trenched, and the whole lines were defended by fallen trees, with their branches sharpened: upon the whole nothing could be stronger of the sort. About a mile beyond the breast work is a saw mill, to which place the river is navigable.*** Here is a slanting fall of water of about 40 feet, and between this and Lake George there is about a mile [by] a carriage.

Lake Champlaine continues from Ticonderoga about 30 miles to the Southeast, this part of it called South Bay. On it there are several Settlements, particularly Skeensborough [Skenesborough], belonging to Major Skeene [Skene].† Into this Bay runs Wood Creek, which comes from the Southward and is navigable within ten miles of Fort Edward. This is now the tract the Post goes to Lake Champlaine and Canada.

At the landing place at Lake George is a Block House in which Lieut. [John] Stoughton, who has a grant of land round it, now lives. Near this place Lord [George Viscount] Howe was killed in [1758].

*The Lotbinière Battery had originally been constructed by the French garrison.

**The brigantine was the *Duke of Cumberland*; one of the schooners was *La Vigilante*; one of the two sloops was the *Boscawen*; and the other *La Brochette, L' Esturgeon* or perhaps the *Waggon*.[6] The sloop that was still in service was *La Musquelongy* which carried William Gilliland to Crown Point in June 1766.[7]

***The sawmill was originally built by the French and later repaired by Amherst in 1759 for use in the construction of the Lake Champlain fleet. Samuel Deall's sawmill was later built on the north side of the LaChute River.

†Philip Skene, a British officer who participated in the Abercromby and Amherst expeditions, received a grant of 25,000 acres in 1765 and 9,000 acres in 1771 at the southern end of Lake Champlain. He had earlier established the settlement of Skenesborough (Whitehall, N.Y.) and was nominally appointed governor of Crown Point and Ticonderoga in 1775.

Sunday, July 19th, 1767. Embarked at 5 A.M. at the landing place, on a batteau; at half past eight got to Sabbath Day Point, distance 12 miles, where there is a Settlement and a tavern. It took its name from an engagement Major [Robert] Rogers had with the enemy at this place on a Sunday.* Proceeded to the narrows, ten miles further; here are a number of small islands with narrow passages between them. At half past five P.M. arrived at Fort George at the end of the Lake, distant from the landing place 36 miles due south. The greatest breadth of the Lake is five miles, but in general it does not exceed two or three. It is surrounded every way by steep rocky mountains, having no flat land anywhere. The islands on it are beds of rocks, so that it never will admit of settling. There are frequent and sudden violent gusts of wind on this Lake from the mountains, which renders the navigation a little hazardous, as there are few places of shelter all along. On this, and Lake Champlaine there is abundance of fish of several kinds. Fort George is situated at the South end of the Lake, nearly fronting the middle of it. There is no fortification except a redoubt amounting 12 guns, about 200 yards from the shore, and some barracks. A large Fort was intended here but it never was executed.** On the other side of a small creek to the Westward of the Fort, which runs through a wide gully, Fort William Henry was situated. It was burnt by Montcalm in [1757], and there is not at present any remains of it to be seen. Between that place and the present Fort are lines thrown up by General Abercromby after the defeat at Ticonderoga extending about two miles. Near the Fort is the field of battle between Sir William Johnson and [Baron de] Dieskau in 1755. The lines Sir William threw up here were nearly parallel to the Lake. The attack of the French was from the land side to the S.E. There is a considerable extent of ground opened here, but the soil is sandy.

Monday, July 20th, 1767. Proceeded from Fort George on horseback for Fort Edward. At three miles from the former is a pond at which began the massacre of the Garrison of Fort William Henry by the Indians, from which it has got the name of 'bloody pond.'*** There were some Settlements on the road, but the soil appears to be very sandy and indifferent. Within three miles of Fort Edward we came to the banks of Hudson's River, running from the N.W. Its source must be considerable distant, as at this place it is of great breadth.

FORT EDWARD is situated in a very pleasant vale through which Hudson's River runs; it is 14 miles distant from Fort George to the Southward.† It is on the East bank of the river which is here divided by two islands. On the opposite shore

---

*During the French and Indian War, a point of land on the west side of the lake just north of the Narrows became known as Sabbath Day Point, but the name is not linked to a battle involving Robert Rogers and his Rangers.

**In 1759 Major General Jeffery Amherst had reassigned workers at Fort George to Crown Point. Amherst described Fort George in 1760 as a neat bastion which "mounts 15 Guns, is very small and a bad defense, but 'twas the shortest, cheapest & best method of finishing what was begun of the Fort."[8] In 1759 the barracks were enclosed by a wooden stockade and located closer to the lake than Fort George. Whether Grant was referring to these wooden barracks or a brick barracks inside the fort is unknown.

***"Bloody Pond" received its name from the Battle of Lake George on September 8, 1755. Canadian troops and Indians, who were looting and scalping the corpses of provincial troops from the ambush of Colonel Ephraim Williams' detachment, were overwhelmed by fresh provincial troops from Fort Lyman. The bodies of the Canadians and Indians were said to have been thrown into the pond.

†Fort Edward was vacated by the British army in 1766 and the stores transferred to Crown Point.

to the Fort is the Hospital, the buildings of which still remain.* At this place we forded the river at its three branches. The soil about Fort Edward is very fine, and we were informed that it is so for many miles to the Eastward. There are numbers of new Settlements about this place, and as far as Saratoga on the banks of the river: these Settlements increase daily.

SARATOGA is thirty miles from Fort George, pleasantly situated in a fine valley, with Hudson's River running through the middle of it, here are many fine farms, and the soil appears to be exceedingly good. At this place are the ruins of an old Fort, which in the war before last was the Frontier of the Province of New York.** At that time this Settlement was cut off by the French and Indians. Mr. Philip Schuyler has a fine Settlement here through which runs a creek, on which he has a fine herring fishery where immense quantities of herring are caught on which in bad years the poor people all around subsist.

Notes

1. Winslow C. Watson, *Pioneer History of the Champlain Valley* (Albany: J. Munsell, 1863), 94.
2. Ibid., 95.
3. Ibid., 128.
4. Jane M. Lape, ed., *Ticonderoga-Patches and Patterns from Its Past* (Ticonderoga, N.Y.: The Ticonderoga Historical Society, 1969), 25; For Samuel Deall's correspondence to John Stoughton and his wife see Flavius J. Cook, *Home Sketches of Essex County-Ticonderoga* (1858, reprint ed., Ticonderoga, N.Y.: Ticonderoga Historical Society, 1989), 24-25; H. P. Smith, ed., *History of Essex County* (Syracuse, N.Y.: D. Mason & Co., Publishers, 1885), 385-86.
5. Francis Grant, "Journal from New York to Canada, 1767," *Proceedings of the New York State Historical Association* 30 (1932): 319-22.
6. Haldimand Papers, "Misc. Papers Relating to the Provincial Navy 1775-1780," National Archives of Canada, Microfilm H-1649, Volume 1, B144, fol.99.
7. Watson, 128.
8. J. Clarence Webster, ed., *The Journal of Jeffery Amherst* (Toronto: The Ryerson Press, 1931), 262.

*Grant is referring to Rogers Island where barracks, Ranger huts, a blockhouse, and a hospital were constructed during the French and Indian War.

**The old fort was Fort Clinton which had been built in 1745 but burned two years later since it was judged impossible to defend against French raiding parties.

Part IV
The American Revolution

Charles Carroll of Carrollton.
(Library of Congress)

9. Charles Carroll 1776

IN 1775 WAR CLOUDS would once again engulf the Lake George and Lake Champlain valleys. Following the capture of Fort Ticonderoga by Ethan Allen and Benedict Arnold on May 10, 1775, Lake George would become a vital link to the northern theater during the American Revolution.

With the capture of Ticonderoga, the patriots set their sights on Crown Point and Fort George. Captain Bernard Romans from Wethersfield, Connecticut, who originally had orders along with others from Connecticut to capture Fort Ticonderoga, left the expedition in Bennington, Vermont, after a disagreement. Romans subsequently took the initiative of seizing Fort George. Unfinished and abandoned, Fort George was nominally under the jurisdiction of Captain John Nordberg, a 65-year-old retired British officer who lived in a cottage near the fort. Although Nordberg later wrote that "Mr. Romans came & took possession of Fort George," Epaphras Bull with the Connecticut troops noted in his journal on May 11 that Romans arrived after the fort had been seized: "we Embark'd [from Ticonderoga] with the Soldiers on board a Large Pettyorger* & 1 Battoe. . .Arri'd at Fort George about 9 OClock P.M. where we met Capt. [John] Stephens with 15 Men Come on from Fort Edward to take Possession of Fort George tho' it Happen'd to be given up to 3 or 4 of our men who we sent forward before they Arr[ive]d. Soon after our Arrival Capt. Roman our Engineer Came up."[2]

In 1775 Lake George quickly became a water highway carrying supplies for the Northern Army during the ill-fated invasion of Canada. Philip Schuyler was commissioned a major general in command of the Northern Army on June 19, 1775, by the Continental Congress. Schuyler, a descendant of one of the most famous

---

*This may have been the two-masted periagua built for Samuel Deall for Lake George in 1769. The vessel was probably built by John Sparding at the Ticonderoga landing.[1]

Dutch families in New York, had participated in the 1755 Battle of Lake George at the onset of the French and Indian War and later accompanied the Abercromby expedition to Fort Carillon (Ticonderoga) in 1758. Arriving at Fort George on July 17, 1775, General Schuyler issued a blizzard of orders regulating the activities, cleanliness, and drinking habits of the 334-man garrison at the southern end of Lake George. To facilitate the movement of men and supplies to Fort Ticonderoga for the Canadian invasion, Schuyler assigned carpenters to Lake George to build bateaux and other vessels. Two weeks after his inspection of Fort George, 30 bateaux were completed at the lake. The American army's invasion of Canada was successful in the capture of Fort St. Jean in early November 1775, which forced the British to evacuate Montreal, but the Americans soon reached a stalemate in the siege of Quebec City.

While the Northern Army continued with its Canadian incursion, Henry Knox was sent to Fort Ticonderoga by George Washington to procure cannon needed to break the British siege of Boston. Knox arrived at Fort George on December 4 at the same time that Lieutenant John André was briefly held a prisoner there following the surrender of Fort St. Jean. André was subsequently paroled and later conspired with Benedict Arnold. Legend suggests that Knox and André stayed in the same cabin at Fort George, but there is little evidence to support the story.[3] Five years later, however, Knox would serve as a member of the military court that would condemn André to death for his part in the Arnold conspiracy.

At Ticonderoga Knox assembled the artillery collected from Crown Point, Fort St. Jean, and Fort Ticonderoga for transfer to Boston. Some of the cannon were transported by vessel a short distance on the LaChute River while the remaining cannon were hauled directly overland to the Lake George landing. According to Knox's notes, 59 cannon, mortars, and howitzers, weighing 119,000 pounds, comprised the artillery train destined for the defense of Boston. On December 9, 1775, Knox recorded the voyage through Lake George:

> 9th. Employ'd in loading the Scow, Pettianger & a Battoe. At 3 o'Clock in the afternoon s[e]t sail to go down the lake in the Pettianger, the Scow in coming after us run aground we being about a mile ahead with fair wind to do down but unfair to help the Scow, the wind dying away we with the utmost difficulty reach'd Sabbath Day Point about 9 o'Clock in the evening—went ashore & warm'd ourselves by an exceeding good fire in an hut made by some civil Indians who were with their Ladies abed—they gave us some Venison, roasted after their manner which was very relishing. . . . We had been there when one of the Battoes which had set out nearly the same time the same day that we had, allur'd by the view of the fire likewise came on shore, & the crew of which inform'd us that the Scow had run on a sunken rock but not in such a manner as to be irretrievable*. . . . The crew of the Battoe after having sufficiently refresh'd themselves told me that, as they were not very deeply loaded, they intended to push for Fort George. I jump'd into the Boat & order'd my man to bring my baggage & we would go with them. Accordingly we s[e]t out it being eleven o'Clock with a light breeze ahead the men row'd briskly, but we had not been out above an hour when the wind sprung up very fresh & directly against us. The men after rowing exceedingly hard for about four hours seem'd desirous

*Nineteen-year-old William Knox, aboard the scow, wrote to his brother Henry on December 14 that his vessel had been freed of the rock and sailed to Sabbath Day Point but had sunk in the shallow water there. The boat was bailed out, repaired, and reached Fort George by December 15.

of going ashore, to make a fire to warm themselves. I readily consented knowing them to be exceedingly weary. . .About half an hour before day break that is about a quarter after six we s[e]t out and in six hours & a quarter of excessive hard pulling against a fresh head breeze we reach'd Fort George.[4]

Knox initially contracted for 42 sleds and 80 pair of oxen to be delivered to Lake George, but dissatisfaction with the high prices quoted resulted in new arrangements through General Philip Schuyler for carriages, sleds, oxen, and 124 teams of horses. The monumental task of transporting the cannon to Boston was completed by the end of January 1776. On March 17, 1776, the British departed from Boston.

"The Noble Train of Artillery" being moved by Colonel Henry Knox and his men from Fort Ticonderoga to Lake George on December 7, 1775. Painting by Tom Lovell.
(Fort Ticonderoga Museum)

Ironically, they abandoned 250 pieces of artillery. Although the cannon had been spiked or disabled by the British, most were later repaired by American craftsmen.

At the same time, the Continental Congress, meeting in Philadelphia, was preparing a mission to Canada to help invigorate the stalemated invasion and persuade the Canadians to form their own independent government allied with the 13 colonies. When the Americans first invaded Canada in late 1775, there appeared to be some support by local inhabitants for the American cause. However, the long siege of Quebec, the anti-Catholic rhetoric by the Continental Congress and some military officers, overdue bills owed Canadians, and the loss of confidence in the American ability to succeed against the British had taken their toll on Canadian support.

One of the commissioners to Canada chosen by Congress was 39-year-old Charles Carroll of Maryland. As an emissary to the French Catholics, Carroll's background included European study, fluency in French, a Roman Catholic up-bringing, and political abilities honed in Maryland. Born in Annapolis in 1737, Carroll had a family heritage of landed aristocracy with roots in the original settlement of the region in the seventeenth century. At the age of 11, Charles Carroll, along with his second cousin, John Carroll, were sent to France for an education at the Jesuit-taught St. Omer College. After six years at St. Omer, Charles Carroll completed further liberal studies at Rheims and Paris. Following a grand tour of Europe, he began the study of English law at London's Middle Temple. Following the completion of his law studies, Carroll became preoccupied with an earnest search for a wife. He returned to America in 1765. His first engagement ended when his fiancé died shortly before their wedding day, but Carroll eventually married in 1769 and settled into managing his property and fortune in Maryland.

In 1773 he penned a series of articles in the *Maryland Gazette* which challenged the governor's proclamation on the support of the Church of England and the concomitant fees placed on the citizenry. Subsequently, Carroll was elected to the Maryland Committee of Correspondence and the Committee of Safety. Although not yet an official delegate to the Continental Congress, by 1776 Charles Carroll had become a respected member of the inner circle of patriot leaders. By the end of January, the Maryland delegates to Congress had informed Carroll of his forthcoming invitation to be one of the three commissioners to Canada and requested that he recommend a priest to accompany the mission. Carroll selected his cousin, John Carroll, who had been a Jesuit in France and at that time was a priest in America. For the two other commissioners, Congress chose Benjamin Franklin, who by then had an international reputation in political circles, and Samuel Chase, a delegate to the Continental Congress from Maryland.

The commissioners had the daunting task of assessing the American military situation in Canada and winning support from the Canadians. In November 1775 the American army under Brigadier General Richard Montgomery had captured Fort St. Jean on the Richelieu River while troops under Benedict Arnold completed an arduous expedition through Maine to attack Quebec City. After the fall of St. Jean, the British fled from Montreal to Quebec. During a bitter snowstorm on December 31, Montgomery was killed and Arnold wounded in an unsuccessful assault on Quebec.

In April 1776 General David Wooster commanded the troops besieging Quebec City. Provisions and troops gradually made their way to the army in Canada for a spring offensive, but the supply lines from Albany were greatly overextended. Ironically, the commissioners reached Montreal just before the American retreat from Quebec. On May 2 Major General John Thomas replaced David Wooster at Quebec, only to retreat hastily from the city four days later when British ships arrived. The Americans fell back to Deschambault (25 miles south of Quebec on the St. Lawrence River) and then Sorel at the mouth of the Richelieu River.

On May 6 the three commissioners wrote to the Continental Congress that unless "hard money" could be sent to Canada to support the army "it would be advisable, in our opinion, to withdraw our army, and fortify the passes on the lake."[5] Realizing the hopelessness of the Canadian campaign and suffering from the swelling of his legs, Benjamin Franklin departed for Albany on May 11, accompanied by Father John Carroll. Father Carroll had been rebuffed by the French Catholic clergy due largely to the tolerant religious policy of the British government. The passage of the liberal Quebec Act of 1774, which allowed unrestricted practice of the Catholic religion and recognized French land tenure, had ended dissent by the Catholic Church's hierarchy in Canada. While in Paris eight years after the Canadian mission, Benjamin Franklin suggested Father Carroll's elevation to Superior of the Catholic Church in America. Carroll was soon appointed to that position by the Pope and subsequently became the first Catholic bishop in the United States. Bishop Carroll delivered the public eulogy at George Washington's funeral in 1799.

Charles Carroll and Samuel Chase wrote to Congress from Canada on May 17, 1776, outlining the problems of supplies, unfit officers, short enlistments, and the general confusion in the army. They concluded that "our stay here [is] no longer of service to the publick" but suggested that they were willing to remain in Canada "for the good of our country."[6] Four days later Carroll and Chase inspected the Sorel camp where they found "the army . . .in a distressed condition. . .in want of the most necessary articles. . .broken and disheartened."[7] On May 31 the two commissioners departed from Chambly for the long trip back to Philadelphia.

Although troubled by the news from Canada, Congress pressed forward with reinforcements. Brigadier General John Sullivan reached Sorel by June 4 with several thousand fresh recruits to assume leadership of an army decimated by smallpox and a lack of supplies. Five days later Brigadier General William Thompson and 300-500 troops were captured in a disastrous foray against the British position at Three Rivers. On June 14 Sullivan evacuated the Sorel camp. Four days later the 7,000-8,000-man army retreated to Isle-aux-Noix in the Richelieu River. On July 2, 1776, the dispirited and broken army reached Crown Point. Two thousand of the sick were later transferred to a hospital at Fort George. Although the Canadian invasion appeared to be a complete misadventure, it resulted in stalling the British advance into the American colonies through Lake Champlain in 1776.

After his return from Canada, Charles Carroll was elected to the Continental Congress, signed the Declaration of Independence, and served on many boards and committees during the war. In 1789 he was elected to the United States Senate under the new Constitution and later served in the Maryland Senate until 1800. When Carroll died at the age of 95, in 1832, he was the last surviving signer of the Declaration of Independence.

BENJAMIN FRANKLIN

Né a Boston le 17. Janvier 1706.

Eripuit coelo fulmen fceptrum que tyrannis.

In April 1776 Benjamin Franklin, at the age of 70, made the trip
across Lake George with Charles Carroll in an open bateau.
(Library of Congress)

Carroll's journal of 1776 provides vivid descriptions of Lake George, Fort George, sailing bateaux, the northern landing, the LaChute River, Montcalm's 1758 breastworks, and Fort Ticonderoga. His views on the future settlement of Lake George and the possibility of a Champlain canal furnish interesting insights into the views of an eighteenth-century chronicler. Carroll began his journal on April 2, 1776, when the commissioners departed from New York City aboard an armed sloop. At one o'clock in the morning the travelers were abruptly awakened by cannon fire from the British warship *Asia*. Benjamin Franklin and others observed the action from the open deck as the American forces attacked British entrenchments on Bedlow's Island.* The following day was rainy with violent winds that split the vessel's mainsail. The weather improved for the next two days, allowing the vessel on April 7 to reach Albany where General Philip Schuyler met the commissioners. As early as October 1775 Schuyler had recommended that a congressional committee travel to Canada to direct future operations.

Carroll noted that Albany appeared larger than Annapolis and that the inhabitants spoke Dutch. After a two-day stay at the Schuyler home, the party departed by wagon for Saratoga, accompanied by Philip Schuyler and his family and Major General John Thomas who was on his way to Quebec. Carroll, along with Schuyler and Thomas, viewed the waterfall at Cohoes on April 9. Late that evening the party reached Schuyler's summer home at Saratoga (later Schuylerville). Schuyler, who had scrutinized the Bridgewater Canal in England in 1761, suggested to Carroll that a canal constructed through Wood Creek could connect the Hudson River to Lake Champlain and Canada. Forty-seven years later the Champlain Canal would be completed.

The day before the commissioners departed from Saratoga, 70-year-old Benjamin Franklin penned an uncharacteristically melancholy letter to his friend Josiah Quincy: "I am here on my way to Canada, detained by the present state of the lakes, in which the unthawed ice obstructs the navigation. I begin to apprehend that I have undertaken a fatigue that, at my time of life, may prove too much for me, so I sit down to write to a few friends, by way of farewell."[8] Franklin, of course, completed the trip and lived to help draft the Declaration of Independence, persuade France to assist the American colonies, and serve as one of the three American commissioners on the peace treaty to end the Revolution. He was later a delegate to the Constitutional Convention and died in 1790.

*The island is today known as Liberty Island, site of the Statue of Liberty.

Journal of Charles Carroll of Carrollton[9]

[April] 16th. This morning we set off from Saratoga; I parted with regret from the amiable family of General [Philip] Schuyler; the ease and affability with which we were treated, and the lively behavior of the young ladies, made Saratoga a most pleasing séjour [stay], the remembrance of which will long remain with me. We rode from Saratoga to McNeill's ferry, (distance two miles and a half), crossed Hudson's river at this place, and rode on to one mile above Fort Miller, which is distant from McNeill's two miles.* A Mr. Duer has a country-seat near Fort Miller; you see his house from the road. There is a very considerable fall in the river at Fort Miller. Just above it our baggage was put into another boat; it had been brought in a wagon from Saratoga to McNeill's, carried over the ferry in a wagon, and then put on board a boat, in which it was conveyed to the foot of Fort Miller falls; then carried over land a quarter of a mile and put into a second boat. At a mile from Fort Miller we got into a boat and went up the Hudson river to Fort Edward. Although this fort is but seven miles distant from the place where we took [the] boat, we were above four hours rowing up. The current is exceedingly rapid, and the rapidity was increased by a freshet. In many places the current was so strong that the batteau men were obliged to set up with poles, and drag the boat by the painter [tow line]. Although these fellows were active and expert at their business, it was with the greatest difficulty they could stem the current in particular places. The congress keeps in pay three companies of batteau men on Hudson's river, consisting each of thirty-three men with a captain;—the pay of the men is £4.10 per month. The lands bordering on Hudson's river, as you approach Fort Edward, become more sandy, and principal wood that grows on them is pine. There are several saw mills both above and below Fort Miller. The planks sawed at the mills above Fort Miller are made up into small rafts and left without guides to the current of the river; each one is marked, so that the raftmen that remain just below Fort Miller falls, watching for them coming down, may easily know their own rafts. When they come over the falls they go out in canoes and boats and tow their rafts ashore, and then take them to pieces and make them again into larger rafts. The smaller rafts are called cribs. The ruins only of Fort Edward remain;** there is a good large inn, where we found quartered Colonel [Arthur] Sinclair's [St. Clair's] regiment. Mr. [William] Allen, son of old Mr. Allen, is lieutenant-colonel; he received us very politely and accommodated us with beds. The officers of this regiment are in general fine sized men, and seemed to be on a friendly footing;—the soldiers also are stout fellows.

17th. Having breakfasted with Colonel Allen, we set off from Fort Edward on our way to Fort George. We had not got a mile from the fort when a messenger from General Schuyler met us. He was sent with a letter by the general to inform us that Lake George was not open, and to desire us to remain at an inn kept by one Wing at seven miles distance from Fort Edward and as many from Fort George.***

*Fort Miller, a staging area during the French and Indian War, was originally located on the west side of the Hudson River.

**Fort Edward was built in 1755 with additional construction through 1758. The fort was abandoned in 1766, but Rogers' Island was reoccupied by American forces during the Revolution.

***Carroll is referring to Abraham Wing who had founded the community a decade earlier (present-day Glens Falls). Until 1788, the settlement was known as Wing's Falls and Wing's Corner.

The country between Wing's tavern and Fort Edward is very sandy and somewhat hilly. The principal wood is pine. At Fort Edward the river Hudson makes a sudden turn to the westward; it soon again resumes its former north course, for, at a small distance, we found it on our left and parallel with the road which we travelled, and which, from Fort Edward to Fort George, lies nearly north and south. At three miles, or thereabouts, from Fort Edward, is a remarkable fall in the river. We could see it from the road, but not so as to form any judgment of its height. We were informed that it was upwards of thirty feet, and is called the Kingsbury falls. We could distinctly see the spray arising like a vapor or fog from the violence of the fall. The banks of the river, above and below these falls for a mile or two, are remarkably steep and high, and appear to be formed or faced, with a kind of stone very much resembling slate.* The banks of the Mohawk's river at the Cohooes are faced with the same sort of stone;—it is said to be an indication of sea-coal. Mr. Wing's tavern is in the township of Queensbury, and Charlotte county; Hudson's river is not above a quarter of a mile from his house. There is a most beautiful fall in the river at this place. From still water, to the foot of the fall, I imagine the fall cannot be less than sixty feet, but the fall is not perpendicular; it may be about a hundred and twenty or a hundred and fifty feet long, and in this length, it is broken into three distinct falls, one of which may be twenty-five feet nearly perpendicular. I saw Mr. Wing's patent [land grant],—the reserved quit-rent is two shillings and sixpence sterling per hundred acres; but he informs me it has never been yet collected.

18th. We set off from Wing's tavern about twelve o'clock this day, and reached Fort George about two o'clock; the distance is eight miles and a half;—you can not discover the lake until you come to the heights surrounding it,—the descent from which to the lake is nearly a mile long;—from these heights you have a beautiful view of the lake for fifteen miles down it. Its greatest breadth during these fifteen miles does not exceed a mile and a quarter, to judge by the eye, which, however, is a very fallacious way of estimating distances. Several rocky islands appear in the lake, covered with a species of cedar called here hemlock. Fort George is in as ruinous a condition as Fort Edward, it is a small bastion, faced with stone, and built on an eminence commanding the head of the lake.** There are some barracks in it, in which the troops were quartered, or rather *one* barrack, which occupied almost the whole space between the walls.*** At a little distance from this fort, and to the westward of it, is the spot where the Baron [de] Dieskau was defeated by Sir William

*This area was first settled in 1768 and became known as Sandy Hill. In 1910 the village of Sandy Hill was renamed Hudson Falls.

**Fort George was begun in 1759 under the direction of Colonel James Montresor, an engineer with General Jeffery Amherst. Although only one stone bastion mounting 15 cannon was completed in 1759, three stockaded bastions and wooden barracks were built near the lake. Additional construction, including a barracks and a hospital, apparently occurred during the Revolution when the fort was garrisoned by American troops. Fort George was occupied briefly by British troops in 1777 and 1780. Many of the stones from the fort were eventually carted away by early settlers. A partial reconstruction of the fort took place in the 1920s; today the site is open to the public.

***In April 1776 Ammi R. Robbins, a chaplain with the American army, recorded that "Fort George is a small stone fort, with convenient brick barrack in the midst, containing six rooms for soldiers."[10] Apparently, new barracks were built in 1776, for Robbins' next sentence mentioned "a convenient wharf at the end and a large number of fine bateaux about it; barracks built for the accommodations of several regiments of soldiers"; and the next day related that he "prayed and sung at night in the large new barrack; great numbers attended."[11] In contrast, the soldiers at Fort George during the previous year did not mention new barracks. Captain Henry Brockholst Livingston of the Third New York

Johnson. About a quarter of a mile further to the westward the small remains of Fort William Henry are to be seen across a little rivulet which forms a swamp, and is the morass mentioned by Sir William Johnson in his account of the action with Dieskau. Fort William Henry was taken last war by Montcalm and destroyed;*—the garrison, consisting of four hundred men, and sixteen hundred others that were intrenched without the fort, capitulated;—a considerable part of these men were murdered by the Indians, on their march to Fort Edward, after they had delivered up their arms, according to the terms of capitulation. The bay in which Montcalm landed is seen from Fort George; he left a guard of five hundred men only to protect his boats and artillery, and marched round over the heights to come to the southward of Fort William Henry. When on these heights, he discovered the intrenched body without the fort, and seeing the great indiscretion he had been guilty of in leaving so small a force to guard his baggage and boats, he rashly marched back to secure them. Had our troops attacked Montcalm's five hundred men, they would probably have defeated them, taken his cannon and boats, and forced him to surrender with his whole army. There was nothing to impede the attack but want of enterprise and conduct in the commanding officer.** The neighborhood of Fort George abounds with limestone, and so indeed does all the country surrounding the lake, and all the islands in it. Their rocky coast and bottom contribute, no doubt, to the clearness of the lake water. Never did I see water more transparent, and to its transparency, no doubt, must be ascribed the excellence of the fish in this lake, which much exceed the fish in Lake Champlain. Lake George abounds with perch, trout, rock, and eels.

19th. We embarked at Fort George this evening, about one o'clock, in company with General Schuyler, and landed in Montcalm's bay about four miles from Fort George.*** After drinking tea on shore, and arranging matters in our boats, we again embarked, and went about three or four miles further, then landed, (the sun being set,) and kindled fires on shore. The longest of the boats, made for the transportation of the troops over Lakes George and Champlain, are thirty-six feet in length and eight feet wide; they draw about a foot [of] water when loaded, and carry between thirty and forty men, and are rowed by the soldiers. They have a mast fixed in them,

Regiment noted in September 1775 that "Fort George is built on an Eminence 300 yards south of Lake George, is much out of repair altho still defensible, being built mostly of stone . . . There is near 3 or 400 acres of cleared land about the fort & a few wretched Hovels that were formerly used as Barracks."[12] However, Sergeant Aaron Barlow in November 1775 noted in his diary that he "lodged this night in the Barracks [at Fort George]."[13] During the summer of 1776 the Fort George post was used as a hospital for the Northern Army. In August 1776 Dr. Lewis Beebe recorded that "the number of the sick in the Hospital was near 2000."[14]

*A replica of Fort William Henry was built between 1954 and 1956. During the excavation of the original fort, archaeologist Stanley Gifford discovered brick-and-stone-lined rooms beneath the remains of the east and west barracks, human skeletons, and thousands of artifacts.[15] Today, the replica of the fort continues to be a major tourist attraction at the southern end of Lake George.

**Carroll's view is at odds with the modern historical analysis of the British defeat at Fort William Henry. Lieutenant Colonel George Monro, the fort's commander, was vastly outnumbered by Montcalm's army. The diversion of troops to the ill-fated Louisbourg campaign by the British commander-in-chief, Lord Loudoun, and Major General Daniel Webb's failure to call for reinforcements in July when scouting reports suggested an impending French offensive were more important reasons that explain the disaster at Fort William Henry.

***In 1757 the Marquis de Montcalm landed his forces in a bay, later named Artillery Cove, located about a mile north of Fort William Henry on the west side of the lake.

to which a square sail, or a blanket is fastened, but these sails are of no use unless with the wind abaft or nearly so.* After we left Montcalm bay we were delayed considerably in getting through the ice; but, with the help of tentpoles, we opened ourselves a passage through it into free water. The boats fitted up to carry us across had awnings over them, under which we made up our beds, and my fellow travellers slept very comfortably; but this was not my case, for I was indisposed the whole night, with a violent sickness at my stomach and vomiting, occasioned by an indigestion. We left the place where we passed the night very early on the 20th.

20th. We had gone some miles before I rose; soon after I got out of bed we found ourselves entangled in the ice. We attempted, but in vain, to break through it in one place, but were obliged to desist and force our passage through another, which we effected without much difficulty. At eight o'clock we landed to breakfast. After breakfast the general looked to his small boat; being desirous to reach the landing at the north end of Lake George, we set off together; but the general's boat and the other boat, with part of the luggage, soon got before us a considerable way. After separating, we luckily fell in with the boat bringing the Montreal and Canada mail, by which we were informed that the west shore of the lake, at a place called Sabatay point [Sabbath Day Point], was much encumbered with ice, but that there was a free passage on the east side; accordingly, we kept along the east shore, and found it free from ice, by which means we got before the general and the other boat; for the general, who was foremost, had been delayed above an hour in breaking through the ice, and, in one place, was obliged to haul his boat over a piece or neck of land thirty feet broad. Dr. Franklin found in the Canada mail, which he opened, a letter for General Schuyler. When we had weathered Sabatay point, we stood over for the western shore of the lake, and a mile or two below the point we were overtaken by the general, from whom we learned the cause of his delay. Mr. Chase and myself went on board the general's boat, and reached the landing place at the [north] end of Lake George near two hours before the other boats. Lake George lies nearly north and south, or rather, as I think, somewhat to the eastward of a due north course. Its shores are remarkably steep, high, and rocky (particularly the east shore), and are covered with pine and cedar, or what is here termed hemlock; the country is wild, and appears utterly incapable of cultivation; it is a fine deer country, and likely to remain so, for I think it never will be inhabited.** I speak of the shores, and I am told the inland country resembles these. The lake, in its greatest width, does not exceed, I think, two miles; the widest part is nearest the north end, immediately before you enter the last narrows, which are not, in their greatest width, above half a mile. There are two places where the lake is considerably contracted, one about the middle of it, the other, as I have said, at the north end; this last gradually contracts itself in breadth to the size of an inconsiderable river, and suddenly, in depth, to that of a very shallow one. The landing place of Lake George is a few yards to the southward of the first fall or ripple in this river, through which the waters of Lake George drain into Lake Champlain. We passed through this ripple, and though our

---

*The bateau, a flat-bottomed, doubled-ended boat with oak frames and pine planks, was the workhorse of eighteenth century armies. Three bateaux were raised from Lake George in 1960. Along the southeastern shore of the lake, seven bateaux are presently in a New York State Submerged Heritage Preserve.

**Obviously, Carroll's prediction missed its mark. By the middle of the nineteenth century, tourist hotels began to dot the very areas that Carroll felt would never be settled.

boat did not draw above seven or eight inches, her bottom raked the rocks; the water ran through this passage about as swift as it does through your tail race [channel from a water wheel]. From the landing place to Ticonderoga is three miles and a half. The boats, in coming through Lake George, pass through the passage just described, and unload at a quarter of a mile below the usual landing place. Their contents are then put into wagons, and carried over to Ticonderoga. General Schuyler has erected a machine for raising the boats when emptied, and then letting them gently down on a carriage constructed for the purpose, on which they are drawn over land to Ticonderoga, on Lake Champlain, to carry the troops over the last mentioned lake, and down the Sorel into the river St. Lawrence.* These carriages consist of four wheels, united by a long sapling, at the extremities of which the wheels are placed; over the axletrees is fixed a piece of wood, on which each end of the boat is supported and made fast by a rope secured round a bolt at the undermost part, and in the centre of the axletree. This bolt is made of iron, and passes through the aforesaid pieces of wood and the axletree. These carriages are drawn by six oxen, and this morning (21st instant) I saw three or four boats carried over upon them. Lake George, from the south end of it to the landing place at the north extremity, is thirty-six miles long. Its average width does not, I think, exceed a mile, and this breadth is interspersed and broken by innumerable little rocky islands formed of limestone; the shores of which are commonly so steep that you may step from the rocks into ten or twelve feet [of] water. The season was not sufficiently advanced to admit of catching fish, a circumstance we had reason to regret, as they are so highly praised by the connoisseurs in good eating, and as one of our company is so excellent a judge in this science. There are no considerable rivers that empty themselves into Lake George. We saw some brooks or rivulets, which, I presume, after the melting of the snows, are almost dry. The lake must be fed, principally, with springs, the melting of snows, and the torrents that must pour into it, from its high and steep shores, after rains. As there is no considerable river that flows into it, so is the vent of its water into Lake Champlain very inconsiderable. In summer you may step, dry-footed, from rock to rock, in the place which I have called the first ripple, and which I said we passed, coming out of Lake George. The water suddenly shallows from a great depth to nine or ten feet or less. This change is immediately discoverable by the great change in the color of the water. The lake water is of a dark bluish cast, and the water of the river of a whitish color, owing not only to difference of the depth, but the difference of the bottoms and shores, which, adjoining the river, are of white clay.

21st. I took a walk this evening to the sawmill which is built on the principal fall of the [LaChute] river flowing from Lake George into Lake Champlain. At the foot of this fall, which is about thirteen feet high, the river is navigable for batteaux into Lake Champlain. From the saw-mill to the place [on Lake George] where the batteaux are put on carriages to be carried over land, the distance is one mile and a half. I saw them unload a boat from the carriage, and launch it, at the same time, into the river; this was performed by thirty-five or forty men. To-day they carried over this portage fifty batteaux. I saw the forty-eighth put on the carriage. A little to the northwestward of the saw-mill, on the west side of the river, I visited the spot

---

*The "machine" may be similar to the mechanism described by James Henderson at Fort Miller in 1759 which lifted bateaux onto carriages to circumvent the falls (see chapter 7).

where Lord [George Viscount] Howe was killed.* At a small expense a continued navigation for batteaux might be made between the Lakes George and Champlain, by means of a few locks. General Schuyler informed me that locks, sufficient and adequate to the above purpose, might be constructed for fifteen hundred pounds sterling. There are but four or five falls in this river, the greatest of which is not above fourteen or fifteen feet. But the general informs me a much more advantageous water carriage may be opened through Wood creek, which falls into Lake Champlain at Skeenesborough, twenty-eight miles south of Ticonderoga.** The general proposes to have this creek accurately surveyed, the heights ascertained, and estimate made of the expense of erecting locks on Wood creek, and the most convenient branch which heads near it and falls into Hudson's river.*** If this water commu-

View of the French lines as they appear today. Charles Carroll
examined the infamous lines in 1776. (Photo by the author)

*Brigadier General George Viscount Howe, the intended field commander for the 1758 Abercromby Expedition, was killed on the first day at Ticonderoga when advance units of British and provincial troops stumbled onto a large French scouting party attempting to return to Fort Carillon.

**In the 1760s Philip Skene had founded the settlement of Skenesborough with 30 families and was subsequently granted two large tracts of land by the British government. Skene remained loyal to the Crown during the American Revolution. American forces captured the area in 1775 and Skene's confiscated sawmills and iron forge were used to build the American fleet that opposed the British armada at Valcour Island in October 1776. The name of the village was officially changed to Whitehall in 1786.

***In 1792 Philip Schuyler became president of the Northern Inland Lock Navigation Company which partially completed a canal that would have connected the Hudson River to Lake Champlain through Wood Creek. In 1817 the state of New York authorized construction of the Champlain Canal which opened for traffic six years later.

nication between Lake Champlain and the province of New York should be perfected, there is little danger of the enemy's gaining the mastery of Lake Champlain, or of their ever having it in their power to invade these colonies in time of war by making this navigation. Trade, during peace, will be greatly benefited by it, as there will then be a continued water communication between New York and Canada, without the inconvenience and expense attending the portages over land.

22nd. I this morning took a ride with General Schuyler across the portage, or from the landing place at the bottom of Lake George, to Ticonderoga. The landing place properly on the [LaChute] river which runs out of Lake George into Lake Champlain, and may be a mile and a half from the place where the former may be said to terminate, i.e., where the lake is contracted into a river, has a current and shallow water. This river, computing its length from the aforesaid spot to the foot of the falls at the saw-mills, and its windings, which are inconsiderable, is not more than four or five miles long. From the foot of the saw-mill falls there is still water into Lake Champlain. It is at the foot of these falls that the batteaux, brought over land, are launched into the water, and the artillery and the apparatus belonging to it are embarked in them; the stores, such as provisions, ball, powder, &c., are embarked from Ticonderoga. At sixty or seventy yards below the saw-mill there is a bridge built over the river:—this bridge was built by the [British] king during the last war;—the road from the landing place to Ticonderoga passes over it, and you then have the river on the right; when you have passed the bridge you immediately ascend a pretty high hill, and keep ascending till you reach the famous lines made by the French in the last war, which Abercrombie was so infatuated [foolish] as to attack with musquetry only;—his cannon was lying at the bridge, about a mile or something better from these lines. The event of the day is too well known to be mentioned; we lost [killed and wounded] near one thousand six hundred men;[*] had the cannon been brought up, the French would not have waited to be attacked;—it was morally impossible to succeed against these lines with small arms only, particularly in the manner they were attacked;—our army passing before them, and receiving a fire from the whole extent;—whereas, had it marched lower down, or to the north-west of these lines, it would have flanked them:—they were constructed of large trunks of trees, felled on each other, with earth thrown up against them. On the side next [to] the French troops, they had, besides felling trees, lopped and sharpened their branches, and turned them towards the enemy; the trunks of the trees remain to this day piled up as described, but are fast going to decay.[**] As soon as you enter these lines you have a full view of Lake Champlain and [the] Ticonderoga fort, distant about a quarter of a mile. The land from thence gradually declines to the spot on which the fort is built. Lake Champlain contracts itself opposite the

---

[*]Major General James Abercromby's official report placed the losses at 1,944 killed or wounded.[16]

[**]The day before Carroll's visit to the old battlefield, Chaplain Ammi Robbins "viewed the place of Abercrombies' defeat in 1758. Saw many holes where the dead were flung in, and numbers of human bones,—thigh, arms, etc.—above ground. Oh, the horrors of war. I never so much longed for the day to approach when men shall learn war no more, and the lion and lamb lie down together."[17] Lieutenant Colonel Joseph Vose from Massachusetts inspected the 1758 breastworks a week after Carroll and noted "mens bones where the battle was fought."[18] On August 23, 1776, Colonel Anthony Wayne penned a letter to a fellow officer which likened Ticonderoga to "the Ancient Golgotha or place of Skulls—they are so plenty here that our people for want of Other Vessels drink out of them whilst the soldiers make tent pins of the shin and thigh bones of Abercrumbies men."[19]

Charles Carroll viewed the schooner *Royal Savage* at Fort Ticonderoga.
From *The History of Our Navy* by John R. Spears (1897).

fort, and runs south twenty-eight miles to Skeenesborough. Crown Point is fifteen miles down the lake from Ticonderoga. The lake is no where broad in sight of the last mentioned place, but the prospect from it is very pleasing; its shores are not as steep as those of Lake George. They rise gradually from the water, and are covered more thickly with woods, which grow in good soils, or at least in soils much better than can be seen on Lake George. There is but one settlement on the latter, at Sabatay point [Sabbath Day Point]; I understood there were about sixty acres of good land at that point. [The] Ticonderoga fort is in a ruinous condition; it was once a tolerable fortification. The ramparts are faced with stone. I saw a few pieces of cannon mounted on one bastion, more for show, I apprehend, than service.* In the present state of affairs this fort is of no other use than as an entrepôt or magazine for stores, as from this place all supplies for our army in Canada are shipped to go down Lake

*Most of the cannon had been hauled to Boston by Colonel Henry Knox.

Champlain. I saw four vessels, viz: three schooners and one sloop;* these are to be armed, to keep the mastery of the lake in case we should lose St. John's [St. Jean] and be driven out of Canada;—in the meantime they will be employed in carrying supplies to our troops in that country. Of these three schooners, two were taken from the enemy on the surrender of St. John's, one of them is called the Royal Savage, and is pierced for twelve guns; she had, when taken, twelve brass pieces—I think four and six pounders; these were sent to Boston. She is really a fine vessel, and built on purpose for fighting; however, some repairs are wanted; a new mainmast must be put in, her old one being shattered with one of our cannon balls. When these vessels are completely rigged, armed and manned, we may defy the enemy on Lake Champlain for this summer and fall at least, even should we unfortunately be driven out of Canada. When our small army last summer, or rather fall, (in number about one thousand seven hundred,) came to Isle aux Noix,** this vessel was almost ready to put to sea, she wanted only as much to be done to her as could easily have been finished in three days, had the enemy exerted themselves. Had she ventured out our expedition to Canada must have failed, and probably our whole army must have surrendered, for she was greatly an overmatch for all the naval strength we then had on the lake. Had [Major Charles] Preston, who commanded at St. John's, ventured out with his garrison, consisting of six hundred men, and attacked our people at their first landing; he would, in all probability, have defeated them, as they were a mere undisciplined rabble, made up chiefly of the offings and outcasts of New York.

23d. We continued this day at the landing place, our boats not being yet ready and fitted to carry us through Lake Champlain. General Schuyler and the troops were busily engaged in carting over land, to the saw-mill, the batteaux, cannon, artillery stores, provisions, &c., there to be embarked on the navigable waters of Lake Champlain, and transported over that lake to St. John's.

24th. We this day left the landing place at Lake George and took [a] boat at the saw-mill. From the saw-mill to Ticonderoga, the distance, by water, is about a mile; the water is shallow, but sufficiently deep for batteau navigation. A little below the bridge before mentioned, the French, during the last war, drove pickets into the river, to prevent our boats getting round from the saw-mill to Ticonderoga with artillery; some of the pickets still remain, for both our boats struck them. [The] Ticonderoga fort is beautifully situated, but, as I said before, it is in a ruinous condition;—neither is the place, in my opinion, judiciously chosen for the construction of a fort; a fort constructed at the saw-mill would much better secure the passage or pass into the province of New York by way of Lake George. Having waited at Ticonderoga an hour or two, to take in provisions for the crews of both boats,

---

*The vessels at Ticonderoga included three vessels captured at St. Jean in 1775: the sloop *Enterprise*, schooner *Royal Savage*, and schooner *Revenge* (originally a row galley). The fourth vessel was the schooner *Liberty*, taken at Skenesborough in May 1775, that had earlier been Philip Skene's schooner *Catherine*. The *Royal Savage* sank during the Battle of Valcour Island on October 11, 1776, and was raised in 1934 by Colonel Lorenzo F. Hagglund.

**Isle-aux-Noix is an island in the Richelieu River north of Lake Champlain that saw military occupation during the French and Indian War, the American Revolution, and the War of 1812. Today, Fort Lennox, built on the island between 1819 and 1829, is a Canadian National Historic Park and military museum.

consisting entirely of soldiers, we embarked at eleven o'clock, and reached Crown Point a little after three, with the help of our oars only.

Notes:

1. B. F. DeCosta, *Notes on the History of Fort George* (New York: J. Sabin & Sons, 1871), 17-18; See also Peter Force, ed., *American Archives*, Fourth Series, Volume 2 (Washington, D.C.: M. St. Clair Clarke and Peter Force, 1839), 873-74.

2. DeCosta, 11-12; Epaphras Bull, "Journal of Epaphras Bull," *Bulletin of the Fort Ticonderoga Museum* 8 (July 1948): 41; See also Allen French, *The Taking of Ticonderoga in 1775: The British Story* (Cambridge, MA.: Havard University Press, 1928), 51; Lincoln Diamant, *Bernard Romans: Forgotten Patriot of the American Revolution* (Harrison, N.Y.: Harbor Hill Books, 1985), 52-53; Edward Mott, "Journal of Capt. Edward Mott," *Collections of the Connecticut Historical Society* 1 (1860): 169.

3. Wm. L. Bowne, *Ye Cohorn Caravan, The Knox Expedition in the Winter of 1775-1776* (Schuylerville, N.Y.: NaPaul Publishers, Inc., 1975), 16; See also Noah Brooks, *Henry Knox: A Soldier of the Revolution* (1900; reprint ed., New York: DaCapo Press, 1974), 41-42; North Callahan, *Henry Knox: General Washington's General* (New York: Rinehart & Company, Inc., 1958), 39-40; Don R. Gerlach, *Proud Patriot: Philip Schuyler and the War of Independence 1775-1783* (Syracuse, N.Y.: Syracuse University Press, 1987), 88.

4. Henry Knox, "Knox's Diary During His Ticonderoga Expedition," *The New-England Historical and Genealogical Register*, 30 (July 1876): 323.

5. Thomas O'Brien Hanley, *Revolutionary Statesman: Charles Carroll and the War* (Chicago: Loyola University Press, 1983), 126.

6. Peter Force, ed., *American Archives*, Fourth Series, Volume 6 (Washington, D.C.: M. St. Clair Clarke and Peter Force, 1846), 588.

7. Alan S. Everest, ed., *The Journal of Charles Carroll of Carrollton* (Fort Ticonderoga, N.Y.: The Champlain-Upper Hudson Bicentennial Committee, 1976), 60-61; See also Force, 6:589.

8. Peter Force, ed., *American Archives*, Fourth Series, Volume 5 (Washington, D.C.: M. St. Clair Clarke and Peter Force, 1844), 947.

9. Brantz Mayer, ed., *Journal of Charles Carroll of Carrollton, During His Visit to Canada in 1776* (Baltimore: Maryland Historical Society, 1876), 58-80. Charles Carroll gave his journal to his granddaughter in 1823 which she bestowed to the Maryland Historical Society in 1844. For a modern version of Carroll's complete diary see Everest (note 7).

10. Ammi R. Robbins, "Journal of the Rev. Ammi R. Robbins," in *History of Norfolk*, comp. by Theron Wilmot Crissey (Everett, MA.: Massachusetts Publishing Company, 1900), 99.

11. Ibid.

12. Henry Livingston, "Journal of Major Henry Livingston, 1775," ed. by Gaillard Hunt, *The Pennsylvania Magazine of History and Biography* 12 (1898): 12-13.

13. Aaron Barlow, "The March to Montreal and Quebec, 1775," ed. by Charles Burr Todd, *American Historical Register* 2 (1895): 649.

14. Lewis Beebe, "Journal of a Physician on the Expedition Against Canada, 1776," *The Pennsylvania Magazine of History and Biography* 59 (October 1935): 344; For additional information on the Fort George hospital see Peter Force, ed., *American Archives*, Fifth Series, Volume 1, (Washington, D.C.: M. St. Clair Clarke and Peter Force, 1848), 232-33, 237, 397, 581, 651, 776, 857.

15. David R. Starbuck, "Anatomy of a Massacre," *Archaeology*, November/December 1993, 42-46; See also *Lake George Mirror*, 16 August 1957.

16. Gertrude Selwyn Kimball, ed., *Correspondence of William Pitt* (New York: The Macmillan Company, 1906), Volume 1, 300; See also Public Record Office, London, 272, 34/30, fol. 23.

17. Robbins, 101.

18. Joseph Vose, "Journal of Lieutenant-Colonel Joseph Vose," *The Colonial Society of Massachusetts* 7 (Transactions 1900-1902): 250.

19. Charles J. Stille, *Major-General Anthony Wayne and the Pennsylvania Line in the Continental Army* (Philadelphia: J. B. Lippincott Company, 1893), 37.

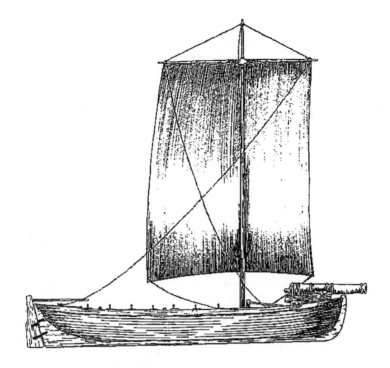

A Draught of a Boat to carry One Carrige Gun, forward
Navy Office   *1 March 1776*

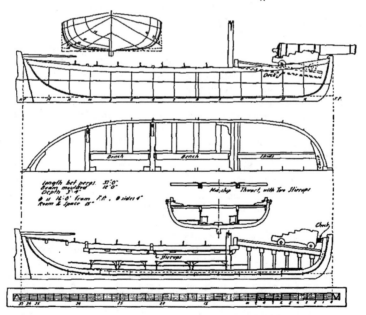

The British gunboats that were assigned to Lake George in 1777 had been used at the Battle of Valcour Island on Lake Champlain the previous year.
Above: Drawing by Aaron Hirsh.
Below: Admiralty draught, Chapelle Collection. (Smithsonian Institution)

10. James M. Hadden 1777

FOLLOWING THEIR RETREAT from Canada in late June of 1776, the American forces were concentrated in the area surrounding Fort Ticonderoga. With the loss of their vessels on the Richelieu River because of the American victories in 1775, the British were forced to engage in a frenzied contest to build a naval fleet during the summer and fall of 1776. Three large British vessels, the *Carleton*, *Inflexible*, and *Maria*, were dismantled and carried overland to St. Jean, Quebec, on the Richelieu River for reassembly. The gondola *Loyal Convert* was dragged over the rapids at Chambly to St. Jean, while the radeau *Thunderer* was built entirely at the St. Jean shipyard. In addition, approximately two dozen gunboats were either constructed at St. Jean from frames transported from England or built completely in Canada. At the same time, the American fleet, consisting of the *Liberty*, *Enterprise*, *Royal Savage*, and *Revenge*, was augmented by new vessels constructed at the Skenesborough shipyard (present-day Whitehall, N.Y.): three galleys, the *Congress*, *Trumbull*, and *Washington*; eight gondolas or gunboats, the *Boston*, *Connecticut*, *New Haven*, *New Jersey*, *New York*, *Philadelphia*, *Providence*, and *Spitfire*; and one cutter, the *Lee*, built from captured British frames.

British plans in 1776 called for an invasion of the colonies through Lake Champlain and Lake George to the Hudson River, to be led by Major General Guy Carleton (Governor of Quebec) and Lieutenant General John Burgoyne. Simultaneously, Major General William Howe's army was to move northward on the Hudson River after the capture of New York City. The Americans amassed a huge army at Ticonderoga and nearby Mount Independence in anticipation of the British attack. On August 24, 1776, Brigadier General Benedict Arnold sailed northward on Lake Champlain with the American fleet in an effort to retard the British invasion. After seven weeks on Lake Champlain, Arnold's fleet met the British armada in the Battle of Valcour Island on October 11, 1776. Outmatched by the more powerful British squadron, the American fleet was devastated at Valcour Bay (near present-day Plattsburgh). After dark the crippled American fleet escaped from the British by passing along the western shore of the lake. On the 13th of October the larger British vessels engaged the Americans once again, whereupon Arnold scuttled five vessels in a bay on the Vermont side of the lake. Only four American vessels escaped the British onslaught. (The schooner *Liberty* also survived, having gone for provisions before the engagement.) Faced with approximately 13,000 American troops at Ticonderoga and Mount Independence, and the prospect of adverse weather, the British army departed for winter quarters in Canada on November 1st and 2nd.

Preliminary plans for the next year at Lake Champlain were formulated by the Continental Congress on December 28, 1776, when orders were given to build a bridge with caissons to connect Fort Ticonderoga with Mount Independence. The caissons would also function to block the advance of British warships on Lake Champlain. Congress further ordered that the passage of Lake George "be also obstructed in [a] like Manner by Cassoons from Island to Island in the Narrows if practicable or by floating Batteries" in order to stop British vessels.[1] In early February Major General Philip Schuyler, commander of the American Northern Department, instructed Colonel Jeduthan Baldwin, the chief engineer at Ticonderoga, to proceed immediately to Lake George to evaluate the possibility of sinking caissons in the Narrows. Upon receiving Schuyler's orders, Baldwin, an officer who served at the lake during the French and Indian War, promptly departed for Lake George from his home in Brookfield, Massachusetts. Between meetings in Massachusetts and duty in New York, Baldwin had spent barely two weeks at home during the winter of 1777 before returning to New York.

After a 10-day journey to Lake George, Baldwin set out on horseback on February 24 from the southern end of the lake: "Crossed 2 very bad [ice] cracks before we got of[f]. Foxes on ye Island. then I walked to ye Narrows with one Frost & Majr. [Ebenezer] Stevens, where we sounded the depth of the water, 7 fathoms in one place & c. and the width of the Chan[n]el is 250 yards between ye two Islands, then rode to Sabbath day point where we made a good fire, fed our horses & Eat some Vituals & then rode of[f] in a Very great Snowstorm wind at N.W. got to Ti about 5 o clock."[2] Apparently Baldwin did nothing further with the Lake George project. Two days later his efforts were devoted to building the bridge to Mount Independence, and he was soon engaged in planning and building a fort and hospital on the Vermont shore.

The winter weather did not end the attacks by the British and their Native American allies on the Americans in the lake valleys. According to Jeduthan Baldwin, an attack occurred on March 19, 1777, at Sabbath Day Point on Lake George:

> Rode out to ye Mills & to Mr Adams.* At Evening he came in after being four Days with the Enemy, he with 2 others were going to Sab[b]ath day point with 13 Horses on ye west side [of] the Lake & were Taken by Capt. McKoy [McKay] with about 18 Cocknewago [Caughnawaga] Indians, about 3 o clock [in the]

---

*This may have been Samuel Adams who had a tavern at Sabbath Day Point prior to the American Revolution. Later Adams' business was relocated to the northern Lake George Landing.

afternoon five miles North of Sab[b]ath day point. Soon after he was taken Capt. [Alexander] Baldwin came along with about 25 Men from Ticonderoga going to Fort George on the Ice. The Indians con[c]ealed themselves in ye Woods until about 3 o clock at night. Capt. Baldwin with his men passed by to Sab[b]ath Day point where they made a fire, L[a]y down & went to sleep, when the Indians attacked them Killed 4 & took 20 which they carried off but Mr. Adams being well acquainted with Capt. McKoy, he pleading that he was only an inhabitant [and] did not belong to the Army obtained Leave to return after marching 30 [miles].[3]

While General Philip Schuyler made preparations to defend Ticonderoga, he also recommended contingency plans in the event that the Americans could not hold their position. On December 30, 1776, Schuyler wrote to John Hancock, president of the Continental Congress, proposing "to build five or six flat Bottomed Vessels of considerable Force on Lake George."[4] On March 17, 1777, Schuyler issued orders that "the schooners there [Lake George] should also be overhauled."[5] A week later Schuyler sent orders to Captain Jacobus Wynkoop to supervise the construction of a new naval force on Lake George. Wynkoop was directed to "employ the carpenters in constructing two strong schooners of sixty feet keel and twenty feet beam. They should be so constructed as not to draw above six feet [of] water, when they have all their cannon and stores on board. . .three other vessels [row galleys] are to be built without decks. These should be so contrived, as to row fast, and to carry a cannon of twelve pound shot in the bow, and as many on each side as possible."[6]

It was not until three months later, however, that Schuyler was able to inform Congress that "one of the schooners at Lake George is launched: She is to carry fourteen guns. Another will be in the lake by the first of next month, and the timber for the [row] gallies is hauled to the spot where they are to be built."[7] On June 26 Schuyler instructed "Commodore" Jacobus Wynkoop to mount the cannon on the new schooner and place cannon on the bows of two bateaux. Eleven days later Schuyler wrote to George Washington, apprising him of the insufficient number of cannon for the two schooners. By then, however, the British incursion was unstoppable. The row galleys were never completed and Schuyler's vessels on Lake George would not be used to block the British advance.

The British invasion plan of 1777 was similar to the strategy of the previous year. General John Burgoyne would lead an army through Lake Champlain to Albany, and General William Howe, in control of New York City, would proceed northward on the Hudson River with his army. At the same time a smaller diversionary force under Brigadier General Barry St. Leger (temporary rank) would push through the Mohawk Valley and join Burgoyne's army in Albany. By the end of June, Burgoyne's expedition had sailed within sight of Ticonderoga. The British fleet was enlarged in 1777 with a new warship, the *Royal George*, and with American vessels captured in 1776. The Americans, on the other hand, had only six vessels, including the row galley *Gates*, completed just after the Valcour engagement. Misjudging the British strategy for 1777, the Continental Congress and George Washington failed to provide the number of troops for the defense of Ticonderoga and Mount Independence that Philip Schuyler had recommended six months earlier.

British gunboat at Ticonderoga before the vessel was transferred to
Lake George. Detail of a watercolor by Lieutenant James Hunter, a British
officer who served in the 1777 campaign. (National Archives of Canada)

On July 2, apprehensive in the face of staggering odds, the Americans opened
their batteries on the advancing British and German troops. Mount Hope,* an
outpost overlooking the LaChute River, was swiftly captured without opposition
and one of the blockhouses on Lake George was burned by the British. The crews
of the American vessels at the northern Lake George landing were ordered to sail
to Fort George, and the troops at the outlet area joined the Ticonderoga garrison.
On July 5, after the British were successful in establishing a battery on the summit
of Mount Defiance overlooking Ticonderoga, the Americans decided to evacuate
their positions at Fort Ticonderoga and Mount Independence. Departing in the
night, the American forces made a frenzied retreat to Skenesborough where their
vessels were immediately destroyed by the escaping troops or captured by the
British. Other American troops retreated toward Castleton. The rear guard, however, was forced to fight a bloody battle at present-day Hubbardton, Vermont,
before fleeing into the wilderness.

With the British army in control of Lake Champlain, General Burgoyne made
a fatal error in choosing to proceed with his troops to the Hudson River through
Wood Creek. This formidable route allowed the American forces to place obstruc-

---

*There is some question whether a blockhouse ever existed at Mount Hope. Most sources do not
indicate that a blockhouse was present. An aide to General Philip Schuyler observed that "it had been
fortified by us the preceding year [1776], but was dismantled."[8] However, on May 6, 1777, Colonel
Jeduthan Baldwin recorded "a Block house ordered to be built near the North mill [LaChute River]
on the hill."[9] Lieutenant Thomas Anburey, a British officer with Burgoyne's expedition, noted "a
block-house upon an eminence above the mills, together with a block-house and hospital at the entrance
of the lake. Upon the right of the lines, between them and the old fort [Ticonderoga], are two new
block-houses and a considerable battery close to the water's edge."[10] Captain Lemuel Roberts with
Lieutenant Colonel John Brown's raiding party in September 1777 noted "they perceived the party
at the block house, on Mount Hope, to whom the sentries belonged."[11]

tions along the way which greatly delayed the British army's progress. The delay would prove calamitous for the British at Saratoga.

The traditional military route through Lake George, however, was to be used for artillery, provisions, and supplies. As early as May 20, Captain Skeffington Lutwidge, commander of the British fleet on Lake Champlain, indicated that once Ticonderoga was captured it would be "necessary immediately to transport the Gun Boats & c. to get possession of Lake George."[12]

From intelligence reports, General Burgoyne learned that the Americans were building a navy to hold Lake George: "They are also building [r]ow-gallies at Fort George, for the defence of that Lake."[13] On Burgoyne's directions, Major General William Philips, second-in-command of the expedition, issued orders to Captain Lutwidge on July 25 "for Lake George and Hudson River: Fourteen Armed Gun Boats at 7 men each. Four Armed Boats with 6 Pounders to Cruize Lake George."[14] On July 27, 1777, Lieutenant James Murray Hadden, a diligent journal keeper, sailed south on Lake George aboard a gunboat.*

Faced with the loss of Ticonderoga and overwhelming odds, Major Christopher Yates, the commander at Fort George, evacuated and burned the fort on July 16 under orders from Philip Schuyler. The newly-constructed vessels were also burned, but "about twenty pieces of artillery from Lake George, together with nearly all the powder, amounting to about thirteen tons" were saved.[15] After the withdrawal, George Washington indirectly questioned Schuyler's judgement by commenting that others had apprised him "that a spirited, brave, judicious officer, with two or three hundred good men, together with the armed vessels you have built, would retard Burgoyne's passage across the Lake for a considerable time."[16] General Schuyler defended his strategy of abandoning Fort George by denigrating its strength:

> The fort was part of an unfinished bastion of an intended fortification. . .In it was a barrack capable of containing between thirty and fifty men; without ditch, without wall, without cistern; without any picket to prevent an enemy from running over the wall. So small, as not to contain above one hundred and fifty men; commanded by ground greatly overlooking it, and within point blank shot; and so situated that five hundred men may lie between the bastion and the Lake, without being seen from this extremely defensible fortress. Of vessels built there, one was afloat and tolerably fitted, the others still upon the stocks; but, if the two had been upon the water, they would have been of but little use, without rigging or guns.[17]

The fortunes of the American army improved in the months following the evacuation from the Lake Champlain and Lake George forts. On August 16 Burgoyne's German troops were decisively defeated at the Battle of Bennington, and a month later American troops were finally able to challenge Burgoyne's main invasion force in the first Battle of Saratoga. At the same time General Benjamin Lincoln deployed three 500-man militia units to Skenesborough, Ticonderoga, and Mount Independence as a diversionary tactic against the rearmost positions of Burgoyne's army.

---

*These same gunboats had been employed at the Battle of Valcour Island in October 1776. Although there were several variants, most of the British gunboats were sloop-rigged, 37 feet in length with a 12-foot beam, and carried a bow cannon.

After freeing 293 prisoners near Ticonderoga, Colonel John Brown "destroyed four Gunboats at this end of Lake George, and two Gun Boats and some batteaux which lay about the bridge on this side of the Sawmill [LaChute River]."[18] Departing with "one Small Sloop mounting 8 Guns & 2 British Gun Boats" and 17 bateaux, Brown decided to attack the British supply depot on Diamond Island in the southern basin of Lake George.[19] Alerted by a sutler (merchant) who had escaped from Brown's flotilla, Captain Thomas Aubrey, with two companies of the 47th Regiment, successfully defended his position on the island with artillery mounted behind breastworks. The battle raged for more than an hour before Brown's crippled sloop had to be towed away, and "one of the Gun Boats [was] so damaged I was obliged to quit her."[20] Brown burned his vessels in a bay on the eastern shore (presumably Dunhams Bay) and escaped to Skenesborough. One gunboat, however, with a 12-pound cannon was retaken by the British.

Remains of Fort George.
(Photo by the author)

After the defeat at Saratoga on October 7, 1777, the British tried to retreat through Fort Edward and Fort George: "a detachment of artificers under a strong Escort were Sent forward to Repair the Bridges, and open the ro[a]ds," but the Americans were able to stymie their attempt at escape.[21] Fort Ticonderoga, Mount Independence, and Fort George were evacuated by the British army soon after their surrender at Saratoga. The 1777 invasion, however, was not the last British military expedition to Lake George. After wreaking havoc in the Champlain Valley, at Fort Anne, Fort Edward, Queensbury, Ballston, and Stillwater, British troops under Major Christopher Carleton reached Fort George on October 11, 1780. When 50 American militia were overwhelmed outside of the fort in an attempt to rescue one soldier, Captain John Chipman, the American commander of Fort George, was forced to accept a capitulation.*

With the end of the American Revolution, Fort George gradually fell into decay, a relic of stormy times that soon became a point of curiosity for travelers and a source of stone for early settlers. Today, as families amble along the sidewalks at the southern shore of Lake George on quiet summer evenings, probably few realize the numbers of soldiers who died at its camps, forts, and hospitals during two wars that determined the fate of a continent.

Lieutenant James Murray Hadden, author of one of the best British journals of the 1776-1777 campaigns, had followed in his father's footsteps by joining the British military. The younger Hadden was admitted into the Royal Military Academy at Woolwich, England, in 1771. Commissioned a second lieutenant in the Royal Regiment of Artillery in 1774, Hadden served at Gibraltar and the Mediterranean before departing for America in 1776. Commanding a gunboat at the Battle of Valcour Island on October 11, 1776, Hadden produced a remarkable eyewitness account of the historic engagement and a detailed map of the positions of the fleets. After the British occupation of Fort Ticonderoga and Mount Independence in July 1777, Hadden was sent with his artillery detachment and an infantry unit under Lieutenant Colonel John Anstruther in a fleet of gunboats to take control of Lake George. His journey on the lake provides an interesting picture of the lake and Fort George. Hadden's comment that "passage across this Lake was very pleasant and it affords many pleasing & romantic prospects" would prove to be a portent of the future era of Lake George history.[25]

*Lieutenant John Enys, a 23-year-old British officer viewed Fort George on October 11, 1780, as a participant of the Carleton expedition: "This fort is Situated not more than two hundred yards from the place that fort William Henry formerly Stood (of which there is very little remains) and is part of a fort Intended to have been built during the latter part of last War. But. . .[only] finished one Bastion. . .The Walls are made of Stone with a thick earth parrapet and good Bomb proofs for the Garrison in case of a seige, togeather with a very good Well. They had also one six pounder Mounted on a feild Carriage and one not Mounted. From this account it may be Supposed the place might make a good defence, but the Walls from being burnt so often were in a very bad way, thro their Negligence they had Suffered [allowed] the Well to be filled with all manner of filth so that it was impossible to drink the Water."[22] Thirty-nine-year-old Austin Wells, a volunteer with the American militia, arrived from Fort Edward soon after the 1780 battle at Fort George and found "twenty-two slaughtered and mangled men. All had their skulls knocked in, their throats cut and their scalps taken."[23] When one officer recognized the bodies of two of his comrades, he "cried like a child beholding them," according to Wells.[24] The bodies of the fallen American soldiers were buried in the vicinity of Fort George.

Journal of Lieutenant James M. Hadden 1777 [26]

July 8th The Gun Boats returned [from Skenesborough] to Tyconderoga, and thence proceeded up the Creek [LaChute River] towards Lake George as far as the Bridge at the Saw Mills. The Brigade of Artillery attached to the Advanced Corps, only, remained with the Army to wait its return, it being determined for the rest to proceed across Lake George.

Wednesday July 9th We began disembarking Guns & Stores from the Gun Boats at the Bridge in Saw Mill Creek.

July 10th Capt [William] Borthwick's Company moved to the other end of the Portage at the entrance of Lake George, carrying with us all the Artillery then landed.

Monday July 14th On the Right. The rest of the Artillery being Landed proceeded from the Saw Mills to the other end of the Portage at Lake George.

July 15th Carriages resembling a Waggon without the Body, (of two sizes, the larger for Transporting Gun Boats, and the lesser for Batteaux's) being put together and some Horses arrived from Canada several Gun Boats and Batteaux's were brought over the Portage and launched in. . .Lake George: This business was much retarded for want of Horses which agreeable to a Contract were to be sent across Lake Champlain in Floats.

Memorandum*

I shall now give an account of the operations of the Detachment to the Right of the Army coming across Lake George, as, the two blended together wou'd have created confusion. From July ye 14th to the 25 We were employed in bringing forward the Guns, Stores, and Provisions; and in transporting Gun Boats & Batteaux's from ye Saw Mill's Creek to Lake George. The Road is tolerably level, and where it wanted repairs the Rebel Prisoners** were employed being furnished with Tools and working under a Guard: We had about Two hundred of them confined in a Barn, and those who were not wanted either for the above purpose or Removing Guns and Stores, amused themselves in beating Hemp: These measures certainly were not justifiable, they were it is true allowed Rum in common with other fatigue Parties and upon the whole 'twas better than close confinement, but it ought to have been optional; they shou'd either have been consider'd as Prisoners of War, or Rebels. The Brutality of Major [Griffith Williams] induced him to bring out these unhappy wretches and parade them in the Rear of the Troops when the Feu de joye [musket] was fired upon our late successes, some of them felt the insult but others threw up their Caps & Huzza'd with the Troops in spite of many pushes from their Comrades. Their Officers were sent to Canada on Parole.

---

*Some of Hadden's entries dealing with General Burgoyne's advance through Wood Creek and the Vermont battles have been omitted.

**Most of the Americans had been captured at the Battle of Hubbardton (Vermont) on July 7, 1777. Two months later these prisoners were freed from a barn located near the eastern shore of Lake George by troops under the command of Lieutenant Colonel John Brown on his raid against Ticonderoga.

Portage, Lake George, Saturday July 26th 1777—Maj'r Gen'l Phillips* was pleased to order me to choose 3 Noncom'd officers & 30 Men from Capt'n [William] Borthwick's Company, of these I was to take Command & proceed with the rest of the Artillery, (except Capt. Borthwick and the remainder of his Company left for the defence of Tyconderoga &c) across Lake George, and this day I embarked with them on board the Gun Boats.

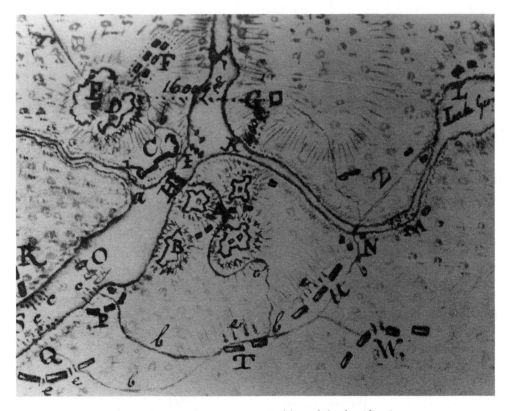

Map drawn by Lieutenant James Hadden of the fortifications at Ticonderoga and the northern section of Lake George. From *Hadden's Journal and Orderly Books* edited by Horatio Rogers (1884).

Sunday July 27th Being embarked on board 26 Gun Boats, we proceeded with 100 Men from the 62nd Reg't and Capt Monins Company of Canadians under the Command of Lt. Col. Anstruther.** This expedition was to have been larger and under the orders of Maj'r Gen'l Phillips, but the Enemy having (a few days since)

*Major General William Phillips was second-in-command to Burgoyne in 1777. Phillips entered the Royal Military Academy at Woolwich as a boy in 1746. He rose to the rank of captain in 1756 and served with distinction during the Seven Years' War. Phillips was in command at St. Jean, Quebec, during 1776 and played a major role in the 1777 campaign.

**Lieutenant Colonel John Anstruther, commissioned an ensign in 1751, was elevated to the rank of lieutenant colonel of the 62nd Regiment of Foot (infantry) in 1773. Serving under Sir Guy Carleton in 1776 and John Burgoyne in 1777, Anstruther was wounded at the battle at Saratoga on September 19 and again during the final engagement on October 7. He was held prisoner in America until 1778.

destroyed their Vessels (5 in number) including two on the Stocks; and destroying the defences of the Fort, abandon'd it retiring towards Fort Edward.*

The first 4 or 5 Miles the water is extremely shallow (4 or 5 Feet deep) but after that it grows very deep and will everywhere admit Vessels of any kind. We passed Rogers's Rock famous for his descending a part of it with his Detachment (during the last War) where it appears almost perpendicular. This was his only alternative to escape falling into the hands of a superior Corps of Savages in the French Interest; It happen'd during the Winter which no doubt facilitated his descent by flakes of Snow &c collected on the Rock, as in its present state one wou'd doubt the fact if not so well authenticated.** He afterwards crossed the Lake on the Ice. We passed Sabaoth day Point so called from an Action which happen'd here on a Sunday. This is the only cleared land we have yet come to; it is Seven Miles from the Portage, & on the Eastern Shore of the Lake.*** In the evening (there being no wind) we came to an Anchor at 14 Mile Island, so called because it is 14 Miles from Fort George: Here we encamped there being only one House on the Island;† we saw and killed a great number of Rattle Snakes, in the Stomach of one of them we found two whole ground Squirrels, on one of which the Hair was quite perfect, it appeared to have been swallowed the preceding day, the effecting of which must have been a work of some time as the Mouth of the Serpent appeared infinitely too small to receive it suddenly; This Snake had 6 Rattles. One was killed which had 13 Rattles. I apprehend one reason for our discovering so many, was the number of Fires and removing old Logs to supply Fuel. On an Island near this, an Artillery Man was stung to Death some years ago, and that Island is so famous for them as to be called Rattle Snake Island. The Rattle is only used when the Snake is coiled, it is then twirl'd round more or less as his fears or anger increase or diminish, and by no means makes so great a noise as people imagine: in fact little more than any other Reptile moving thro. dry Leaves. (The inhabitants dry and eat the snakes.) We met with no accidents, and having a fair wind arrived at Fort George about Noon on the 28th July. Lake George is 36 miles in length, and a little more than two in width; it lays in a Valley between two immense Ridges of Mountains the bottoms of which border on the Lake, from this circumstance it is extremely deep quite up to the landing near Fort George, and has seldom more than two prevailing winds but is very liable to sudden squals, in one of these the Rev'd Mr [Edward] Brudenell [chaplain] was very near lost in a Man of War's Barge. Towards the middle there are a great number of small Islands uninhabited, nor are there above 5 or 6 Settlements on the whole Lake. The

*The British had intelligence reports of the Fort George evacuation. The vessels probably included two schooners in the water and two row galleys on the stocks.

**On May 3, 1777, Colonel Jeduthan Baldwin also referred to the mountainside as "Rogerses Rock."[27] (See chapter 5 for more discussion of the Rogers Rock story.)

***Sabbath Day Point is located on the western shore. The origin of the name remains rather elusive. One story relates the name to the Indian chief Sabatis and others tie it to Abercromby's or Amherst's expeditions.[28] However, Sabbath Day Point was known by that name before either expedition. Soldiers with the Abercromby expedition recorded the name upon landing at Sabbath Day Point on Wednesday, July 5, 1758.[29]

†Fourteen Mile Island was used often by soldiers in both the French and Indian War and the American Revolution. The *Connecticut Courant* reported an incident on the island in July 1779 when an American detachment from Fort George was "attacked by some Savages and Tories. Major [Wright] Hopkins, two sergeants, three privates, and two ladies were shot dead and scalped; two captains, one lieutenant [Michael Dunning] and the rest were captured and led away."[30]

Mountains are plentifully supplied with Deer the few Inhabitants hunt them with Dogs 'till they take the Water and in attempting to cross the Lake are picked up by People laying wait in Boats or Canoes. Our passage across this Lake was very pleasant and it affords many pleasing & romantic prospects. Were we to retain a Post at Tyconderoga the little depth of water towards that end of Lake George wou'd be a great obstacle to our keeping up a Fleet. Gun Boats appear to be well calculated for this Lake the water being in general so smooth that they could always act; and at the Fall of the Year they might take advantage of the encrease of Water in the Saw Mill Creek [LaChute River] to pass the Rapids and Shallows which interrupt the communication with Lake Champlain, and be secured under the Guns in Tyconderoga,or Mount Independence. So soon as we arrived at Fort George The Infantry were employed in clearing a post on Gage's Hill which commands the Fort at the distance of about 1500 Yards, on the Road to Fort Edward.* This is a very strong position, the Road being in a manner cut thro. the height on which the post is taken.

Fort George which stands near the water at the end of the Lake, is a small square Fort faced with Masonry and contains Barracks for about a hundred Men secured from Cannon Shot.** This Fort cou'd not stand a Siege, being commanded, & too confined not to be soon reduced by Bombardment. The Rebels before they abandon'd it had endeavour'd to destroy the defences and actualy blew up the Magazine on the side next the Water, which demolish'd that Face.

The Ruins of Fort [William] Henry are on the [southwestern] shore of the Lake, this was never much more than a small stockaded Fort. The Land is cleared for about a Mile Round the Fort on both sides of the Lake, and on it are built 5 Farm Houses. We found that the Enemy had carried off a large Magazine of Flour & other Provisions, during the time the British Army lay at Skeensborough to repair the communications to Fort Anne, destroyed by the Enemy's felling Trees across them after the 9th Reg't were withdrawn: Had a large Corps been advanced to the Cross Roads near Fort Edward, or more properly the greater part of the Army leaving a Detachment at Skeensborough we shou'd have got an immense supply of Provision's thus far on our Route, and gained much time; Gen'l Burgoyne had intelligence of these circumstances, as the Storekeeper of Fort George (originally in the British service & whose Son was with us) came in, and saw him. From what we cou'd learn the Enemy had made two or three trips with 40 or 50 Waggons; having full time they carried off or destroyed the minutest articles, and also drove with them the Cattle belonging to the Inhabitants: Indeed, an attempt was made on the last Division

---

*Fort Gage was a stockaded outpost built under Major General James Abercromby in 1758 to protect the military road to Fort Edward. Located on the high ground southwest of Lake George, the site of the fort is now a Ramada Inn adjacent to Interstate 87.

**Major General Friedrich Riedesel, commander of the German troops with Burgoyne's forces, recorded notes on Fort George based on earlier intelligence reports. Although the notes are not quite accurate, his writings provide some idea of the relative location of some of the buildings. "1st. The citadel has only recently been repaired and provided with two nine-pounders. It contains, also, twelve cannons, which are not yet mounted. Barracks for 1,000 men lie twenty yards east of it.

"2d. Close to the shore is a large magazine in which there is an abundance of provisions.

"3d. To the west of this magazine, where Fort William Henry formerly stood, is the large hospital, a building of great dimensions, and used for the sick from Fort Carillon. This is said to be surrounded by palisades, and to have a small redoubt [Fort Gage] on the hill south of it. A strong guard is posted here every night. The rebels at Fort George are very busy in cutting down trees and carrying them to the shore to be used in the construction of six strong vessels on the lake."[31]

of Waggons by a Detachment of Savages, they Seized one Waggon which had broken down, began to plunder it of the Horses &c, and cou'd not be prevailed on to pursue the rest of them. July 28th (continued) we landed and encamped. I was taken very ill this night.

July 30th most of the Guns & Stores being disembarked, I was order'd with my Detachment and Six Pieces of Lt. Artillery to join Capt. Jones & remain attached to the Right Wing of the Army. I was attacked with the Ague [fever] when I set out, but recover'd on changing the Air, which from the Fires to destroy the Storehouses, Barracks, Shipping on the Stocks &c [at Fort George] and a quantity of bad Provisions dispers'd about, was very hot & unpleasant, the Soil being sandy encreased these. Here I first tasted Windsor Beans of any size, those in Canada being scarce and very small. We also took great quantities of Trout in a Creek near here. I marched 14 Miles this day & encamped at the cross Roads about 2 Miles short of F't Edward.

Thursday. July 31st I marched to Fort Edward and encamped with the first Brigade British. Fort Edward; here are the Ruins of a small Fort thrown up near the Hudson River to cover a part of it which is here Fordable. This is at present totally dismantled and does not appear ever to have been calculated for a further purpose than repelling a sudden attack being commanded on both flanks within Cannon Shot; The Army encamped on these heights, The Advanced [Corps] being on the far side (towards Albany) and the Right Wing about the same distance in the Rear of the Fort; The fires of these encampments were uncommonly beautiful at Night. A small Detachment remained at the Cross Roads to prevent small parties of the Enemy crossing a Ford there and interrupting our communications with Fort George, Skeenesborough &c. The Germans remained at Fort Anne.

Notes

1. William James Morgan, ed., *Naval Documents of the American Revolution* (Washington, D.C: Naval History Division, Department of the Navy, 1976), Volume 7, 1190; "The Trial of Major General Schuyler, October 1778," *Collections of the New-York Historical Society* 12 (1879): 78-79.
2. Jeduthan Baldwin, *The Revolutionary Journal of Col. Jeduthan Baldwin 1775-1778*, ed. Thomas Williams Baldwin (Bangor, ME.: DeBurians, 1906), 93.
3. Ibid., 95-96; See also John Calfe, "Capt. John Calfe's Book" in *A Memorial of the Town of Hampstead, New Hampshire*, comp. by Harriette Eliza Noyes (Boston: George B. Reed, 1899), 289.
4. Morgan, 7: 627.
5. William James Morgan, ed., *Naval Documents of the American Revolution* (Washington, D.C.: Naval History Division, Department of the Navy, 1980), Volume 8, 135.
6. Morgan, 8: 187-88; See "Trial of Schuyler," 88.
7. "Trial of Schuyler," 116.
8. "The Trial of Major General St. Clair, August 1778," *Collections of the New-York Historical Society* 13 (1880): 115.
9. Baldwin, 101; See also Thomas Hughes, *A Journal By Thos: Hughes* (Cambridge, U.K.: Cambridge University Press, 1947), 13.
10. Thomas Anburey, *Travels Through the Interior Parts of America* (Boston: Houghton Mifflin Company, 1923), Volume 1, 186.
11. Lemuel Roberts, *Memoirs of Captain Lemuel Roberts* (1809; reprint ed., New York: The New York Times & Arno Press, 1969), 59.
12. Morgan, 8: 1000.

13. F. J. Hudleston, *Gentleman Johnny Burgoyne* (Garden City, N.Y.: Garden City Publishing Co., 1927), 137.
14. William James Morgan, ed., *Naval Documents of the American Revolution* (Washington, D.C.: Naval History Division, Department of the Navy, 1986), Volume 9, 332.
15. "Trial of Schuyler," 162; See also Calfe, 291; General James Wilkinson, *Memoirs of My Own Time* (1816; reprint ed., New York: AMS Press Inc., 1973), 193.
16. Jared Sparks, *Writings of George Washington* (Boston: Russell, Odiorne, and Metcalf, 1834), Volume 4, 494; See also B. F. De Costa, *Notes on the History of Fort George During the Colonial and Revolutionary Periods* (New York: J. Sabin & Sons, 1871), 36.
17. Sparks, 494; In a subsequent letter, Washington withdrew his questioning of Schuyler's orders to evacuate Fort George. John C. Fitzpatrick, ed., *The Writings of George Washington* (Washington, D.C.: United States Government Printing Office, 1933), Volume 8, 449.
18. "General Powell to Sir Guy Carleton, 19 September 1777," *The Bulletin of the Fort Ticonderoga Museum* 7 (July 1945): 32; Some of the remains of these gunboats may still exist at the northern end of Lake George. Brown mentioned a total of 17 gunboats above the falls, Morgan, 9: 939.
19. Morgan, 9: 968; Another version of the same letter noted three guns on the sloop. Peter Nelson, "The Battle of Diamond Island," *Quarterly Journal of the New York State Historical Association* (January 1922): 47.
20. Morgan, 9: 968.
21. James Minor Lincoln, *The Papers of Captain Rufus Lincoln of Wareham, Mass.* (1904; reprint ed., Arno Press, Inc., 1971), 21.
22. Elizabeth Cometti, ed., *The American Journal of Lt. John Enys* (Syracuse, N. Y.: Syracuse University Press, 1976), 46-47.
23. Winston Adler, ed., *Their Own Voices: Oral Accounts of Early Settlers in Washington County, New York* (Interlaken, N.Y.: Heart of the Lakes Publishing, 1983), 101.
24. Ibid, 102.
25. Horatio Rogers, ed., *Hadden's Journal and Orderly Books: A Journal Kept in Canada and Upon Burgoyne's Campaign in 1776 and 1777, by Lieut. James M. Hadden, Roy. Art.* (Albany: Joel Munsell's Sons, 1884), 106. The original journal and orderly books of Lieutenant Hadden are presently in the Fort Ticonderoga Museum Collection.
26. Rogers, 90-91, 96, 100-10.
27. Baldwin, 100.
28. M. J. Powers, *A Summer Paradise* (Albany: Delaware and Hudson Co., 1930), 159; *Nelson's Guide to Lake George and Lake Champlain* (London: T. Nelson and Sons, 1866), 18; Benson J. Lossing, *The Pictorial Field-Book of the Revolution* (1851; reprint ed., Freeport, N.Y.: Books for Libraries Press, 1969), 115.
29. Lemuel Lyon, "Military Journal for 1758," in *The Military Journals of Two Private Soldiers, 1758-1775*, by Abraham Tomlinson (1854; reprint ed., New York: Books for Libraries Press, 1970), 20; Benjamin Jewett, "The Diary of Benjamin Jewett - 1758," *National Magazine* 17 (1892-93): 62.
30. J. F. Wasmus, *An Eyewitness Account of the American Revolution and New England Life*, trans. Helga Doblin (New York: Greenwood Press, 1990), 146.
31. William L. Stone, trans. *Memoirs, Letters, and Journals of Major General Riedesel* (1868; reprint ed., New York: The New York Times & Arno Press, 1969, Volume 1, 295-96.

Part V
Travelers In A New Century

Ruins of Fort Ticonderoga
(Print, author's collection)

11. Abigail May 1800

BEFORE SETTLERS and peacetime travelers returned to the Lake George Valley, one final military trek of the American Revolution occurred in July 1783. While awaiting the signing of the peace treaty ending the war, General George Washington undertook a tour of military posts in New York which included an inspection of Fort Ticonderoga. Washington notified Philip Schuyler on July 15, 1783, that he had sent Lieutenant Henry Dinker, the assistant quarter master general, "to make arrangements, and particularly to have some light Boats [bateaux] provided and transported to Lake George that we may not be delayed on our arrival there."[1] After visiting Fort George and the remains of Fort William Henry, Washington and his inspection party crossed Lake George in three bateaux to survey Fort Ticonderoga and Crown Point. Seven weeks later, the Treaty of Paris officially ended the American Revolution.

In 1787 James Caldwell, a merchant from Albany, was granted a patent for 1,595 acres adjacent to the southern end of Lake George and later purchased additional acreage in the same vicinity. Smaller land patents were also granted to former soldiers who served in the Revolutionary War. James Caldwell was able to lure settlers to the lake, and his son William subsequently constructed a grist mill and iron forge in the area. Although some early plans called for a village near the site of Fort George, the settlement of Caldwell was located along the southwest shoreline of the lake. In 1792 John Thurman, a New York City merchant, acquired a huge tract of land (800 square miles) which extended over much of present-day Warren County. John Thurman, more than James Caldwell, was responsible for attracting settlers to the region. From the original Thurman grants and other land patents, the towns of Bolton (1799), Rochester(1807, renamed Hague in 1808), and Caldwell (1810) were delineated by the state legislature.

Two early travelers to the Lake George Valley, James Madison and Thomas Jefferson, were both destined to become presidents of the United States. Writing in a birch bark notebook, Thomas Jefferson wrote a letter to his daughter Martha Jefferson Randolph on May 31, 1791, describing his passage through Lake George. Traversing the wilderness of the lake, Jefferson noted "the most beautiful water" that he had ever seen:

> its water limpid as crystal, and the mountain sides covered with rich groves of thuja, silver fir, white pine, aspen, and paper birch down to the water-edge; here and there precipices of rock to checker the scene and save it from monotony. An abundance of speckled trout, salmon trout, bass, and other fish, with which it is stored, have added to our other amusements, the sport of taking them. Lake Champlain, though much larger, is a far less pleasant water. It is muddy, turbulent, and yields little game.[2]

After sailing a half day on Lake Champlain, Jefferson and Madison returned to Lake George and then proceeded through Vermont to the Connecticut River on their way south.*

"Lake George." Detail of a painting by Alfred Thompson Bricher.
(Albany Institute of History and Art, gift of Averill Harriman)

*In his letter to his daughter, Jefferson reflected on the disadvantages of the climate in the northeast compared to his beloved Virginia. "Here they are locked up in ice and snow for six months. Spring and autumn, which make a paradise of our country, are rigorous winter with them; and a tropical summer breaks on them all at once. When we consider how much climate contributes to the happiness of our condition, by the fine sensations it excites, and the productions it is the parent of, we have reason to value highly the accident of birth in such a one as that of Virginia."[3]

Abigail May's visit to Lake George in July 1800 was one of the first detailed accounts of a tourist's impression of the lake. Her journal not only presents an interesting insight into life in 1800 and the state of medical care at the time but also reveals her innermost thoughts and feeling on the trip. Accompanied by her mother, a younger brother, and a family friend, 24-year-old Abigail May departed from Boston for Ballston Spa, New York, on May 19, 1800.* The trip to Ballston Spa was a vain attempt to find a remedy for Abigail's unspecified affliction that resulted in "spasms" and a hand rendered nearly useless by an apparent nerve disorder.

By the turn of the nineteenth century, Ballston Spa had a national reputation for its therapeutic springs. The spring waters of Ballston Spa had been frequented by deer and were later discovered by a surveyor in 1771, although nearby High Rock Springs had been known to Native Americans for centuries for its healing powers.** In 1787 a new era commenced with the construction of a log tavern at Ballston Spa, a resort community founded on the medicinal qualities of the spring water. By 1800 Ballston Spa had become a popular resort with several hotels, while neighboring Saratoga Springs was still in its infancy with only a tavern and two log huts for accommodations.*** Several years later, however, the opening of Union Hall (later named the Grand Union Hotel) advanced Saratoga Springs to the forefront of the early tourist trade.

Abigail's journal also offers a glimpse into travel along the early roads in the northeast. Her carriage trip included passage through Worcester, Brookfield, Belchertown, and Northampton, Massachusetts (along a road that follows present-day Route 143). At Pittsfield the May family spent the night at an inn hosted by a physician. Abigail conferred with the doctor, who "was positive [that] he could entirely cure me, and offer'd to try if the waters fail'd. I have had enough of *Quackery* one would think—but tis adding a slender string to the bow of expectations, and I will not snap it off prematurely."[8] In the morning the passengers boarded their carriage, journeyed through Lebanon, New York (following a road that parallels present-day Route 20), and eventually crossed the Hudson River by ferry for a stopover in Albany. Accompanied by Mr. Howard, a family friend, Abigail viewed Albany, observing that "many of the houses are very elegant, and the new Church is a splendid building but the little old pick'd dutch houses pleased me with their novelty more."[9]

The next day, only a half-hour into the trip north of Albany, it was discovered that Abigail's younger brother George might have been exposed to smallpox while staying at the inn in Albany the previous night. In Schenectady a doctor was quickly summoned to inoculate the young boy. Although inoculation for smallpox was a

---

*Born in Pomfret, Connecticut, in 1775, Abigail May was the oldest daughter of Colonel John and Abigail May.

**The therapeutic value of springs was endorsed by Sir William Johnson who visited "the Springs near the Frontiers of N[ew] England [Lebanon Springs, New York]" in August 1767 and again the following year.[4] Johnson later sought relief at the Ballston Spa spring in 1771 for a lingering wound received during the Battle of Lake George (1755).[5]

***In September 1790 Elkanah Watson visited Saratoga and Ballston when the area was still undeveloped and predicted that "the remarkable medicinal qualities of these Springs, and their accessible position, must render this spot, at some future period, the Baths of America."[6] At Ballston Spring, Watson observed "two or three ladies walking along a fallen tree to reach the fountain, and was disgusted to see as many men washing their loathsome sores near the barrel. There was also a shower bath with no protection except a bower of bushes."[7]

controversial procedure during the American Revolution, it was apparently a more accepted practice by the turn of the nineteenth century. Following the publication in 1798 of Edward Jenner's successful vaccination experiments, smallpox inoculation gained greater acceptance in the medical community.

After a five-day journey, the May party reached the Aldridge House at Ballston Spa just before sunset on May 23, 1800.* The hotel, which held as many as 80 boarders during the summer, had been enlarged since Abigail's aunt had visited there the previous year. While at the height of the summer season the resort catered to "the fashionable world," off-season Abigail was greeted with the afflicted: a four-year-old child unable to walk with "something resembling. . .St. Vitas's dance"** and another guest "troubled with Epileptic fits."[11] Reflecting on the irony of the two disparate groups of pilgrims at Ballston, Abigail mused: "it is and ever has been a strange circumstance to me that people should resort to a watering-place for pleasure —that they can dance and sing, while disease and death continually stare them in the face."[12] Her cure would involve a regimen of drinking two to four tumblers of salty mineral water daily and showers in the graffiti-covered bathhouse. Sundays brought more visitors to the magic waters: "I was amused at the concourse of people who flock'd in waggons, on horseback, and on foot—to drink the waters, the seats round the spring were constantly fill'd and resemble'd the booths upon the common [on] Election day."[13] Although Abigail found the mineral water disagreeable and questioned its value, she nevertheless noted some miraculous recoveries: "Maj[o]r Keizes. . .came there about 4 weeks ago—with his crutches—and so weak he could not ride above ten miles a day—he now skips about without help."[14]

Within two days of their arrival at the hotel, Joshua Aldridge, the innkeeper, heard of George's inoculation and feared that it might hurt his business. On June 1 Abigail's mother accompanied George to Schenectady for a short stay under a doctor's care. Mr. Howard, the friend who had escorted the May family to Ballston Spa, had set out on foot for Boston a few days earlier. Although most of Abigail's sojourn would be relatively cheerful, her initial state of mind turned melancholy: "I have been young but now am old. . .24 years. Long enough have I lived to see the insufficiency of earthly things; to have my fairest prospects blasted; to experience old age in all its helplessness and to find myself an useless being in society."[15]

Abigail's mother and brother began their return trip to Boston on July 10, leaving Abigail in the care of Dr. Anderson from Schenectady. Anderson carefully monitored Abigail's hand, manipulating the joints and offering words of encouragement. Anderson also attended to other affluent guests at the Aldridge House and administered the accepted medical techniques of the day including bloodletting. For the most part, Abigail's mental state improved in the summer "for I can walk, *play*,

---

*The Aldridge House was first constructed in 1792 by Benajah Douglas and sold in less than three years to Joseph Westcot. Within a year of the death of Westcot in 1795, his widow married Joshua B. Aldridge. After building a sawmill on the property, Aldridge substantially enlarged the hotel. At the time of Abigail May's visit in 1800, the Aldridge House had become the first fashionable hotel at Ballston Spa. By the late nineteenth century the building had seen a series of owners and had become known as Brookside by 1893. The Saratoga County Historical Society persuaded the town to purchase the building in 1971 as a home for the society.[10]

**Saint Vitus Dance, characterized by involuntary spasmodic muscle movements, was a neurological disorder thought to stem from a rheumatic infection that chiefly affected children. The name originated in the Middle Ages when the afflicted made pilgrimages to the shrines of Saint Vitus.

drink, and eat with the best of them. . .weeks fly away with astonishing rapidity."[16] Her activities included horseback riding, playing cards, visiting a nearby Native American wigwam to observe basketweaving, and enjoying the company of the guests at the hotel. Abigail's long stay at the Aldridge House also allowed her to hobnob with the rich and famous, including the governor of New York, the attorney general, the mayor of Albany, and the family of a former governor.* While there is little direct evidence in Abigail's journal of her own family wealth, her three-month pilgrimage to New York suggests affluence.

On July 14, 1800, one of the guests invited Abigail on a trip to Lake George with some of the other hotel boarders.** With the approval of her doctor, she set out with the group for the lake on a Sunday afternoon in a motley caravan of carriages. Stopping for the night at a primitive hotel on the banks of the Hudson River (a few miles north of present-day Saratoga Springs), the travelers spent an uncomfortable night warding off mosquitoes and other insects. Passing through present-day Hudson Falls, the party of tourists reached the southern end of Lake George the following day in time for a grand view of the lake and surrounding mountains. After spending that evening at a prison-like inn on the southern shore, one of the party proposed crossing Lake George for a visit to Fort Ticonderoga. Fearful of the hazardous journey across the lake, half of the group refused to embark on the voyage the next morning. Abigail and five other guests plus a servant and the boatmen made the eventful trip to Ticonderoga. Her description of the ruins of Fort Ticonderoga provides a noteworthy picture of the remnants of the historic fortress in 1800. The travelers were so enthusiastic with their journey that they briefly entertained the notion of going on to St. Jean, Canada. On the return trip across Lake George, the adventurers braved another primitive inn located on the shore of the lake and a stormy voyage. When the group returned to the Aldridge House, they were greeted by a crowd of other guests who congratulated them on their escape from drowning. Abigail's journal is the first tourist account of Lake George in the nineteenth century. The excursion would be the highlight of her journey to New York.

Later, during the summer, Abigail's hand grew more painful, despite the continued manipulation by her doctor. Upon the recommendation of another doctor who was also a guest at the Aldridge House, Abigail was willing to undertake a new approach to treating her illness: "Dr. Stringer of Albany prepares the Oxygen Gas—or vital air according to the latest and most approved method—he has made several extraordinary cures."[18] With the concurrence of Dr. Anderson, her physician from Schenectady, Abigail traveled to Albany for the gas. Dr. Stringer, however, postponed the oxygen treatment and recommended the use of opium. Previously, Abigail had occasionally used laudanum, a mixture of opium in liquid form, for her illness. Placing her confidence in Dr. Stringer, Abigail began taking opium in pill form but the dosage quickly disoriented her: "Oh this opium! my senses sealed in

*In the years that followed, other luminaries lodged at the Aldridge House, including Washington Irving in 1802 and 1803. Irving was not impressed by the spring during his last visit: "The Springs are intollerably Stupid owing to the miserable deficiency of female company I took the warm bath this Morning and drank the waters which however do not agree with me."[17] James Fenimore Cooper stayed at Aldridge's in 1824 while researching the geographical setting for *The Last of the Mohicans*.

**Abigail's dates and days did not always correspond in her July journal.

forgetfullness my frame tottering."[19] Her reaction to the opium grew worse which led Dr. Stringer to reduce the dosage.

With "various medicines" in hand, Abigail departed from Albany for the long trip back to Boston.* While lodging at an inn in Lebanon, New York, on the journey home, Abigail unhappily found "those twitches and tremors returning again—w[h]ether it was owning to my bathing [at Lebanon] in the warm bath (that was too relaxing for me) or that Opium I took in Albany caused these distressing sensations I am unable to say—but I passed a wretched day—and at seven o clock took 15 drops of Laudanum."[21]

In Boston Abigail was content to be reunited with her family and friends. While she conjectured that her health had benefited from the trip, she was resigned to the inability to use her hand. After some revisions, Abigail planned to publish the journal of her adventure in New York. On September 9, 1800, only ten days after returning to Boston, Abigail May died. Six months later, her sister Lucretia "in compliance, with the wishes of my honor'd mother, and many other *dear* friends. . .have undertaken the painfully pleasing task of transcribing the journal of my dear, and regretted Sister. . .I have undertaken to retrace those lines her hands have pen'd, not with any idea of improving: (for that is beyond my power) but merely to preserve. What is to her friends an inestimable treasure: she wrote from the warm and genuine impulses of her feeling heart."[22]

The Aldridge House, known as Brookside today,
houses the Saratoga County Historical Society
(Photo by the author)

*Before leaving Albany, Abigail and others "went to see the vertical car—about half a mile from town."[20] Whether this referred to some type of crude elevator or amusement wheel (Ferris Wheel) is unknown.

The Journal of Abigail May 1800 [23]

I was preparing to dress for the Day—when called into the Piazza to Mrs. Bowers, and the two Cochrans [Andrew Cochran and Walter Cochran] she came to invite Mrs Amory, Miss Bowen, and myself to Tea with her in the afternoon, soon after as we were conversing, Mr A[mory] and Mr B[owers] came up, and said they had agreed to go to Lake George. and proposed setting of[f] immediately after dinner—I told him I came here for the benifit of the waters and should not feel easy to leave them—he called Mrs Bowers in, she brought Doct[o]r A[nderson]'s opinion, that the journey would do me good, and all urged my being of the party so strongly I could not refuse. twas then past 12. we dined at one, and started at two —I however put on my habit made up a small bundle, and after dinner walk'd to Mrs Westerns, prefering to get into the carriage from her door, to our public Piazzas—the cavalcade came on in the following order—Mr [Thomas] Amory, and Mr Baldwin on horseback, Mr J Bowers, and McMasters in a curricle [two-wheeled carriage]—Mr Bowers and Miss May in a chaise [hooded two-wheeled carriage]—Mrs Bowers and Miss Gibbs in a Phaeton [four-wheeled carriage]—Mrs Amory and Miss Bowen ditto—Mr Lyman and Hunt in two Sulkies [two-wheeled carriages drawn by one horse]—and two servants on horseback brought up the rear—we made a very handsome appearance, I assure you.

At Saratoga springs we stop'd near half an hour—I then rode with Miss Gibbs in the Phaeton—till we reach'd—(I forget) 2 miles from the spot w[h]ere General Burgoyne surrender'd—the house did not promise much but Mrs B[owers] had a most distressing headache, and we agreed to make the best of it—twas a one story building, and our room communicated with the one oc[c]upied by Mr. and Mrs. B[owers]—indeed the partition was so thin we could hear even a whisper—and that alone seperated them—we 3 Girls had two beds in this room, and as we felt very fatigued, hop'd for rest, but rest was denied us—innumerable bugs and musquitoes— tormented us—we drew our bed upon the floor, and tossed and groaned till morning—Mr B[owers] continually calling and talking to us—we thought this bad enough, but it was only the beginning of sorrow as you shall hear in due time—at 5 we swallow'd a little refreshment and prepar'd for our journey—the house w[h]ere we slept was delightfully situated upon the North River [Schuylerville]— command- ing a most extensive and delightful prospect—we crossed the ferry at this place and rode to Sandy hill [later Hudson Falls], 30 miles from Ballstown, to breakfast—we had tolerable accommodations—and were enchanted with our ride, which all the morning was on the banks of the [Hudson] river, whose delightful shores presented an evervarying but improving perspective—I rode with Mrs Bowers, and found her an elegant woman in conversation, as well as looks.

From Sandy hill, we rode 17 miles, thro[ugh] a wild interesting country, to Queensbury, on the banks of Lake George*—the first view of this Lake is most noble—A long sweep of mountains, extending as far as the eye can reach embosom- ing this smooth tranquil p[i]ece of water, which like a mirror reflected every object upon its banks, and visible at only one opening, w[h]ere the road wound thro[ugh]

---

*A considerable portion of the end of Lake George was part of Queensbury and Thurman until the formation of Caldwell in 1810.

a hollow—the surface of the Lake unruffled except round the many little woody islands that embellish it—I was struck with awe—and could not give utterance to my feelings—we alighted at the *only* house that could accommodate us—and which indeed did not promise much—a one story building which had very much the appearance of a Goal [gaol or jail]*—we however had a good din[n]er of Bass and Perch—which our gentlemen praised highly as being alive but half an hour before caught from the Lake—I could not eat any of them after this recommendation, and made my dinner of mutton—tho[ugh] I know every thing must die before it can be eaten , I hate to have it brought to my rememberance.

The afternoon pass'd very pleasantly, in reading, sleeping, talking, playing & cc—in the evening Mr Bowers declared his intention of crossing the Lake to Ticonderoga—some ridiculed him, but he was inflexible—Mr Amory said at once it was hazardous, and he *would not go*—but return to Albany the next morning, I grieve'd on hearing this, that I had not brought my writing with me—as I could not tell when another opportunity might present—but grieving did no good, I scratch'd a few hasty lines to Mammar—purporting our intentions, and situation; but in the midst of laughter and gabble—that I [k]now not as it was intelligible, again, the inhabitants of bedsteads drove us from their territory—and we sought repose upon the floor, their flea regiment follow'd us even there—but we worried thro[ugh] the night—presenting pretty haggard countenances to each other in the morning—but a view of this delightful Lake and a glorious morning dispelled our gloomy looks—and we prepar'd for our voyage against the wishes and advice of all but the Bowers party—we were assur'd of a wat[e]ry grave—but Hunt (a true original) promised to write an elegy [eulogy] upon us, and actually pretended he had made the two first lines.

After a fine breakfast, about half past eight, we ascended our bark, a small Boat I should say—which with close stowing and accurate balanceing, took in Mr and Mrs Bowers, Miss Gibbs, Miss May, Mr J Bowers, Mr Baldwin, one servant, four men to row, a box of provisions and liquor, and fishing apparatus—the rest of the party remain'd on shore "bawling good luck" till we were out of hearing,—when the Amory party went to Albany the Gents to Ballstown. We had a most pleasing row of it to the 14 mile island, when we landed**—and had a fire kindled, fish caught, and cook'd, which with our cold provision gave us an excellent dinner, while at our repast, the thunder mutter'd at a distance, and the blackness of the clouds indicated a shower, we felt rather unpleasant at the idea of witnessing a tempest upon the Lake; however we had no alternative, our men made a tent for us of some sails "and we spread ourselves into a clump" under it. The lightning was severe, but could we have divested ourselves of all fear, the scene would have been inexpressibly pleasing to me—as it was, it was terribly, awfully, grand and sublime—the hills enveloped in clouds, the Lake late so calm and serene, now tempestuously dashing against the rocks at our feet—the pattering of rain upon the trees over us—the thunder echoing among the mountains, all form'd a scene truly noble—we staid under our tent about an hour, when the rain subsided, and we once more committed

---

*There is some debate regarding the inn at the southern end of Lake George. By one account, the hotel was between Fort George and the lake and may have originally been a barracks.[24]

**Fourteen Mile Island, located on the east side of the lake at the entrance to the Narrows, was a traditional stopping point from the eighteenth century through the steamboat era.

The Narrows of Lake George.
(Photo by the author)

ourselves to the waters—we stop'd again at a fountain about 14 miles distant—re-markable cold and pleasant—(we did not go [on] shore from fear of rattlesnakes which our Capt[ai]n said were plenty here) the boat was fastened to a tree upon shore, while the men rested—and we contemplated the scenery which was enchant-ing—over our heads frown'd the buck mountain or rather rock 600 feet high, and projecting into the Lake—on the opposite side a point of land form'd a most beautiful bay*—and the shore on either side as far as we could see, presented the richest verdure—while tremendous mountains from'd the back ground, innumer-able islands, were dispersed over the Lake—some rocky and barren, others cover'd with trees and shrubbery—presented a most pleasing variety but my feeble pen cannot *now* do anything like justice to its beauties—at the time my eyes were fascinated by it—I could have written a more lively description, but now I recollect it was a most delightful scene, that I was fully sensible of it—but that is all the impression it has left on my mind, the grand and pleasing I cannot transmit to you—so I will not attempt saying anything more about it.

We arrived at Ticonderoga at eight in the evening hungry, tired, sleepy and wet—we tried to think our home a good one, our supper really was, but a *small* difficulty arose about our lodging**—our hostess could spare us three beds (2 feather

*Abigail could not have been looking at Buck Mountain since she would have passed that area before reaching Fourteen Mile Island. She may have viewed Deer Leap (Bloomer Mountain) with the adjacent shoreline at Sabbath Day Point and the opposite shore of present-day Huletts Landing.

**At this time a tavern existed near the landing on the east side of Lake George in Ticonderoga. The Alexandria Hotel was built after the turn of the century in the same vicinity.

one straw) and two bedsteads—but only one room—what could we do? I said [sit] up—but Mrs B[owers] checked me and I held my peace—the room we were to occupy had an old fashion'd chest of drawers in it we push'd our bed against the wall and placed this at its feet—then mov'd Mrs Bowers's bed which had curtains, close too—and hem'd ours in—the curtains were fasten'd together—and our two Beaus [fellow travelers, Mr. J. Bowers and Mr. Baldwin] took the straw bed upon the floor on a line with the others—'tis true we were effectually hid from sight, but it was something unpleasant to me—however, I was so sleepy I slept perfectly sound—and waking and finding myself cold in the morning (intirely forgetting there was any one in the room) I said to Miss Gibbs as I have often to you "do hug me for I am almost frozen" in a moment I recollected and could have hid myself—I heard a suppressed laugh—but could not help it—our gentlemen were perfectly delicate, and did not allude to our "case of delicacy."

We [ate] a fine breakfast, rambled upon the rocks, and about 9 oclock got into a wagon to cross to Lake Champlain—tis about 8 miles and every step is interesting—our driver a smart shrewd young man satisfied our curiosity as to 'whats that' and 'whats this'—the old French war was described, and we [were] sh[o]wn vestigates [vestiges] of that calamity, but how shall I convey any idea to you of the delight I experienced, when the ruins of Fort Ticonderoga, and Lake Champlain appear'd in view—never in my life did I see such a prospect—our waggoner stop'd—to the right and in front of us, lay the Lake smooth and tranquil—its banks romantically sloping to its verge—and in a much higher state of cultivation than the borders of Lake George—a distant range of blue almost indistinct mountains, in the back ground, on our left lay the ruins, much more magnificent then I supposed existed in our new country, built of stone, and the stone alone remaining—wood, glass, all devour'd by the insatiable monster*—but the chimnies are intire, the walls of the houses, and peaks of the roof—the windows and door frames—the ramparts, fortifications (or whatever name they bear) yet remain—but over grown with nettles and weeds, such a scene of desolation I never beheld—we alighted, I paced over the stones awe struck—this, said our guide was the house of the commanding officer—I paus'd—w[h]ere now is thy distinction, thought I, as I passed what once was the threshold, a cold chill ran through my veins, Ah! thought I, how often has a proud step and a gay heart passed thee, that now beats no more—we were sh[o]wn the sally ports [gates]—the Guard room—the bakers room—and descended into some subterraneous cells supposed to be places of confinement—A powder room &cc— our guide though he knew a great deal—but I wish'd he knew more, I wanted to know. . .every particular, of a spot that interested my feelings so much—but could obtain very imperfect information—that a vast sight of blood has been spilt on [this] spot, all agree—for several miles round, every object confirms it—the heaps of stones on which the soldiers used to cook—the ditches, now grass grown, and forsaken graves!! all, every thing makes this spot teem with melancholy reflections—I knew not how to leave it, and ascended the waggon with regret—I should like to pass a day there alone.

We rode about half a mile and alighted at the house of our guides Mother—her name is Hay—we said she had seen better days, and we were right—she has been one of the gayest and wealthiest women in Montreal, but now, widow'd and old—

---

*Doors, windows, flooring, etc. were carted away by early settlers and reinstalled in their homes.

reduced to keep a tavern on the banks of Lake Champlain*—her house however is delightfully situated, and she has the *comforts* of Life as they are called—she gave us a fine dinner, of Chickens, Ham, green Peas, Cucumbers, Custards &cc—after which we amused ourselves with reading, and viewing the Lake—the Piazza stands over it, and commands a view charming indeed—we were all so much pleased with it—we talked seriously of going to Montreal—for my own part I should have admired it of all things, but our scanty wardrobe was on the further banks of Lake George—this, and this alone prevented our immediately crossing Lake Champlain to St Johns [St. Jean, Quebec]—tis a much pleasanter tour then the one we have taken, and I really regretted we could not prosecute it—I gazed on the beautiful scene around me with an odd mixture of sensations, such a prospect always gives me pleasure, and yet I felt something like pain, when I reflected I probably should never see it again—and more than pain when I contemplated that I was so many long miles from my Friends and had yet to encounter *many dangers* as all seem'd to agree it was very dangerous to cross the Lake as we had done, yet we had no other way to get back, I turn[e]d my eyes to the Fort—I regretted I had no drawing implements with me—I should have attempted a sketch if I had—I feel persuaded [that] pappar would have been pleased with it—our landlady too came in for a share of my thoughts—and the persecuting attention of Mr Bowers quite vexed me**—I thought myself secure from all, even civilities from him, as I had heard he "detested ugly women" and thought a woman who pretended to sense and sentiment, the greatest bore in the creation—as I make pretentions to all three—I placed my security there—however as there were only 3 females of us—one married, the other an "old acquaintance"—I was gifted at once with every power of pleasing—and tormented with unmeaning compliments which not all my stock of gravity could save me from laughing at—tho[ugh] vexed.

At four in the afternoon we resumed our waggon—Mr B[owers] the elder had walk'd on, to take another view of the Fort—I regretted not knowing it as I should have asked to accompany him, we passed thro[ugh] the yet remaining gates of the fortress, but saw nothing of him—supposing he had walked on, we did not stop—we went near a mile and an half when we saw him running towards us, he was tired and almost angry, had been again in the subterraneous rooms, and discover'd two more which were lock'd—and found some human bones in one of the cells—and in short, was so much interested that had we not got thus far—he intended staying another day to inspect the ruins more accurately—I would willingly have gone back but it was thought best to proceed—we arrived at the house w[h]ere we lodged the night before, and waited only to rest us and have our boat prepar'd.

*The widow of Judge Charles Hay operated a hotel in the "Old King's Store near the present steamboat landing from [Lake] Champlain at Ticonderoga."[25] Charles Hay had been a wealthy merchant in Montreal at the beginning of the American Revolution. Refusing a commission in the fight against the American colonists, Hay was imprisoned for several years during the war. He sued for false imprisonment and later moved to Poughkeepsie, New York. He next spent two years in business in the Fort George area before moving to Lake Champlain. As one of the early important settlers in Ticonderoga, Hay was made a judge soon after his arrival. In 1796 Isaac Weld, a British traveler, described the tavern "as a large house built of stone. . . . The man of this house was a judge, a sullen demure old gentleman, who sat by the fire, with tattered clothes and dishevelled locks, reading a book, totally regardless of every person in the room."[26]

**Mr. J. Bowers of New York City was the son of Mr. and Mrs. Bowers of Swansea, Massachusetts. Abigail's confrontations with the younger Bowers continued after the excursion to Lake George.

As we were told, we could have good accommodations 8 miles down the Lake—we saw a log hut upon shore to which our Capt[ain] appear[e]d to steer*—we all exclaim'd "is that the house"? Being answer[e]d in the affirmitive, some of us anxiously wish'd to proceed and pass the night upon the Lake—it was however at last determined we should go on shore—the house consisted of only two miserable rooms—pine knots were burning in the stone chimney for light—the fire out of doors at which our cakes and coffee were made, more dirt than ever I saw before in one house was here—we swallow'd and hem'd [paused], and but for extreme hunger, and fatigue, could neither have eaten or slept in such a place—Mr and Mrs Bowers, Miss Gibbs and myself occupied one room—our beaus and all the family the other—the woman own'd but 3 sheets, so we could not expect more—one thing disturb'd us, a ladder which led to the roof was down in our room, and several cats kept constantly going up and down—we however lived thro[ugh] it, at 5 [ate] a poor breakfast, and consoled ourselves with the prospect of dining at Queensbury upon fine fish &cc but alas! how vain are all our plans,—a strong head wind, and rough sea, made our voyage most unpleasant, oh! how sick and melancholy we look'd—about noon our Capt[ain] said it was vain to strive, against wind and tide—and landed us upon a solitary island, 20 miles from w[h]ere we expected to dine, we had nothing on board but some stale bread and horrid mutton—a little gin and brandy—carpets and mats were spread upon the grass—and we try'd to sleep by way of amusement, but in vain—a pack of cards was all we had to beguile time with—nothing to eat, read, or smoke—and to comfort us we had no prospect of leaving it that night—unless the wind subsided, the waves dash'd with great fury around us—and our little bark could never have sustain[e]d such a sea—and hour before sunset the fury of the waves abated, the wind lull'd and we again commit[t]ed ourselves to the unstable element.

We arrived safe and happy at Queensbury—made a delicious meal of supper and complain'd not of Bugs or Fleas or anything else, we rose at 5 and at seven were in our carriages, on our way to Balls town, had a delightful ride thro[ugh] woods stop'd to view Glens falls on the North river, which even now the river is so low, are elegant—and arrived at Kings tavern 13 miles from the spring w[h]ere we dined—poorly enough—I assure you I experienced a very delightful sensation as the bridge, the bathing house, Mrs Westerns Cottage, and lastly Aldridges house, met my sight—Mrs Bowers went with me home, and I alighted amid a cro[w]d of Beaus, who all flew to welcome me, and congratulate me on my escape from drowning—I felt very much confused and embarr[as]sed, up stairs I made my escape as soon as possible, the ladies lock'd round, and warm, dirty, tired as I was, I could not get away to change my dress, Mr Hunt had assured them we were out in a dreadful thunder storm, that our escape from the Lake would be a miracle, and Rattle snakes, and Bears awaited us on Shore.

---

*The house was probably located at Sabbath Day Point. Captain Sam Patchin, a Revolutionary War soldier, built a log house there just before 1800. Mrs. Adolphus Sheldon, at the age of 74, wrote her reminiscences of the region. At age 13 in 1797, she traveled north by sleigh across the ice: "On neither side of the lake was there any settlement except at Sabbath day point. There both sides and whole length of the lake the great pines stood, all around on the mountains, one unbroken wilderness."[27] Like many early settlers in America, her family was misled by stories of an easy life: "We had heard that Ti was a Paradise, that we should find pigs and fowls ready cooked running about with knives and forks stuck in their backs, crying 'Eat us!' But when we got there it was all bushes."[28]

Notes:

1 John C. Fitzpatrick, ed., *The Writings of George Washington* (Washington, D.C.: United States Printing Office, 1938), Volume 27, 66; See also John H. G. Pell, "General George Washington's Visit to Fort Ticonderoga in July 1783," *The Bulletin of the Fort Ticonderoga Museum* 14 (Fall 1983): 260-62.

2. Sarah N. Randolph, *The Domestic Life of Thomas Jefferson* (New York: Harper & Brothers Publishers, 1871), 201; Madison noted that the tour "was a very agreeable one, and carried us thro an interesting country new to us both." Gaillard Hunt, ed., *The Writings of James Madison* (New York: G. P. Putnam's Sons, 1906), Volume 6, 53.

3. Randolph, 202.

4. Alexander C. Flick, ed., *The Papers of Sir William Johnson* (Albany: The University of the State of New York, 1927), Volume 5, 631; Milton W. Hamilton, ed., *The Papers of Sir William Johnson* (Albany: The University of the State of New York, 1957), Volume 12, 515.

5. Alexander C. Flick, ed., *The Papers of Sir William Johnson* (Albany: The University of the State of New York, 1933), Volume 8, 258.

6. Winslow C. Watson, *Men and Times of the Revolution; or Memories of Elkanah Watson* (New York: Dana and Company, Publishers, 1856), 290; See also Valentine Seaman, *A Dissertation on the Mineral Water's of Saratoga Including an Account of the Waters of Ballston* (New York: Collins & Perkins, 1809).

7. Ibid., 291; See also William Strickland, *Journal of a Tour in the United States of America, 1794-1795*, ed. by J. E. Strickland (New York: The New York Historical Society, 1971), 143.

8. Abigail May, "The Journal of Abigail May," printed copy, New York State Historical Association, No. 1, 7 (see original in the Schlesinger Library of Radcliffe College of Harvard University).

9. Ibid., No. 1, 9.

10. Field Horne, *The First Respectable House: Brookside and the Growth of Ballston Spa* (Ballston Spa, N.Y.: Saratoga County Historical Society, 1984), 13, 16-17, 51, 70-71; See also Edward F. Grose, *Centennial History of the Village of Ballston Spa* (Ballston, N.Y.: The Ballston Journal, 1907), 55-56.

11. May, No. 1, 11-12, see also 29.

12. Ibid., No. 1, 12.

13. Ibid., No. 1, 13.

14. Ibid., No. 1, 23.

15. Ibid., No. 1, 14.

16. Ibid., No. 1, 58.

17. Horne, 20-21.

18. Ibid., No. 2, 19.

19. Ibid., No. 2, 32.

20. Ibid.

21. Ibid., No. 2, 39.

22. Ibid., No. 1, 1.

23. Ibid., No. 1, 67-73.

24. Benjamin Silliman, *Remarks Made on a Short Tour Between Hartford and Quebec in the Autumn of 1819*, 2nd ed. (New Haven: S. Converse, 1824), 150; See also Betty Ahern Buckell, *Old Lake George Hotels* (Lake George, N.Y.: Buckle Press, 1986), 30.

25. Flavius J. Cook, *Home Sketches of Essex County: Ticonderoga* (Keeseville, N.Y.: W. Lansing & Son, 1858), 29.

26. Isaac Weld, Jr., *Travels Through the States of North America and the Provinces of Upper and Lower Canada, During the Years 1795, 1796, and 1797* (London: John Stockdale, 1800), Volume 1, 292-93.

27. Ibid., 34.

28. Ibid.

Timothy Dwight in 1817. Painting by John Trumbull.
(Library of Congress)

12. Timothy Dwight 1802

TWO YEARS after Abigail May's visit to Lake George, Timothy Dwight, the president of Yale College, journeyed to the lake and surveyed the historic landmarks of the eighteenth century. Published 20 years later, *Travels in New-England and New-York* would become a classic early description of the history, geography, economics, agriculture, religion, and politics of an emerging nation seeking its own national identity. Although Dwight modestly suggested that his book "professes nothing more than to give a description of a country and a people," the four volumes were destined to become a unique historical account of America in the early nineteenth century.

Born in 1752 in Northampton, Massachusetts, Dwight was a member of the sixth generation of a family whose roots in Massachusetts began in 1635. Young Timothy Dwight showed early signs of academic brilliance, and in 1764, at the age of 12, was sent to Middletown, Connecticut, to pursue the study of Greek and Latin under the tutelage of Reverend Enoch Huntington, a recent Yale College graduate. At 13, Dwight easily passed the college entrance examination for Yale and entered the college in the fall of 1765. Although Yale had been established early in the eighteenth century, the teaching staff at the time of Timothy Dwight's entrance was comprised of only four faculty members. During his first two years, Dwight passed with little effort, but he excelled in the last two years with a self-imposed regimen of study. Dwight's graduation in 1769 was followed by further studies at Yale as a resident graduate while teaching in a grammar school in New Haven. Two years later, at the age of 19, Dwight was appointed a tutor at Yale and completed his Master of Arts degree in 1772. Nathan Hale was among Dwight's students during his first years as a Yale tutor. Dwight's zealous dedication to his teaching and study, however, soon resulted in a schedule of only four hours of sleep each night, a lack of exercise, and a minimal diet limited to vegetables. Within a short period of time, Dwight's general health and eyesight failed. Hopelessly ill, Dwight was taken home to Northampton by his father, where a slow, uneven recovery extended over many months. His treatment included proper nutrition, exercise, doses of "Hull's Colic Powder," and "free use" of Madeira wine (one bottle daily).[2] Dwight returned to his tutorial duties at Yale, but his eyesight never fully recovered. In 1777 Dwight married and, with the aid of his uncle, became qualified for the ministry.*

On October 6, 1777, the Continental Congress approved the appointment of Timothy Dwight as chaplain to the First Connecticut Brigade of the Continental Army under General Samuel H. Parsons. A fervent supporter of the American Revolution, Dwight found a forum for his nationalistic views through sermons, patriotic songs, and poems. During his service Dwight witnessed the gritty realities of war in the contested areas of southern New York. Dwight would later recall the emotion of war in his narration of a deer hunting episode during his 1802 trip to Lake George. His career with the army was cut short in November 1778 when he received word of his father's death. Harassed because of his loyalist sentiments, his father had purchased land with the intention of resettling in present-day Mississippi. The land was part of a grant to his brother-in-law, General Phineas Lyman, who had served at Lake George during the French and Indian War. Lyman and his eldest son died in 1774 and were buried along the Big Black River in Mississippi. In 1776 Timothy Dwight, Sr., accompanied his sister Eleanor, the widow of Phineas Lyman, to the Mississippi territory. The elder Dwight and his sister both died of illness there in 1777. It took a year, however, before news of the deaths reached Northampton. Leaving the Continental Army, Timothy Dwight returned to Northampton early in 1779 to support his mother and younger brothers and sisters.

Over the next few years Dwight's stature in Massachusetts grew as his sermons were heard in surrounding communities and his voice in Northampton and colonial politics influenced events. Although supporters tried to convince him to become a candidate for the Continental Congress, he decided to pursue a career in the ministry. On November 5, 1783, Dwight was ordained pastor of the Greenfield Hill Church in Fairfield County, Connecticut. Following the experience of his earlier school in Northampton, Dwight began a more ambitious school in the village of Greenfield Hill in 1786. Dwight's academy, offering a diverse curriculum, attracted 50 to 60 students of varied ages from the entire eastern seaboard. As the only instructor, Dwight spent six hours a day teaching his young scholars.

In 1795 Timothy Dwight was elected president of Yale College. At a time when a minister often continued at his post for life, Dwight prudently solicited his church's leaders for their guidance in accepting the Yale position. The members of the parish, however, met beforehand and voted not to release Dwight, but the church leadership later reluctantly approved his dismissal from the Greenfield Hill Church. At Yale Dwight found a struggling college that had barely grown since his own graduation 30 years earlier. With only two professorships and three tutors, the college conferred 34 bachelor of arts degrees, 6 master of arts degrees, and 6 honorary master's degrees in 1795. Within two years, Dwight began making additions to the existing four buildings of the Yale campus and doubled the number of students in his first five years at the school.

*There are some conflicting views on whether Timothy Dwight left Yale voluntarily.[3]

Dwight's effectiveness was shown most clearly by the augmentation of professorships staffed by talented faculty. Dwight's persistence resulted in approval by the Yale Corporation for a professorship of law in 1801, followed by a professorship of languages and another in chemistry the next year. The chemistry position would prove to be a significant step in Yale's progress toward university status. Dwight's selection of Benjamin Silliman, a gifted 1796 Yale graduate and a tutor at Yale, was unexpected since the 22-year-old Silliman had nearly completed his preparation for the Connecticut Bar. Assured of ample time for preparation in chemistry, Silliman studied under distinguished faculty in America before beginning his first lectures at Yale and later studied in England.

The chemistry position and new laboratory were prerequisites for the long-range plan for a medical school at Yale. After years of preparation, including his earlier work to help charter the Connecticut Medical Society, Timothy Dwight realized his dream when a medical school opened at Yale in 1813. At the time there were only three colleges with operational medical programs in the United States. As the number of professorships and the student body increased under Dwight, Yale's reputation as a distinquished institution of higher learning in America was solidified.

In September 1796 Timothy Dwight began a series of trips that would extend over much of the rest of his life. With a notebook in his pocket, Dwight resolved "to devote the vacations, particularly that in the autumn, which includes six weeks, to a regular course of travelling."[4] Often lodging in rudimentary taverns and frontier log houses, Dwight regularly journeyed over 600 miles during his fall excursions with shorter trips during the winter and spring. Accompanied by one of his sons, colleagues, or students, Dwight traveled approximately 18,000 miles in America over a period of two decades. Dwight's motivation for his extensive adventures included physical fitness since "I was very near losing my life [in 1774] by inaction, and too intense application to study. A long course of unremitted exercise restored my health."[5]

Dwight's intention was to observe and write about a unique society built from the forests of America: "The scene is a novelty in the history of man. The colonization of a wilderness by civilized men, where a regular government, mild manners, arts, learning, science, and christainity have been interwoven in its progress from the beginning."[6] From his youth, Dwight had always been a fervent booster of the American experience. For that reason he wished to rectify the "misrepresentations, which foreigners, either through error or design had published of my native country."[7] To Dwight, earlier writings resulted in an "injustice done. . . by European travellers. The United States have been regarded by this class of men as fair game, to be hunted down at pleasure."[8] In particular, Dwight was offended by English writers whose "numerous errors" about America had been published.[9] Dwight's portrayal of the United States would emphasize the culture, inventiveness, and persistence of its settlers.

Dwight adopted a broad-based view of America and integrated every aspect of society into the book. He especially endeavored to recount accurately the history of each area that he visited. His research was remarkable not only for its scrutiny of contemporary historical chronicles but also for its use of firsthand accounts of events. Dwight had planned to limit his "observation to New-England: but, as my excursions were in several instances made chiefly in New-York; as a considerable majority of its inhabitants are derived from New-England; as the rest are intimately connected with New-England by business. . .I determined to include it in my remarks."[10] His emphasis on New England served to demonstrate his provincialism. For Dwight, New Englanders were an exceptional group, superior to Englishmen and even other settlers in America.[11] New England villages, in Dwight's opinion, were "one of the most delightful prospects which this world can afford."[12] In Dwight's view, New England was notable for an equalitarian environment compared to Europe: "Immense private wealth is rare; and the style of building and living is rather neat and comfortable than manificient. . .poverty is almost unknown."[13]

While Timothy Dwight's views may be regarded as provincial, others might see a shade of bias.[14] However, his perceptions must be viewed in the light of the thoughts of his own day. Dwight attempted to analyze nearly every aspect of the New World, including the first colonization, Native Americans, wartime events, and the history of settlements in each region, as well as contemporary descriptions of communities in the nineteenth century. His thoughts on Native Americans, were consistent with his enthnocentrism. While Dwight recognized positive qualities in Native Americans, including "a natural understanding, sagacity, and wit, equal to the same attributes in other men," he nevertheless applied the European standard for material possessions to their culture.[15] Dwight mused that "crimes against property must have been very few" among Native Americans since they owned nothing more than a wigwam and a few belongings.[16] "Their houses, through a succession of several thousand years, were still weekwams [wigwams], and their hoes and axes clumsy pieces of stone."[17] Dwight's analysis of this failure to achieve European-style economic development stressed a lack of motivation: "With minds not less capable of improvement than those of the rest of mankind, they stopped at a goal, a little advanced from complete ignorance. The reason of this is, obviously, the absolute want of any motives, which they could comprehend and feel, to rouse them from their lethargy and prompt them to go forward."[18]

Although Dwight noted that "there was no fixed intention formed of publishing, during my life-time, the book which I projected, " he had investigated the potential publication for his book as early as 1801.[19] When Professor Benjamin Silliman visited London in 1805, further queries on publication were made on Dwight's behalf. To correct the negative image of America and reach recognized literary circles, Dwight was most interested in having his travels published in England. Dwight's commitment to his travels was unwavering and continued for another decade. With his eyesight failing, Dwight needed others to help him with the writing. The Yale class of 1802 "spontaneously offered to write for me in succession."[20] The War of 1812 delayed Dwight's bid to find a British publisher, and in 1814 his son wrote to London in an unsuccessful attempt to seek assistance in finding a publishing house.

Early in 1816 Timothy Dwight's health deteriorated. Despite severe pain, Dwight continued his duties at Yale. By the end of the year, however, he was nearly incapacitated. On his deathbed, Dwight sent for Professor Benjamin Silliman to make his final request known: "I do not seem to have any directions except as to publication of books. . .these travels of mine."[21] The following day, January 11,

1817, Timothy Dwight died at the age of 65. An autopsy revealed bladder cancer as the cause of death. His family arranged the publication of *Travels in New-England and New-York* in four volumes in 1821 and 1822 through a printer in New Haven, Connecticut. In 1823 the four volumes were published in London. Dwight's style, which combined history with a tourist's view of scenery, would soon be followed by other travel writers in the nineteenth century.

Dwight's *Travels* is in the form of a series of letters. His "First Journey to Lake George" in 1802 consists of four letters. The first letter is the actual journey to the lake while the second is a separate description of its vivid scenery, a narrative somewhat reminiscent of Peter Kalm's 1749 journal. Dwight fervently believed in elaborate descriptions of the scenery. He was unequivocal in his praise of the panorama of "Lake George [which] is universally considered as being in itself, and in its environs, the most beautiful object of the same nature in the United States."[22] His account is perhaps the most artistic depiction of the beauty of Lake George ever written. His third and fourth letters deal with battles of the French and Indian War at Lake George and Ticonderoga. Dwight's "Second Journey to Lake George" in 1811 consists mainly of his travels through Connecticut, Massachusetts, and New York. His visit to Caldwell, unfortunately, was very brief and did not include a voyage on the lake because of inclement weather.

Dwight, accompanied by a member of the senior class at Yale, departed from New Haven for Lake George on September 18, 1802. The travelers rode northward to Goshen, Connecticut, where Reverend Asahel Hooker, married to Dwight's cousin, joined the excursion party. Following a turnpike (a route duplicated by present-day Route 7), the travelers passed through Sheffield, Great Barrington, and Stockbridge, Massachusetts. Delayed by rain, the party stayed in Stockbridge for two days before departing on September 23 for Albany along the same route followed two years earlier by Abigail May (present-day Route 20). After lodging within five miles of Albany, Dwight and his traveling companions arrived in the city on Sunday morning, September 26.

First Journey to Lake George[23]

In the morning we reached Albany in sufficient season for divine service. Here we continued till Tuesday. Then, visiting the Cohoes [on] our way, we rode to Ensign's at Stillwater; and the next day, having dined at Sandy Hill [later Hudson Falls], alighted from our horses at the head of Lake George, and lodged in an inn, kept by a Mr. Verner.*

The country, as far as Glen' falls, I found much improved in its appearance. The forests, which heretofore bordered the road in many places, were gone. The ground was inclosed. The houses were better, and more numerous; and every thing wore the aspect of increasing prosperity. The road from Sandy Hill to Lake George passes along the Hudson [River], as you may remember to Glen's falls, three miles. Throughout the remaining distance, it crosses a pine ground, generally poor and barren. The road is indifferent, being alternately encumbered with sand, and stones: and the settlements are few, recent, and very unpromising.

The next morning, Thursday September 30th, our host very readily, and very civilly, offered to conduct us over the lake. Preparations were, therefore, immediately made for our voyage; and we set out between ten and eleven o'clock. The boat, which conveyed us was built the preceding year at Schenectady, for the use, and under the direction, of General [Philip] Schuyler.** Thence it was removed, partly by water, and partly over land, into the Hudson; up that river to Fort Edward; and thence over land into Lake George. Here this gentleman, then more than seventy years of age, embarked with a part of his family; and crossing the several portages, proceeded down Lake Champlain, and the river St. Lawrence, to Quebec. By the same route he returned to this place; and, leaving the boat for the accommodation of future passengers, proceeded by land to Albany. No vehicle could be lighter, or more convenient. It was built in the form of a batteau; and was thirty feet in length, and about eight or nine in breadth. Over the middle half, a canopy of painted canvass, with curtains of the same material descending from it, sheltered passengers from the sun, wind, and rain. This room; for such it was when the curtains fell; was neatly floored; and furnished with seats and other accommodations, perfectly fitted for ease, and pleasure. The day was fine; and the scenery above, beneath, and around us

*On his second visit to Lake George in 1811, Dwight noted:"When I wrote these observations, I little thought, that, within ten years, there would be raised up a beautiful village, exhibiting, with a brilliancy almost singular, many of these elegancies. Such, however, is the fact. Few settlements of the same size have a more cheerful, and thrifty appearance than that of Caldwell; erroneously named Fort George; which has within this period been built on the Western side of the lake, immediately after turning its Southern boundary, and almost literally at its South-Western corner. A number of neat, and even handsome, houses have started up here, under the direction, and by the enterprize, of a Mr. Caldwell of Albany, the proprietor, as I understand, of this township. In one of them we found all the accommodations, which are usually found in the most populous parts of the United States. Another was a country seat, a pretty building, surrounded by handsome appendages."[24] Dwight probably stayed at the first Lake House located on the property of the present-day Shepard Park.

**Philip Schuyler served as an officer during the French and Indian War at Lake George and as a major general in command of the Northern Department during the American Revolution. As president of the Northern Inland Lock Navigation Company in the 1790s, Schuyler oversaw the building of a canal from the Hudson River to Lake Champlain through Wood Creek. Although the canal was not successfully completed, the project provided needed experience that would be used by the builders of the Champlain Canal.

enchanting. We were in the best spirits. Our conductor was exceedingly obliging; and the rowers followed his example. No excursion could be pleasanter than this; except that, during the latter part of the voyage, and of the day, the wind, for about two hours, blew from the North with sufficient strength to retard our progress, and to prevent us from reaching the landing till the evening was somewhat advanced. During the last two or three miles the air, in this manner became cold enough to be disagreeable.

From the [Ticonderoga] landing we proceeded to the house of Judge K.* The family were in bed: but they rose immediately and entertained us with the utmost hospitality.

Very early the next morning we took a waggon, and rode to the peninsula, so often mentioned in American history by the name of Ticonderoga. Our driver, who was perfectly acquainted with the spot, conducted us sedulously [diligently] to every thing, which we wished to see. We first examined the old French lines; a mound raised by a body of that people across the isthmus, while they we[re] in possession of it, for the purpose of defending the approach to the fort.** Across these, the principal object of my curiosity in visiting this place, lay our road to the fort. We

Ruins of Fort Ticonderoga.
(Postcard, author's collection)

*Although Dwight's reference to "the house of Judge K." implies that the hotel was operated by the widow of Judge Charles Hay, the inn must have been in the village of Ticonderoga, given the distance to the fort by wagon.

**In his letter on the historical background of the region, Dwight noted that Montcalm's 1758 breastworks were "not more than four [feet high]" in 1802.[25] Referring to the crushing defeat of Abercromby's forces at Ticonderoga in 1758, Dwight remarked: "Probably there was never a more ill-devised, and ill-conducted enterprise. This opinion I had heard given by my own countrymen of all descriptions from my childhood."[26]

then surveyed the fort itself; and then the grenadiers' battery. Thence we proceeded to the shore of Lake Champlain; that we might see the difference between the waters of the two lakes; the one pure as [crystal]: the other turbid with clay, and disgusting to the eye. After our curiosity was satisfied, we returned to the house of Mr. K.; breakfasted; bade adieu to this worthy family; and began our voyage to the head of the Lake.

The morning had been foggy; but the vapour was dispersed, and the weather became bright, serene, and soft, like that of the preceding day. Our voyage was in the highest degree delightful.

On our way we called at a house, standing upon the Western shore, to supply ourselves with bread. The man and his wife had just taken, not a solemn, but very violent resolution to part forever; and were busied in preparing for their separation. They were, it seems, veterans in this species of contest; and had adopted a similar resolution very often before. The man was a sot [drunkard]; and the woman, a termagant [violent shrew].

Two or three miles higher up the lake, we saw at a considerable distance what appeared to us to be a bear, mounted upon a tall, dry tree, leaning towards the lake, on the extremity of one of the points, which stretched out from the Western shore. As we approached the place: we found the beast changed into a stout boy, about sixteen years of age: who had taken possession of this watch-tower, for the purpose of observing the first entrance of the deer, which some neighbouring huntsmen were endeavouring to drive into the water. We were all forcibly struck with the position, attitude, and general appearance, of this stripling[youth]; nor did I ever before mistrust how much a human being can resemble a monkey.

Deer abound in the mountains on both sides of Lake George. To me the manner, in which they are taken was new. The huntsmen with their hounds rouse them from their retreats in the forest: when they immediately betake themselves to the water, and swim towards the opposite shore. Other huntsmen, engaged in the business, place themselves on the points, to watch their entrance into the lake. Each of these is provided with a small, light batteau, which he is able to row faster than the deer can swim. When he has overtaken the deer; he dispatches him with a stroke, or two, of his oar, and then tows him back to the beach.*

We landed on the point, next above. Here we found a huntsman, who had a little before taken a handsome buck, three years old, which was then lying by him on the shore. He informed me, that his companion, who was then with a pack of hounds at a small distance in the interiour, and whom he expected every moment, usually took from twenty to thirty in a year.

Bears are caught here in the same manner, except that they are shot: as being too dangerous to be closely approached.

On this point we dined without ceremony, or dainties; but we had keen appetites, and were satisfied. Before our departure we heard the hounds advancing near to us. Our hunting companion instantly took fire at the sound. His eye kindled; his voice assumed a loftier tone; his stride became haughty: his style swelled into pomp; and his sentiments were changed, rapidly, from mildness to ardor, to vehemence, and to rage. The boy above mentioned, whose aerial stations was in full

---

*This deer-hunting technique was in use at least as early as the Revolutionary War. See *Journal of Lieutenant James M. Murray* (chapter 10, page 185).

view from this point, had disappeared. Wrathful at this desertion, and assured of the immediate appearance of the deer, he vented his mingled emotions in a singular volley of magnificent promises, impious oaths, and furious execrations.

I was forcibly struck with the sameness of the emotions, produced by hunting, and by war. The ardor of battle, the glitter of arms, the roaring of cannon, the thunder of shouts, and the shock of conflict, could scarcely have produced, in a single moment, more lofty, more violent, or more fierce, agitations, than were roused in this man by the approach of the hounds, the confident expectation of a victim, and the brilliant prospect of a venatory triumph. To him, who has been a witness of both objects, it will cease to be a wonder, that the savage should make the chase his darling substitute for war, and a source of glory, second only to that acquired in battle: or that Nimrod,* and his fellow hunters, were speedily changed into warriors, and learned from preying on beasts to fasten upon men.

All human expectations, however firmly founded, or confidently entertained, are liable, alas! to disappointment. Our hunter was not exempted from the common lot of man. His partner came up with the hounds; but, sad to tell, without a deer. The magnificence of our companion dwindled in a moment. The fire vanished from his eye; his voice fell to the natural key; and the hero shrunk into a plain farmer.

From this point we easily made our way to the house of a blacksmith, named Edmund, on the Western side of the lake, eleven miles from Fort George. We arrived just as it became dark. The man had heard the sound of the oars; and with a civility,

Mohican House. A frame house which existed in 1802 on Mohican Point (Bolton Landing) was subsequently enlarged and became known as the Mohican House.
(Bolton Historical Society)

*Dwight is making a reference to the biblical Nimrod, the great-grandson of Noah, who was known as a great hunter.

common among new settlers, came, with a candle, to aid us in landing: the shore being rough, and inconvenient. He readily consented to lodge us, and both he and his family entertained us with as much hospitality, and kindness, as we could have expected from particular friends.

These people furnished a complete contrast to the pair, mentioned above. The man was six feet, and two or three inches in height; and a Sampson in his appearance. His wife also was tall, and of a vigorous frame: and, had a controversy arisen, they would together have been no ill match for our whole company. But they were gentle-minded, affectionate, and even polite, both to each other and to those around them. This character was not assumed, but habitual; as was evident from the easy and native appearance, which it uniformly wore. Plain, indeed, they were in their manners; but there is something in the unaffected civility of plain people, which is peculiarly pleasing and amiable; and to my eye, at times, peculiarly graceful.

This man had a framed house, of two stories, with two rooms on a floor.* He told us, that he raised it on the first of the preceding March, and removed his family into it, on the 13th of the same month. He further informed us, that he had sown twenty-seven bushels of wheat the preceding year; from which in ordinary seasons he would probably have reaped twenty bushels per acre, and in good seasons thirty; and that, although he had gathered all, which was worth the labour, he should not get more than fifty bushels from the whole. This disappointment, to him a very serious one, he bore with entire equanimity, and even with cheerfulness. A blast in this region is uncommon; and such a one, as has prevailed the present year, was never before known.

In the morning, Saturday, October 2nd, I took a survey of our landlord's farm, and was pleased to see it exhibit all the proofs of fertility and thrift, which could be expected on so new a plantation. We breakfasted early; and taking our leave of this friendly family, began our voyage homeward. The weather was a mere continuation of that fine serenity, which had smiled upon us the two preceding days. Scarcely had we advanced two miles on our way, when we saw a buck, swimming in the lake half a mile before us. As soon as he perceived us; he exerted all his strength to gain the point of an island, which a little Southward of our course projected far into the water. To my great satisfaction, he reached it before we came up with him. As soon as he struck the shore; he flew, rather than ran, into the forest; and was out of sight in a moment. Our conductor, and his men, were much less satisfied with the disappointment than we were. But fortune, if I may use their language, soon made them amends. When we had proceeded about half a mile farther, another animal of the same species, but still larger, appeared at a little distance, making his way across the lake, and too far advanced to retreat. Our companions pursued him with no small degree of the spirit mentioned above, generally however with entire decency; and speedily coming up, made him their prisoner after having given him a few strokes with the oar. They then drew him into the bow of the boat; where he lay just by my side, in a posture, and with an eye of. . .affecting supplication, as I almost ever beheld. Indeed it was a stronger resemblance of the suppliant aspect, and attitude, of a suffering infant than can easily be conceived.

*The location of this house is uncertain. However, Roger Edgecomb reportedly had a frame house in 1802 on Mohican Point in Bolton Landing. The house was subsequently enlarged and became known as the Mohican House.[27]

At the first sight of this animal I was convinced, that we should overtake him; and therefore hardened my heart, as well as I could, in order to be prepared for the event. I recollected that it was as vindicable to kill a buck, as an ox; and that his flesh would be a substitute for other meat, which must be obtained at the same expense of life and happiness. Nor could I deny that our companions were uncensurable for their wishes to possess themselves of such a dainty; or refuse to exculpate [clear] them from the charge of any peculiar cruelty. I acknowledged, that they felt, and did, exactly what their fellowmen, as a body, would in the same circumstances have felt, and done. But all my efforts were to no purpose. The appearance of the unfortunate animal put my philosophy to flight; and made so strong an impression upon my mind, that for several days his image, in spite of every exertion, was almost incessantly before my eyes; and is at this distance of time fresh and vivid in my remembrance. "Poor unhappy creature," I thought within myself, "like Christianity, without an earthly friend, and every where denied a safe, quiet retreat. Wherever thou wanderest, thou art persecuted; and thy persecutors are every where wolves, catamounts, and men; the last, thy worst persecutors: the two first, symbols of the men, and the fiends, who have ever combined to persecute Christianity also."

Our conductor, however, and his rowers exulted in their victory. Amid many other expressions of joy he remarked, that he would not for a considerable sum have failed of meeting with this adventure, that I might mention it in the journal, which he perceived I kept. He also informed us, with an air of no common panegyric [oration], that a Mrs. D. of Sandy Hill, had caught one of these animals with her own hands, and brought it to the shore. Mrs. D. I presume, is of the true Amazonian breed; and, had the register of her genealogy been correctly kept, would find her ancestry reaching directly to the Thermodon [ancient Greece].

The buck, which we had taken, was five years old; the largest, and fattest, that I ever saw.

A fine breeze now sprung up from the North-West. We hoisted our sail, and made the rest of our way as easily, and pleasantly, as can be conceived. We landed at the South-West corner of the lake, for the sake of seeing the remains of Fort William Henry. This fortress stood on a small eminence, rising gradually, and immediately, from the beach. It was a regular square work; with three, and I presume with four, bastions: for I had not curiosity enough to examine. On the North is the lake; on the West, a valley; on the South and South-East, a thick swamp; and on the East, a beach, very little elevated above the water. The immediate access was therefore difficult; but the spot is entirely commanded by more distant grounds; particularly by the eminence, on which Fort George was afterwards erected.* The walls were built of earth, rather sandy and loose; yet, having been always covered with the verdure, which spontaneously springs up every where in the Eastern parts of the Union, are chiefly entire, except where they are broken down by the great road, which passes into the North-Western parts of this State, and runs directly over

---

*In another letter Dwight observed that the site of Fort William Henry was "almost on a level with the waters of the lake. . .overlooked, and perfectly commanded by the eminence on which Fort George was afterwards built. . .so far as its situation is concerned, appears to have been the least fitted to answer the design for which it was built."[28] Eighteen years earlier, Peter Sailly, a Champlain Valley pioneer, observed "the remains of the old ramparts of earth [at Fort William Henry]. . .covered with wild cherry trees. . .[and] the remains of an entrenched camp. . .in the center a graveyard."[29] Sailly also noted that Fort George in 1784 "is yet in good repair."[30]

them. In their best state they would have been a defence, only against desultory attacks of Canadians, and savages.*

After we had satisfied our curiosity, we returned directly to the inn; mounted our horses; and set out for Sandy Hill. Before we began our voyage over the lake, we had examined with minute attention Fort George, and the remains of the works erected in its neighbourhood. On our return we surveyed several places which we had before passed in the evening; particularly the pond, called Bloody Pond;** a name, which it received from the fact; that the French, and probably the English also, who fell in the [1755] battle between Baron [de] Dieska[u], and the detachment of English, and Indians, under Col. [Ephraim] Williams and the great [Mohawk chief] Hendrick, were thrown into its waters. We also marked the rill [brook], called Rocky brook,*** where this battle began. At Glen's Falls we turned aside, and viewed this fine piece of Nature's workmanship. At Sandy Hill, where we arrived about three o'clock, we took, a light dinner and then without any inconvenience, except the heat, reached Carpenter's a little after sunset: our whole journey having been forty miles.

Description of Lake George

Lake George lies between 43° 25' and 43° 55' N. lat. and between 73° 25' and 73° 43' W. long. from London. Its Southern termination is in the township of Queensbury; its Northern, in that of Crown Point. Its length is thirty-four miles; its greatest breadth four. At the head, or Southern end, its breadth is about one mile. From this place it increases to a remarkable point, called fourteen mile point, (being at that distance from the head of the lake) to three miles and a half. Here it opens on the left hand into a large Bay, called North-West bay, running back six miles into the country. Above fourteen mile-point to Scotch bonnet-point, (ten miles,) the whole distance is called the Straits [Narrows]: being generally, from a mile to a mile and a half in breadth. Here it expands again into an opening called, Macdonald's bay [Hague]; five miles in length, and four in breadth. After this it gradually narrows into a river; which. . .it may fairly sustain for a mile and an half above the landing. Here it is not more than forty or fifty yards in breadth.

The depth of this lake is very various: the greatest is sixty fathoms.

Its water is perfectly pure; inferiour in this respect to none, perhaps, in the world. All travellers remark this fact; a strong proof that it is nearly singular. By the inhabitants on its borders, who freely drink it at all times, it has been abundantly

---

*Dwight revealed the strong feelings aroused in the colonies following the defeat of the British and provincial forces at Fort William Henry in 1757: "I was a little child, when it took place; and distinctly remember the strong emotions, which it every where excited, and which, hitherto, time has not been able to efface. From that day to the present it has been familiarly known by the emphatical appellation of the massacre at Fort William Henry."[31]

**Dwight's original note: "Bloody-Pond is at a small distance from the road on the Eastern side, somewhat more as I should judge than three miles South of Fort George. It received its name from the fact that the French threw their slain into it, after the engagement with Col. Williams' party."[32] Bloody Pond was known by that name during the French and Indian War. See the diary of Abel Spicer (chapter 6).

***Dwight's original note: "Rocky-Brook, or Four-mile Brook, crosses the road about four miles South of Lake George, near where the rocky ground terminates."[33]

proved to be entirely salubrious [healthy]. We drank it often; and found it to be of the best taste, and quality. On the surface it was, at this time too warm to be agreeable. Six feet below, it was cool, and lower still, cold. These facts result from its formation by subjacent springs.

North-East winds are here frequent; and often violent; blowing nearly in the longitudinal direction of the lake. Winds from the East are rare; as they are also from the South-East: but, when coming from this quarter they are usually tempestuous. In the winter they blow almost wholly from the North-East or the North-West. From the latter point, they have the same character, as in the New-England States. A West wind is scarcely known. The South-West winds prevail principally in the summer; and are generally mild and pleasant.

The snow usually begins to lie, permanently, about the middle of November; and continues till the first of April. There is however, a great difference in this respect, in different years. During the winter, preceding our journey, very little snow fell. That, which falls, is as frequently blown into drifts, as in the country near the ocean.

The lake is commonly frozen between Christmas, and the 1st of January. It continues frozen from three and an half to four months, and once within the knowledge of my informant, was frozen till the 3d of May. The ice does not sink, as in Lake Champlain; but gradually dissolves.

There is no perceptible current in its waters, except within a small distance from the North landing. A log, thrown into it, floats with the winds, and the waves, with equal ease in every direction; and in still weather is perfectly quiescent.

The fish of this lake which are brought upon the table are trout, bass and perch. The first are large but not numerous. Our landlord informed me, that he had seen one, which weighed thirteen pounds; and that some had been caught which weighed eighteen. I ate of them several times; and found them good. The bass seldom exceed five pounds; and the perch, two. Both are in sufficient plenty.

Few water-fowl frequent this spot except the loon; which is not eaten. The common birds of the country abound on the borders. Eagles are numerous. Of this, the number, which we saw, furnished sufficient evidence.

The surface of Lake George is said by Dr. Morse* to be one hundred feet higher than that of Lake Champlain. The inhabitants on its borders estimate it at three hundred. So far as I was able to judge from a loose observation of the falls, I thought this estimate not very remote from the truth. There are three sets of falls in the stream [LaChute River], which carries the waters into Lake Champlain. The lower falls, with the rapid at the bottom, cannot be less, but are probably more, than one hundred feet in perpendicular height; and in the Spring, when the lake is full, must be a cataract of uncommon magnificence. Now they were a collection of small, and beautiful, cascades. The bottom of the lake is probably about the same level with the surface of Lake Champlain. Its waters must, I think, be almost all supplied by subjacent springs. This is evident from two considerations. The first is, that the streams, which flow into it, are so few, and so small, as scarcely to supply the waste, occasioned by evaporation. The other is, that the water of this lake differs materially

---

*A personal friend of Dwight, the Reverend Jedidiah Morse of Charlestown, Massachusetts, had written a geography book used in the Yale curriculum. Jedidiah Morse was the father of inventor Samuel F. B. Morse.

from those of all the neighbouring country. The waters of the Hudson, of Lake Champlain, and generally of the whole region between the Green Mountains and the Mississippi, are impregnated with lime. Those of Lake George are pure and potable; as are almost all others which are Eastward of the Green Mountains. The vast ranges on both sides of this lake furnish ample reservoirs; and the earth, and the rocks, of which they are composed, are, both, of the kinds, whence pure waters are usually derived.

When the snow dissolves in the spring, the water of Lake George rises, at the utmost, only two feet. The variation is distinctly marked on the rocky parts of the shore, which, between two horizontal lines, are in a small degree discoloured. It is said, that before the erection of the upper dam, near the North landing [Ticonderoga] the variation was only one foot. About a mile and a half, South of the landing, the soil changes to clay; and the water becomes somewhat turbid and disagreeable; though far less so than that of South Bay [Lake Champlain]; and, like that bay, is deformed by bulrushes [aquatic weeds]. This is the part, which I have mentioned, as assuming the appearance of a river.

On each of these falls mills are erected; and forges also, in which a considerable quantity of iron is manufactured.* The ore is brought from the border of Lake Champlain in boats; which come to the bridge, built over this river about half way between the two lakes. It is said, a method of blowing the fire, peculiarly ingenious, is adopted here; and, it is supposed, here only. We were not able to visit the place, where this operation is performed.

The shores are composed of two ranges of mountains; sometimes meeting the water abruptly, and sometimes leaving a horizontal, or very gradually rising, margin, extending from a few rods to as many miles. Upon this margin settlements are begun on the Eastern, and much more frequently on the Western, side. The lands are said to be generally good; being chiefly loam, mixed with gravel; and yield, abundantly, every product of the climate.

The forested grounds contain no animals, which are not common to the country at large.

The borders are eminently healthy; and the fever and ague [severe fever and chills] is unknown.

The rocks, so far as I had opportunity to observe them, were chiefly granite, and generally stratified. In contradiction to all other strata in this State, lying in the same longitude, the strata, here, lie obliquely. They are formed of the common grey granite of this country. On the mountain, called Anthony's Nose, on Buck mountain, and in several other places, they are stained with iron.

Limestone, exactly the same with that at Glen's falls, and elsewhere in this region, blue, horizontally stratified, and fantastically seamed by the weather, abounds at the head of the lake.

By persons, who love the fine scenes of nature, and probably all, who have visited this spot, I should be thought unpardonable, were I to omit a particular description of those, which are here presented to the eye.

Lake George is universally considered as being in itself, and in its environs, the most beautiful object of the same nature in the United States. Several European travellers who have visited it, and who had seen the celebrated waters of Switzerland,

---

*At least two iron forges, located at the upper falls in Ticonderoga, were operating in 1802.[34]

have given it the preference. The access from the South is eminently noble; being formed by two vast ranges of mountains, which, commencing their career several miles South of Fort George, extend beyond Plattsburg, and terminate near the North line of the State; occupying a distance of about one hundred miles. Those on the East are high, bold, and in various places naked and hoary. Those on the West are somewhat inferiour, and generally covered with a thick forest to their summits. The road for the three or four last miles passes through a forest; and conceals the lake from the view of the traveller, until he arrives at the eminence, on which Fort George was built. Here is opened at once a prospect, the splendour of which is rarely exceeded.

The scenery of this spot may be advantageously considered under the following heads: The Water, the Islands, the Shore, and the Mountains.

View of the Narrows from Bolton Landing.
(Bolton Historical Society)

The water is probably not surpassed in beauty by any in the world; pure, sweet, pellucid [translucent], of an elegant hue when immediately under the eye, and at very small, as well as at greater distances presenting a gay, luminous azure, and appearing as if a soft lustre undulated every where on its surface with a continual and brilliant emanation. This fine object, however, is visible only at certain times, and perhaps in particular positions. While employed on its shores, or in sailing upon its bosom, the traveller is insensibly led into an habitual, and irresistible, consciousness of singular salubrity [healthiness], sweetness, and elegance. During the mild season he finds an additional pleasure. The warmth of the water on the surface diffuses a soft and pleasing temperature; cooler in the day, and warmer in the evening, than that of the shore; and securing the traveller alike from inconvenience, and disease. A fresh North wind met us in our voyage down the lake in McDonald's bay [Hague]; and the coolness of the atmosphere became disagreeable. When we reached the river [Ticonderoga], the wind had ceased; but the cold was very sensibly augmented in a moment. When we landed, it was suddenly increased a second time.

The islands are interesting on account of their number, location, size, and figure. Their number is very great; fancifully computed at 365. Few pieces of water, and none within my knowledge, are so amply furnished. Their location is exquisite. They are solitary; in pairs; and in groups, containing from three to perhaps thirty; arranged with respect to each other, and the neighbouring shores with unceasing variety, and with the happiest conceivable relations.

Both the size, and the figure, of these islands are varied in the same delightful manner. The size changes from a few feet to a mile and a half in length. The figure of most of them is oblong. A small number are round. But the variety of their appearance is peculiarly derived from their surface. A small number of them are naked rocks, and by the power of contrast are very interesting features in the aspect of the group. Some are partially, and most are completely, covered with vegetation. Some are bushy; others ornamented with a single tree,—with two, three, or many; and those with, and without, their bushy attendants. Others still, the greater number, exhibit an entire forest. Some of them, of a long and narrow structure, present through various openings in their umbrage [foliage] the sky, the mountains, the points, and other distant, beautiful objects, changing to the eye, as the traveller approaches, and passes, them. On some stand thick coppices [bushes], impenetrably interwoven. On a great multitude the lofty pine, with its separate boughs, lifts its head above every other tree, waving majestically in the sky. On others the beech, maple, and oak, with their clustering branches, and lively verdure, present the strongest examples of thrifty vegetation. At the same time, on a number, not small, decayed, bare, and falling trees are finely contrasted to this vivid appearance. He, who wishes to know the exquisite and diversified beauty, of which islands are capable, must, I think cross Lake George.

The shores of this lake exhibit a similar, and scarcely less striking, aspect. On one part of the lake you are presented with a beach of light coloured sand, forming a long, extended border, and showing the purity of its waters in the strongest light. On another you see a thick, dark forest, rising immediately from the rocky shore, overhanging, and obscuring the water with their gloomy umbrage. Here the shore is scooped by a circular sweep. The next bend is perhaps elliptical, and the third, a mere indent. The points, also, are alternately circular, obtuse, and acute, angles. Not a small number of them are long, narrow slips, resembling many of the islands, shooting either horizontally, or with an easy declension [slope], far into the lake; and covered, as are all the others, with a fine variety of forest. In many places a smoothly sloping margin, for the distance of one, two, or three miles presents a cheerful border, as the seat of present or future cultivation. In many others, mountainous promontories ascend immediately from the water.

The beauties of the shore, and of the islands are at least doubled by being imaged in the fine expanse below; where they are seen in perpetual succession depending with additional exquisiteness of form, and firmness of colouring.

The mountains, as I have already remarked, consist of two great ranges, bordering the lake from North to South. The Western range, however, passes

Westward of the North-West bay; at the head of which a vast spur, shooting towards the South-East, forms the whole of the peninsula [Tongue Mountain] between that bay and the lake. On the latter it abuts with great majesty in a sudden and noble eminence, crowned with two fine summits. From this spot, fourteen miles from fort George, it accompanies the lake uninterruptedly to the North end; and then passes on towards Canada. Both these ranges alternately approach the lake, so as to constitute a considerable part of its shores; and recede from it to the distance, sometimes, of three miles. They are visible, also, in smaller portions, and greater, from one to twenty miles in length. Generally, they are covered entirely with forests; but in several instances are dappled with rocks, or absolutely naked, wild, and solitary. This appearance is derived chiefly, if not wholly, from [geological] conflagrations.

The summits of these mountains are of almost every figure, from the arch to the bold bluff, and sharp cone; and this variety is almost every where visible. In some instances they are bald, solemn, and forbidding; in many others, tufted with lofty trees: While casting his eye over them, the traveller is fascinated with the immense variety of swells, undulations, slopes, and summits, pointed, and arched, with their piny crowns; now near, verdant, and vivid; then gradually receding, and becoming more obscure, until the scene closes in misty confusion. Nor is he less awed, and gratified, with the sudden promontory, the naked cliff, the stupendous precipice, the awful chasm, the sublime and barren eminence, and the vast heaps of rude and rocky grandeur, which he sees thrown together in confusion, and piled upon each other by the magnificent hand of nature.

The three best points of view are Fort George, a station a little North of Shelving Rock, fourteen miles; and another at Sabbath-day Point, twenty-one miles; from the head of the lake. The last view is to be taken Southward; the other two, Northward.

From Fort George the best prospect is taken of the lake itself; which is here seen to the distance of fourteen miles, together with the North-West bay. Here the mountains on both sides are visible twenty-five miles. Six fine islands are also in full view; and the mountain at the end of the peninsula, which I shall take the liberty to call Mount Putnam [Tongue Mountain], rises in the back ground with the utmost advantage; as does Shelving Rock, a promontory shooting out from the East far into the lake.

The scenes of the two remaining prospects are, however, clearly superiour to these, both in beauty and variety. The islands are far more frequent, and abrupt; the summits more lofty, and masculine. Between these views I was unable to form a preference.

From Sabbath-day point, advancing Northward, the scenery evidently declines in beauty. Still it is fine; and some of it exquisite. Rogers' Rock* and Anthony's

---

*Dwight's original note: "Rogers' Rock rises on the Western side of the lake: a naked, bold, and rough promontory of a very fine figure. Our guide informed us that it derived its name from the following facts. Major [Robert] Rogers, who commanded a party of Rangers in the last Canadian war; and who, with very little merit, acquired by his activity a considerable reputation; was attacked on this height by a body of Indians, and defeated. With his usual adroitness, and when his personal safety was concerned, with his usual success, he escaped down a narrow and steep valley at the South end of the rock, thirty or forty rods from the precipice which abuts upon the lake. The Indians supposed him to have fallen down the precipice, and therefore gave over the pursuit. Rogers made his way on the ice, near the shore, to a garrison, kept at a little distance on Friends Point; but according to his usual fortune, lost a great part of his men. Colonel Cochrane, then young, and an officer in Rogers' corps, made his

Nose,* uncouth as the latter name may seem, are among the most interesting objects
in the whole group. Even at the North end, the landscape is of a superiour cast, and
in most other regions would present uncommon attractions.

The whole scenery of this lake is greatly enhanced in beauty and splendor by
the progressive change, which the traveller, sailing on its bosom, perpetually finds
in his position, and by the unceasing variegations of light and shade, which attend
his progress. The gradual, and the sudden, openings of scoops and basins, of islands
and points, of promontories and summits; the continual change of their forms; and
their equally gradual, or sudden, disappearance; impart to every object a brilliancy,
life, and motion, scarcely inferiour to that, which is seen in the images, formed by
the camera obscura, and in strength and distinctness greatly superiour. Light and
shade are here not only far more diversified, but are much more obvious, intense,
and glowing, than in smooth, open countries. Every thing, whether on the land or
water, was here affected by the changes of the day: and the eye, without forecast,
found itself, however, disposed on ordinary occasions to inattention, instinctively
engaged, and fastened, with emotions approximating to rapture. The shadows of the
mountains, particularly on the West, floating slowly over the bosom of the lake,
and then softly ascending that of the mountains on the East, presented to us, in a
wide expanse, the uncommon, and most pleasing, image of one vast range of
mountains, slowly moving up the ascent of another.

As a specimen of the peculiar variegation of light in this region, you may take
the following. On Thursday the 30th of September, a little before the setting of the
sun, I saw one of the mountains on the East, arrayed in the most brilliant purple,
which can be imagined. Nothing could surpass the lustre, which overspread this
magnificent object, and which was varied through innumerable tints, and softenings,
of that gorgeous colour.

The dim lights, frequently seen in the night upon the shore, sometimes of
candles, feebly starring the midnight gloom of the forest, and sometimes of fires,

---

escape in the same way, together with several others. This gentleman, being employed to run the line
between the Counties of Essex and Washington, told his attendants, when he came to this rock, that
he would show them a tree in which was lodged a musket-ball shot at himself between thirty and forty
years before, in this encounter. Accordingly he pointed out the tree; and his men cut out the ball."[35]

*Dwight's original note: "Anthony's nose seems to have been a favourite name with the former
inhabitants of this State, for mountains distinguished by bold precipices. There is a mountain of this
name on the Hudson [River], forming the Southern limit of the Highlands on that river; two more on
the Mohawk [River]; and a fourth on this lake. The first and last are lofty summits, faced with
perpendicular precipices. As I am very little versed in legendary lore, I know not whether the Nose of
St. Anthony was or was not so remarkably precipitous, as in a striking manner to resemble the figure
of these mountains. Something extraordinary must have induced the inhabitants of New-York to make
them perpetual memorials of the shape and size of this prominence on the face of the Saint.

"Some years before our excursion, a fisherman was pursuing his business near the foot of this
mountain; when a huge rock fell from the precipice, and plunging into the lake at a little distance from
his canoe, came very near sinking him by the surge which it produced.

"On a rock opposite to Anthony's Nose, our guide, who had seen them, informed us, that there
were about a dozen mortars, wrought in the solid stone by the Indians, for the purpose of pounding
their corn; some of them are capable of containing half a barrel; and others of inferiour capacities down
to half a peck. They are very smooth, and exactly circular [Indian Kettles in Hague].

"Such a mortar exists on a summit of a high rock in the parish of Greenfield, Connecticut. If I
remember right, it would contain about three gallons. The rock is hard granite, and by Indians must
have been formed with great difficulty."[36]

"Lake George." Print by J. & F. Tallis, London (ca. 1830). On the evening of September 30, 1802, Timothy Dwight noted the setting sun on the eastern mountains of Lake George "arrayed in the most brillant purple, which can be imagined."
(Author's collection)

glimmering from fields and mountains, presented a strong contrast to the cheerful splendour of the day.

On the evening of Friday, the 1st of October, while we were returning from Ticonderoga, we were presented with a prospect, superiour to any which I ever beheld. An opening lay before us between the mountains on the West, and those on the East, gilded by the departing sunbeams. The lake, alternately glassy and gently rippled, of a light and exquisite sapphire, gay and brilliant with the tremulous lustre, already mentioned, floating upon its surface, stretched in prospect to a vast distance, through a great variety of larger and smaller apertures. In the chasm, formed by the mountains, lay a multitude of islands, differing in size, shape, and umbrage, and clothed in deeply shaded green. Beyond them, and often partly hidden behind the tall and variously figured trees, with which they were tufted, rose, in the West and South-West, a long range of distant mountains, tinged with a deep misty azure, and crowned with an immense succession of lofty pines. Above the mountains, and above each other, were extended in great numbers, long, streaming clouds, of the happiest forms, and painted with red and orange light, in all their diversities of tincture. Between them the sky was illumined with a vivid, yellow lustre. The tall trees on the Western mountains lifted their heads in the crimson glory; and on this back-ground displayed their diversified forms with a distinctness, and beauty, never surpassed. On a high, and exactly semi-circular, summit, the trees, ascending far without limbs, united their crowns above; and thus formed a majestic, and extensive, arch in the sky; dark, exactly defined, and exactly corresponding with the arch of the summit below. Between this crown, and the mountain, the vivid orange light, shining through the grove, formed a third arch, equally extended, and elegantly striped with black by the stems of the trees.

Directly over the gap, which I have mentioned, and through which this combination of beauty was presented to us; the moon, far Southward, in her handsomest crescent, sat on the Eastern, and the evening star, on the Western, side of the opening, at exactly equal distances from the bordering mountains; and, shining from a sky, perfectly pure and serene, finished the prospect.

The crimson lustre, however, soon faded. The mountains lost their gilding; and the clouds, changing their fine glow into a dull, leaden-coloured hue, speedily vanished. The lake, though still brilliant, became misty and dim. The splendour of the moon, and of Hesper [planet Venus], increased, and trembled on its surface, until they both retired behind the Western mountains, and just as we reached the shore, left the world to the darkness of night.

To complete the scenery of this lake, the efforts of cultivation are obviously wanting. The hand of the husbandman has already begun to clear these grounds: and will, at no great distance of time, adorn them with all the smiling scenes of agriculture. It does not demand the gift of prophecy to foresee, that the villas of opulence and refinement will, within a half a century, add, here, all the elegances of art to the beauty and majesty of nature.

Notes:

1. Timothy Dwight, *Travels in New-England and New-York* (London: William Baynes and Son, 1823), Volume 1, xx.
2. Charles E. Cuningham, *Timothy Dwight: 1752-1817* (New York: The Macmillan Company, 1942), 45.
3. Timothy Dwight, *Travels in New England and New York*, ed. Barbara Miller Solomon (Cambridge, MA.: The Belnap Press of Havard University Press, 1969), xii, n. 6.
4. Dwight, 1: iii.
5. Ibid.; For Dwight's earlier health problems see Cuningham, 43-46.
6. Dwight, 1: xii.
7. Ibid., iv.
8. Ibid., xvi, see also 4: 497-98.
9. Ibid., xix.
10. Ibid., vi.
11. Solomon, xxxv; see also xxiv, xxv.
12. Dwight, 1: xv.
13. Ibid., xi, xv.
14. Ibid., xxxvi, xxxviii, xxxix.
15. Ibid., 86.
16. Ibid., 92.
17. Ibid., 95.
18. Ibid.
19. Ibid., iv; Solomon, xxvii.
20. Dwight, 1: v.
21. Solomon, ix.
22. Timothy Dwight, *Travels; in New-England and New-York* (New Haven, CT.: S. Converse, 1822), Volume 3, 353.
23. Ibid., 340-60.
24. Ibid., 411-12.
25. Ibid., 383.
26. Ibid., 384.
27. Betty Ahearn Buckell, *Old Lake George Hotels* (Lake George, N.Y.: Buckle Press, 1986), 44; *Warren County: A History and Guide* (Glens Falls, N.Y.: Warren County Board of Supervisors, 1942), 168; See also Wallace E. Lamb, *The Lake Champlain and Lake George Valleys* (New York: The American Historical Company, Inc., 1940), Volume 2, 538.
28. Dwight, 3: 376.
29. Peter Sailly, "Diary of Peter Sailly on a Journey in America in the Year 1784," *New York State Library History Bulletin*, no. 680 (1919): 64.
30. Ibid.
31. Dwight, 3:378.
32. Ibid., 347.
33. Ibid., 348.
34. Flavius J. Cook, *Home Sketches of Essex County: Ticonderoga* (Keeseville, N.Y.: W. Lansing & Son, 1858), 42.
35. Dwight, 3: 357.
36. Ibid., 357-58.

"Carter's Tavern at the Head of Lake George."
Detail of a painting by Francis Guy (1817/1818). See page 246.
(Founders Society Purchase, Detroit Institute of Arts)

13. Benjamin Silliman 1819

IN 1819 PROFESSOR BENJAMIN SILLIMAN, a protégé of Timothy Dwight, made the first of two trips to Lake George. From his hotel balcony, on September 28, 1819, Silliman admired "the fine outline of the mountains. . .[as] the sky and the lake conspired to exalt every feature, of unrivalled landscape."[1] By that time Lake George had changed as settlements grew along the western shoreline of the lake. The village of Caldwell, Silliman noted, "contains five or six hundred inhabitants, with neat buildings, public and private, and a very large commodious public-house."[2]

Although some early businesses, including lumbering, appeared in the southern basin, the tourist trade soon dominated the economy of the region. Located on the route linking the Hudson River to Lake Champlain, Caldwell would provide a natural stopping point for travelers in the nineteenth century. At the time of Silliman's visit, Caldwell hosted a number of taverns, including Carter's Tavern, the subject of a painting by Francis Guy.[3] James Caldwell, the founder of the village, occupied a home on the present site of Shepard Park on the southwest side of the lake. The structure was subsequently enlarged and became known as the Lake House. The Lake George Coffee House, also located in this area, served as a makeshift court house before 1817. Caldwell was designated the county seat in 1815, and a new court house was built on the adjacent land two years later.[4]

One of the first large commercial boats on Lake George in the nineteenth century was the *Queensbury Packet*, built in 1815 by Elijah Dunham of Dunham's Bay. The vessel was used "for carrying lumber and was from sixty to seventy feet long."[5] The dominance of sailing vessels, however, was eventually displaced by steam-powered craft. With the knowledge gained from steamboat construction on Lake Champlain, John Winans began construction of the first steamboat on Lake

George in 1816. Winans and his brother had built the steamer *Vermont* in 1809 at Burlington. The *Vermont* had sunk in the Richelieu River (north of Lake Champlain) in 1815, when her connecting rod broke a hole through the hull. At the time of the sinking, the newly-chartered Lake Champlain Steam-boat Company had begun operation of the steamer *Phoenix*. To avoid any potential competition, the Lake Champlain Steam-boat Company contracted with John Winans for the salvaged boilers and engine from the *Vermont* to be placed in their new steamer, the *Champlain*. The *Champlain*'s engine was replaced the following year and the original engine and boilers from the *Vermont* were then transported to Lake George for installation in the *James Caldwell*.

The Lake George steam boat company (the company had four slightly different names between 1817 and 1872) was chartered by the New York legislature on April 15, 1817, until 1838, with James Caldwell and John Winans among the directors. The *James Caldwell* was built at Ticonderoga which minimized the transfer of the engine and boilers from Lake Champlain. Completed in 1817, the 120-ton *James Caldwell* was 80 feet in length, 20 feet wide, and had an 8-foot draft. The vessel cost $12,000, exclusive of the 20-horsepower, third-hand engine and two boilers. The vessel's design was similar to that of early Lake Champlain steamers, including a bowsprit, but no actual drawing of the vessel has been found to date.

With a speed of only four miles per hour, the *James Caldwell*, commanded by Captain John Winans, required a full day to reach the northern end of the lake, making its return trip on the following day. The Harris dock, adjacent to the site of present-day Shepard Park, was the berth of the *James Caldwell*. Passenger traffic, however, "was so small that the boat did not pay," according to a newspaper report.[6] Inexplicably, the vessel burned to the waterline at her dock in 1819. Shortly thereafter, Professor Silliman noted "the wreck of a steam-boat, recently burnt to the waters edge, lay near the tavern: it gave great facility in going up this beautiful lake to Ticonderoga; parties and individuals, were much in the habit of making this tour;. . .and were the steam-boat re-established, [Lake George] must become as great a resort" as those of European fame.[7]

Benjamin Silliman was the most renowned American professor of science in the early nineteenth century. Silliman's family roots on his father's side could be traced back to Italy while his mother, a direct descendent of John and Priscilla Alden, was linked to the Pilgrims of the *Mayflower*. Born in North Stratford (present-day Trumbull), Connecticut, in 1779, Silliman started life in the midst of the American Revolution. Three months before Benjamin's birth, his father, Brigadier General Gold Selleck Silliman, and Benjamin's brother William had been captured by the British at the Silliman homestead. It was not until a year later that the family was reunited.*

Young Silliman was raised in relative affluence for the eighteenth century; both his father and grandfather had graduated from Yale College and pursued prominent careers in law . In September 1792, two years after his father's death, Benjamin Silliman entered Yale College at the age of 13. Timothy Dwight assumed the presidency of Yale during Silliman's senior year and immediately impressed the young student as a person to emulate, and Dwight himself recognized the potential

---

*A 1993 movie, "Mary Silliman's War," was loosely based on the capture and captivity of Gold Selleck Silliman.

of his bright student as a future faculty member at Yale. Silliman graduated from Yale in 1796, but remained at home for a year organizing his father's financial matters while recovering from an infection in his foot incurred as a result of an accident chopping firewood. Still affected by the lingering injury and "in danger of lockjaw," Silliman spent a month at the Aldridge House in Ballston Spa.[8]

With the return of his health in 1797, Silliman accepted the post of headmaster at a small private school in Wethersfield, Connecticut. Following family tradition, Silliman and his brother Selleck, who had attended Yale College with Benjamin, began their instruction in law in New Haven during the fall of 1798. A year later, Benjamin Silliman became a tutor at Yale College at the behest of President Timothy Dwight. Just as Silliman was completing his legal studies, Dwight convinced him to become a professor at Yale College. On September 7, 1802, the Yale Corporation appointed Silliman to a professorship of Chemistry and Natural History, a field that would require extensive preparation by Silliman. Following a whirlwind tour of study with the most distinguished scholars and medical practitioners in America, Silliman, then 24 years old, delivered his first chemistry lecture before the senior class at Yale. Dispatched to London in 1805 to procure equipment and books for Yale's fledgling science program, Silliman spent a year abroad, studying at Edinburgh University in Scotland.

Three years after his return from Europe, Silliman married Harriet Trumbull, daughter of Governor Jonathan Trumbull of Connecticut. Her family's lineage also included a grandfather, Jonathan Trumbull (the elder), who had been governor of Connecticut (1769-84), and two prominent uncles: Joseph Trumbull, the first commissary general of the Continental Army, and John Trumbull, known as "the painter of the Revolution." The Sillimans settled in a spacious house in Lebanon, Connecticut, which Benjamin subsequently purchased with a loan from Yale College. By 1816 Silliman's family had grown to four with the birth of a second son, Benjamin, in early December.

In this period, Silliman's academic career as an outstanding American scholar in the sciences was solidified. In 1818, Silliman founded *The American Journal of Science and Arts* which would subsequently advance American science immeasurably under his editorship. His teaching endeavors were no less remarkable. Upon attending one of Silliman's lectures at Yale in 1814, a Havard graduate commented on "a vigor, a spirit, and a freshness of manner to which I had not been accustomed, and which I think I have seldom seen equalled since."[9] Silliman also presented popular lectures on chemistry and geology to the general public, including several in Boston before audiences of 1,500 where the "charm in his cordial manner. . .[and] earnestness" was able to hold the listeners' attention for two hours.[10] Over 50 years later, the president of Yale University eulogized Silliman with the remark that "as a lecturer he was almost unsurpassed."[11]

Silliman's pleasant family life was altered in 1818 with the illness of his four-year-old son, Jonathan Trumbull Silliman. In the spring of 1819, after the boy had experienced a winter of continued respiratory problems, Silliman accompanied him to the estate of his brother-in-law, Daniel Wadsworth, near Hartford, Connecticut. Since there was no sign of improvement, the boy with his father returned home where the child died shortly thereafter. Two weeks before Jonathan Trumbull's death, Mrs. Silliman had given birth to a girl, but the baby died two months later.

"My spirits dropped and my health began to be affected," Silliman later recounted.[12] Silliman's depression was not easily reversed.

Concerned with Silliman's mental state, his brother-in-law suggested a trip to raise his spirits. Benjamin Silliman, accompanied by Daniel Wadsworth, began a journey to Quebec in the fall of 1819. "Neither Mr. Wadsworth or myself had ever visited Canada, and we resolved on this journey as a tour of refreshment and observation, without any motives of business."[13] Despite his intentions of avoiding any "business," the erudite professor kept a meticulous journal of his travels which was subsequently published in two editions. Although Timothy Dwight had traveled through the Lake George region 17 years before Silliman, the latter excursionist had his journal published first. Silliman, however, had earlier success with the publication of *A Journey of Travels in England, Holland and Scotland* based on his 1805-1806 European tour. The northern tour of 1819 was successful in easing Silliman's melancholy state of mind.

As a result of a lingering respiratory illness in the spring of 1821, Silliman once again embarked on a journey to restore his health and spirits. His second trip to Lake George allowed a closer scrutiny of the geology and scenery of the lake. Accompanied by Samuel F. B. Morse, a former student at Yale and the future inventor of the telegraph, Silliman visited Albany and Ticonderoga. While the journey did not ameliorate his health problems, it did provide new material for the second edition of his book.

Heartaches were not yet over for the Silliman family. Two children, one born in 1820 and another in 1821, died after a few months. Silliman later reflected that "four children had been removed from us within three years and anxiety, watching and sorrow had worn upon the health of both parents."[14] Once more Silliman's physical and mental well-being faltered as a gastric ulcer and insomnia plagued him. Again Daniel Wadsworth provided advice on a cure for his ills. Silliman abandoned his "oxide of bismuth" remedy, as well as wine, and adopted a bland diet. Two healthy daughters, born in 1823 and 1826, further raised his spirits and improved his emotional state.

Silliman's academic career flourished at Yale College as his books, including *First Principles of Chemistry* and *An Introduction to Geology*, continued into multiple editions. After 50 years at Yale, Silliman informed the president of the college on August 8, 1849, that he would retire after the 1850 commencement. He acceded to a request from the Yale Corporation, however, and agreed to continue his professorship.

On January 18, 1850, Harriet Silliman, his wife of 40 years, passed away after a long illness. Two months later Silliman's family convinced him to visit Washington, D.C., where he met with President Zachary Taylor and Secretary of State Clayton, the latter a former student at Yale. The next year Silliman embarked on a grand tour of Europe with an entourage of family and friends. Soon after returning home, he entered into a second marriage. His new wife, Sarah Isabella Webb, was a family friend and relative of his first wife. For the next 13 years, Silliman's life was both fulfilling and active as he continued his scholarly pursuits and close relationship with his family. The day before Thanksgiving in 1864, Silliman enjoyed entertaining some of his friends but the next morning died in bed of an apparent heart attack.

The following account of Silliman's trip to Lake George was written in 1819, with additional remarks added after his 1821 visit to the lake. Silliman and Daniel Wadsworth departed from Hartford, Connecticut, on September 22, 1819. Reaching Albany in two days, the travelers lodged at the home of Judge James Kent. Upon leaving Albany, Silliman observed a horse ferry in operation at Troy that had been invented by Barnabas and Jonathan Langdon of Whitehall, New York.* At Stillwater, Silliman spent the night at a house where Brigadier General Simon Fraser, one of General John Burgoyne's officers, had died following the British defeat by the American forces at Saratoga on October 7, 1777. Silliman was guided through the old Saratoga battlefields by 75-year-old Ezra Buel who was an eyewitness to the 1777 engagements.

Silliman and Wadsworth crossed the Hudson River at Fort Miller and proceeded to the town of Fort Edward, viewing the Champlain Canal under construction. The ruins of Fort Edward, according to Silliman, included "walls. . .in some places still twenty feet high, notwithstanding what time and the plough have done to reduce them; for the interior of the Fort, and in some places, the parapet are now planted with potatoes."[16] Sandy Hill (present-day Hudson Falls), Silliman noted, was "composed of neat and handsome houses, many of which surround a beautiful central green. . .formerly the scene of Indian barbarities."[17] The story of an Indian massacre during the French and Indian War was told to Silliman's guide, an unnamed Mr. H. from Sandy Hill, by a Mr. Schoonhoven who had survived the ordeal.**

*Silliman's original description of the horse boat is a rare glimpse of these unique vessels. "The ferry-boat is of a most horizontal solid wheel which extends to the sides of the boat; and there the platform, or deck, is cut through, and removed so as to afford sufficient room for two horses to stand on the flat surface of the wheel, one horse on each side, and parallel to the gunwale of the boat. The horses are harnessed, in the usual manner for teams—the whiffle trees being attached to stout iron bars, fixed horizontally, at a proper height, into posts, which are a part of the fixed portion of the boat. The horses look in opposite directions, one to the bow, and the other to the stern; their feet take hold of channels, or grooves, cut in the wheels in the direction of radii; they press forward, and although they advance not, any more than a squirrel in a revolving cage, or than a spit dog at his work, their feet cause the horizontal wheel to revolve, in a direction opposite to that of their own apparent motion; this, by a connexion of cogs, moves two vertical wheels, one on each wing of the boat, and these being constructed like the paddle wheels of steamboats, produce the same effect, and propel the bow forward. The horses are covered by a roof, furnished with curtains, to protect them in bad weather; and do not appear to labour harder than common draft horses, with a heavy load."[15]

**Silliman related the following story. "Old Mr. Schoonhoven, recently living in this vicinity, and probably still surviving, although at the great age of more than four score, informed Mr. H. that during the last French war, he, and six or seven other Americans coming through the wilderness, from Fort William Henry, at the head of Lake George, to Sandy Hill, had the misfortune to be taken prisoners by a party of the savages. They were conducted to the spot which is now the central green of Sandy Hill, and ordered to sit down in a row, upon a log. Mr. Schoonhoven pointed out to Mr. H. the exact place where the log lay; it was nearly in front of the house where we dined. The Indians then began, very deliberately, to tomahawk their victims, commencing at one end of the log, and splitting skulls of their prisoners, in regular succession; while the survivors, compelled to sit still, and to witness the awful fate of their companions, awaited their own, in unutterable horror. Mr. Schoonhoven was the last but one, upon the end of the log opposite to where the massacre commenced; the work of death had already proceeded to him, and the lifted tomahawk was ready to descend, when a chief gave a signal to stop the butchery. Then approaching Mr. Schoonhoven, he mildly said, 'do you not remember that (at such a time) when your young men were dancing, poor Indians came, and wanted to dance too; your young men said 'no!—Indians shall not dance with us;' but you (for it seems, this chief had recognized his features only in the critical moment,) you said, Indians shall dance—now I will shew you that Indians can remember kindness.' This chance recollection (providentially, we had better call it,) saved the life of Mr. Schoonhoven, and of the other survivor."[17]

The format of Silliman's book, combining observations of the lake with historical narratives of the war periods, is similar to Timothy Dwight's *Travels in New-England and New-York*. To avoid repetition, some of Silliman's historical sections have been omitted in the following text.

Cascade at Glens Falls.
(Postcard, author's collection)

Excursion to Lake George[18]

This interesting region lay to the left of our proposed route to Lake Champlain; to visit it would demand nearly twenty miles of additional travelling, through very bad roads; Mr. W[adsworth] was already familiar with the scene; I therefore took an extra conveyance, with which I was furnished at Sandy Hill [later Hudson Falls], by the civility of Mr. H. who did me the favor to accompany me on the excursion, (for there was no public vehicle,) and leaving Mr. W[adsworth] to pursue his journey to Fort Anne, where I agreed to meet him, I parted with him four miles above Sandy Hill, at Glenn's Falls.

Glenn's Falls

We stopped for a few moments at this celebrated place. It is not possible that so large a river as the Hudson is, even here, at more than two hundred miles from its mouth, should be precipitated over any declivity, however moderate, without a degree of grandeur. Even the various rapids which we had passed above Albany, and still more, the falls at Fort Miller Bridge, and Baker's Falls, at Sandy Hill, had powerfully arrested our attention, and prepared us for the magnificent spectacle now before us. I regretted that I could not, more at leisure, investigate the geology of this pass, both for its own sake, and for its connexion with this fine piece of scenery.

Down these platforms, and through these channels, the Hudson, when the river is full, indignantly rushes, in one broad expanse; now, in several subordinate rivers, thundering and foaming among the black rocks, and at last dashing their conflicting waters into one tumultuous raging torrent, white as the ridge of the tempest wave, shrouded with spray, and adorned with the hues of the rainbow. Such is the view from the bridge immediately at the foot of the falls, and it is finely contrasted with the solemn grandeur of the sable ledges below, which tower to a great height above the stream.

I do not know the entire fall of the river here; but should think, judging from the eye, that it could not be less than fifty feet, including all its leaps, down the different platforms of rock.

Through an uninteresting country, partly of pine barren, and partly of stony hills, I arrived at nightfall, at the head of Lake George, and found a comfortable inn, in the village of Caldwell, on the Western shore.

As we approached Lake George, fragments of primitive rocks began to appear, and I observed numerous loose masses of granite, on the steep stony hills, near the lake. I was much struck with the formidable difficulties which General [John] Burgoyne had to encounter in transporting his stores, and his boats, and part of his artillery, over this rugged country: at that time [1777], without doubt, vastly more impracticable than at present.

Prospect From the Head of Lake George

Sept. 28. [1819]—In the first gray of the morning, I was in the balcony of the Inn, admiring the fine outline of the mountains by which Lake George is environed, and the masses of pure snowy vapour, which, unruffled by the slightest breeze, slumbered on its crystal bosom. During all the preceding days of the tour, there had not been a clear morning, but now, not a cloud spotted the expanse of the heavens, and the sky and the lake conspired to exalt every feature of this unrivalled landscape.

The morning came on with rapid progress; but the woody sides of the high mountains, that form the eastern barrier, were still obscured, by the lingering shadows of night, although, on their tops, the dawn was now fully disclosed, and their outline, by contrast with their dark sides, was rendered beautifully distinct; while, their reversed images, perfectly reflected from the most exquisite of all mirrors, presented mountains pendent in the deep, and adhering by their bases, to those, which at the same moment were emulating the heavens.

A boat had been engaged, the evening before, and we now rowed out upon the lake, and hastened to old Fort George, whose circular massy walls of stone, still twenty feet high, and in pretty good preservation, rise upon a hill about a quarter of a mile from the southern shore of the lake. I was anxious to enjoy, from this propitious spot, the advancing glories of the morning, which, by the time we had reached our station, were glowing upon the mountain tops, with an effulgence [brilliance], that could be augmented by nothing but the actual appearance of the king of day.

Now, the opposite mountains—those that form the western barrier, were strongly illuminated down their entire declivity, while the twin barrier of the eastern shore (its ridge excepted) was still in deep shadow; the vapour on the lake, which was just sufficient to form the softened blending of light and shade, while it veiled the lake only in spots, and left its outline and most of its surface perfectly distinct, began to form itself into winrows,* and clouds and castles, and to recede from the water, as if conscious that its dominion must now be resigned.

The retreat of the vapour formed a very beautiful part of the scenery; it was the moveable light drapery, which, at first, adorning the bosom of the lake, soon after began to retire up the sides of the mountains.

At the distance of twelve or fourteen miles, the lake turns to the right, and is lost among the mountains; to the left, is north-west Bay, more remote and visible from the fort.

The promontory [Tongue Mountain], which forms the point of junction between the lake and the bay, rises into lofty peaks and ridges, and apparently forms the northern termination of the lake.

Up these mountains, which are even more grand and lofty, than those on the sides of the lake, the vapour, accumulated by a very slight movement of the atmosphere from the south, rolled in immense masses, every moment changing their form; now obscuring the mountains almost entirely, and now veiling their sides, but permitting their tops to emerge, in unclouded majesty.

Anxious to witness, from the surface of the lake, the first appearance of the sun's orb, we regained our boat, and, in a few moments, attained the desired position. Opposite to us, in the direction towards the rising sun, was a place or notch, lower than the general ridge of the mountains, and formed by the intersecting curves of two declivities.

*Silliman's original note: "This, possibly is an American word, (meaning the rows of hay, that are raked together in a meadow, before the hay is thrown into heaps;) it exactly describes the vapour, as it appeared in some places, on the lake, and I knew no other word that did."[19]

Precisely through this place, were poured upon us the first rays, which darted down, as if in lines of burnished gold, diverging and distinct, as in a diagram; the ridge of the eastern mountains, was fringed with fire, for many a mile; the numerous islands, so elegantly sprinkled through the lake, and which recently appeared and disappeared, through the rolling clouds of mist, now received the direct rays of the sun, and formed so many gilded gardens; at last came the sun, "rejoicing in his strength," and, as he raised the upper edge of his burning disk into view, in a circle of celestial fire, the sight was too glorious to behold;—it seemed, when the full orb was disclosed, as if he looked down with complacency, into one of the most beautiful spots in this lower world, and, as if gloriously representing his great creator, he pronounced "it all very good." I certainly never before saw the sun rise with such

"Lake George from Fort George" (Print No. 4) by Daniel Wadsworth
from Benjamin Silliman's *Remarks, Made on a Short Tour,*
Between Hartford and Quebec in the Autumn of 1819.

majesty. I have not exaggerated the effect, and, without doubt, it arises principally from the fact, that Lake George is so completely environed by a barrier of high mountains, that it is in deep shade, while the world around is in light, and the sun, already risen for some time, does not dart a single ray upon this imprisoned lake, till, having gained a considerable elevation, he bursts, all at once, over the fiery ridge of the eastern mountains, and pours, not a horizontal, but a descending flood of light, which, instantly piercing the deep shadows, that rest on the lake, and on the western side of the eastern barrier, thus produces the finest possible effects of contrast. When the sun had attained a little height above the mountain, we observed a curious effect; a perfect cone of light, with its base towards the sun, lay upon the water, and, from the vertex of the cone, which reached half across the lake, there shot out a delicate line of parallel rays, which reached the western shore, and the whole very perfectly represented a gilded steeple. As this effect is opposite to the common form of the sun's effulgence, it must probably depend upon some peculiarities in the shape of the summits of the mountains at this place.

In [a] print, No.4 [by Daniel Wadsworth], the observer being at Fort George, situated, as I have already remarked, at some distance from the southern shore of the lake, and in a direction, about mid-way between its eastern and western sides, contemplates a prospect, considerably different from that seen in the other position. The eastern barrier is now much less in view: the promontory, where the lake turns off to the right, and is lost among the mountains, and where northwest bay stretches to the left and appears bounded by very high mountains, is immediately before him, at the distance of about twelve miles; the islands, in view, are more numerous, and give greater variety to the now more extended surface of the lake; and, immediately at the observer's feet, is the acclivity [ascending slope], by which we ascend from the lake, to the old fort, upon the walls of which we are supposed to stand, and they, of course, are not in view. On the very shore, we observe one of the old barracks, formerly belonging to the fort, now exhibiting a tavern sign, and, till within a few years, constituting the only place of accommodation to those who visited Lake George.* At this place, although principally covered by the water, are the ruins of the old military quay or pier, formerly extending a good way into the lake, and affording important facilities to the numerous expeditions, that have sailed upon Lake George.

Remarks On Lake George and Its Environs

Every one has heard of the transparency of the waters of Lake George. This transparency is, indeed, very remarkable, and the same, (as we might indeed well suppose it would be,) is the fact with all the streams that pour into it. After the day light became strong, we could see the bottom perfectly, in most places where we rowed, and it is said, that in fishing, even in twenty or twenty-five feet of water, the angler may select his fish, by bringing the hook near the mouth of the one which he prefers.

Bass and trout are among the most celebrated fish of the lake; the latter were now in season, and nothing of the kind can be finer; this beautiful fish, elegantly decorated, and gracefully formed, shy of observation, rapid in its movements, and delighting, above all, in the perfect purity of its element, finds in Lake George, a residence, most happily adapted to its nature. Here it attains a very uncommon size, and exhibits its most perfect beauty and symmetry. The delicate carnation of its flesh, is here also most remarkable, and its flavour exquisite.

---

*Silliman based his conclusion that the tavern had been an old barracks from Fort George on a letter from Judge James Kent of Albany who had visited Lake George in 1795. "We returned through Lake George in a small sailboat, and lodged at a dismal old house which had been a military barrack on the shore below Fort George. It was all woods where the beautiful village of Caldwell now stands, and we ran over the ruins of Fort William Henry, then most fearfully interesting from historical recollections, for it appeared not to have been disturbed by the hand of man since 1757."[20]

If the lovers of the sublime and beautiful, visit Lake George, for its scenery, and the patriotic, to behold the places where their fathers stemmed the tide of savage invasion; the epicure [connoisseur], also, will come not to cherish the tender and the heroic, nor to admire the picturesque and the grand, but to enjoy the native luxuries of the place.

The lake is about a mile wide near its head, and is sometimes wider, sometimes narrower than this, but rarely exceeding two miles, through its length of thirty-six miles. It is said to contain as many islands, as there are days in the year.*

I had scarcely any opportunities of observing the mineralogy and geology of this region.

The beautiful crystals of quartz, which all strangers obtain at Lake George, are got on the islands in the lake; one about four miles from its head, (and called, of course, the diamond island,) has been principally famous for affording them; there is a solitary miserable cottage upon this island, from which we saw the smoke ascending;—a woman, who lives in it, is facetiously called "the lady of the lake," but, probably no Malcolm Groeme, and Roderick Dhu will ever contend on her account.**

Crystals are now obtained from other islands, I believe, more than from this, and they are said no longer to find the single loose crystals in abundance on the shores, but break up the rocks for this purpose. Poor people occupy themselves in procuring crystals, which they deposit at the public house, for sale.

The crystals of Lake George, are hardly surpassed by any in the world, for transparency, and for perfection of form; they are, as usual, the six-sided prism, and are frequently terminated at both ends by six-sided pyramids.*** These last must, of course, be found loose, or, at least, not adhering to any rocks, those which are broken off, have necessarily only one pyramid.† I procured specimens of the rocky matrix, in which the crystals are formed; it is of a quartzoze nature, and contains cavities finely studded with crystals.

The crystals of Lake George frequently contain a dark coloured foreign substance, enclosed all around, or partially so; its nature, I believe, has not been ascertained; it may be manganese, titanium, or iron.

The mountains are extensively, or rather almost universally in dense forest; rattle snakes and deer abound upon them, and hunting is still pursued here with success.

In some places, the mountains, contiguous to the shores, are rocky and precipitous. Tradition relates, that a white man, closely pursued, in the winter season, by two Indians, contrived to reach the ice, on the surface of the lake, by letting himself down one of these precipices, and, before the Indians could follow, he was on his skaits[skates], and darting, "swift as the winds along," was soon out of their reach.‡

---

*Lake George is 32 miles long with 200 islands.

**Silliman is referrring to characters in Sir Walter Scott's *The Lady of the Lake* (1810).

***Apparently, troops during the French and Indian War were aware of the diamond crystals in the lake. Amos Richardson, a provincial soldier from Massachusetts stationed on Diamond Island in 1758, "went to Looking [for] Dimons in the Lake."[21]

†Silliman's original note: "I have a crystal from Lake George, obtained by a soldier, and presented to the late President Dwight, which is between five and six inches long, by three broad, and is perfectly limpid, and well crystalized."[22]

‡Undoubtedly, this was a version of the story of Robert Rogers at Rogers Rock after the second Battle on Snowshoes in 1758.

I am not informed that the height of the mountains, about Lake George, has ever been measured; they appeared to my eye, generally, to exceed one thousand feet, and probably the highest may be fifteen hundred, or more.

The wreck of a steam-boat,* recently burnt to the waters edge, lay near the tavern: it gave great facility in going down this beautiful lake to Ticonderoga; parties

"Lake George" by William Momberger, engraved by Robert Hinshelwood.
(New York State Historical Association)

and individuals, were much in the habit of making this tour; and, were there a good road, instead of a very bad one, from Glenn's falls to Lake George, and were the steam-boat re-established, it must become as great a resort, as the lakes of Westmoreland and Cumberland, or as Loch Katrin[e], now immortalized by the muse of [Sir Walter] Scott.

The village of Caldwell, built entirely since the American war, contains five or six hundred inhabitants, with neat buildings, public and private, and a very large commodious public house, well provided and attended, so that strangers, visiting the lake, can have every desired accommodation. This village, I am informed, has arisen principally from the exertions of one enterprising individual [James Caldwell], from whom it derives its name, as well as its existence. He has lived to see his labours crowned with success, and a pretty village now smiles at the foot of the western barrier of Lake George, on ground where the iron ramparts of war are

*The wreckage of the steamer *James Caldwell*, built in 1817, lay near the site of present-day Shepard Park.

still visible; for, on this very ground, the Marquis [de] Montcalm's army was entrenched, at the siege of Fort William Henry, in 1757.

Battles of Lake George

In the wars of this country, Lake George has long been conspicuous. Its head waters formed the shortest, and most convenient connexion, between Canada, and the Hudson, and hence the establishment of Fort William Henry, in 1755, and, in more recent times, of Fort George, in its immediate vicinity.

This most beautiful and peaceful lake, environed by mountains, and seeming to claim an exemption from the troubles of an agitated world, has often bristled with the proud array of war, has wafted its most formidable preparations on its bosom, and has repeatedly witnessed both the splendors and the havoc of battle.

Fort William Henry

The remains of this old fort are still visible; they are on the verge of the lake, at its head; the walls, the gate, and the out-works, can still be completely traced; the ditches have, even now, considerable depth, and the well that supplied the garrison, is there, and affords water to this day; near, and in this fort, much blood has been shed.

The neighbouring mountain, in which the French so suddenly made their appearance [in 1755], is to this day, called French Mountain, and this name, with the tradition of the fact, will be sent down to the latest posterity. I was shown a rock by the road at which a considerable slaughter took place. It was on the east side of the road near where Col. [Ephraim] Williams fell, and I am informed is, to this day, called Williams' Rock.*

The Bloody Pond

Just by the present road, and in the midst of these battle grounds, is a circular pond, shaped exactly like a bowl; it may be two hundred feet in diameter, and was, when I saw it, full of water, and covered with the pond lilly, Alas! this pond, now so peaceful, was the common sepulchre of the brave; the dead bodies of most of those who were slain on this eventful day [September 8, 1755], were thrown, in undistinguished confusion into this pond; from that time to the present, it has been called the bloody pond, and there is not a child in this region, but will point you to the French mountain, and to the bloody pond.—I stood with dread, upon its brink, and threw a stone into its unconscious waters.** After these events, a regular fort was constructed at the head of the lake and called Fort William Henry.

*Colonel Ephraim Williams of Deerfield, Massachusetts, was killed in the first of three battles on September 8, 1755. After the battle, his troops buried the fallen officer four miles from Lake George along the side of the military road and marked the site with a large irregular stone (west side of Route 9 today). A marble monument was placed on a large stone by Williams College alumni in 1854 to mark the spot where Colonel Williams had been slain (located on the east side of Route 9).

**A fierce battle occurred late on the day of September 8, 1755, when 210 provincial troops from Fort Lyman (Edward) surprised a party of Canadian troops and Native Americans who were engaged in looting and scalping the dead soldiers from Colonel Ephraim Williams' detachment. The Canadians and Indians killed in the ensuing battle were said to have been thrown into the pond. "Bloody Pond" is situated on the east side of Route 9 today.

Massacre of Fort William Henry

The three battles of September 8th [1755], were not the end of the tragedies of Lake George. The Marquis de Montcalm, after . . .ineffectual attempts upon Fort William Henry, made great efforts to besiege it in form, and in August, 1757, having landed ten thousand men near the fort summoned it to surrender. The place of his landing was shown me, a little north of the public house; the remains of his batteries and other works are still visible; and the graves and bones of the slain are occasionally discovered.

Having occupied a very busy morning in visiting the memorable places at the head of Lake George, and having procured specimens of the mineral productions of this region, I proceeded on my journey to Fort Anne. Mr. H——, my obliging companion, attended me, and we were necessitated to return some miles through the gorge of the mountains, and again to view the bloody pond, the French Mountain, and the bloody defile [narrow passage]. Rarely, I presume, have such scenes of horror been exhibited so often, within so narrow a space. We may confidently trust, that they will never be repeated; that Lake George, traversed no longer by armies, its forests and its mountains undisturbed by the roar of cannon, and its waters polluted no more by blood; but visited in peace, by the lovers of the sublime and beautiful, and arrayed in its own grandeur and loveliness, will hereafter exhibit the tragical history of other times, only to impart a pensive tenderness and a moral dignity to the charming scenes with which the story of these events is associated.

As we emerged from the defile, and turned to the left, around the base of the mountains that form the eastern barrier of Lake George, we had many opportunities of admiring the grandeur of that barrier, and of contemplating all that wildness of [the] landscape, which, it may be presumed, has undergone little change, since it was traversed by the prowling savage, intent on the chase, or on his more beloved employment, the destruction of his fellow creatures. In this dreadful occupation he has, however, been more than rivalled by the polished nations of America and of Europe; who, if they do not pursue war with the atrocity of the savage, seem to have followed it with all his eagerness, and have often identified themselves with his most horrid cruelties, by calling him in as an ally and a friend, and marching by his side to slaughter those who are connected by the common, (it ought to be by the sacred), tie of Christianity.

In the progress of our ride, we emerged from mountain scenery, and saw many good farms, and much arable and pasture land. The country became much less rugged, although the roads were little improved by art; for they were common and often obscure cross roads.

We met with no adventure, and the failure of one of our waggon wheels, which obliged us to walk, and to sustain the vehicle for the last two miles, did not prevent our arriving at the appointed hour of dinner at old Fort Anne, which Mr. Wadsworth had already reached before me.

Fort Anne was another post established in the French wars. It stood about midway between Fort Edward and the most southern point of Lake Champlain, and at the head of batteaux navigation on Wood Creek. I did not go to its site, the ruins of which, I am told are almost obliterated; its well, however, is still to be seen. There is a considerable village here, which bears the name of the Fort.

In May, 1821, I again visited Lake George and its environs, and passed in an open boat down the whole length of the Lake, by water, to Ticonderoga.

Quartz crystals in the Islands of the South end of Lake George. These are commonly obtained by visitors; they are now become much more rare than formerly, and those which are procured are small, although still very limpid and beautiful. On visiting the Island called Diamond Island, three or four miles from the village of Caldwell, and which has afforded most of these crystals we found them occurring in the same compact limestone, which forms the ledges at the head of the lake. This small island scarcely covering the area of a common kitchen garden is inhabited by a family who occupy a small but comfortable house, and constantly explore the rocks for the crystals. These are found lining drusy [incrusted] cavities, and forming geodes in the limestone; these cavities are often brilliantly studded with them and doubtless it arose from their falling out by the disintegration of the rock that the crystals were formerly found on the shores of the island and in the water. At present they are scarcely obtained at all except by breaking the rocks.

Crystals of Diamond point.—We passed down the whole length of the lake (thirty-six miles) in a very small open boat—a fisherman's skiff rowed by two men. We stopped at a place on the north shore of the lake called Diamond Point, from the fact that crystals are found also at this place.—It has been recently opened by the man who lives on the Island and who was our guide on the present occasion.— The rock and its associated minerals are the same as on the Island, only we observed a greater variety of siliceous minerals.

Transparency and purity of the Waters of Lake George.—The fact is notorious and the degree in which it exists is most remarkable: the bottom and the fish are seen at a great depth: the fisherman who rowed us asserted that they could at particular times see the fish at the depth of 50 feet: if even half this statement be admitted, it is sufficiently remarkable. The water is also very pure, salubrious [healthy] and agreeable to the taste. It is well known that the French formerly obtained and exported this water for religious uses, and that they called the lake St. Sacrament.

The cause of the transparency and purity of these waters is obvious. With the exception of small quantities of transition limestone, its shores as far as we saw them, are composed of primitive rocks, made up principally of siliceous and other very firm and insoluble materials. The streams by which the lake is fed, flow over similar substances, and the waves find nothing to dissolve or to hold mechanically suspended. Clay which abounds around the head waters of the contiguous lake (Champlain) and renders them turbid, scarcely exists here. It is remarkable, however, that as we approach Lake Champlain in the vicinity of Ticonderoga, the waters of Lake George become, for a few miles somewhat turbid, and near the efflux [outlet] they are very much so.

Mountains of Lake George.—There can be no doubt that whenever they are thoroughly explored they will abundantly reward the geologist and mineralogist. We however saw them only as picturesque objects; as such they are certainly very fine. Particularly as we proceed north from the Tongue Mountain, which is twelve miles from Caldwell. For twenty miles beyond this, on the way to Ticonderoga, the scenery combines in an uncommon degree, both richness and grandeur. The mountains are all primitive: they form a double barrier, between which the lake, scarcely a mile wide, but occasionally expanding into large bays, winds its way. They are steep and precipitous to the very water's edge: they are still clothed with grand trees, and possessed by wild animals—deer, bears, &c. They give in some places, the most distinct and astonishing echoes, returning every flexion of the voice with the most faithful response. We saw them hung with the solemn drapery of thunder clouds, dashed by squalls of wind and rain, and soon after decorated with rainbows, whose arches did not surpass the mountain ridges, while they terminated in the lake and attended our little skiff for many miles. The setting sun also gilded the mountains and the clouds that hovered over them and the little islands, which in great numbers rise out of the lake and present green patches of shrubbery and trees, apparently springing from the water, and often resembling, by their minuteness and delicacy,

"Lake George" by John William Hill.
(New York State Historical Association)

the clumps of a park, or even the artificial groups of a green house. Fine as is the scenery at the southern end of the lake and in all the wider part of it, within the compass of the first twelve miles from Fort George—its grandeur is much augmented, after passing Tongue Mountain and entering the narrow part where the mountains close in upon you on both sides, and present an endless diversity of grand and beautiful scenery. It is a pleasing reflection, that even after this part of the United States, shall have become as populous as England or Holland, this lake will still retain the fine peculiarities of its scenery, for they are too bold, too wild, and too untractable, ever to be materially softened and spoiled by the hand of man. Deer are still hunted with success upon the borders of this lake. The hounds drive them from the recesses of the mountains, when they take refuge in the water, and the huntsmen easily overtaking [them] in an element not their own, seize them by the horns, knock them on the head, and dragging their necks over the side of the boat, cut their throats.

There is a celebrated mountain about fourteen miles from Ticonderoga, called the Buck mountain [Deer Leap], from the fact that a buck, pursued by the dogs leaped from its summit over-hanging the lake in the form of a precipice, and was literally impaled alive upon a sharp pointed tree which projected below.*

Ticonderoga**

The remains of this celebrated fortress, once so highly important, but no longer, an object either of hope or fear, are still considerably conspicuous. As we came up with, and, from the narrowness of the lake, necessarily passed very near them, I was gratified, as much as I could be, without landing, by a view of their ruins, still imposing in their appearance, and possessing, with all their associations, a high degree of heroic grandeur.

They stand on a tongue of land, of considerable elevation, projecting south, between Lake Champlain, which winds around and passes on the east, and the passage into Lake George, which is on the west.

The remains of the old works are still conspicuous, and the old stone barracks, erected by the French, are in part standing.

This fort was built by the French; and the Lord [George Viscount] Howe, and many other gallant men, lost their lives in the enterprize against it in 1758.

From this fortress, issued many of those ferocious incursions of French and Indians, which formerly distressed the English settlements; and its fall, in 1759, (when, on the approach of General [Jeffery] Amherst with a powerful army, it was abandoned by the French, without fighting,) filled the northern colonies with joy.

In 1777, great hopes were reposed upon this fortress, as a barrier against invasion; it was regarded as being emphatically the strong hold of the North; and when General [John] Burgoyne, with astonishing effort, dragged cannon up the precipices of Mount Defiance, and showed them on its summit, Ticonderoga, no longer tenable, was precipitately abandoned.

Mount Defiance stands on the outlet of Lake George, and between that and Lake Champlain, and most completely commands Ticonderoga, which is far below, and within fair cannon shot. On the slightest glance at the scene, it is a matter of utter astonishment, even to one who is not a military man, how so important a point came to be overlooked by all preceding commanders: probably it arose from the belief, which ought not to have been admitted till the experiment had been tried, that it was impossible to convey cannon to its summit.***—On the right is Mount Independence [Vermont], where there was a formidable fort at the time of General Burgoyne's invasion.

---

*Silliman's original note: "This circumstance was mentioned to me by the man whose dogs drove the buck to this desperate extremity. He stated that he had sometimes taken forty deer in a season."[23]

**This description of Fort Ticonderoga was written by Silliman in 1819 after traveling from Whitehall on Lake Champlain with Daniel Wadsworth.

***Mount Defiance was not entirely overlooked by American officers. In 1776 Colonel John Trumbull, deputy adjutant general to General Horatio Gates, had recommended a battery for Mount Defiance and climbed the summit with Benedict Arnold and Anthony Wayne. A year later Thaddeus Kosciuszko made the same suggestion, but none of the recommendations were ever followed.

The shadows of the night were descending on the venerable Ticonderoga, as we left it; and when I looked upon its walls and environs, so long and so often clustering with armies—formidable for so great a length of time in all the apparatus and preparations of war, and the object of so many campaigns and battles; but now, exhibiting only a solitary smoke, curling from a stone chimney in its half-fallen barracks, with not one animated being in sight; while its massy ruins, and the beautiful green declivities, sloping on all sides of the water, were still and motionless as death, I felt indeed that I was beholding a striking emblem of the mutability of power, and the fluctuations of empire. Ticonderoga, no longer within the confines of a hostile country—no longer a rallying point for ferocious savages and for formidable armies—no more a barrier against invasion, or an object of siege or assault, has now become only a pasture for cattle.

Ruins of Fort Ticonderoga (1831). Painting by Thomas Cole from
The Champlain Tercentenary by Henry Wayland Hill (1913).

The next season but one after the above remarks were written, I enjoyed the opportunity which I had long desired of examining the ruins of Ticonderoga.* Mr. S. F. B. Morse and myself after having proceeded (as already mentioned,) by water from the head of Lake George to its outlet, landed at the village of Ticonderoga, and proceeded to view the interesting objects of the peninsula. The first thing that will strike the traveller, is a fine cascade [LaChute River] produced by the waters of Lake George rushing down the ledges of rock which form the barrier between it and Lake Champlain. The difference of level between the two lakes is variously stated by different authors. Worcester's Gazetteer, and Morses Geography (the Edition of

*The following account of Silliman, which describes Fort Ticonderoga, was written on his second trip to Lake George in 1821.

1822,) place it at about 100 feet.* As the waters of Lake George perform the greater part of this descent, within a very short distance, they form a very fine cataract, and at the same time furnish ample water power for mills and manufactories, several of which are established upon the bank. The village of Ticonderoga is uninteresting; but it will furnish the traveller with a waggon and a guide for the purpose of exploring the peninsula. The voyager on Lake George will of course carry with him, interesting recollections of its military history, and especially of the ill-fated expedition [in 1758] of General [James] Abercrombie whose departure from the head of the Lake, I have already mentioned.

As we advanced from the mills over the same ground still covered (as it was then) in a great measure by wood, we descried [discovered] the lines,** still in fine preservation, running quite across the peninsula, and winding down its shores on both sides, making a circuit of 3-4 of a mile, we were forcibly struck with the madness of the attempt. The parapet [elevated main wall], especially in the front of the work, where the principal assault was made, is still tenable, and would at this moment, without repair, form a better defence than the Americans enjoyed at Bunker's Hill. The ditch is even now very deep—I descended into it and found that the parapet was higher than the top of my head, so that I can readily believe that it was originally, as stated by historians, eight or nine feet high.*** In front of this work, the trees were felled so as to interweave their branches, and present their points (sharpened by axes) in every direction, so as to form the most impenetrable abattis.

After entering the old French lines, which are nearly half a mile distant from the fort of Ticonderoga, we come to a fine parade ground sufficient for the evolutions of many thousands. It slopes gently to the south,and terminates at the walls of Ticonderoga, the ancient fortress erected by the French. This fortress, although in ruins, is well worthy of being visited by every traveller. After all the dilapidations of time and of man, Ticonderoga, with its mutilated walls and barracks, and with its picturesque environs, presents one of the finest ruins in America. Happily the garrison ground, constituting a farm of about six hundred acres, and including the old French lines, as well as the forts and barracks, has fallen into the hands of a gentleman, whose good sense and just taste will not permit a stone to be removed.†— This scene, fine in its natural beauty and grandeur, and still finer in its historical associations, may therefore go down to posterity without further mutilation. The rock of which the walls and barracks of Ticonderoga are built, is a black fetid [odorous] compact limestone. It abounds in this region, and constitutes the ledges on the shores of the contiguous part of Vermont. Its stratification is nearly horizontal, and it is filled with organized remains, corallines [coral-likes], bivalves [mollusks], &c.—At New Shoreham [Vermont], which is immediately opposite to Ticonderoga, they informed us that the water of wells dug in this limestone is

*Silliman is referring to the writings of Reverend Jedidiah Morse, father of Samuel F. B. Morse.

**The defensive breastwork was built by Marquis de Montcalm's troops in 1758.

***Silliman's original note: "Doct. Dwight (*Travels*, p. 383,) remarks that when he saw the lines, they were not more than four feet high, and expresses a doubt whether they were ever more than six—this is true of the wings—But in front where, alone the attack was made, their appearance was still very formidable."[24]

†William Ferris Pell, a New York businessman involved in the import business, had acquired the fort and grounds from Union College and Columbia College in 1820 and ended the piecemeal destruction of the fort.

offensive, and unfit for use. Hence the inhabitants use the water of the lake, and they provide ice houses, that the water may, in warm weather, be rendered agreeably cool.

The walls, the barracks, the subterraneous magazines, the kitchens and store rooms, the covered ways and advanced works of Ticonderoga are of solid masonry. When this fortress was precipitately abandoned in the Revolutionary war, by the army under Gen. [Arthur] St. Clair, it was blown up and set on fire.* The explosion removed the roof and overthrew a part of the walls of the barracks; but enough remains to give one a perfect idea of the structure, and to form a ruin well worthy of the pencil. The half burnt timbers still remain in the walls, and the subterraneous structures as well as the proper walls of the fort have escaped with little injury from the hand of violence and of time. The south gate of the fort, is the one which Gen. [Benedict] Arnold [and Ethan Allen] entered, when he surprised the British garrison at the commencement of the American war. The Grenadier's battery, as it is still called, is at the southern point of the peninsula at the water's edge, and is terminated by perpendicular cliffs of limestone rock. On the shore at the landing place is one of the old stone store-houses which is now used as a tavern.** On the continent, on the opposite side of the lake, are the remains of the fort on Mount Independence, to which the main body of the American army retreated in July, 1777, when pursued by Gen. Burgoyne.

"Carter's Tavern at the Head of Lake George." Painting by Francis Guy (1817/1818).
(Founders Society Purchase, Detroit Institute of Arts)

*American plans to blow up Fort Ticonderoga after the evacuation of General St. Clair's troops in 1777 were never carried out.

**The old King's Store had been operated by the Hay family as a hotel/tavern.

Notes:

1. Benjamin Silliman, *Remarks, Made on a Short Tour, Between Hartford and Quebec in the Autumn of 1819* (New Haven, S. Converse, 1820), 143.
2. Ibid., 154.
3. Carter was also mentioned in H. P. Smith, ed., *History of Warren County* (Syracuse, N.Y.: D. Mason & Co. Pub., 1885), 566.
4. Betty Ahearn Buckell, *Old Lake George Hotels* (Lake George, N.Y.: Buckle Press, 1986), 25; See also Smith 566-67; William H. Brown, ed., *History of Warren County New York* (Glens Falls, N.Y.: Board of Supervisors of Warren County, 1963), 209.
5. *Glens Falls Republican*, 19 May 1857.
6. Ibid.
7. Silliman, 153.
8. George P. Fisher, *Life of Benjamin Silliman* (New York: Charles Scribner and Company, 1866), Volume 1, 308.
9. Fisher, 2: 321.
10. Ibid., 323.
11. Ibid., 320.
12. Fisher, 1: 277.
13. Ibid.
14. John F. Fulton and Elizabeth H. Thomson, *Benjamin Silliman 1779-1864: Pathfinder in American Science* (New York: Henry Shuman, 1947), 113.
15. Silliman, 74; See also Fisher 1: 291.
16. Silliman, 133.
17. Ibid., 138-39.
18. Benjamin Silliman, *Remarks Made on a Short Tour Between Hartford and Quebec in the Autumn of 1819*, 2nd ed. (New Haven: S. Converse, 1824), 142-76.
19. Ibid., 146.
20. Fisher, 1: 293-94.
21. Amos Richardson, "Amos Richardson's Journal, 1758," *The Bulletin of the Fort Ticonderoga Museum* 12 (September 1968): 284.
22. Silliman, 2d ed., 153.
23. Ibid., 154.
24. Ibid., 176.
25. Ibid., 201.

Cooper's Cave at Glens Falls. James Fenimore Cooper viewed the cavern in 1824
and subsequently used it for a scene in his novel, *The Last of the Mohicans.*
Thereafter the cave became a favorite tourist attraction.
(Detail of postcard, author's collection)

14. Theodore Dwight, Jr. 1831

USING A FORMAT similar to the earlier books of Benjamin Silliman and Timothy Dwight, Theodore Dwight's first of six editions of *The Northern Traveller* was published in 1825. Theodore Dwight, who had studied at Yale College under his uncle Timothy Dwight, combined an historical narrative with a detailed description of the scenery in his travel guidebook. Theodore Dwight traveled extensively himself and was a firm believer in the educational value of travel: "the wider the range [of travel] he has enjoyed, the greater the opportunities he has had to learn by that most satisfactory mode—personal observation, the more evident is the effect on his character."[1] Like others who visited Lake George before him, Theodore Dwight had only praise for "this beautiful basin, with its pure crystal water" and mused that "a more delightful place can hardly be found in the United States."[2]

With the publication of James Fenimore Cooper's sixth novel, *The Last of the Mohicans*, in 1826, the history and scenery of Lake George achieved a new prominence in the itineraries of excursionists. Dwight's *Northern Traveller* was the first tour guide to make reference to the landmarks described in *The Last of the Mohicans*. Cooper's novel, filled with adventure, violence, and suspense, was based on the siege and massacre at Fort William Henry in 1757. In his boyhood, Cooper had a keen interest in Indians, especially after Native American relics were discovered at his father's Lake Otsego (N.Y.) home. As a young student in Albany at the turn of the nineteenth century, Cooper witnessed the relocation of Lieutenant Colonel George Monro's grave. Monro, the commander at Fort William Henry during the 1757 siege, would become one of Cooper's principal characters in the book. Although a novel, the book was fact-based and included several characters who had actually existed, including Monro (spelled Munro by Cooper), the Marquis de Montcalm, and Lieutenant Colonel John Young, who was portrayed as Duncan Heywood in the book. Obviously, Cooper took liberties with the events and failed to distinguish properly the actual allegiance of the Native American tribes in their support of the English and French.[3]

Cooper also changed the name of Lake George to Horicon in his book. In an 1851 preface to *The Last of the Mohicans*, Cooper noted that "we took the liberty of putting the Horicon. . .as a substitute for Lake George" based on " an ancient map [which indicated] that a tribe of Indians called 'Les Horicans' by the French, existed in the neighborhood of this beautiful sheet of water."[4] A closer examination of the map, however, did not show the "Horicans" anywhere near Lake George.[5] Cooper endeavored to change the name of the lake to Horicon and a few contemporary writers adopted the name.

In writing *The Last of the Mohicans*, Cooper relied heavily on Jonathan Carver's *Travels Through the Interior Parts of North America* and David Humphrey's *An Essay on the Life of the Honourable Major General Israel Putnam*.[6] While both books were written in the eighteenth century and Carver was an eyewitness at Fort William Henry in 1757, some question of exaggeration was later raised.[7] Cooper was also influenced by Timothy Dwight's description of the battle and massacre at Fort William Henry in *Travels in New-England and New-York* which had been published a few years before the completion of *The Last of the Mohicans*.[8]

In August 1824, prior to the writing of *The Last of the Mohicans*, Cooper visited Glens Falls and Lake George in the company of four English travelers. One of his four traveling companions, Edward E. Stanley, would later become prime minister of England. Departing from Congress Hall in Saratoga, the excursionists viewed the caves at Glens Falls where Stanley noted in his journal that "Mr. Cooper, the American Novellist, who was of our party on this occasion, was much struck with the scenery which he had not before seen; and exclaimed, 'I must place one of my old Indians here.' "[9] The party later lodged "at a large unfinished wooden house, immediately upon the borders of. . .Lake [George] & very beautifully situated. From hence a steamboat plies. . .to the neighborhood of Fort Ticonderoga."[10] Stanley also mentioned the "remains of old forts. . .in which are collected as relics buttons, bullets, [and] tomahawks."[11]

Cooper, Stanley, and the rest of the group crossed Lake George in the new 100-foot steamboat *Mountaineer*, completed in 1824 at Caldwell by Captain Jahziel Sherman.* The *Mountaineer*, the second steamboat on the lake, made several round trips to Ticonderoga each week and could be chartered on most other days. Under

---

*A nineteenth-century newspaper article noted the unusual construction of the *Mountaineer* which had "no timber employed. . .except the Ke[e]lson. The hull was made of inch oak plank which ran fore and aft. The next course ran, the other way, bent up by steaming to fit, also shaped to the hull, and fastened with cedar pins; a quilting of tarred paper was placed between each tier of Plank, the last tier of Plank ran fore and aft and was pitched."[12] The peculiar construction of the vessel was due to the influence of naval architect William Annesley. In March 1823 Annesley spent two weeks in Vergennes, Vermont, where he designed a schooner-rigged canal boat without traditional frame timbers that was completed under Captain Sherman's direction. In March 1824 Annesley traveled to Caldwell to "set up the moulds of the Mountaineer Steam Boat, 100 feet extreme length, 17 feet wide, and 8 feet deep, measuring 130 tons."[13] Captain Sherman, Annesley recorded, "superintended the planking and finishing of this vessel, which performs well with an inferior quality of engine of 15 horse power."[14] As a youngster, Elias S. Harris, a future Lake George captain, had his first steamboat ride on the *Mountaineer*. Harris's comment that the steamer would "weave and twist like rubber" was no doubt due to the frameless hull.[15]

the command of Captain Lucius C. Larabee, the *Mountaineer* held to a faster schedule than the ill-fated steamer *James Caldwell* because of the routine of transferring passengers from rowboats to the steamer's yawl while underway. At Cook's Landing at the northern end of the lake, travelers boarded carriages for a trip to view the remains of Fort Ticonderoga.

Theodore Dwight's *Northern Traveller* provides coverage of the steamboat tour to Ticonderoga, the historic sites along Lake George, and a delineation of the magnificent scenery of the lake. Writing a tour book would seem to have been second nature to Dwight, who was both a prolific writer and avid traveler. Born in 1796, Theodore Dwight would follow in the footsteps of his father, Theodore Dwight, Sr., who wrote several history books and edited *The Connecticut Mirror* and *The Hartford Courant* and later founded *The Daily Advertiser* in Albany and *The New York Daily Advertiser*. Theodore Dwight graduated from Yale in 1814 and authored 15 books during his lifetime and also edited many publications, including his father's paper, *The New York Daily Advertiser*.[16] He traveled extensively in Europe and was fluent in French, Spanish, and Italian. His social consciousness was demonstrated through support for European and South American political exiles seeking political independence for their countries, the championing of the infant school movement (an early version of day-care centers), acting as director of the New York Asylum for the Blind, and helping to settle Kansas as a free state. As the father of six children, his commitment to the family was evident in his advice book for fathers on child rearing, *The Father's Book* (1834), and his editorship (1845-52) of a family-oriented periodical, Dwight's *American Magazine and Family Newspaper*.

Although *The Northern Traveller* proved to be his most popular travel book, *Sketches of Scenery and Manners in the United States* (1829) more fully illuminated his views on the importance of travel as education and the instillment of moral ideals. "After a return from our journey," Dwight mused, "the important question is not what we have enjoyed. . .but what knowledge have we obtained which may be applied to some useful purpose."[17] Dwight submitted that the "uninstructed" traveler returned home with "little more than their own ignorance and the prejudices or vices of others," but those who made the effort to understand the culture and land would bring back "more unprejudiced minds, with a large and continually increasing fund of valuable information."[18] Dwight recommended that parents, at the beginning of a journey, offer instruction to their children to enhance the educational opportunities of the trip. Children should be encouraged to keep a daily diary of their journey which would provide "great gratification" upon reflection after their return.[19] Dwight's interest in travel was again manifested with the publication of *A New Gazetteer of the United States* (co-authored with William Darby in 1833).[20] Ironically, this experienced traveler, at the age of 70 (in 1866), died as a result of an injury received in a train accident.

The following tour description was first written in 1825 and updated in 1831 to include the latest information available on the region. Dwight's narration begins with a stagecoach ride from Saratoga Springs, with a stop at Glens Falls, where the cavern used in *The Last of the Mohicans* was scrutinized. Familiar landmarks, including Colonel Ephraim Williams' battle site, Bloody Pond, Fort William Henry, Fort George, and Montcalm's trenches (at Caldwell), were on the itinerary of the trek northward. Readers are provided with vivid descriptions of the islands, including a farm on Long Island, the Narrows, and the mountainsides. In describing Ticonderoga, *The Northern Traveller* furnishes a detailed view of the French lines, the fort, the Lotbinière battery, and Mount Defiance. A few of Dwight's passages dealing with the battles at Lake George and Ticonderoga have been omitted since this material was covered in earlier chapters.

"Carillon and the Ruins of Ticonderoga" by M. Welsh (ca. 1832-1836) shows The Pavilion on the shore of Lake Champlain. The lithograph, printed by Mesiers Lith., New York, was later used as an advertisement for The Pavilion Hotel.
(Fort Ticonderoga Museum)

Excursion to Lake George[21]

This is by far the most delightful, as well as fashionable excursion which can be made from the Springs in any direction, as it abounds with some of the finest scenery in the United States, and in numerous sites and objects intimately connected with the history of the country.

A stage coach leaves Saratoga Springs every morning for Caldwell, at the south end of the lake, passing through Glenn's Falls.

From the time of the earliest wars between the British colonies and the French in Canada, to that of 1755, the tract over which part of our route lies was the high road of war. It was traversed by many a hostile expedition, in which the splendour and power of European arms mingled with the fierce tactics of savage warriors; the ruins of fortresses are still to be traced in several places, and tradition points to many a spot that has been sprinkled with blood. During the Revolution, also, some of the important events in our history, took place in this neighbourhood. The battle of Saratoga, and the defeat of General [John] Burgoyne have been already dwelt upon; but we shall have to refer more than once to his expedition as we pass other scenes with which the events of it are connected.

The journey to Montreal may be made by the way of Lake George; and this route the book will pursue, to Montreal and Quebec, whither the reader, it is hoped, will accompany it.

The Road from Saratoga to Glenn's Falls

Wilton, 7 m.—Here take the left-hand road, where a small house stands at the angle. This will prove the better route, and meets the other branch twice, at four and six miles distance. Thirteen miles beyond, the road branches off eastward for Sandy Hill [later Hudson Falls].

Half a mile before reaching the village, the road enters a rich plain, probably once overflown by the river, which is now discovered on the left, dividing it in its course, while the village appears in front, with a handsome church spire, and a number of neat white houses, all backed by the mountains, which here stretch off towards the north.

French Mountain is the most prominent eminence, of which more anon [later]. A more distant range is likewise seen further to the right.

Glenn's Falls.—If the traveller is going on immediately to the lake, he should stop a few moments on the bridge, to see the falls in the Hudson, which are in full view below. The river here makes a sudden descent of 37 feet, over a rock of dark blue limestone, which has been worn into so many forms as to break up the current in a very singular manner. The projection of two large masses of rock divides the water into three sheets (except when it is much swollen by floods). Of these, the northern one is much the largest, and the other two unite and pass through a deep channel, about 15 feet wide. A man jumped off the bridge here, twice, a few years ago, yet escaped without serious injury. The most water passes through the other channel.*

A dam is thrown across just above the falls, which supplies a Cotton Manufactory. . .with water, as well as several mills. On the north side of the river is a canal, which is intended for a feeder to the Champlain canal, and passes along the elevated bank.** It now furnishes water for several mills, and an artificial cascade.

The great flat rock which supports the bridge, projects beyond it, and affords space for a small garden on its highest part, although the greater part of it is overflown in high floods. Like the other rocky strata there, it has a gentle dip towards the south, and a perpendicular fracture running nearly north and south.

Caverns.—Passing through the garden, and turning to the left, the mouths of two caverns are found facing the north, in different places among the rocks. They have been cut through by the rushing of water, in a direction across the river's course, and corresponding with the natural fracture. The first is just large enough to permit the passage of a man, and is cut with surprising regularity for a distance of about 25 feet. This place is made the scene of some of the most interesting chapters of Mr. [James Fenimore] Cooper's novel *The Last of the Mohicans*. The cavern (perhaps altered since 1757) was the place where the wanderers secreted themselves, and were made captives. The cavern conducts to one of the river's channels, where it opens on the side of a precipice, directly over the water.*** The banks of the river are perpendicular rocks as far as can be seen; and nearly opposite the caverns, under the north bank, is an abundant spring of fine, pure water, which pours from a hole in the rock, a few feet from the surface of the river.

About half-way between this place and Sandy Hill, a convoy of wagons was attacked in the French war, on their way to Lake George.†

Nearly north of Glenn's Falls, is Luzerne Mountain; and a little to the right of it, French Mountain. Between them passes the road to Lake George. Towards the west, a range of high hills encloses the view, and in the east, the Vermont Mountains make a fine appearance.

Near the foot of French Mountain is a small tavern, on the east side of the road; and near this place Gen. [Baron de] Dieskau's advanced guard struck the route from Glenn's Falls and Fort Edward to Fort William Henry. The valley through which we pass is narrow for some distance beyond; and after about half an hour's ride (for there are no mile stones [mile markers]), a little circular pond is discovered on the east side, and close by the road. It is generally almost concealed with water plants.

---

*Dwight's original note: "Sandy Hill, 3 miles eastward.—This village is pleasantly situated at the next fall in the river below. The cascade is less remarkable as an object of curiosity and interest, but it is still worthy of attention if the stranger have sufficient time at his disposal. He will find a pleasant road onward; and if he should be on his return from Lake George, and wishes to visit this part of the river, the Field of Surrender, or the Battle Ground, before reaching Saratoga or Ballston, he will find it convenient to follow the course of the river. The village has a good inn."[22]

**The Glens Falls Feeder Canal was opened to navigation in 1832. The canal was widened in 1845 but eventually traffic declined with the extension of the railroads in the late nineteenth century.

***A set of wooden stairs to reach the caverns was erected in the nineteenth century and was later replaced by iron steps. A concrete spiral stairway was completed in 1915 but was removed in 1962 because of safety concerns.[23]

† In July 1758 an attack by 400-500 Canadians and Indians under the leadership of St. Luc de la Corne killed many provincial troops and noncombatants and destroyed approximately 40 wagons.

This was near the place of action [in 1755] between Colonel [Ephraim] Williams and General Dieskau. The latter had extended his troops across the path, and advanced his wings some distance in front, the left wing occupying the rising ground on the west side of the road near this place. A small cleared spot may be noticed on the other side, a little beyond the pond (in 1825 a hut stood upon it), that is said to have been the principal scene of action; and a singular rock near by is pointed out by tradition as the mark of Col. Williams' grave. This, however, is considered very doubtful; by others, it is said that he ascended the rock to reconnoitre, and was shot from its summit.*

The little pond above mentioned was the place where most of the dead were thrown, and it bears the name of, Bloody Pond to this day. It is probably much smaller than formerly. In 1825 the skeleton of a man was dug up from a depth of one and a half feet, near the pond, with a marble pipe, and some silver eyed buttons bearing the royal stamp. This pond is nearly circular, and is covered, in its season, with the Pond Lily (Nymphea Alba), which expands its flowers on the surface of the water.

Lake George

Coming to the brow of a high hill, the prospect opens, and the lake appears, enclosed by mountains, many of which, at this distance, are of a deep blue. The side of French Mountain is near at hand on the east, covered with thick trees to the summit, while the smoothness of the lake, the beauty of its nearest shore, with the neat white buildings of Caldwell, communicate to the scene a degree of beauty and seclusion, which can hardly be found in any other spot. Directly at the south end of Lake George, are the remains of Forts George and William Henry, famous in the history of the French war; and on the site of the former was General [William] Johnson's camp, when he was attacked by [Baron de] Dieskau. The particulars of the action will be given hereafter.

Caldwell

The village of Caldwell is the place at which the visiter will stop to take a view of this charming lake, and from which he will make his excursions across its beautiful waters. The village stands at the south end of the lake, and on its shore, commanding a fine view of the neighbouring sheet of water and the mountains by which it is almost enclosed. The inn to which strangers resort, occupies a spot peculiarly fitted to gratify the eye of taste, as it overlooks the lake for several miles, and the view is not interrupted by any neighbouring obstacle.** A more delightful place can hardly be found in the United States, for the temporary residence of one who takes delight

---

*Dwight is probably referring to a large rock said to be the place where Colonel Ephraim Williams received his fatal wound (east side of present-day Route 9).

**The inn was the Lake House owned by John Baird on the present site of Shepard Park. In 1825 Henry Dilworth Gilpin noted that Caldwell contained "about sixty houses, a printing office, a neat church, and the public buildings of the country. The hotel is large, commodious and well furnished, so that travellers who visit the lake will not suffer for want of accommodation. It is named after James Caldwell."[24]

in scenery of this description, and loves to recur to deeds long past, and to exploits great in themselves and important in their results even to the present day.

Lake George is 34 miles long, and its greatest breadth 4. At the south end it is only about one mile broad. The greatest depth is sixty fathoms. The water is remarkable for its purity—a fish or a stone may be seen at the depth of 20 or 30 feet.

"Caldwell, Lake George." Drawn by William Henry Bartlett (1838),
engraved by Charles Cousen.
(New York State Historical Association)

It is undoubtedly supplied by springs from below, as the water is coldest near the bottom. It contains trout, bass, and perch. There are deer in the neighbouring forest. The outlet which leads to Lake Champlain contains three large falls and rapids. The lake never rises more than two feet.

The three best points of view are at Fort George, a place north of Shelving Rock, 14 miles, and another at Sabbath Day Point, 21 miles from the head of the lake.* The last view is taken southward, the other two northward.

This beautiful basin, with its pure crystal water, is bounded by two ranges of mountains, which, in some places rising with a bold and hasty ascent from the water, and in others descending with a graceful sweep from a great height to a broad and level margin, furnish it with a charming variety of scenery, which every change of weather, as well as every change of position, presents. . .new and countless beauties. The intermixture of cultivation with the wild scenes of nature is extremely agreeable; and the undulating surface of the well-tilled farm is often contrasted with the deep

---

*This passage and others are borrowed directly from his uncle's book, *Travels in New-England and New-York*.[25]

shade of the native forest, and the naked, weather-beaten cliffs, where no vegetation can dwell.

The situation of the hotel [Lake House] is delightful, surpassing that of almost every other to be found in this part of the country. The traveller may hereafter take pleasure in comparing the scene enjoyed from his window, with those he may witness from the walls of Quebec, Masonic Hall at Montreal, and Forsyth's at Niagara. The house is very large, having been increased within a year or two by the addition of a long wing, three stories high, so that it is now capable of furnishing lodgings for one hundred persons, and the apartments are so arranged, that half of them look out upon the lake. A green and handsome slope descends about 200 yards to the very margin, where there is no obstruction but a few trees and scatter[ed] buildings. There is the wharf, at which the steamboat [*Mountaineer*] receives and lands her passengers, often adding much variety to the place by an addition of company. The discharge of the signal gun makes fine echoes among the mountains in a clear night.

The lake is here about three-quarters of a mile wide, and the range of mountains opposite, which are high and uninterrupted, are quite uncultivated, with the exception of a few farms near the shore; the other parts being covered with trees almost to the water.

On the right is seen the south end of the lake, which is formed of low land for some distance back, succeeded by French Mountain in the rear. On a little point, half covered with trees, and rising only about 25 feet above the water, is the site of Fort William Henry; and about a mile towards the south-east from it, on a considerable elevation, are the ruins of Fort George.

Excursions on the Lake, Fishing, &c.

Boats are kept at the wharf to convey passengers to any part of the neighbouring shores and islands. Fine perch, or black bass, (Perca Franklinia), are caught in abundance almost every where; and trout, at the mouth of a small stream near the south end. Fishing rods and tackle may be obtained at the hotel; and a variety of other fish are to be found.

Diamond Island is a few miles down the lake, and is famous for abounding in crystals of quartz, which are found in a loose rock by digging a little under the surface. They are found, however, in equal numbers in several of the other islands; and it is, after all, the easier way to purchase them, and not to permit the labour of searching for them to interfere with the pleasure of the excursion, particularly as that labour is often ineffectual. A poor family lived on Diamond Island, subsisting partly on a small spot of tilled land, and partly on the produce of the crystals sold to visit[o]rs.

Tea Island, about 2 miles down the lake, is another favourite retreat. The little bay in which the boats land is remarkably retired and beautiful, and there is an old hut standing which affords something of a shelter.

Long Island contains about 100 acres, and has been inhabited and cultivated. Besides these, there are many other islands on the neighbouring parts of the lake; and those who are fond of such excursions would be highly delighted with devoting several days to visit them. The finest cluster is in the Narrows, about 12 miles distant. These will be spoken of hereafter.

One steamboat [*Mountaineer*] usually goes three times a week to the north end of the lake; but is always ready to perform that excursion and will take a party of twenty or more for $1 each.

West of the village is a remarkable conical eminence, called Rattlesnakes' Cobble, or Prospect Hill. This, as well as the mountains beyond it, is the habitation of bears and deer, and much infested with rattlesnakes. The view from the top is very fine. It is the place from which Hawk-eye, in the *Last of the Mohicans*, leads his companions into Fort William Henry through the mist.

The French Approaches. The village of Caldwell is of recent date. In the French war, during the siege of Fort William Henry, the ground which it now occupies was crossed by the trenches and batteries with which [Marquis de] Montcalm finally succeeded in forcing the capitulation of that little fortress [in 1757].

The place where he landed with his army is the little cove just behind the new stone building, a few steps north of the hotel. He erected his battery near the shore, and ran his first trench across the street into the fields in front of the hotel. The remains may still be traced, as well as the marks of a small mortar battery, near the bars of a fence leading to a small house. Another line runs to the bank of the lake, on his side of the brook, where [there] was also a battery; and another borders the swamp to the right, and another turns southward along the high ground. Behind this, in a pine wood, are the graves of about 1000 French soldiers, who died in the fort.*

Fourteen Mile Island and Shelving Rock at the entrance of the Narrows.
(Photo by the author)

---

*Obviously, this is an exaggeration. Louis Antoine de Bougainville, an aide-de-camp to the Marquis de Montcalm in 1757, listed the French dead as 17 with 40 wounded.[26]

Voyage Down Lake George

Leaving Caldwell, and passing Mr. Caldwell's house at a quarter of a mile, the steamboat passes Tea Island, Diamond, Long, and other islands, particularly the Two Sisters; and then the lake becomes wider, and the surface more uninterrupted, the course of the boat being directly towards a remarkable eminence, with a double summit, called Tongue Mountain. That which partly shuts it in from this direction on the right, is Shelving Rock; and Black Mountain shows its rounded summit beyond it, a little to the right. This last is supposed to be about 2200 feet high, and is considered the highest mountain on the lake.

Twelve Mile Island [Dome Island] appears to be at the foot of Tongue Mountain, and is seen just ahead for a great distance after leaving Caldwell. It is of a singularly rounded form, covered with trees, with the utmost regularity, and protected from the washing of the waves by a range of large stones along the shore, so well disposed as to seem like a work of art.

A rich and cultivated slope is seen on the western shore, before reaching Tongue Mountain, which belongs to a new township.*

The Narrows

The lake is very much contracted where it passes between the mountains just mentioned, and their surface is for several miles broken by innumerable islands. These are of various sizes, but generally very small, and of little elevation. A few of them are named, as Green, Bass, Lone-tree islands. Some of them are covered with trees, others with shrubs, some show little lawns or spots of grass, heaps of barren rocks, or gently sloping shores; and most of them are ornamented with graceful pines, hemlocks, and other tall trees, collected in groups, or standing alone, and disposed with most charming variety. Sometimes an island will be observed just large enough to support a few fine trees, or perhaps a single one, while the next may appear like a solid mass of bushes and wild flowers; near at hand, perhaps, is a third, with a dark grove of pines, and a decaying old trunk in front of it; and thus, through every interval between the islands as you pass along, another and another labyrinth is opened to view, among little isolated spots of ground, divided by narrow channels, from which it seems impossible for a person who should have entered them, ever to find his way out. Some of the islands look almost like ships with their masts; and many have an air of lightness as if they were sailing upon the lake.

After passing the Narrows, the lake widens again, and the retrospect is, for several miles, through that passage, with Tongue Mountain on the west, and Black Mountain opposite, the Luzerne range appearing at a great distance between them. The mountains in view have generally rounded summits; but the sides are in many places broken by precipitous ledges. They are inhabited by wolves, deer, rattle-snakes, &c.

Sabbath Day Point.—This is a low neck of land, stretching into the lake from the Western shore, and containing the little village of Hague. That on the opposite shore is Putnam.

---

*The town of Bolton was organized in 1799.

On Sabbath Day Point, Lord Amherst, with his numerous host, stopped for refreshment upon the morning of the Sabbath, and gave this beautiful point the name by which it is now known: it is a charming spot, and susceptible of the greatest embellishment.*

"The Narrows, Lake George." Drawn by William Henry Bartlett (1838),
engraved by Francis William Topham.
(New York State Historical Association)

Rogers' Rock and Anthony's Nose

These are two mountains at which the lake again contracts itself to pass between them. The shores of the lake still continue elevated, and but a few cultivated farms are distinguishable here and there. Anthony's Nose presents a precipice, on the eastern shore as we enter the strait; and the firing of a gun produces a fine echo. Rogers' Rock or Rogers' Slide is a still more formidable one, on the other hand, a little further on. The last retrospect up the lake is still very fine, even from this point—Black Mountain being yet clearly to be seen.

Rogers' Slide has its name from Capt. [Robert] Rogers, a partisan officer, who distinguished himself in the French war by his boldness, activity, and success. He commanded an expedition which left Crown Point in the year [1759], against the Canadian frontiers, and cut off the Indian village of St. Francis, afterward returning, with the severest hardships, by the way of Connecticut River. Tradition says, that

*Sabbath Day Point had its name prior to General Jeffery Amherst's 1759 expedition. (See footnote in chapter 10, page 184.)

Boating party on Lake George (untitled). Painting by Alfred Thompson Bricher.
(Adirondack Museum)

Rogers Slide.
(Print, author's collection)

he was, at another time [March 1758], closely pursued by a party of Indians, and forced to retreat to the verge of this mountain. Finding no other way to escape, he descended half down by the ravine which opens towards the south, and then by a sudden turn came to the east side, where is a precipice about two hundred feet high of smooth rock, and nearly perpendicular, down which he slipped upon his snow shoes to the lake, escaping upon the ice. The water is deep at the bottom, and fine trout are caught there with a long line.

The lake here assumes the appearance of a narrow pond for three or four miles, and seems closed at both ends. The ground is still elevated on both sides, but hills have succeeded to mountains, and some of these are at length overtopped by Black Mountain, which, although at such a distance, at length makes its appearance again, and continues in sight. The lake at length diminishes to a very narrow stream, and the bottom becomes gradually covered with weeds.

Lord Howe's Landing is just behind an island of three acres, on the left-hand at the entrance of the creek. Here is the spot where the unfortunate expedition of [General James] Abercrombie [in 1758] effected their landing. . .on their way to the attack of Ticonderoga.

Ticonderoga

The steamboat [*Mountaineer*] passes on some distance beyond this place, and lands her passengers on the other side, where, at her regular voyages, carriages are found in waiting to convey them to Ticonderoga, three miles, over a rough road.*

Those who intend to take a steamboat on Lake Champlain, should be careful to inquire the hour when it passes, and regulate their time accordingly. Ticonderoga has become one of the stopping places, which will prove a great convenience to the numerous travellers attracted to this interesting spot.

Abercrombie's army passed for some part of the way along the route we travel. Passing the Upper Falls, which are the highest, he forded the creek above the second. At the Falls near the bridge which we cross, and there was a redoubt on the north side of the stream near the bridge, where, as in several other places, there was some fighting to carry the French outposts.

At the Upper Falls are several valuable sawmills and forges, and the scenery is highly picturesque.

The Fortress of Ticonderoga

This famous old fortress, or rather its remains, are distinctly seen from Lake Champlain, though, from the direction by which we approach it, they are discovered only at a short distance. An elevated piece of land, gently sloping towards the south, and ending abruptly over a bend of the lake, appears, partially covered with trees, and crowned near its extremity with a cluster of broken walls and chimneys. There is a meadow on the eastern side, running to the base of the ridge, and across this is a footpath from the ferry to the fort by the nearest way. A carriage road also leads from the ferry to the ridge, and thence down to the same place.

*Cephas Atherton operated a carriage service at 50 cents per passenger to Fort Ticonderoga and the steamboat landing on Lake Champlain.

The outlet of Lake George in Ticonderoga (ca. 1830)

Above: The Upper Falls. *Below:* The Lower Falls.
(Ticonderoga Historical Society)

The Old French Lines,

where General Abercrombie was defeated in 1758, are the only part of the fortification which was ever the scene of a battle. They commenced on the east side, at a battery of heavy cannon on the shore, about a quarter of a mile south of the ferry. The remains of the breastwork can yet be seen. The lines were drawn in a zig-zag; first stretching off to the right, along the side of marshy ground to a cluster of bushes where was a battery; and then to the left to the verge of a wood, where was another.*

Their course may be distinctly traced in this manner, across the ridge of land at its highest elevation, over to the brow of a steep bank looking towards the outlet of Lake George. The ground is so high on the top of this ridge, that it must have been a commanding position when clear of trees. The woods that now so much interrupt the sight, have grown since the evacuation of the fortress, after the Revolutionary War.

There is a fine spring of water near the western part of the French lines, where a bloody engagement occurred between two hostile parties during the battle. Bodies of men have been dug up hereabouts within a few years, and shot were formerly very frequently found in old timber.

Mount Hope is a hill about a mile north from this place. It was occupied by General [John] Burgoyne's British line, which formed the right wing on his approach to Ticonderoga, on the 2d of [July], 1777.

In proceeding from the French lines south towards the fortress, by a gentle descent, the surface of the ground appears to have been in some places smoothed in former times by the plough, and by the removal and cutting away of rocks, to render it convenient for the evolutions of troops, and the use of artillery. A close observer will also remark that he passes the remains of several distinct lines of small redoubts, placed at equal distances, and ranged in the form of a quincunx [one in each corner of a square with one in the middle]. These were intended to [slow] still further the approach to the fortress, which assumes the air of a more important work as you approach it.

There are two old intrenchments, 270 and 150 yards from the fortress; and then comes the edge of the outer ditch or counterscarp, where there was a row of palisadoes [palisades or pointed stakes]. Five steps more bring you to the walled side of the ditch, which is still eight feet deep in some places, and therefore impassable except where it has been partly filled up. Its breadth is generally about 8 or 9 yards, and the wall of the fortress on the other side in some places 20 or 25 feet high.

The fortress is of an angular form, and embraces a large tract of ground, being divided into parts [demi-lunes] by deep ditches, which were defended by cannon and musketry, and added very much to the security of the place. The communication between these different parts was kept up by stone staircases, placed in convenient positions of the angles, all so calculated as to make the descent into the ditches and the ascent circuitous and intricate, and open to the cannon and small arms. A glance at some of those that remain will show the plan. The walls were originally much higher than at present, being raised by superstructures of logs filled in with earth, to such a height as to protect the barracks.

---

*The lines were strengthened by French troops after Abercromby's defeat and later by the Americans during the Revolution.

The Barracks formed an oblong, and the walls still remain of all except those on the eastern side; their form is plainly distinguishable. The parade [ground], which they include, appears to have been formerly carefully smoothed. This area is about 52 1/2 yards long, and 8 in breadth. The barracks, &c., the walls of which remain on the north, south, and west sides, are built on the rough blue limestone, of which the neighbouring rocks are formed, two stories high; and these, with the chimneys, several of which are standing, are the principal objects seen from a distance. By the southern entrance, Ethan Allen entered with his 83 raw soldiers, when he surprised the fortress on the [10th] May, 1775; and on reaching the court yard and calling on the commander to surrender, the British officer, Capt. [William] De[la]place, made his appearance at a window and submitted, delivering up 3 officers and 44 rank and file. In consequence of this coup de main, this important place was in the hands of the Americans until the arrival of Burgoyne, in 1777.

The battlements of Ticonderoga first bore the flag of independence. This circumstance should of itself render this ruin, so fine in other associations, interesting to the traveller.

At each corner was a bastion or a demi-bastion; and under that in the north-eastern one is a subterranean apartment, the access to which is through a small entrance near that corner of the court yard. It communicates with two magazines at the further end: that on the left, which is the larger, being 19 or 20 feet long. The room is also arched, measures about 35 feet in length, 21 breadth, and 10 or 11 in height, and like the magazines was bomb proof. The cellars south of this, which belonged to the demolished buildings, and are almost filled up, have a room or two with fireplaces still distinguishable.

The Grenadiers' Battery

This important outwork is situated on a rocky point towards the east from the main fortress. They were connected by a covered way, the traces of which are distinctly visible. It was surrounded by a wall faced with stone, with five sides, one of which measures about 180 feet; but that towards the lake has been undermined by time, and slipped down the bank. The remaining parts are nearly entire, and about 10 feet high.

Still in advance of the Grenadiers' Battery is a small work of earth, which might have contained five or six guns; while in front of it, and on the extreme point, two or three more guns appear to have been placed between the rocks, to fire down upon the water, about 40 feet below. A little further east, and under the bank, is an old stone house, formerly a store belonging to the fort, and now occupied by the tenant of Mr. [William Ferris] Pell, the proprietor of the whole peninsula of Ticonderoga.* On a spot formerly occupied as the King's Garden, Mr. P.[ell] has a fine garden, abounding in the choicest fruits imported from Europe, and transported from the celebrated nurseries of Long Island. If it is the intention of the traveller to cross the lake, to the neighbouring Vermont shore, where are still some slight remains of Burgoyne's entrenchments [from 1777], he will be much pleased with a walk across the meadows to the upper ferry, a distance of about three-quarters of a mile.

*In 1826 William Ferris Pell built a large summer home with a Greek revival facade called "The Pavilion" along the shore of Lake Champlain. The building still graces the area between the "Kings Garden" and the lake.

Between the Grenadiers' Battery and the fortress, the shore retains traces of many terraces, breastworks, and buildings, such as were probably workshops, barracks, stores, &c.

The great mountain which rises dark and abruptly from the opposite shore is Mount Defiance, about 800 feet high, on the summit of which Gen. Burgoyne's troops showed themselves on the morning of July [5th], 1777, with a battery of heavy cannon, which they had drawn up along the ridge by night, and planted in that commanding position, whence they could count the men in the fort.* The distance to the summit in a straight line is about a mile, so that the defence of Ticonderoga would have been impossible; and on the firing of a few shots by the British upon a vessel [sloop *Enterprise*] in the lake, which proved the range of their guns, the Americans made preparations to evacuate the place, and effected their retreat to the opposite shore during the night.

The ascent of Mount Defiance is laborious, but the view is extremely fine from its summit. There are the remains of Burgoyne's battery, with holes drilled in the rocks for blasting, and the marks of a large blockhouse.

Mount Independence is a hill of comparatively small elevation east of Mount Defiance, and separated from it by the lake, which has here reduced its size to that of a small river. On a bank, just above the water, are the remains of a zig-zag battery for about 40 or 50 guns, running across a little cornfield behind a house, and making five or six angles. The Horseshoe Battery is traceable on an elevation about a quarter of a mile in the rear. A bridge once connected Ticonderoga with Mount [Independence], the buttresses of which are remaining, to the great annoyance of the navigators of the lake; the steamboat passes to the south of them. On the west shore (near the stone storehouse), Arnold, when pursued by the British, caused his flotilla to be run on shore. These [h]ulks remain almost as sound as when first stranded.** A forty-two pounder is said to have ranged from the Horseshoe over this channel (now marked by a buoy) and the fortress.

After the Revolutionary War about 500 cannons were lying about the fortress, lines, &c. many of them as left by the English with their trunnions [swivels] knocked off.

The mountainous region on the west side of the lake abounds with deer, and considerable numbers are killed every season.

*After a reconnoitering report by Lieutenant William Twiss, a British engineer, General William Phillips established a battery on Mount Defiance (called Sugar Loaf Hill) on July 5, 1777, forcing a hasty evacuation of Fort Ticonderoga by the American forces.

**After the Battle of Valcour Island, Benedict Arnold abandoned four gunboats and the galley *Congress* on October 13, 1776, in Ferris Bay (present-day Arnold's Bay) on the east side of Lake Champlain. Dwight apparently confused the hulks of Amherst's fleet, from the French and Indian War at the old military dock at Ticonderoga, with the remains of Arnold's fleet.

Notes

1. Theodore Dwight, *Sketches of Scenery and Manners in the United States* (New York: A. T. Goodrich, 1829), 178.

2. Theodore Dwight, *The Northern Traveller and Northern Tour* (New York: J. & J. Harper, 1831), 167; Dwight's guidebook in 1831 was nominally combined with Henry Dilworth Gilpin's book, *A Northern Tour*, published in May 1825. Dwight's passages on Lake George, however, contain little of Gilpin's earlier work. Gilpin's description of Lake George largely consisted of long quotes from Benjamin Silliman's book. See Henry Dilworth Gilpin, *A Northern Tour* (Philadelphia: H.C. Carey & I. Lea, 1825), 73-76.

3. For a discussion on Cooper's inaccuracies on Native Americans see Robert Emmet Long, *James Fenimore Cooper* (New York: The Continuum Publishing Company, 1990), 54; See also Paul A. W. Wallace, "Cooper's Indians," in *James Fenimore Cooper: A Re-Appraisal*, ed. by Mary E. Cunningham (Cooperstown, N.Y.: New York State Historical Association, 1954), 60-61; Arthur C. Parker, "Sources and Range of Cooper's Indian Lore," in Cunningham, 85.

4. James Austin Holden, "*The Last of the Mohicans*, Cooper's Historical Inventions, and His Cave," *Proceedings of the New York State Historical Association* 16 (1917): 219.

5. Ibid., 219-26.

6. Jonathan Carver, *Travels Through the Interior Parts of North America in the Years 1766, 1767, and 1768* (1778; reprint ed., Minneapolis: Ross & Haines, Inc., 1956); David Humphreys, *An Essay of the Life of the Honourable Major General Israel Putnam* (1778; reprint, Boston: Samuel Avery, 1818); Thomas Philbrick, "The Sources of Cooper's Knowledge of Fort William Henry," *American Literature* 36 (May 1964): 211-14.

7. Ian K. Steele, *Betrayals: Fort William Henry & the "Massacre"* (New York: Oxford University Press, 1990), 158-60, 165-67.

8. Timothy Dwight, *Travels; in New-England and New-York* (New Haven, CT.: S. Converse, 1822), Volume 3, 376-81.

9. Edward E. Stanley, *Journal of a Tour in America 1824-1825* (London: R & R Clark, Ltd., 1930), 34.

10. Ibid., 35.

11. Ibid.

12. *Glens Falls Republican*, 19 May 1857.

13. John L. Sullivan, *Commentary on the New System of Naval Architecture of William Annesley* (Troy, N.Y.: William S. Parker, 1823), Appendix, 2.

14. Ibid.

15. Captain E. S. Harris, *Lake George: All About It* (Glens Falls, N.Y.: Glens Falls Republican, 1903), 26.

16. For a list of Theodore Dwight's other books see Benjamin W. Dwight, *The History of the Descendants of John Dwight* (New York: John F. Trow & Son, 1874), 232.

17. Dwight, *Sketches*, 175.

18. Ibid., 179, see also 184.

19. Ibid., 182.

20. William Darby and Theodore Dwight, Jr., *A New Gazetteer of the United States of America* (Hartford, CT.: Edward Hopkins, 1833), see 80-81, 246-47, for coverage of Lake George.

21. Dwight, *Northern Traveller*, 162-84.

22. Ibid., 164.

23. Holden, 250-52; Dennis Johnson, "Cooper's Leatherstocking Lore," *Adirondack Life*, September/October 1992, 22.

24. Gilpin, 73.

25. Timothy Dwight, *Travels*, 356.

26. Louis Antoine de Bougainville, *Adventure in the Wilderness: The American Journals of Louis Antoine de Bougainville 1756-1760*, trans. and ed. Edward P. Hamilton (Norman, OK: University of Oklahoma Press, 1964), 178.

Portrait of Harriet Martineau (ca. 1835).
(British Museum)

15. Harriet Martineau 1835

AT THE AGE OF 32, Harriet Martineau was already a well-known literary figure when she arrived in America in 1834 for a two-year visit. As a sagacious witness of her day, Martineau gravitated toward controversial topics in her writing but also appreciated the ordinary observations of the countryside. Despite the hardships involved in early nineteenth-century travel, she never vacillated in her thirst for new horizons and rarely complained. Martineau was an accommodating and versatile traveler, filled with energy, who often rose at sunrise and walked several miles each day. She was eager to see America and journeyed to the Great Lakes, Midwest, New England and New York. In particular, Martineau wished to visit Lake George which "of all others, I most desired to see."[1] Her expectations were fulfilled, and she mused that "the time will never come when my memory will not be occasionally treated with some flitting image of Lake George."[2]

Harriet Martineau was born in 1802 to Thomas and Elizabeth Martineau. Her father, a textile manufacturer of silk and wool blend fabrics in Norwich, England, associated with an intellectual circle of friends which included a few contemporary writers. His political and economic ideas would help shape Harriet Martineau's views in her subsequent prolific writing career. Her mother, although intelligent and well-informed, had little formal education. According to Harriet, her own emotional needs were sadly neglected by a stern, unaffectionate mother. Harriet herself, like many female children of the day, had only a short period of formal schooling, but was a voracious reader by the age of seven. Beginning at the age of 12, Martineau gradually began to suffer a hearing loss that became noticeable to others by the time she had reached 15. At 28, she began using an ear trumpet that allowed her to carry on conversations with others. Her hearing impairment never interfered with her social dealings, and she vowed early "never to ask what was said."[3]

Her first writing endeavors, which were fervently supported by her older brother Thomas, were published in the *Monthly Repository*, a Unitarian periodical, in 1822 and 1823. Shortly thereafter, her personal life was beset with misfortune when her brother Thomas died in 1824, followed by her father's death two years later. Her father had narrowly avoided bankruptcy in the economic downturn of 1825-26, but the family investments totally collapsed by 1829. Her precarious engagement to John Worthington ended in 1826 when he succumbed to insanity following persistent health problems.

With a need to sustain herself financially, Harriet Martineau began sewing during the day and writing at night. She moved to London in 1829 in an effort to earn an income from her literary work, but her mother soon summoned her home to make a living with her needlework. She continued her writing in the evenings, submitting three essays for a writing contest sponsored by the *Monthly Repository*. Finally recognizing her daughter's talent and ambition, her mother allowed Harriet to reside in London for three months each year. When she returned to London, she discovered that she had won all three prizes in the *Monthly Repository* writing contest.

Harriet Martineau soon drafted an idea for a number of fictional tales to explain the concepts of political economy. The result, *Illustrations of Political Economy*, would solidify Martineau's writing career and raise her to luminary status. Actually, Martineau's interest in political economy had materialized by the age of 14. Her ideas were shaped by Adam Smith's *An Inquiry in the Nature and Causes of the Wealth of Nations* (1776), which provided a comprehensive and integrated view of the benefits of a free competitive economy. David Ricardo's *Principles of Political Economy and Taxation* (1817) further honed the ideas of a self-regulating market system while developing the theories of comparative advantage and free trade. *An Essay on the Principle of Population* (1798) by Thomas Malthus and his *Principles of Political Economy* (1820) added to the fledgling subject of economics. Martineau's laissez-faire economic philosophy was tied to "a belief that economic benefits to manufacturers would inevitably benefit workers."[4] Her faith that the benefits from an unfettered business sector would trickle down to workers was undoubtedly related to her family's background in textile manufacturing. She did not comprehend the profound unrest of industrial workers in Britain until much later in her life. After drawing a conclusion on an issue, Martineau was unwilling to entertain other opinions and would sometimes lower her ear trumpet when people disagreed with her views.

Martineau's reading of Jane Marcet's *Conversations on Political Economy* (1816), which focused on a young audience, had a direct impact on Martineau's political economy treatises. After contemplating Marcet's work, Martineau decided to write a similar book that would show the operation of the economy in "selected passages of social life."[5] Ultimately, Martineau would succeed in popularizing the ideas of political economy by aiming her work at a mass audience. Published between 1832 and 1834, the short, preachy fictional stories involved stilted dialogues on particular issues of political economy. Sales swiftly ballooned.

Martineau's thoughts on the economy reflected a laizzez-faire view of capitalism and economic individualism which decried public health measures, public assistance, government regulation of worker safety, child labor laws, and legislation regulating wages. On the other hand, free trade and the abolition of the English Corn Laws (duties on grain imports) were favored. At the time of the writing of *Illustrations of Political Economy,* she concluded that political economy was a "complete science" but years later admitted that it "is no science at all."[6] Recognizing the real world of capitalism, Martineau subsequently modified her stance on a number of issues, including her earlier opposition to legislation mandating a ten-hour day for women and children. Nevertheless, the political economy tales (1832-1834) succeeded in eliciting widespread discussion of economics by the public and made Martineau financially secure.

Completing her last tale of *Illustrations of Political Economy,* Martineau embarked for Liverpool on the first leg of her trip to America. To Martineau, America, with its individualism and democracy, would be the ideal laboratory to verify the tenets of political economy. Martineau was accompanied by Louisa Jeffrey, a well-educated and even-tempered traveling companion, who received expenses in return for assisting Martineau with her hearing problems. Martineau departed from Liverpool on August 8, 1834, on a voyage to America aboard the packet ship *United States,* a trip which took nearly a month and a half. Martineau's thoughts on the long passage exemplified her optimistic, resilient attitude toward life. While others grew weary of the crossing, Martineau delighted in "careening along in the most exhilarating style" and never tired of "watching the dashing and boiling of the dark green waves."[7] When a hurricane transformed waves into "huge wandering mountains," Martineau fastened herself to the binnacle post on deck and took refuge below only when the ship had "nearly half her length under water."[8] The packet *United States* arrived safely in New York City on September 19, 1834, after an "agreeable voyage of forty-two days,"Martineau noted.[9]

Although Martineau denied that her trip to America was for a "book-making expedition" and had turned down publishers' advances for a manuscript, she wrote two books, *Society in America* and *Retrospect of Western Travel* (three volumes each), after her return to England.[10] It was a prevailing practice in this period for English writers to recount their observations of America in book form upon returning home. Martineau's visit, however, came at a time when Americans were particularly sensitive to criticism, due to the current harsh treatment at the hands of English writers. Captain Basil Hall, an individual unsuitable in temperament for travel, wrote the faultfinding *Travels in North America in the Years 1827 and 1828.* Hall and his wife fundamentally disagreed with American principles of equality and democracy and were out of their element in a country with little class distinction.*

* Although Basil Hall was critical of many things in America, he had only praise for Lake George except for his ride on the steamboat *Mountaineer.* "On the 8th of September [1827], we made a delightful voyage along Lake George, freely acknowledging that we had come at last to some beautiful scenery in the United States—beautiful in every respect, and leaving nothing to wish for. I own that Lake George exceeded my expectations as far as it exceeds the power of the Americans to overpraise it, which is no small compliment. . .Of all kinds of navigation that by steam is certainly the most unpleasant. . .Fortunately our passage down Lake George was in the day-time, for just as we had reached almost the end of this splendid piece of water, we heard a fearful crash—bang went the walking beam of the engine to pieces, and there we lay like a log on the water. But the engineer had no sooner turned off the steam, than the prodigious fizzing, together with the sound of the bell, which was instantly set

Applying the conventional upper-class standards of the time, Mrs. Francis Trollope was likewise highly critical of America in *Domestic Manners in America* (1832). The controversial book was a best seller in England and was considered the "most prejudiced and most hotly discussed of all British books of travel in the United States."[11]

After reading Trollope's work, Martineau was determined to avoid the pitfalls of negativism. She arrived with an optimistic view of American society and its political institutions. In contrast to early English excursionists, Martineau made a point of meeting with the common men and women of America. Although she often lodged with the rich and famous, she frequently stayed at ordinary boarding houses during her 10,000-mile sojourn in America. Martineau emphasized the commonplace social and economic aspects of daily life, rather than the geological wonders of the New World. Because of the limited access to travel, except for the well-to-do, the authors of travel books in this era tended to emphasize spectacular scenery. Despite her emphasis on everyday realities in America, Martineau did observe the renowned sights on her tour including Lake George and Niagara Falls.

Although Martineau found much to appreciate in America, she was frank in her criticism of slavery, the displacement of Native Americans, the lack of opportunity for women and the emphasis on materialism. Martineau ultimately came to the unhappy conclusion that laizzez-faire economics and individual liberty were not completely compatible.[13]

After completing her two American books, Martineau continued her productive writing career by finishing more than a dozen books over the next decade and a half. One habit that aided her prolific work was the custom of sending her manuscripts directly to the publisher without rewriting, editing, or even recopying. Early in the 1840s Martineau's health problems, related to a uterine tumor, initiated varying periods of invalidism. When traditional nineteenth-century medical techniques such as blood letting with leeches and opiates failed, Martineau turned to a controversial "Mesmeric Cure," consisting of hypnotic trances. Martineau experienced a temporary remission, probably due to psychological suggestion, but in 1854 her problems reoccurred. Feeling that she was near death, Martineau began to write an autobiography. She lived, however, for another 22 years, in which she championed many causes and collaborated with Florence Nightingale to repeal the Contagious Diseases Acts which required coercive physical examinations for venereal diseases of all women living in military communities. Martineau continued her writing, including pieces for the *Daily News* (London) which advocated equal education for women as well as other feminist causes, support for oppressed minorities, opposition to monopolies in the economy, and facilitated public opinion on the side of the Union during the American Civil War. Martineau was living on a meager income at her home near Lake Windermere in England when she died on June 27, 1876.

The following description of Lake George appeared in Martineau's second book on America, *Retrospect of Western Travel* (1838). While her first book, *Society in America* (1837), dealt with the political institutions, economics, and social aspects

a-ringing, aided by the shouts of the crew, gave alarm to those on shore. In a few minutes half a dozen boats shot out from under the high bank near the village of Caldwell, and towed us speedily to land. This was a shortlived distress, therefore, and rather picturesque and interesting upon the whole, as the twilight was just about to close, and the magnificent scenery of Lake George, being reduced to one mass of deep shade, became still more impressive, I thought, than it had been even in full daylight."[12]

of American society, *Retrospect of Western Travel* was mainly a book of travel. Reaching Saratoga by rail on May 12, 1835, Martineau proceeded a few days later to Glens Falls and Caldwell by carriage. She lodged at the Lake House in Caldwell and explored the ruins of Fort William Henry, enjoyed a carriage ride along the western bank of the lake, walked the eastern shore and viewed a portion of the southern basin of the lake from a rowboat. As had other travelers before her, Martineau marvelled at the combination of mountains and water and the transparency of the lake.

"Lake George." Etching by John William Casilear, engraved by Robert Hinshelwood.
(New York State Historical Association)

Lake George[14]

Everybody who has heard of American scenery has heard of Lake George. At one time I was afraid I should have to leave the States without having visited the lake which, of all others, I most desired to see, so many hinderances had fallen in the way of my plans. A few weeks before I left the country, however, I was fortunate enough to be included in a party of four who made a trip to the Springs and the lake. It was not in the fashionable season, and for this I was not sorry. I had seen the Virginia Springs and Rock-away in the plenitude of their fashionable glory, and two such exhibitions are enough for one continent.

It was about noon on the 12th of May [1835]when we alighted shivering from the railcar at Saratoga. We hastened to the Adelphi [Hotel], and there found the author of Major Jack Downing's Letters* and two other gentlemen reading the newspapers round a stove. We had but little time to spare and, as soon as we had warmed ourselves and ascertained the dinner hour, we set forth to view the place and taste the Congress [Spring] water. There is nothing to be seen but large white frame houses, with handsome piazzas, festooned with creepers (at this time only the sapless remains of the garlands of the last season). These houses and the wooden temple over the principal spring are all that is to be seen, at least by the bodily eye. The imagination may amuse itself with conjuring up the place as it was less than half a century ago, when these springs bubbled up amid the brush of the forest, their qualities being discovered by the path through the woods worn by the deer in their resort to it.** In those days the only edifices were a single loghut and a bearpound; a space enclosed with four high walls, with an extremely narrow entrance, where it was hoped that bears might get in during the dark hours, and be unable to find their way out again. Times are much changed now. There are no bears at Saratoga but a two-legged species from Europe, dropping in, one or two in a season, among the gentry at the Springs.

The process of bottling the Congress water was in full activity when we took our first draught of it.*** Though the utmost celerity [bubble] is used, the water loses much of its virtue and briskness by bottling. The man and boy whom we saw filling and corking the bottles with a dexterity which only practice can give, are able to despatch a hundred dozen per day. There are several other springs, shedding waters of various medicinal virtues; but the Congress fountain is the only one from which the stranger would drink as a matter of taste.

The waterworks are just at hand, looking like a giant's shower-bath. At the top of the eminence close by there is a pleasure railroad; a circular track, on which elderly children may take a ride round and round in a self-moving chair; an amusement a step above the old merry-go-round in gravity and scientific pretension. But for its vicinity to some tracts of beautiful scenery, Saratoga must be a very dull place to

---

*Martineau was probably referring to Charles Augustus Davis who used the pseudonym Major Jack Downing in his droll political commentaries in the *Daily Advertiser* (New York).

**The traditional story of the springs suggests that deer were the first to drink from the waters before the appearance of early settlers.

***The Congress Spring in Saratoga Springs became more widely known with the bottling and shipping of its water after 1824.

persons shaken out of their domestic habits, and deprived of their usual occupations; and the beauties of the scenery must be sought, Saratoga Lake lying three miles, Glen's Falls eighteen, and Lake George twenty-seven miles from the Springs.

At dinner Mr. R., the gentleman of our party, announced to us that he had been able to engage a pretty double gig,* with a pair of brisk ponies, for ourselves, and a light cart for our luggage. The day was very cold for an open carriage; but it was not improbable that, before twenty-four hours were over, we might be panting with heat; and it was well to be provided with a carriage in which we might most easily explore the lake scenery if we should be favoured with fine weather.

The cart preceded us. On the road, a large white snake made a prodigious spring from the grass at the driver, who, being thus challenged, was not slow in entering into combat with the creature. He jumped down and stoned it for some time with much diligence before it would lie down so that he might drive over it.** As we proceeded the country became richer, and we had fine views of the heights which cluster round the infant Hudson [River], and the Green Mountains of Vermont.

"View of Caldwell" (1835) shows the Lake House and the steamboat *Mountaineer.*
(Print, author's collection)

We were all astonished at the splendour of Glen's Falls. The full though narrow Hudson rushes along amid enormous masses of rock, and leaps sixty feet down the chasms and precipices which occur in the passage, sweeping between dark banks of shelving rocks below, its current speckled with foam. The noise is so tremendous that I cannot conceive how people can fix their dwellings in the immediate neighbourhood. There is a long bridge over the roaring floods which vibrates incessantly, and clusters of sawmills deform the scene. There is stonecutting as well as planking done at these mills. The fine black marble of the place is cut into slabs, and sent

---

*A light two-wheeled carriage.
**Such cooperation by snakes in the North Country is quite unusual!

down to New-York to be polished. It was the busiest scene that I saw near any water-power in America.

Lake George lies nine miles beyond Glen's Falls. We saw the lake while we were yet two miles from Caldwell, the pretty village at its southern extremity. It stretched blue among the mountains in the softening light; and we anticipated what our pleasures were to be as we looked upon the framework of mountains in which this gem is set. We had just emerged from a long and severe winter. We had been walking streets in every stage of thaw; and it was many months since we had loitered about in the full enjoyment of open air and bright verdure, as we hoped to do here. This trip was to be a foretaste of a long summer and autumn of outdoor delights.

The people at the inn were busy cleaning, in preparation for summer company; but they gave us a welcome, and lodged and tended us well. Our windows and piazza commanded a fine view of the lake (here just a mile broad), of the opposite mountains, and of the white beach which sweeps round the southern extremity of the sheet of waters, as transparent as the sea about the Bermudas.

As we had hoped, the next morning was sunny and warm. We employed it in exploring the ground about Fort William Henry, which stands on an eminence a little way back from the water, and is now merely an insignificant heap of ruins. The French and Indians used to pour down upon the settlements in the plains by the passes of the Lakes Champlain and George, and near these passes were fought some of the severest battles recorded in American history. The mountain opposite our windows at the Lake House is called French Mountain, from its being the point where the French showed themselves on the bloody 8th of September, 1755, when three battles were fought in the neighbourhood on the same day. It was two years later when the Marquis of Montcalm conducted an army of 10,000 men to invest Fort William Henry. Colonel Monro, who held it for the British, was obliged, after a gallant defence, to capitulate. He marched out with 3000 men, and many women and children. The Indians attached to the French army committed outrages which it is thought the marquis might have prevented. But it is probable that, when the guilt of taking savages for allies in offensive warfare is once incurred, any amount of mischief may ensue which no efforts of the commander can control. Every one knows the horrible story of Miss [Jane] McCrea, the young lady who was on the way to be married [in 1777] to her lover in the British army, and who was tomahawked, and scalped by the Indians in whose charge she was travelling. During the recrimination between the commanders on this occasion, General [John] Burgoyne explained his inability to control the movements of passionate savages; and it must be supposed that Montcalm had no more power over the Indians who plundered and then murdered almost the whole number of the British who evacuated Fort William Henry.* It was a horrible scene of butchery. We went over the ground, now waste and still, tangled with bushes, and inhabited only by birds and reptiles.

After wandering for some hours on the beach, and breaking our way through the thick groves which skirt it, dwelling upon the exquisite scene of the blue lake, with its tufted islands shut in by mountains, we wished to find some place where

---

*From a total of approximately 2,300 soldiers and civilians, the actual number killed in the 1757 massacre at Fort William Henry has been estimated at between 69 and 184, with several hundred missing or taken prisoner.[15]

we might obtain an equally good distant view, and yet enjoy the delights of the margin of the water. By climbing a fence we got to a green bank, whence we could reach a log in the water; and here we basked, like a party of terrapins [turtles], till dinnertime. The foliage of the opposite woods, on French Mountain, seemed to make great progress under the summer warmth of this day; and by the next morning the soft green tinge was perceptible on them, which, after the dry hardness of winter, is almost as beautiful as the full leaf.

"Pleasant Day, Lake George." Painting by William Bliss Baker.
(Adirondack Museum)

After dinner we took a drive along the western bank of the lake. The road wound in and out, up and down on the mountainous barrier of the waters, for there was no beach or other level. One of the beauties of Lake George is that the mountains slope down to its very margin. Our stout ponies dragged us up the steep ascents, and rattled us down on the other side in charming style; and we were so enchanted with the succession of views of new promontories and islands, and new aspects of the opposite mountains, that we should have liked to proceed while any light was left, and to have taken our chance for getting back safely. But Mr. R. pointed to the sinking sun, and reminded us that it was Saturday evening. If the people at the inn were Yankees, they would make a point of all the work of the establishment ceasing at sunset, according to the Sabbath customs of New-England; and we must allow the hostler a quarter of an hour to put up the ponies. So we unwillingly turned, and reached Caldwell just as the shutters of the stores were in [the] course of being put up, and the last rays of the sun were gushing out on either side [of] the mountain in the rear of the village. At the Lake House the painters were putting away their brushes, and the scrubbers emptying their pails; and by the time twilight drew on, the place was in a state of Sunday quietness. We had descried [discovered] a church standing under the trees close by, and the girl who waited on us was asked what services there would be the next day. She told us that there was a regular service during the summer season when the place was full, but not at present; she added, "We have no regular preacher now, but we have a man who can make a very smart prayer."

The next day was spent in exploring the eastern side of the lake for some distance on foot, and in sitting on a steep grassy bank under the pines, with our feet overhanging the clear waters glancing in the sun. Here we read and talked for some hours of a delicious summer Sunday. I spent part of the afternoon alone at the fort, amid a scene of the profounded stillness. I could trace my companions as they wound their way at a great distance along the little white beaches and through the pine groves; the boat in the cove swayed at the end of its tether when the wind sent a ripple across its bows; the shadows stole up the mountain sides; and an aged labourer sauntered along the beach, with his axe on his shoulder, crossed the wooden bridge over a brook which flows into the lake, and disappeared in the pine grove to the left. All else was still as midnight. My companions did not know where I was, and were not likely to look in the direction where I was sitting; so, when they came within hail—that is, when from mites they began to look as big as children—I sang as loud as possible to catch their attention. I saw them speak to each other, stop, and gaze over the lake. They thought it was the singing of fishermen, and it was rather a disappointment when they found it was only one of ourselves.

On the Monday we saw the lake to the best advantage by going upon it. We took boat directly after breakfast, having a boy to row us,* a stout boy he must be, for he can row twenty-eight miles on the hottest summer's day. The length of the lake is thirty-six miles; a long pull for a rower; but accomplished by some who are accustomed to the effort. First we went to Tea Island.** I wish it had a better name, for it is a delicious spot, just big enough for a very lazy hermit to live in. There is a teahouse to look out from, and, far better, a few little reposing places on the margin; recesses of rock and dry roots of trees, made to hide one's self in for thought or dreaming. We dispersed; and one of us might have been seen, by any one who rowed round the island, perched in every nook. The breezy side was cool and musical with the waves. The other side was warm as July, and the waters so still that the cypress twigs we threw in seemed as if they did not mean to float away. Our boatman laid himself down to sleep, as a matter of course, thus bearing testimony to the charms of the island; for he evidently took for granted that we should stay some time. We allowed him a long nap, and then steered our course to Diamond Island.*** This gay handful of earth is not so beautiful as Tea Island, not being so well tufted with wood; but it is literally carpeted with forget-me-not. You tread upon it as upon clover in a clover-field.

*The steamboat *Mountaineer* was still in operation at Lake George in 1835, making two round trips to Ticonderoga each week and daily charters on most other days. Since Martineau visited the lake in May, the vessel was probably not operating on her normal summer schedule.

**Close to the western shore, Tea Island is only a mile and one quarter from the southern shore of Lake George. The island is the subject of surviving legends of the burial of gold during the French and Indian War. One version suggests that Montcalm's troops buried the gold on the island in 1757; another that Abercromby's forces buried it in 1758. Neither story is supported by documented eyewitness accounts.

***Apparently the dwelling occupied by a family on Diamond Island that had been observed by Benjamin Silliman in 1821 was not present in 1835.

We coasted the eastern shore as we returned, winning our way in the still sunshine under walls of rock overhung by projecting trees, and round promontories, across little bays, peeping into the glades of the shore, where not a dwelling is to be seen, and where the human foot seems never to have trod. What a wealth of beauty is there here for future residents yet unborn! The transparency of the waters of this lake is its great peculiarity. It abounds with fish, especially fine red trout. It is the practice of the fishermen to select the prime fish from a shoal, and they always get the one they want. I can easily believe this, for I could see all that was going on in the deep water under our keel when we were out of the wind; every ridge of pebbles, every tuft of weed, every whim of each fish's tail, I could mark from my seat. The bottom seemed to be all pebbles where it was not too deep to be clearly seen. In some parts the lake is of unmeasured depth.

It was three o'clock before we returned; and, as it is not usual for visiters to spend six or seven hours of a morning on the lake, the good people of the Lake House had been for some time assuring one another that we must have been cast away. The kind-hearted landlady herself had twice been out on the top of the house to look abroad for our boat. I hope the other members of my party will be spared to visit this scene often again. I can hardly hope to do so; but they may be sure that I shall be with them in spirit, for the time will never come when my memory will not be occasionally treated with some flitting image of Lake George.

Notes:

1. Harriet Martineau, *Retrospect of Western Travel* (London: Saunders and Otley, 1838), Volume 2, 221.
2. Ibid., 227
3. Gillian Thomas, *Harriet Martineau* (Boston: Twayne Publishers, 1985), 5; See also Harriet Martineau, *Harriet Martineau's Autobiography with Memorials by Maria Weston Chapman* (London: Smith, Elder, & Co., 1877), Volume 1, 74.
4. Thomas, 60.
5. Ibid., 9; Martineau, *Autobiography*, 1:138.
6. Valerie Kossew Pichanich, *Harriet Martineau: The Woman and Her Work, 1802-76* (Ann Arbor: The University of Michigan Press, 1980), 49; See also Martineau, *Autobiography*, 3:245.
7. Harriet Martineau, *Retrospect of Western Travel* (London: Saunders and Otley, 1834), Volume 1, 17.
8. Ibid., 28-29.
9. Ibid., 35.
10. Vera Wheatley, *The Life and Work of Harriet Martineau* (London: Secker & Warburg, 1957), 147.
11. Allan Nevins, *American Social History: As Recorded by British Travellers* (New York: Henry Holt and Company, 1923), 159.
12. Basil Hall, *Travels in North America* (1829; reprint ed., Akademische Druck, 1964), Volume 2, 2-5.
13. Pichanich, 80-81.
14. Martineau, 2:221-27.
15. Ian K. Steele, *Betrayals: Fort William Henry and the "Massacre,"* (New York: Oxford University Press, 1990), 144, 138-39.

Francis Parkman
(Library of Congress)

16. Francis Parkman 1842

FRANCIS PARKMAN was one of the most renowned American historians of the nineteenth century. Despite serious physical disabilities, Parkman traveled throughout North America to research historic sites and to Europe in search of original manuscripts. His interest in the "Old French War" began in his sophomore year at Harvard College and culminated with the publication of his most highly regarded work, *Montcalm and Wolfe*, in 1884. To prepare for his writing pertaining to the French and Indian War, Parkman "visited and examined every spot where events of any importance with the contest took place."[1] Although Parkman observed breathtaking scenery across America and Europe, Lake George remained a favorite destination. When Parkman beheld Lake Como in Italy, he remarked that nothing was "more beautiful than this lake. It reminds me of Lake George," but Lake Como had "none of that shaggy untamed aspect in the mountains. . .none of those little islands, covered with rough and moss-grown pine trees, which give it a certain savage character to the beauties of Lake George. . .Give me Lake George, and the smell of the pine and fir!"[2]

Born in Boston on September 16, 1823, Parkman had the benefit of social position and affluence. The son of Reverend Francis and Caroline (Hale) Parkman, his lineage included a long line of Puritan clerics on both sides of the family. His roots could also be traced to family members who had participated in the French and Indian War and the American Revolution. His great uncle, William Parkman, left a diary written during the 1758 Abercromby expedition against Fort Carillon (Ticonderoga) which Francis Parkman used a century later in *Montcalm and Wolfe*. As a youngster at home, Parkman was fidgety and restless, which resulted in his long stay, beginning at the age of eight, at his grandfather's farm in Medford, Massachusetts. For four years young Parkman had the run of a rocky, densely-wooded area known as the "Five Mile Woods," adjacent to his grandfather's property. It was here that he developed his great love of the wilderness as he wandered the woodlands exploring cliffs, ravines, and marshes while hunting with his bow and arrow.

At the age of 13, Francis Parkman returned to Boston where he attended Gideon Thayer's academy, Chauncy Hall, in preparation for Harvard. Parkman's interests included scientific pursuits, amateur acting, and a passion for books. Under the tutelage of an exacting, dedicated teacher at Chauncy, Parkman learned "to write good and easy English" and was "encouraged. . .to write translations in prose and verse" of the classics.[3] The oldest child in the family, Parkman had close bonds with his mother and was indulged by his three younger sisters. Parkman also had a younger brother who later made the U.S. Navy a career and served during the Civil War.

Lake George (untitled). Painting by George Wellington Waters.
(Adirondack Museum)

In the fall of 1840 at the age of 17, Parkman began his studies at Harvard College. His close friends at Harvard had similar backgrounds, and Parkman was an active member of the Institute of 1770, a debating and literary club, president of the Hasty Pudding Club, and an officer of the Natural History Society. Despite Harvard's academic orientation, Parkman found sufficient time to pursue a demanding regimen of physical activities including gymnastics, horsemanship, boxing, and marksmanship. Irrespective of college rules against guns in student dormitories, Parkman's room resembled the quarters of a hunter. Parkman's college vacations were a series of excursions through the wilds of America. In his first summer vacation (1841), Parkman began his wilderness travels with a walking and climbing trek with a college friend through the White Mountains of New Hampshire. It was here that he had his first brush with adventure when he found himself stranded alone high above a ravine while rock climbing. Using a jackknife, Parkman created handholds to reach safety.

In his sophomore year of college, Parkman's "schemes had crystallized into a plan of writing the story of. . .the 'Old French War.'"[4] Seeking bibliographical sources, Parkman wrote to Professor Jared Sparks at Harvard, a noted authority on American history, that he was "desirous of studying the history of the Seven Years' War. . .I wish particularly to know the details of military operations around Lake George—the characters of the officers—the relations of the Indian Tribes—the history, the more minute, the better, of partisan exploits—in short, all relating to the incidents of the war in that neighborhood."[5] This passion would consume much of Francis Parkman's life, and his subsequent writings would materially add to the knowledge of the Seven Years' War in America. The first step in his pursuit of information on the war led Parkman to Lake George in the summer of 1842. The summer of 1843 would again bring Parkman through Lake George on his way to Canada.

In the fall of 1843 at the beginning of his senior year at Harvard, Parkman suffered the first collapse of his health. As a formula for renewing his well-being, Parkman sailed on the merchant vessel *Nautilus* for a tour of Europe. After a long voyage marked by unfavorable weather, Parkman landed at Gibraltar and thereafter began a camping trip in Sicily before his grand tour of Italy, the Alps, Paris, London, and Scotland. Parkman still managed to return home in time to take his senior examinations and graduate with his class in 1844. Prior to the commencement, however, Parkman set out on foot with his rifle to explore western Massachusetts and research the areas connected with the French and Indian War. Parkman visited the site of Fort Massachusetts near North Adams, viewed original diaries and other materials from the war, and interviewed those who recollected stories that had been told to them by participants in the war.

Although Parkman did not demonstrate any exceptional academic ability in college, he did graduate 20th in a class of 62 and achieved "high distinction" in history. Fulfilling his father's expectations for a professional career, Parkman immediately entered Harvard Law School in 1844. In law school Parkman still found time for a general history course and another in Indian history and ethnology. After his first year in law school, Parkman embarked on a trip to research materials for a book dealing with the life of Pontiac, the chief of the Ottawa and leader of the confederacy of tribes in the Ohio Valley and the Great Lakes region during the French and Indian War. In the summer of 1845 Parkman traveled through Pennsylvania, western New York, Michigan, and the Great Lakes area. The trip bore fruit with his examination of trunks of historical documents, meetings with Native Americans, and interviews with authorities and storytellers on the French and Indian War. In 1845 Parkman published his first writings in the form of four prose pieces and one in verse that appeared in the *Knickerbocker Magazine,* relating to his wilderness experiences. The following year (1846), Parkman received his law degree from Harvard but never practiced law.

Parkman's remedy for eyestrain, as a result of studying for his law degree, was to join a hunting expedition along the Oregon Trail with his cousin, Quincy A. Shaw. In St. Louis, Parkman contracted the services of Henry Chatillon, a hunter and guide with a Sioux wife, who had recently returned after four years in the wilderness. On April 28, 1846, Parkman and Shaw and their party departed from St. Louis for the Oregon Trail. The journey allowed Parkman to devote three weeks to buffalo hunting and living with a roaming party of Oglala Sioux warriors. Parkman's journey through the West did not end until October 1846. Although Parkman had prepared himself physically for the trip by strenuous exercise, he suffered from a host of other maladies on the trip including dysentery, injury to his eyes from the sun, and insomnia.

Upon his return from the Oregon journey, Parkman's health collapsed from illness that would continue throughout the rest of his life. Parkman's afflictions involved a "whirl" in the brain, "resembling the tension of an iron band," sleep-lessness, water on the knee, and a serious weakness of sight.[6] Although Parkman tried rest cures, water cures, and saw a brain specialist in Paris, the symptoms recurred throughout his life. Although no exact diagnosis of his disorders was possible, given the limited medical knowledge of the nineteenth century, some of his maladies were actually linked to migraine headaches, arthritis, depression, and hypochondria. Parkman's problems, however, never prevented him from writing, and he characteristically shunned the image of an invalid. After having his notes from his western trip read aloud, Parkman dictated his classic *The Oregon Trail* to one of his sisters and his cousin Quincy Shaw in the fall of 1846. His condition often limited him to two hours or less of work per day. Despite his physical problems, Parkman began work on *The Conspiracy of Pontiac* in the spring of 1848. Documents and books were read to him for a half hour at a time. He had a "gridiron," or wire writing frame, constructed at that time which allowed him to write in the darkness with a black crayon. With an emphasis on scholarship and authenticity, the two volumes of *Pontiac* were well received upon publication in 1851.

In 1850, after some improvement in his health, Parkman married Catherine Scollay Bigelow of Boston. The marriage was a happy one with a daughter born in 1851 and a son in 1854. When his father passed away in 1852, Parkman's inheritance enabled him to maintain his life as a writer. Both his wife and her sister, Mary Bigelow, read copies of historical materials on the French and Indian War to Parkman. The marriage must have been stable since his wife took the dictation of Parkman's only novel, *Vassall Morton*, in which the heroine was Parkman's thinly disguised lost love interest, Pamela Prentis of Keene, New Hampshire, whom he had first met on his 1841 trip to the White Mountains. Published in 1856, the novel was a failure. Tragedy struck the Parkman's in 1857 when their son Francis died at the age of four. The following year, Parkman's wife, Catherine, died during the birth of their second daughter.

Parkman's mental state deteriorated to such an extent that he traveled to Paris in the winter of 1858-1859 to have his condition evaluated by an eminent brain specialist. During his protracted illness, his daughters became the responsibility of his unmarried sister-in-law, Mary Bigelow. After returning from Paris, Parkman lived in Boston with his mother and sisters during the winter and stayed at his cottage on Jamaica Pond with them in the summer.

For the next three decades Parkman produced a remarkable series on France and England in North America: *The Pioneers of France in the New World* (1865), *The Jesuits in North America* (1867), *LaSalle and the Discovery of the Great West* (1869),

The Old Régime (1874), *Count Frontenac and New France* (1877), *Montcalm and Wolfe* (1884, two volumes), and *A Half-Century of Conflict* (1892, two volumes). A dominant theme in most of his works was the eventual end of the forest and the Indian way of life as the onslaught of English settlers pressed westward and northward. Parkman's afflictions, however, continued with varying degrees of severity during his prolific years of writing. The help of his devoted sister, Lizzie, who never married and spent her life assisting Parkman's literary efforts, made it possible for Parkman to produce his impressive historical volumes. Parkman's books never diminished in the public's attention and his status as a literary luminary continued all his life.

Parkman's abilities included a keen memory, organizational capabilities, dedication, and a graphic imagination. One biographer has characterized his writing style as "brilliant gifts of narrative" with "an uncanny sympathy with all forms of physical movement. . .the motion of the wind in the dip and rise of the grass, the onward impetus of the groaning bullet, the physical plunge of the water in the stream, the bound and rebound of the gun barrel down the rocks."[7] His narrative tomes entertained readers much the same way that novels do. Parkman brought a sense of scholarship to his books as he ferreted out original documents on the French and Indian War in North America, England, and France. As an example of his diligent research, he spent 15 years pursuing documents relating to the Marquis de Montcalm. He traveled to Europe several times for documents and spent time in the French colonial archives during the winter of 1858-1859 even when he was suffering his greatest mental problems. Because of the limitation of his eyesight, he often employed assistants abroad to read the documents to him in the library. Parkman also retained students in Paris, London, and Canada to copy original materials and send the copied manuscripts to him in Boston.* As a result of his research and travel expenses, the net income generated from his books was modest. But Parkman was quite satisfied with the simple things in life and never pursued a life of luxury.

Parkman's health fluctuated, and in later life he resorted to the use of a cane or crutches. Nevertheless, as late as 1886, Parkman camped in the wilderness along the Batiscan River in Canada and made his seventh and last trip to Europe the following year. He remained active in a number of social clubs in Boston and served as an Overseer and Fellow of Harvard. From 1871-1893 Parkman shared the family home in Boston with his sister Lizzie and spent summers with a married daughter on the New Hampshire coast. After a relatively healthy summer with his daughter, Parkman died on November 8, 1893, from appendicitis.

The journal that follows was written by eighteen-year-old Francis Parkman during his 1842 expedition to Lake George. Parkman was accompanied by Henry Ore White, a fellow student from Harvard, who was a skilled cook but was not always willing to follow Parkman's lead on the trip. Parkman had the habit of tiring out traveling partners who did not share his passion for the wilderness and historical forays. After one disagreement with White, Parkman spent the night camping alone on an island in Hague. Parkman's trip in 1842 occurred at a time when much of the

---

*Although Parkman has been cited by biographers for the meticulous accuracy of his research, his quoted material often differed from the original documents. It is debatable as to whether this was done to embellish the narrative or because of different translations from the French archives or simply errors in copying.[8]

lake was still unsettled and travel itself still somewhat of a novelty to the general public. Parkman and White had traveled by railroad from Boston to Saratoga where they boarded a stagecoach for the last leg of the trip to Caldwell. At Caldwell, Parkman scrutinized the ruins of the two forts, observed sunken bateaux, and climbed Prospect Mountain. The young adventurers rented a rowboat and camped first on Diamond Island. After camping in the Narrows, Parkman and White lodged at Sabbath Day Point and listened to the stories of Captain Sam Patchin, a Revolutionary War veteran. Rowing to Hague, the two stayed at Garfields where they met William Caldwell, son of the founder of the village of Caldwell and the unofficial "lord of the manor" of Lake George. After speaking to a local resident in Ticonderoga who did not know where Fort Ticonderoga was located, Parkman managed to find the French lines and the fort. Parkman lamented that "senseless blockheads in the neighborhood have stolen tons and tons of the stone [from the fort]."[9] Parkman and White later boarded a steamboat at Ticonderoga for Burlington.

"Lake George, from the top of Fort George, Caldwell Village."
Woodcut by W. R. Miller.
(Print, author's collection)

Parkman at Lake George[10]

July 16th. Caldwell.—This morning we left Albany—which I devoutly hope I may never see again—in the cars for Saratoga. My plan of going up the river to Fort Edward I had to abandon, for it was impracticable—no boat beyond Troy. Railroad the worst I was ever on; the country flat and dull; the weather dismal. The Catskills appeared in the distance. After passing the inclined plane and riding a couple of hours, we reached the valley of the Mohawk and Schenectady. I was prepared for something filthy in the last-mentioned, venerable town, but for nothing quite so disgusting as the reality. Canal docks, full of stinking water, super-annuated, rotten canal-boats and dirty children and pigs paddling about, formed the delicious picture, while in the rear was a mass of tumbling houses and sheds, bursting open in all directions; green with antiquity, dampness, and lack of paint. Each house had its peculiar dunghill, with the group of reposing hogs. In short, London itself could exhibit nothing much nastier. In crossing the main street, indeed, things wore an appearance which might be called decent. The car-house here is enormous. Five or six trains were on the point of starting for the North, South, East, and West; and the brood of railroads and taverns swarmed about the place like bees. We cleared the babel at last, passed Union College [Schenectady], another tract of monotonous country, Ballston, and finally reached Saratoga, having travelled latterly at the astonishing rate of seven miles an hour. "Caldwell stage ready." We got our baggage on board, and I found time to enter one or two of the huge hotels. After perambulating the entries, filled with sleek waiters and sneaking fops, dashing through the columned porticos and enclosures, drinking some of the water and spitting it out again in high disgust, I sprang onto the stage, cursing Saratoga and all New York. With an unmitigated temper, I journeyed to Glens Falls, and here my wrath mounted higher yet at the sight of that noble cataract almost concealed under a huge, awkward bridge, thrown directly across it, and with the addition of a dam above, and about twenty mills of various kinds. Add to all, that the current was choked by masses of drift logs above and below, and that a dirty village lined the banks of the river on both sides, and some idea may possibly be formed of the way in which the New Yorkers have bedeviled Glens. Still the water comes down over the marble ledges in foam and fury, and the roar completely drowns the clatter of the machinery. I left the stage and ran down to the bed of the river, to the rocks at the foot of the falls. Two little boys volunteered to show me the "caverns," which may be reached dry-shod when the stream is low. I followed them down, amid the din and spray, to a little hole in the rock, which led to a place a good deal like the "Swallow's Cave," and squeezed in after them. "This is Cooper's Cave sir; where he went and hid the two ladies." They evidently took the story in *The Last of the Mohicans* for gospel. They led the way to the larger cave, and one of them ran down to the edge of the water, which boiled most savagely past the opening. "This is Hawley's Cave: here's where he shot an Indian." "No, he didn't, either," squalled the other, "it was higher up on the rocks." "I tell you it wasn't." "I tell you it was." I put an end to the controversy with two cents.*

*James Fenimore Cooper had visited the cave at Glens Falls in 1824. In his novel, *The Last of the Mohicans*, Hawkeye, Chingachgook, and Uncas use the cave as a hiding place for Cora, Alice, Duncan, and David. James Fenimore Cooper's novels were favorites of Parkman.[11]

Dined at the tavern and rode on. Country dreary as before; the driver one of the best of his genus I ever met. He regaled me, as we rode on with stories of his adventures with deer, skunks, and passengers. A mountain heaved up against the sky some distance before us, with a number of smaller hills stretching away on each hand, all wood-crowned to the top. Away on the right rose the Green Mountains, dimly seen through the haze, and scarcely distinguishable from the blue clouds that lay upon them. Between was a country of half-cultivated fields, tottering houses, and forests of dwarf pines and scrub oaks. But as we drew near, the mountain in front assumed a wilder and loftier aspect. Crags started from its woody sides and leaned over a deep valley below. "What mountain is that?" "That ere is French Mounting"—the scene of one of the most desperate and memorable battles in the old French War.* As we passed down the valley, the mountain rose above the forest half a mile on our right, while a hill on the left, close to the road, formed the other side. The trees flanked the road on both sides. In a little opening in the woods, a cavity in the ground, with a pile of stones at each end, marked the spot where was buried that accomplished warrior and gentleman, Colonel [Ephraim] Williams, whose bones, however, have since been removed.** Farther on is the rock on the right, where he was shot, having mounted it on the lookout***—an event which decided the day; the Indians and English broke and fled at once. Still farther on, is the scene of the third tragedy of that day, when the victorious French, having been, in their turn, by a piece of great good luck, beaten by the valorous [General William] Johnson at his entrenchment by the lake, were met at this place on their retreat, by [Captain William] McGinnis, and almost cut to pieces. Bloody Pond, a little dark, slimy sheet of stagnant water, covered with weeds and pond-lilies, and shadowed by the gloomy forest around it, is the place where hundreds of dead bodies were flung after the battle, and where the bones still lie.† A few miles farther, and Lake George lay before us, the mountains and water confused and indistinct in the mist. We rode into Caldwell, took supper—a boat—and then a bed.

July 17. Caldwell.—The tavern is full of fashionable New Yorkers—all of a piece. Henry (White) and myself both look like the Old Nick [the devil], and are evidently looked upon in a manner corresponding. I went this morning to see [Fort] William Henry. The old fort is much larger than I had thought; the earthen mounds cover many acres. It stood on the southwest extremity of the lake close by the water. The enterprising genius of the inhabitants has made a road directly through the ruins, and turned bastion, moat, and glacis into a flourishing cornfield, so that the spot so celebrated in our colonial history is now scarcely to be distinguished. Large trees are growing on the untouched parts, especially on the embankment along the

---

*Parkman is referring to the first engagement on September 8, 1755, when 1,000 troops commanded by Colonel Ephraim Williams and 200 Native Americans led by King Hendrick were attacked south of Lake George by a French force under Baron de Dieskau.

**Colonel Williams' bones were reinterred in the Thompson Memorial Chapel at Williams College on June 20, 1920.

***In 1854 the alumni of Williams College erected a marble obelisk upon the rock as a memorial.

†A detachment of 120 New Hampshire troops under Captain Nathaniel Folsom and 90 New York troops led by Captain William McGinnis from Fort Lyman (Edward) surprised a French force of Canadians and Indians who were scalping and looting the dead bodies from Colonel Williams' detachment. The French who were killed in the ensuing battle were said to have been thrown into "Bloody Pond."

"View of the Town of Caldwell" by Mallory showing a steamboat,
probably the *William Caldwell*, at the Lake House dock.
(New York State Historical Association)

lake shore. In the rear, a hundred or two yards distant, is a gloomy wood of pines, where the lines of [Marquis de] Montcalm can easily be traced. A little behind these lines is the burying-place of the French who fell during that memorable siege. The marks of a thousand graves can be seen among the trees, which, of course, have sprung up since. Most of them have been opened, and bones and skulls dug up in great numbers.* A range of mountains tower above this pine forest—Cobble Mount—The Prospect, etc., the haunt of bears and rattlesnakes. The ruins of Fort George** are on a low hill of limestone, a short distance southeast of William Henry—of stone and in much better preservation than the other, for they are under the special protection of Mr. [William] Caldwell, the owner of the village; but they have no historical associations connected with them. I noticed some curious marks of recent digging in William Henry, and asked an explanation of an old fellow who was hoeing corn in a field close by. He said that some fools had come up the lake with a wizard and a divining rod to dig for money in the ruins.*** They went at

---

*Apparently, bones from the eighteenth century were often found in the next century. "While digging cellars for his house (1860) and vault for ice-house (1867) [Dr. James Cromell of Lake George] exhumed thirteen skulls."[12]

**Observing Fort George the next year (1843), Parkman recorded that "near Ft. George I saw a flat rough stone with an inscription as follows '1776 Here lies Stephen Hodges' and more unreadable. Other apparent graves are near."[13] Built in 1759 under General Jeffery Amherst, Fort George was also occupied during the American Revolution. Parkman's 1878 journal written at Lake George noted "the ruins of Fort George [are] chiefly stone laid in mortar. The work is small, but the walls are of very considerable height & thickness."[14]

***The legends of lost gold payrolls from the French and Indian War continue to the present day. The stories apparently began in the early nineteenth century.[15]

midnight for many successive nights and dug till daylight. I undertook to climb the Prospect [Mountain]—three miles high, without a path. I guided myself by the sun and the summits of the mountains, and got to the top almost suffocated with heat and thirst. The view embraced the whole lake as far as Ty [Ticonderoga]. All was hazy and indistinct, only the general features of the scene could be distinguished in the dull atmosphere. The lake seemed like a huge river, winding among mountains. Came down, dined, and went to church. The church is a minute edifice, with belfry and bell exactly like a little school-house. It might hold easily about sixty. About thirty were present—countrymen; cute, sly, sunburnt slaves of Mammon [wealth]; maidens of sixty and sixteen; the former desperately ugly, and black bonnets, frilled caps, peaked noses and chins, and an aspect diabolically prim and saturnine [gloomy]; the latter for the most part remarkably pretty and delicate. For a long time the numerous congregation sat in a pious silence, waiting for the minister. At last he came, dodged into a door behind the pulpit, and presently reappeared and took his place, arrayed in a white surplice [vestment gown] with black facing. He was very young, and Yankee ploughboy was stamped on every feature. Judge of my astonishment when he began to read the Episcopal service in voice so clear and manner so appropriate that I have never heard better in Boston. He read the passage in Exodus quite appropriate to the place, beginning "The Lord is a Man of war." In his sermon, which was polished and even elegant every figure was taken from warfare.

One of Montcalm's lines ran northwest of the tavern toward the mountains.* Two or three years ago, in digging for some purpose, a great quantity of deer, bear, and moose bones were found here, with arrows and hatchets, which the tavern-keeper thinks marked the place of some Indian feast. The spikes and timbers of sunken vessels may be seen in strong sunlight, when the water is still, at the bottom of the lake, along the southern beach. Abercrombie sunk his boats here.** There are remains of batteries on French Mount, and the mountain north of it, I suppose to command the road from Fort Edward. This evening visited the French graves. I wrote this at camp, July 18th. Just turned over my ink-bottle and spilt all the ink.

July 18th. Camp at Diamond Island.—Set out this morning in an excellent boat, hired at Caldwell. The sun rose over the mountains like a fiery ball of copper—portending direful heat. The lake was still as glass, the air to the last degree sultry and oppressive. Rowed to the western side and kept to the banks, which were rocky and covered with birch, spruce, cypress, and other trees. We landed occasionally, and fished as we went along. About ten o'clock stretched across Middle Bay, and got bread, pork, and potatoes at a farmhouse, with which our fish we regaled ourselves at a place halfway down the bay. Here I wrote my journal for yesterday; we slept an hour or two on the ground, bathed, and read [a book of Oliver] Goldsmith, which Henry brought in his knapsack. At three we proceeded to explore the bay to its

---

*In 1757 troops under the Marquis de Montcalm dug siege lines at the southwest corner of the lake in the attack on Fort William Henry.

**General James Abercromby sank bateaux and other vessels in late 1758 for winter storage. Parkman viewed some of the sunken bateaux along the southeastern shore of the lake.[16] Undoubtedly, he also observed the remains of a 44-foot military sloop in 15 feet of water near the present-day steamboat dock at Lake George Village. The vessel of unknown origin was raised in 1903 and dismantled for souvenirs.[17]

bottom, returned, made for Diamond Island, which is now uninhabited, prepared our camp, and went to sleep.

July 19th—I woke this morning about as weak and spiritless as well could be. All enterprise and activity was fairly gone; how I cannot tell, but I cursed the weather as the most probable cause. Such has been the case with me, to a greater or less degree, for the last three or four weeks. Rowed today along the eastern shore. Explored several beautiful bays, in one of which was a curious cave in the rock. Heat suffocating. The water of the lake is equal to most spring water, and we drank it in great quantities. The scenery thus far, though extremely fine, had disappointed me, probably on account of the extravagant ideas I had formed of it; but now it grew

"Lake George Looking North from Tongue Mountain Shore."
Painting by David Johnson.
(Adirondack Museum)

continually more imposing. A strong south wind, too, sprang up and raised the glassy flat surface of the lake into waves, and, in part, dissipated the mists that hung over all the mountains. The boat began to pitch and plunge with an enlivening motion, and the motion in the air strengthened and invigorated us. We dashed through the water at a rapid rate. At last we saw a little white flag fluttering among the trees, by way of sign to a tavern [in Bolton Landing]. We landed, dined, and set out again. The wind almost blew a gale. The little boat was borne up and down with such violence that we judged best to keep near the shore, so as to be able to get our baggage in case of an overturn. White sat in the stern grunting a German song, about as intelligible to me as to him, while I rowed. We reached what in the War-time was Gankasky [Northwest] Bay, close to the Narrows. Here the storm grew so furious that we landed at the point of the bay—the extremity of Tongue Mt. The lake plunged and foamed like the ocean. At this point it is full of islands and flanked by noble mountains. This is the scene of the canoe-chase in *The Last of the Mohicans*.* While White had gone off shooting, I swam across the strait to one of the islands, from which the view down the lake was the finest water scene I ever saw. It was a perspective of mountains towering above the narrow sheet filled with islands, against which the white breakers were now fiercely dashing. But everything was obscured with mist. When the wind became less violet we rowed to an island in the middle, where we are now encamped.[18]

July 20th—Entered the narrows this morning and rowed among all the islands and all along the shores. White trailed a line behind the boat, by which means he caught a large bass. Scenery noble, but mists still on the mountains. Passed along the rocky and precipitous shore of Tongue Mount[ain], stopped and fished and caught so many that we flung several dozen away. About eleven o'clock landed on a little island, built a fire and prepared dinner, White officiating as cook with considerable skill. We rowed down the lake again and soon cleared the narrows. On our right rose the ridges of Black Mount[ain], the loftiest summit on the lake. We stopped at a log cabin at its base, where an old man of eighty was splitting shingles under a shed, surrounded by a group of women and children, who, with becoming modesty, fled at our approach. The old man lost no time in informing us that he

"Black Mountain." Painted by Thomas Creswick from a sketch (1838) by William Henry Bartlett, engraved by Robert Wallis. The print shows the steamboat *William Caldwell* in the background and a deer about to be clubbed following a chase by hunting dogs.
(Author's collection)

*In chapter 20 of James Fenimore Cooper's *The Last of the Mohicans*, Hawkeye, Chingachgook, and Uncas, with Colonel Munro and Duncan Heyward, are chased by Huron and Mingos through the Narrows in canoes.

did not belong there, but had only come to work for the family. We went up to the house—one of the most wretched cabins I ever saw—inhabited by two families, French and American...We left and kept down the lake, with a fierce wind sweeping down after us and driving the mists before it. The water was a dark glistening blue, with lines of foam on the crests of the waves; huge shadows of clouds coursed along the mountains. The little islands would be lighted up at one instant by a stream of sunshine falling on them, and almost making their black pines transparent, and the next moment they would be suddenly darkened, and all around be glittering with a sudden burst of light from the opening clouds. We passed under Black Mount[ain], whose precipices and shaggy woods wore a very savage and impressive aspect in that peculiar weather, and kept down the lake seven miles to Sabbath Day Point. High and steep mountains flanked the lake the whole way. In front, at some distance, they seemed to slope gradually away, and a low green point, with an ancient dingy house upon it, closed the perspective. This was Sabbath Day Point, the famous landing-place of many a huge army.* We noticed two abrupt mountains on our left, and steering under them, found the most savage and warlike precipices we had yet seen. One impended over the lake like the stooping wall of an old castle.** Its top was fringed with trees, which seemed bushes from the height, and great fragments of broken rock were piled around its base. We ran our boat on the beach of Sabbath Day Point and asked lodgings at the house. An old woman, after a multitude of guesses and calculations, guessed as how she could accommodate us with a supper and bed, though she couldn't say nohow how we should like it, seeing as how she warn't used to visitors. The house was an old, rickety, dingy shingle palace, with a potato garden in front, hogs perambulating the outhouses, and a group of old men and women engaged in earnest conversation in the tumble-down portico. The chief figure was an old gray-haired man, tall and spare as a skeleton, who was giving some advice to a chubby old lady about her corns.

"Well, now," said the old lady, "I declare they hurt me mighty bad."

"I'll give you something to cure them right off."

"What is it? I hope it ain't snails. I always hated snails since I was a baby, but I've heard say they are better for corns nor nothing else at all," etc., etc.

The old man was a revolutionary pensioner, Captain [Samuel] Patchin by name, and stouthearted, hale, and clever by nature.*** He is the owner of the place, but the house is occupied by another family—old man, old woman, and a numerous progeny of youthful giants and ogresses, but the whole "calculated on" removing to Illinois in the fall. There were visitors of the family also, the most conspicuous of whom was a little Canadian Frenchman, with his family, who professed himself a mighty adept at angling, but whose pretensions were found on trial to be greatly above his merits. The whole household presently gathered under the old portico, where stories of revolutionary campaigns, rattlesnakes, deadly beasts, and deadly diseases flew from mouth to mouth with awful rapidity. After a few rifle trials with

*General James Abercromby's 15,000-man expedition against Fort Carillon occupied Sabbath Day Point for six hours on July 5, 1758.

**Parkman probably observed Deer Leap.

***Captain Samuel Patchin, a veteran of the American Revolution, had built a home on Sabbath Day Point prior to 1800. Patchin died on March 18, 1844, and is buried in a cemetery adjacent to Route 9N in Hague.

the aforesaid youthful giants we took supper, and went on the lake after bass, with the Frenchman in our boat, and the young men following in their own. We had good success—Henry and I caught a dozen apiece, some of very large size, while the vainglorious Frenchman had to be content with one wretched perch. The Captain to-night sent his dogs to the mountains in the care of a neighbor of his in hopes that a deer may be roused and driven to the lake in the morning. One of the children is playing with the tail of a rattlesnake, killed last night by one of the men in the middle of the road.

"Sabbath Day Point." Sketch by William Henry Bartlett (1838),
engraved by H. Adlard.
(Author's collection)

July 21st.—Fished for bass off shore with rifle and fowling piece ready, in case the deer should take to the lake. But we waited in vain. It turned out afterwards that the hound had proved unmanageable and refused to follow the scent. We caught fish enough, landed, and with Myrtle Bailey, one of the young Brobdingagians [giants from *Gulliver's Travels*], a simple, goodnatured, strong-handed, grinning son of the plough, set out on a rattlesnake hunt on the mountain back of the Point. Here was the summer den of a swarm of these beasts, who thence infested the whole country. Myrtle told us that they went to their winter den in autumn; then repaired to their summer den in spring, where they educated their children; which parental office being discharged, the[y] scattered at large over the rocks. We climbed through tangled woods and steep sunscorched ledges till we came to the edge of a lofty precipice which towers above the lake. We looked down upon piles of confused rocks and forests of blasted and stunted trees along the foot of the cliff and washed by the lake on the other side. Some crows were wheeling and cawing over the tree tops, looking like black beetles from the height above. Steadying myself by putting one arm round a gnarled tree I leaned from the precipice and discharged "Satan" [Parkman's name for his rifle] into the gulf. The crows ceased their cawing and took themselves off with all speed. We soon reached a still higher point, which commanded the noblest view of the lake I had yet seen. It stretched north and south between its mountains, visible for two thirds of its length, its waters glistening in the sun, dotted with a hundred green islands. As it wound down through the huge

"Lake George." Painting by Andrew W. Melrose.
(Adirondack Museum)

valley, it seemed like a still clear stream in the bottom of a deep glen, rather than a lake. The waters dwindled to nothing in comparison to the towering mountains that environed them. There would be no finer place of gentlemen's seats than this, but now, for the most part, it is occupied by a race of boors about as uncouth, mean, and stupid as the hogs they seem chiefly to delight in. The captain's household is an exception.

We found the den, but no snakes—they had already dispersed. We looked long and anxiously among the rocks, but in vain, and we had to descend. Near this Mt. is another—mentioned before—still more steep and rocky, called Buck Mt. [Deer Leap] from the exploit of a hunted deer, many years ago, who being hard pressed on the top by hunters, leaped from the precipice for the lake, but fell whirling upon the rocks at the bottom and sprinkled them with his blood for rods around. Afternoon: fished again—evening: fished again, and caught a very large bass—all in company of Myrtle, whose luck not satisfying him, he cursed the "darned cursed fish" in most fervent style.[19]

July 22nd.—Left old Patchin's this morning, he having previously exhorted me to come and buy his place, which he says I may have for $5,000. A strong south wind compelled us to run toward Ty. We rowed six miles down the lake—mountains less high than before, lake broad. In front lay a confused mass of precipitous mountains, apparently stretching across and barring the passage. On the left was a hamlet [Hague] at the foot of a range of hills, for which we steered, in order to put a letter into the post-office, which we knew to be there. We broke an oar when within about half a mile, and paddled to shore with great difficulty through a great surf which was dashing against the beach like the waves of the ocean. We found the post-office a neat little tavern, kept by one [Nathaniel] Garfield, entitled the Judge.* He referred us to a carpenter who promised to make an oar forthwith, and worked six hours upon it, an interval which I spent chiefly in wandering about the country. I followed the course of a rocky brook, which came down a valley, with a little road running along its side, with an occasional cabin or mill, or narrow clearing breaking upon the forest.** One old mill stood by the roadside where the stream tumbled in a broken line of foam over a mass of rock into a basin beneath, above which the building stood. Fantastic rocks, crowned with trees and shrubs, leaned above the basin and darkened the whirling waters below, while the dripping logs and walls of the mill on the other side, and the high rocks and waterfall in front,gave a sort of picturesque aspect to the place that I never hoped to see the companion of any Yankee edifice. Going on farther, I found other mills in abundance, and at last one which stood on the top of a deep descent of rock, flanked by the woods, down the surface of which the water came gliding in a thread so small that I wondered what had become of the stream I had seen so large before. Listening, I heard the heavy plunging of water, apparently from under ground. I looked all about, and could see no channel; but the noise grew louder as I approached the woods on the left. I force my way among the trees and came to the edge of a ravine not ten feet wide, but so deep that, leaning over, I could distinguish nothing but dark moss-grown rocks, while the noise of the water came up from the gulf with an appalling din. I went to the foot of the rocks and found the place where the water came glancing furiously out from the shelter of rocks and bushes, and following this guide by means of fallen logs and timbers, entered what seemed to be the mouth of a damp, gloomy cavern. The rocky walls of the ravine rose on each side some sixty or seventy feet, dripping with continual moisture. When I had got a little farther on, I could see a mass of rocks piled up in front, with the water tumbling over it in a sheet of foam. The cliffs leaning toward each other overhead, and the bushes that projected from them, rendered the place almost dark, though here and there the jagged rocks were illumined by a faint stream of sunshine. Just above the cataract could be seen the old green timbers and wheels of a mill, built across the ravine. The whole very much resembled the Flume at Franconia [N.H.].

*Nathaniel Garfield built a two-story tavern in Hague about 1810 on a 122 1/2-acre parcel of land near the lake. Garfield was a justice of the peace and had served as the town supervisor in 1825, 1830, and 1836. Garfield died on September 22, 1853, at the age of 60 and is buried in an old Hague cemetery next to Route 9N. A large room on the second floor of Garfield's tavern provided space for town meetings and social gatherings. The tavern burned in 1863 and subsequently became the site of the three-story Phoenix Hotel. The Phoenix burned in 1956 and was replaced by the Beachside which was razed in 1991.

**Parkman was following the course of present-day Route 8 along Hague Brook.

Returned to Garfield's and found there Mr. Gibbs, with his wife, the "vocalist." Presently the man appeared with the oar finished. White undertook to pay him with a Naumkeag Bank bill, the only bills we had.*

"Don't know nothing about that money. Wait till Garfield comes, and he'll tell whether it's genuine or not."

"There's the paper," said I. "Look and see." He looked; all was right.

"Well, are you satisfied?"

"How do I know but what that ere bill is counterfeit? It has a sort of counterfeit look about it to my eyes. Deacon, what do you say to it?"

The Deacon put on his spectacles, held the bill to the light, turned it this way and that, tasted of it, and finally pronounced that, according to his calculation, it was good. But the carpenter was not contented.

"Bijah, you're a judge of bills. What do you think?"

Bijah, after a long examination, gave his opinion that it was counterfeit. All parties were beginning to wax wroth [wrathful], when the Judge entered and decided that the bill was good.

We pushed from the beach and steered down the lake, passed some islands, and beheld in front of us two green mountains, standing guard over a narrow strait of dark waters between. Both were of solid granite, rising sheer from the lake, with a few stunted trees thinly clothing their nakedness. Behind each stretched away a long train of inferior mountains, like satellites of some gloomy despot. One of these mountains was the noted Roger's Slide, the other almost as famous, Anthony's Nose. Both had witnessed in their day the passage of twenty vast armies in the strait between, and there was not an echo on either but had answered to the crack of rifles and screams of dying men. We skirted the base of the Nose—for which sentimental designation I could find no manner of reason—till we arrived opposite the perpendicular front of his savage neighbor. About a mile of water was between. We ran the boat ashore on a shelving rock, and looked for a camping-place among the precipices. We found, to our surprise, at the side of a steep rock, amid a growth of cedars and hemlocks, a little enclosure of logs, like a diminutive cabin without a roof. We made beds in it of hemlock boughs—there was just space enough—brought up our baggage and guns, ate what supper we had, and essayed to sleep. But we might as well have slept under a showerbath of melted iron. In that deep sheltered spot, bugs, mosquitoes and "no-see-ems" swarmed innumerable. Our nets protected us from mosquitoes only. A million red-hot needles were gouged into hands, faces—everywhere. White cursed the woods and me for leading him into such a scrape. I laughed at him and the bugs as long as I could, but as last my philosophy gave way, and the utmost point of my self-command was to suffer in silence. It grew dark, and the wind came rushing along the side of the mountain, and stirring the trees over our heads with a lulling sound, and we were well tired with the labor of the day, so we fell at last into a sort of unquiet and half-conscious doze, ever and anon [later] interrupted by a muttered grumble or a motion to scratch some severely affected part. Late in the night I was awaked from this blissful state by sounds rather startling in that solitude—the loud voices and shouts of men close by. I sat up and listened,

---

*Henry paid the bill with a note issued by a bank in Salem, Massachusetts. Before checking accounts, banks issued bank notes in various denominations which circulated in the economy as a medium of exchange and could be redeemed for specie (gold or silver) at the bank of origin. Because there were so many bank notes in circulation, counterfeit notes were fairly common.

"Rogers' Slide." Painted by Thomas Creswick from a sketch by
William Henry Bartlett (1838), engraved by Charles Cousen.
(Author's collection)

but the moaning of the wind and the dash of the water against the shore prevented
my distinguishing a syllable, until there came, louder than the rest, "Now then,—
damn it, pull for your lives; every stroke helps." In an instant it flashed across my
bewildered brain that some scoundrels were making off with our boat, and I got
clear of my blanket and ran down to the shore, first shaking White to wake him.
All I could see through the darkness was that our boat was safe, and that another
was drawn up beside it, when a man sprung up suddenly from the grass, with a
muttered curse, and demanded who I was. We made mutual explanations. He had
tried to run up the lake from Ty, with a companion in another boat, but his strength
had failed against a strong contrary wind, and he had landed, leaving his friend, who
had a long distance to go, to keep on.

The wind drove the bugs from the shore and made it a much more comfortable
resting-place; so thither we adjourned and spread our blankets near the ragamuffin
boatman. We built a little fire, and our new friend and White enjoyed a social pipe
together.* As the light fell on his matted hair; his grisly, unshorn countenance,
haggard with drinking; and his battered and patched clothes, and then again flared
high upon the cliffs and savage trees, and streamed across the water, I thought that
even that shore had seldom seen a more outlandish group—we in our blankets, he
in his rags. He told us that the camp where we had been sleeping was made by a man
last summer who lived here for the purpose of fishing. "He was a sort of a villain-like
character," said our acquaintance; "he went and stole fish off my ground, damn him;

*Before the widespread use of cigarettes, tobacco was smoked in long-stemmed clay pipes.

and then again he killed his own son right down here in this place. The old man got drunk, and said he would have the boy over to this camp, and so he got him in his old boat with him, though the boy's mother cried about it, and said she'd keep him at home, and the boy himself felt afeared to go. Well, the old fellow was so far gone that when he got to the landing place—there, just where your boat is drawed up on the rock—he forgot he had his son with him, and ran his boat again the rock and tumbled himself out of it in such style that she overset, and pitched the boy into the deep water. The instant the old man heerd his son holler, it sobered him up in no time, but he nor the boy neither couldn't swim a mite, and so he stood on the rock and seed him drown, and then came over and told the folks of it in the morning. That ere cured him of his tricks for one while, but within a week or two he has been up to them agin, and I ketched him on my fish grounds last Sunday—may I be d—d if I didn't dress him."

With this dismal legend did our new friend beguile the hours of the night-watch. At length we all fell asleep and did not wake till day. The ragamuffin said he was hungry, on which we gave him a piece of bread, got all things on board our boat, and set out again for Patchin's, where we had left some linen to be washed. That morning was the most toilsome we have passed. The wind was dead against us; the waves ran with a violence I had never seen before except on the ocean. It required the full force of both arms to hold the boat on her course. If we slackened our efforts for a single moment, she would spin round and drive backward. We had about twelve miles to row under these agreeable auspices. "Well," said White, "you call this fun, do you? To be eaten by bugs all night, and work against head winds all day isn't according to my taste, whatever you may think of it."

The Cooks Islands in Hague where Parkman camped in 1842.
(Photo by the author)

"Are you going back out?" said I. "Back out, yes; when I get into a bad scrape I back out of it as quickly as I can"—and so he went on with marvellous volubility to recount his grievances. Lake George, he called a "scrubby-looking place" —said there was no fishing in it—he hated camping and would have no more of it—and he wouldn't live so for another week to save his life, etc. Verily what is one man's meat is another man's poison. What troubles me more than his treachery to our plans is his want of cash, which will make it absolutely necessary to abandon our plan of descending through Maine. His scruples I trust to overcome in time.

We reached Patchin's at last, and were welcomed by the noble old veteran as cordially as if we were his children. We dined, and sat in his portico, listening to his stories. He is eighty-six. Three years ago he danced with great applause at a country party, and still his activity and muscular strength are fully equal to those of most men in the prime of life. He must once have been extremely handsome; even now his features are full and regular, and when he tells his stories he always sets his hat on one side of his head, and looks the very picture of an old warrior. He was several times [a] prisoner. Once, when in Quebec, an English officer asked him, as he tells the story, "What's your name?" "Patchin." "What, Hell-Hound Patchin?" says he.

At another time an officer struck him without any provocation but that of his being a rebel. Patchin sprang on him and choked him till he fainted, in the streets of Quebec. He served in the Indian campaigns [against] Butler and Brant about Fort Stanwix,* at the recovery of Fort Ann[e] after it was taken by [General John] Burgoyne; was present when Sir John Johnson fled from the Mohawk with his property, and tells how narrowly that Tory made his escape from the pursuing party on [Lake] Champlain.** He wants us to come back and hear more of his stories.

We left him and his family and ran down the lake again, bathed at an island, and, White still continuing contumacious [disagreeable] I left him at Garfield's, and proceeded to camp by myself at an island two or three miles off.*** I hauled the boat on shore and prepared to wash my pantaloons, an operation I could commit to no one else, since I should have to wander breechless in the interim. I put the breeks in the water to the windward of the island, and, having suitably pounded them down with stones, left them to the operation of the waves while I made ready my camp. Presently, taking them out and wringing them, I strung them on a tree hard by to dry, wrapped myself in my blanket and laid down. I read a book of White's as long as I could see. Two boats passed by me as I lay, and the occupants turned a wondering gaze upon me, especially an old lady in green spectacles, whom her son was rowing down the lake. I slept comfortably and in the morning went back to Garfield's, where I found White, Gibbs, and his wife. The Judge was

---

*Colonel John Butler, who had served on the New York frontier during the French and Indian War, led Butler's Rangers against Mohawk Valley settlements during the American Revolution. Joseph Brant, or Thayendanegea, a Mohawk chief and brother-in-law to Sir William Johnson, also fought for the British during the French and Indian War and the American Revolution. Fort Stanwix, built in 1758 in present-day Rome, New York, was successfully defended by American troops against a three-week siege by a British force under Barry St. Leger.

**Sir John Johnson, son of Sir William Johnson, was Barry St. Leger's second-in-command in 1777. In the spring of 1780, Johnson led a 500-man raiding party through Lake Champlain to attack villages in the Mohawk Valley; Johnson's party returned to Crown Point with American prisoners and traveled back to Canada.

***Parkman probably camped in the Cooks Islands adjacent to the Hague shoreline.

hospitable and kind, and we instantly planned a fishing party for the next day. To-day, being Sunday, I have stayed at home for the most part, written letters, journals,etc. The family are essentially "genteel" in the true sense of the word, the Judge a gentleman, his wife a lady, both polite by nature. The lady has a pretty flower garden—with no sunflowers in it. There is an old Irish gardener, whose department is managed in a most exemplary manner, and who has spent half the afternoon in expounding the superiority of the shamrock over the rose and thistle. In short, the whole establishment is to the dwellings around it what Mr. Cushing's place is to a common farm.*

Monday, July 25th. Breakfasted at nine, and went shooting with Gibbs—the ostensible object being a robin pie, the true one of our own amusement. We made a great destruction among the small birds. The weapon I carried was used in the Revolution by Garfield's father. It was six feet long, slender, small bore, light breech of polished oak, flint lock. It had sent many a fatal charge of buckshot. In the afternoon went fishing with Gibbs and White, and witnessed the arrival of the great Nabob, Mr. [William] Caldwell, the founder and owner of the village of that name, who comes here on a long-promised visit in a little barge of his own, with flags at prow and stern, and a huge box of wines for his private refreshment.** Ask anybody here what kind of a man Mr. Caldwell is, and he will answer with a shrug of the

"Fort Ticonderoga in 1848." Painting by Russell Smit.
(Fort Ticonderoga Museum)

*A. Loring Cushing, a noted Boston attorney, apparently owned an impressive estate.

**William Caldwell, son of the original founder of the village of the same name and an entrepreneur in his own right, owned a good deal of property in Caldwell and also held mortgages on other real estate in the area.

"Ticonderoga Village, From the Road to the Fort" by W. R. Miller. Detail
of a print from *Gleason's Pictorial Drawing-Room Companion*, 1854.
(Author's collection)

shoulders, or if he is unusually delicate or cautious, it will be, "Oh, he is a very good sort of a man," or else, in the emphatic tone of one defending an accused person, "He is a very clever man, sir, a very clever man." But the truth is that he is a consummate tyrant and fool. He refused to patronize the steamboat unless it was called after his name, and fired a salute on approaching the village, whenever he was present, which is accordingly done. It is impossible to get any favor from him without the humblest deference. He treats the townsmen, his vassals, with favor or the contrary according as they yield him due reverence. To-night, the report of a piece from his boat gave the signal of his approach. Patrick, the Irishman, stood on the beach with the Judge's best gun and answered with a salute, for so it must be, or the great man would be displeased. Somehow or other, the Judge himself, though I believe him as sensible a man as I ever met, seems to regard his humble roof as honored by the mighty presence. [William] Caldwell is of course reported vastly rich, as perhaps he is, but he got all his property from his father [James Caldwell], an Irish emigrant who built himself a fortune by trading at Albany.[20]

We were to have gone toward Ticonderoga to-night, but an easterly storm with rain prevents us, and compels us to remain here and sleep under a roof.

Tuesday, July 26th. The great man [William Caldwell] and his retinue occupied every nook and corner of the little tavern. Two of his satellites were quartered in the same room with us and entertained us all night with snorings so diversified and so powerful that I wished myself at camp in spite of the storm. Garfield has a very good rifle, which he wanted to "swap" for mine. As his has some important advantages over mine, in size of bore, and is only inferior to it in roughness of mounting and in being rather worn by use, I agreed to make a trial with him, which occupied half the morning, and showed no marked superiority in either gun. I therefore declined the "swap." Left Garfield's at noon, and rowed down to Ticonderoga. Passed close under Roger's Slide, whose bare perpendicular sheets of granite, with their deep gullies and weather stains, and stunted shrubs in their crevices, present as dismal and savage an aspect as ever I saw, except at the White Mountains. Found the steamboat* at the wharf at the outlet of the lake, and were welcomed on board by old Dick,** whose acquaintance we made at Caldwell, who now composed her whole crew, the rest being seated under a tree on shore. Dick showed us his rattlesnakes again, and told us how a fellow once stole them, shut up in their box, mistaking the rattling for the sound of some valuable piece of machinery; but when he examined his prize and found the truth of the case, he dropped the box in the woods and ran for his life. We consigned our boat to the Captain to be carried back to Caldwell and got on a stage we found at the wharf, which carried us to the village of Ty. It is a despicable manufacturing place, straggling and irregular—mills, houses, and heaps of lumber—situated in a broad valley with the outlet of Lake George running through the middle—a succession of fierce rapids, with each its sawmill. I bespake me here a pair of breeches of a paddy tailor, who asked me if I did not work on board the steamboat, a question which aggravated me not a little. I asked a fellow the way to the fort. "Well," said he, "I've heerd of such a place, seems to me, but I

*Built in 1837 at Cooks Landing in Ticonderoga, the 110-foot steamboat *William Caldwell* offered the first through service via land connections by carriage to Lake Champlain.

**Richard Shear, or "Old Dick," made a meager living at Lake George doing odd jobs and charging tourists a fee to see his box of rattlesnakes.

never seen it, and couldn't tell ye where it be." "You must be an idiot," thought I; but I found his case by no means singular. At last, I got the direction and walked about two miles before I saw the remains of a high earthen parapet with a ditch running through a piece of wood[s] for a great distance. This, I suppose was the place where the French beat off Abercrombie's army [in 1758]. Farther on, in a great plain scantily covered with wood[s], were breastworks and ditches in abundance, running in all directions, which I took for the work of Amherst's besieging armies [of 1759]. Still farther, were two or three square redoubts. At length, mounting a little hill, a cluster of gray, ruined walls, like an old château, with mounds of earth and heaps of stones about them, appeared crowning an eminence in front.* When I reached them, I was astonished at the extent of the ruins. Thousands of men might have encamped in the area. All around were ditches of such depth, that it would be death to jump down, with walls of masonry sixty feet high. Ty stands on a promontory, with [Lake] Champlain on one side and the outlet of Lake George on the other; his cannon commanded the passage completely. At the very extremity is the oldest part of the fortress—a huge mass of masonry with walls sinking sheer down to the two lakes. All kinds of weeds and vines are clambering over them. The senseless blockheads in the neighborhood have stolen tons and tons of the stone to build their walls and houses of—may they meet their reward.

Remains of barracks at Fort Ticonderoga.
(Postcard, author's collection)

*Seven years earlier Nathaniel Hawthorne visited the ruins of Fort Ticonderoga and sat down "in one of the roofless barracks. . .The one in which I sat was long and narrow, as all the rest had been, with peaked gables. The exterior walls were nearly entire, constructed of gray, flat, unpicked stones, the aged strength of which promised long to resist the elements, if no other violence should precipitate their fall. The roof, floors, partitions, and the rest of the wood-work, had probably been burnt, except some bars of staunch old oak, which were blackened with fire, but still remained imbedded into the window-sills and over the doors."[21]

Notes:

1. Francis Parkman, *Montcalm and Wolfe* (1884; reprint ed., New York: Atheneum, 1984), xxxii.
2. Charles Haight Farnham, *A Life of Francis Parkman* (Boston: Little, Brown, and Company, 1901), 66-67.
3. Ibid., 73.
4. Ibid., 187; See also Samuel Eliot Morison, *Francis Parkman (1823-1893)* (Boston: Massachusetts Historical Society, 1973), 3.
5. Howard Doughty, *Francis Parkman* (1962; reprint ed., Cambridge, MA.: Havard University Press, 1983), 29.
6. Farnham, 327-28; See also Doughty, 141-44.
7. Doughty, 370, 97.
8. As an example, compare Parkman's quotation of Father Roubaud at Fort William Henry in *Montcalm and Wolfe*, 294, to the version in Reuben Gold Thwaites, ed., *Travels and Explorations of the Jesuit Missionaries in New France* (Cleveland: The Burrows Brothers Company, 1900), Volume 70, 179; See also Francis P. Jennings, "Vanishing Indian: Francis Parkman Versus His Sources," *Pennsylvania Magazine of History and Biography* 87 (July 1963): 306-23; Modern writers have suggested that Parkman fabricated some of his research: "Parkman entirely invented the image of Indians demanding rum" prior to the 1757 massacre at Lake George. See Ian K. Steele, *Betrayals: Fort William Henry & the "Massacre"* (New York: Oxford University Press, 1990), 174. However, Parkman relied on French sources, whether correct or not, that made such an assertion. See "An Account of the Attack and Taking of Fort William Henry to the Marquise de Montcalm," in *Report of the Public Archives for the Year 1929*, ed. by Arthur G. Doughty (Ottawa: Public Archives of Canada, 1930), 96; See also E. G. O'Callaghan, ed., *Documents Relative to the Colonial History of the State of New York* (Albany: Weed, Parsons and Company, 1858), Volume 10, 633.
9. Parkman Collection, "Diary July - August 1842," 2nd Series, Volume 3, 31, Massachusetts Historical Society, Boston.
10. Francis Parkman, "Parkman at Lake George," *Scribner's Magazine*, July 1901, 23-30; See also "Diary," 7-31.
11. Mason Wade, ed., *The Journals of Francis Parkman* (New York: Harper & Brothers Publishers, 1947), Volume 1, 335.
12. A. W. Holden, *A History of the Town of Queensbury* (Albany: Joel Munsell, 1874), 311.
13. Wade, 1: 90.
14. Ibid, 2: 570.
15. Ibid., 1: 337.
16. *Lake George Mirror*, 10 June 1893.
17. Ogden J. Ross, *The Steamboats of Lake George 1817 to 1932* (Albany: Press of the Delaware and Hudson Railroad, 1932), 33; See also B. F. DeCosta, *Lake George: Its Scenes and Characteristics* (New York: Anson D. F. Randolph & Co., 1869), 63.
18. The preceding entry of July 19 was omitted from *Scribner's Magazine*; See "Diary," 10-12.
19. The July 21 entry came from "Diary," 16-18.
20. A portion of the July 25 entry came from "Diary," 28-29.
21. Nathaniel Hawthorne, "A Visit to Ticonderoga 100 years Ago," *The Bulletin of the Fort Ticonderoga Museum* 4 (January 1936): 14.

Part VI
Tourism Comes of Age

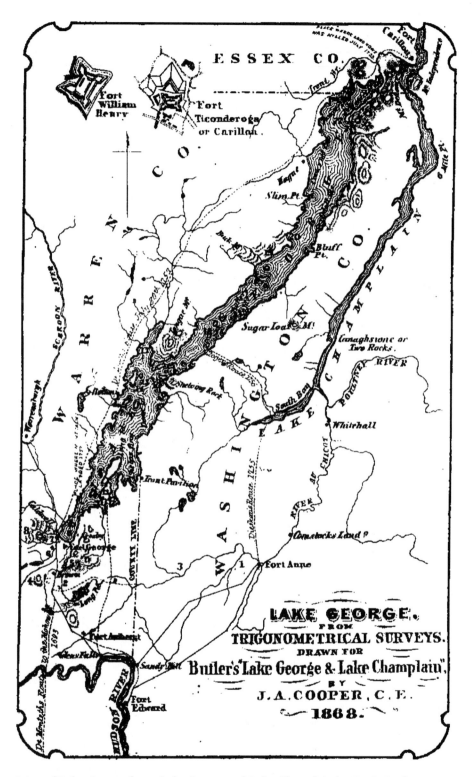

Map of Lake George from *Lake George and Lake Champlain* by B. C. Butler, 1868.

17. Thomas Nelson 1866

T HOMAS NELSON'S 1866 GUIDE to Lake George and Lake Champlain was one of the earliest travel books to feature the region as a separate entity. Nelson's guide appeared at a time when there were barely a dozen hotels and boarding houses at Lake George and just prior to the great hotel boom that would spread throughout the basin in the ensuing two decades. Nelson's guidebook was soon followed by the travel books of B. F. DeCosta, S. R. Stoddard, R. S. Styles, Charles H. Possons, and others.

After Francis Parkman's 1842 visit, many new inns were built along the lake. The most notable, the Fort William Henry Hotel, would dominate the travel scene at the southern end of the lake for the next century. Completed in 1855, the three-story, 200-foot long hotel had several additions constructed before the Nelson guide was published. By 1866 the facade had been lengthened to 337 feet, and a rear wing extended 250 feet.[1] Adjacent to the ruins of Fort William Henry, the luxurious hotel exhibited a fountain in the front yard facing the lake with accompanying walkways to a steamboat dock. Located on the southeastern shore of the lake, the United States Hotel was also built in the 1850s. According to Henry Marvin, author of *A Complete History of Lake George* published in 1853, the hotel had "the finest view of any point on Lake George" with bells that communicated with each room and baths connected to the main house.[2] The hotel, however, was not financially successful and was eventually sold to Francis Crosby who enlarged the inn to accommodate 200 guests and renamed it Crosbyside. The Trout Pavilion at Kattskill Bay in the town of Queensbury was known as "one resort of those who are fond of fine fish."[3] Originally built as a log cabin in 1810 for fishermen and hunters, the structure was later reconstructed as a three-story frame building. In Bolton Landing the old Mohican House and the Wells House continued to operate in the 1860s.

Following a fire in 1863, a rebuilt Garfields (possibly named the Lake George House) and the newly-opened Trout House accommodated travelers in the hamlet of Hague. A number of hotels in Ticonderoga served excursionists on the northern tour during this period, including The Pavilion adjacent to the ruins of Fort Ticonderoga. The Pavilion, originally built for William Ferris Pell in 1826, was rented as a fine hotel after 1838. A line of stagecoaches owned by William G. Baldwin connected the northern landing of Lake George to the Ticonderoga steamboat dock on Lake Champlain. Baldwin was noted for his cogent narrations of the historic sites along the way.

Caldwell, however, was still the center of the tourist industry at Lake George. Writing in the late 1860s, Benjamin F. DeCosta remarked that "the majority of transient visitors congregate at Caldwell, and here, all day long, the water is covered with boats containing parties engaged in fishing, rowing, and in excursions to the islands."[4] In addition to the new Fort William Henry Hotel and the United States Hotel, there were several smaller public houses, including the Caldwell House and the Central Hotel in Caldwell. The Lake House, the oldest, sizable hotel in the village, was still the preferred place of lodging for many tourists in the area. Amelia M. Murray, an English traveler visiting Lake George in September 1855, chose the Lake House which she described as "much pleasanter and less staring than a new place [Fort William Henry Hotel]."[5] Murray commented that the Lake House had "easy access to the water from a lawn, for bathing, fishing, or boating, and bowling and billiards."[6] Murray's journey coincided with the one hundredth anniversary of the 1755 victory of General William Johnson's provincial army over the French forces. The celebration involved a church ceremony and a cannon firing, followed by "a beautiful array of. . .twenty-four boats marshalled in line upon the lake or sweeping along in succession. . .when night came on, the darkness was illuminated by a liberal display of rockets and Roman candles."[7] At the time, a proposal was made to build a monument on the battlefield to William Johnson and King Hendrick, the fallen Mohawk chief. However, it was not until 1903 that a monument was erected.

A succession of steamboats catered to the tourist trade during this era. The steamboat *William Caldwell*, in service at the time of Francis Parkman's Lake George tour in 1842, was retired in 1850 and dismantled in the bay north of the Lake House. In 1853 Henry Marvin observed that the *William Caldwell* had been "stripped of all her valuable necessaries and was left lying upon the strand, where she has been subjected to the action of the elements for the past three years."[8] The vessel's saloon deck, however, survived for a time on the lawn of the Mohican House. Following the retirement of the *William Caldwell*, the *John Jay* provided the only passenger steamboat service on the lake. Completed in 1848 at Ticonderoga, the 142-foot *John Jay* plied the lake until the evening of July 29, 1856, when the 250-ton steamboat caught fire and sank in Hague. Six of the 80 passengers aboard

Opposite. Top: "Caldwell Village, New York." Woodcut by W. R. Miller from
   Gleason's Pictorial Drawing-Room Companion, 1854.
Middle: "Lake House" by H. Ferguson.
Bottom: Stern section of the steamboat *John Jay*, sunk in Hague on July 29, 1856.
(Photo by the author)

lost their lives in the disaster. Traveling on the *John Jay* three years earlier, Henry Marvin had ironically remarked that the "staunch vessel. . .[was] managed. . .with a due regard to speed, and to the higher importance, of confident safety to the traveller."[9] Within two weeks of the catastrophe in Hague, the directors of the Lake George Steam Boat Company authorized the construction of a new steamboat for the lake. With the engine, boilers, and machinery recovered from the *John Jay*, the 140-foot *Minne-Ha-Ha* was launched on May 12, 1857. The 75-horsepower engine propelled the sidewheeler at a speed of 13 miles per hour. The vessel burned six cords of wood on her ten-hour round trip of the lake and eventually required the purchase of wood lots by the steamboat company to supply the voracious appetite of the steam engine. In service during the period covered by the Nelson guidebook, the *Minne-Ha-Ha* had regularly scheduled stops at Caldwell, the Trout Pavilion, Bolton, Hague, and Cook's Landing (Baldwin) in Ticonderoga.

Roads continued to serve the traveling public in the region throughout the nineteenth century. In 1844 a plank road was constructed from Glens Falls to Caldwell. Plank roads in New York were built with 4-inch thick carved planks fastened to wooden rails or"sleepers." The eight-foot wide timbered roads or "farmer's railroads" made it much easier for horses to pull wagons and stagecoaches. By 1875 there were nearly 3,000 miles of plank roads in New York State. From Caldwell to Bolton Landing, however, a dirt/gravel roadbed had been in existence since the early nineteenth century. By the middle of the century, a rough road allowed carriages to carry some visitors over Tongue Mountain to Hague. Writing for *Harper's New Monthly Magazine* in 1853, Addison Richards mentioned that the road "sullenly winds its rugged and laborious way across the mountains. . . until it again descends to the lake near Garfield's [Hague]—a tedious traverse of a score of miles or more. . .From Sabbath-Day Point and Garfield's, the road again jogs merrily in the neighborhood of the water."[10] Richards noted, however, that the trip could "much more rapidly and pleasantly [be] made on the steamer."[11]

Nelson's guidebook to Lake George was similar to several dozen tourist and history tomes that the company produced in the late nineteenth century. Their books covered much of America and Europe, and many focused on British and American cities. In the decade following the Lake George and Lake Champlain volume, the company would publish two more books about the region: *Views of Saratoga* and *Views of the Hudson*. The Lake George and Lake Champlain book was illustrated with 12 remarkable oil-colored engravings that were prepared in London from photographs taken at the lake. The guidebook encompassed the historical sites around the lake, the hotels, and a panorama of images as seen by a visitor traveling from Caldwell to Ticonderoga aboard the steamboat *Minne-Ha-Ha*. Nelson incorporated a considerable amount of material from Addison Richards' earlier article on the lake.

Lake George[12]

It has been remarked that, in America, Lake George holds the place of Loch Katrine in Scotland—that it is the Tros[s]achs on a larger scale.* There is much truth in this. The scenery of this charming district is indeed most beautiful;—mingling the soft and gentle with the bold, magnificent, and picturesque. Historical association also lends additional interest to Lakes George and Champlain. In days long gone by, these wild solitudes were frequently disturbed by the savage wars of the Indian tribes who then possessed the land; and in later years, the peace of these beautiful lakes was broken by the loud artillery of modern warfare. Civilized soldiers and savages have fought side by side upon their shores, while fleets have contended on their waters. Indians, Americans, French, and British, have each played their part in the thrilling dramas and tragedies that have been enacted on and around these romantic waters.

Besides being in themselves extremely grand and beautiful, the lakes are easy of access; being situated near the head waters of the celebrated Hudson River, and on the route between New York and Canada.

We will take it for granted that the traveller has reached Saratoga Springs, that celebrated resort of lovers of mineral waters, fresh air, and amusement. We will suppose that he has visited the springs, tasted the health-giving waters, wondered at the extraordinary powers of the invalids, who rise early in order to drink, and sit up late in order to dance, and we will conclude that he is now desirous of visiting the two romantic lakes which form the subject of this little volume.

Let us proceed, then, by rail and plankroad, to Caldwell, at the head of Lake George. The distance is twenty-eight miles,—fifteen miles from Saratoga to Moreau Station, by the Troy and Whitehall line, and thirteen from thence to Caldwell. On the way we pass two spots of great interest and beauty,—Glen's Falls, nine miles and the Bloody Pond, four miles from the lake. These spots ought to be visited from Caldwell, and should have a day devoted to them. We have only time to glance at them in passing onward to the lakes, but we will pause to describe them particularly here.

Glen's Falls

are situated in the upper Hudson River, about nine miles distant from Lake George. The total descent is 72 feet, and width of the river at the top of the fall is about 900 feet. The water descends in a succession of leaps over rugged rocks, amid which it boils and foams, spirts and thunders, in magnificent style, especially when the river is in full-flood as it finds its way through the wild ravine, and emerges into the quiet lands below.

It was here that Cooper laid some of the scenes in his well-known tale, *The Last of the Mohicans*. Here the brave yet gentle Uncas, the stalwart Hawk-eye, and the other dramatis personoe of that exquisite novel, enacted some of their finest parts; and the caves below the bridge are associated with these stirring incidents of savage

*The Trossachs refers to a wooded valley in Scotland surrounding Loch (lake) Katrine. The Trossachs was the subject of several Nelson guidebooks from 1857 to 1884.

warfare. The traveller must be prepared, however, to throw himself rather violently into these memories of the past, and to indulge romantic associations under difficulties; for modern civilization, and progress, and peace, have planted on the stream mills of stern utility, and manufactories of sentiment-expelling common-placeness, which are apt to damp[en] the spirits of all, save the most ardent enthusiasts. Clank, whirl, and spin, have taken the place of the rifle-crack, the stealthy tread, and the war-whoop of the savage! Shortly after leaving Glen's Falls, the road passes near the

Bloody Pond

Here, in 1755, Colonel [Ephraim] Williams was killed in an engagement with the French and their Indian allies, under General Dieskau. An old boulder in the neighbourhood is still known as Williams' Rock. The slain, on both sides of this sanguinary fight, were thrown into the pond, which derives its name from this circumstance.

A little farther on, we obtain our first view of Horicon [Lake George], and a surpassingly beautiful view it is. Descending the hills towards the lake, we soon arrive at the village of

Caldwell

The view in our Engraving is taken from [the] Fort William Henry Hotel, which stands near to the ruins of the Old Fort. Here we will take up our abode, as the views from this new and elegant building are most exquisite, and the entertainment is admirable. The Lake House, is also a first rate establishment, commanding a very fine view of the lake, with its beautiful islands and the hills beyond.

We may remark here that Toole's Inn, a few miles along the eastern shore is conveniently situated for fishing quarters, and is more secluded than those at Caldwell.* Bolton and Garfield may also be mentioned as good spots for a pleasant sojourn. The former is a particularly charming spot. Here, in the Mohican House, we may enjoy the comforts of a well-appointed hotel, while outside, all that is beautiful and attractive in nature awaits us. We stongly recommend a halt at this place.

The village of Caldwell is beautifully situated at the southern end, or head, of Lake George. It contains two churches, a court-house, a jail, and a number of elegant private residences. There are above two hundred inhabitants, and, during the summer months, it is crowded with visitors in search of health, or pleasure, or both. It is delightfully and conveniently situated for being our head quarters while engaged in exploring the beauties of the lake.

The Ruins of Fort William Henry, which was built by the English in 1755, are close to the hotel of the same name. A short distance from the village, and about a mile to the south-east of this, are the Ruins of Fort George. A steamboat plies

---

*Toole's Inn seemingly refers to the Trout Pavilion noted for its excellent fishing. In 1853 Henry Marvin referred to the hotel as "Low's Trout Pavilion," while Addison Richards in the same year noted that Toole's, "some miles beyond [the United States Hotel], on the eastern shore, is well known to the hunting and fishing visitors."[13]

Above: Grounds of Fort William Henry.
(Postcard, author's collection)

Below: Looking north on Canada Street in Caldwell. From
Caldwell, Lake George by the Lake George Printing Company.

regularly between this village and the landing near Ticonderoga, at the other end of the lake, the distance being 36 miles. The trip there and back can be accomplished in a day, but we would strongly recommend a more leisurely survey of this Queen of Waters. In the summer of 1856, the steamer *John Jay* was destroyed by fire near Sabbath-day Point.* It has been replaced by the present handsome vessel, the boiler and furnace of which have been placed in a fire-proof iron case. Her name *Minne-Ha-Ha*, which signifies laughing water, is taken from Longfellow's poem, *Hiawatha*.

Lake George

It may, perhaps, be advisable, before launching ourselves upon the placid and beautiful waters of this lake, to make a few brief statistical observations in regard to it. Lake George, then, is situated close to the eastern border of the State of New York, and its waters discharge in a northerly direction, into Lake Champlain. It is 36 miles long, lying north and south, and from 2 to 3 miles wide. It is 243 feet above the tide-waters of the Hudson River. The water of the lake is remarkably pellucid[lucid or clear], and the basin in which it rests is covered with a yellow sand, so that the bottom is visible at a depth of seven fathoms.** The surface of the lake is everywhere dotted with the most romantic-looking islands, and its shores are encompassed by picturesque hills, clothed with rich vegetation, and, many of them, rising to a height that entitles them to rank as mountains. The islands are said to equal in number the days in the year.*** Many are large and fertile, others are mere barren rocks.

There are thousands of fish in the lake. Salmon-trout, silver-trout, brook trout, perch, pike, &c., are abundant, and of the finest quality.

Fish may be caught in all parts of Horicon [Lake George], but the best fishing grounds are at the head of the lake, near Bolton Landing and Shelving Rock.

The Indian name of this lake is Horicon, or the silvery waters, and we cannot help expressing regret that this euphonious [pleasing] appellation has not been exclusively retained.† The natives also called it Caniderioit, or, the tail of the lake, in reference to its position near the southern termination of Lake Champlain.‡ It was named by the French Lac [St.] Sacr[e]ment,on account of the purity of its waters.

This singular transparency of the water is the more remarkable that the waters on every side—those of Lake Champlain, of the Hudson, and of the whole region between the Green Mountains and the Mississippi,—are more or less impregnated with lime.

---

*The *John Jay* burned and sank south of the Cooks Islands beside a large rock(later called Calamity Rock) on the Hague shoreline.

**In 1853 Henry Marvin remarked that "the water is so transparent that a white object may be seen at the depth of near forty feet."[14]

***This is an often repeated statement. However, the lake has 200 islands, not 365.[15]

†Many writers of this period also used the name Horicon, including Addison Richards.[16] In 1858 Flavius Cook's *Home Sketches of Essex County* noted that "Lake George, throughout these sketches, is called by its original and only appropriate name, and the one which writers now generally adopt, L. Horicon, or the Silver Water."[17] The use of the Horicon name was the result of James Fenimore Cooper's campaign to change the name of the lake. Horicon was used in his novel *The Last of the Mohicans*.

‡The Iroquois were said to have called the lake "Andiatarocté. . .there where the lake is shut in."[18]

The Head Waters of Lake George,
From the Grounds of Fort William Henry Hotel

This view is exceedingly fine and animated,—the islands in the distance resting, if the weather be calm, on their own reflected images, and beyond these, the graceful outline of the hills cutting against the clear sky. The grounds of the hotel and the wharf in front are usually crowded with gaily dressed visitors, especially when the bright-looking steamer [*Minne-Ha-Ha*] darts from the shore on its trip down the lake. This steamer is a graceful little boat, elegantly fitted up, and, in the beauty of its appearance, very much in keeping with the lovely lake over which it darts with arrow-speed. She is 145 feet long, by 26 feet wide. During the summer season her decks are crowded with gay tourists, whose joyful voices, ringing over the lake, make the name of "laughing water" seem very appropriate. As the steamer rushes away, the flag that floats from the stern waves adieu to the stripes and stars that flutter from the flag-staff in front of the hotel.*

Islands of Lake George

As we have before remarked, these are very numerous as well as varied in size and form. Some are of considerable extent, level and cultivated; others rise in rugged cliffs from the water, their summits crowned with tufts of vegetation, and their crevices filled with clinging shrubs and stunted trees: some are bare rocks, on which the water-fowl make their nests; and many are mere points, rising but a few feet above the water: but all are beautiful and interesting to those who have the good fortune to traverse their labyrinths.

There are plenty of skiffs and boats on the lake in which we may row and dream upon the placid waters and among the sweet islets of Horicon, until we have forgotten the present, and are revelling in the romantic memories of the past,—when these crystal ripples were cut only by the light bark-canoe of the red man, as he glided noiselessly through the vast solitudes in search of game, perchance of enemies. The pictures that are seen, in a retrospective glance, are generally strongly defined in powerful light and shade. The sunbeams of romantic association and adventure may be broad and vivid; but the shadows of evil deeds and savage warfare are terribly dark and sombre. The woodman's axe now awakens the echoes which were wont to answer to the ring of the pioneer's rifle and the yell of his Indian foe; while the canoe has given place to the more convenient boat and the rapid steamer. Yet we may get out of the way of civilized sights and sounds, and find spots here where the descendant of the first owners of the soil might wander and dream until he should fancy the time of his forefathers had returned, and that he was still alone in the vast wilderness.

But however pleasant dreaming may be, we are constrained to interrupt it. The steamer is rapidly sweeping us through the midst of the most fairy-like scenes, and opening up to our view prospects of ever-changing grandeur and beauty, which claim our undivided attention.

---

*A portion of the text is omitted here since it dealt with the 1757 siege and massacre at Fort William Henry which was covered earlier in the book.

Illustrations from *Nelson's Guide to Lake George and Lake Champlain* (1866).

Above: "Fort William Henry Hotel, Caldwell."
Below: "Lake George--Entrance to the Narrows from the South"
with the steamboat *Minne-Ha-Ha.*

Illustrations from *Nelson's Guide to Lake George and Lake Champlain* **(1866).**

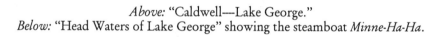

Above: "Caldwell—Lake George."
Below: "Head Waters of Lake George" showing the steamboat *Minne-Ha-Ha.*

"With every changing hour," writes Addison Richards—"dawn, sunset, and night—with the varying weather—from the calm of drowsy morning to the eve of gathering storm—these islands are found in everchanging phases. As they sleep for a moment in the deep quiet of a passing cloud-shadow, you sigh for rest in their cooling bowers. Anon [later] the sun breaks over them, and you are still as eager to mingle in their now wild and lawless revelry. You may shake up the lake like a kaleidoscope, seeing with every varying change a new picture, by simply varying your relative position to these islands. Now you have a fore-ground of pebbly beach, or, perchance, of jagged rock or of forest debris, with the spreading water and the distance-tinted hills, to fill up the canvass; or , peeping beneath the pendent boughs of the beech and maple, and Arcadian bower discloses vistas of radiant beauty."*

Description attempts in vain to convey an accurate idea of beautiful scenery. We quote the opinion of others, in order to tempt the traveller to visit this lovely spot—to go and see that which is so well worthy of being seen, but cannot be adequately described.

The first island of interest that we pass, after leaving Caldwell, is Diamond Island, near Dunham Bay. It was a depot of military stores for [General John] Burgoyne's army in 1777, and the scene of a sharp skirmish between the garrison and a body of Americans[led by Colonel John Brown].

On Dome Island, twelve miles from Caldwell, Putnam's men took shelter while he went to acquaint General Webb with the enemy's movements.**

North-west Bay, just beyond Bolton, is an exceedingly beautiful part of the lake.

Bolton itself is nothing, a mere "huddle" of huts, as its inhabitants appropriately term it. Its inn [Mohican House] is everything, and that is everything to us! The vicinity of Bolton is the favourite resort of the hunter and the piscator [fisherman]. The trout and bass taken here are frequently of enormous size. From the Pinnacle and other elevations in the neighbourhood, splendid views of the surrounding country and of Lake Champlain may be obtained, by those who love to tread the mountain-tops at [the] break of day. This is one of the broadest parts of the lake, and the islands are numerous.

Tongue Mountain protrudes itself into the water here, cutting off North-west Bay from the main passage; and hard by, on the eastern shore, is

Shelving Rock, a bold semicircle of pallisades, famed for its dens of rattlesnakes and its good fishing.

Black Mountain rises immediately behind Shelving Rock. It is a bold, prominent, and ever-visible object in the scenery of the lake, 2200 feet high.

Fourteen-Mile Island, in front of Shelving Rock, is the favourite temporary residence of those who chase the deer among the crags of Tongue Mountain.

But let us prepare for a change in the scene, for our little vessel is now approaching.

---

*This passage was taken from Addison Richards' 1853 article on Lake George that appeared in *Harper's New Monthly Magazine*.[19]

**Just before the 1757 siege of Fort William Henry, Israel Putnam of the Connecticut provincial Rangers was sent north on a scouting mission on Lake George with eighteen volunteers in three whaleboats. There is no definitive evidence, however, that his men landed on Dome Island at that time.

Above: "Study of Nature—Dresden, Lake George." Painting by David Johnson.
(Albany Institute of History and Art)

Below: Mohican House in Bolton Landing.
(Bolton Historical Society)

The Narrows

The hills extend into the lake at this point, and contract it very considerably, while the height of the mountains renders the contraction more impressive and apparent. The Black Mountain rears his bulky form here to a height of above 2200 feet, and around are the boldest and most picturesque parts of the shores of Lake George. The water here is 400 feet deep, and wonderfully pellucid, permitting the eye to penetrate far down into its mysterious depths.*

The passage of the Narrows is a most interesting part of our voyage. There are few scenes more enchanting or more romantic than the intricacies of an island-studded lake. In passing through such scenery every faculty of the mind is roused to an unusual state of activity. Like the moving pictures of a panorama, scene follows scene with a rapidity that gratifies and excites the mind, filling the eye with ever-changing visions of beauty, and raising expectation[s] to its utmost pitch, as each point or headland is passed, and the prospect is slowly unveiled. Scenery of this kind, even though the land be unpicturesque or barren, is always interesting from its novelty and variety; but when, like the Narrows of Lake George, all around is grand, verdant, and lovely, the scene becomes one which it is beyond the power of language to describe.

Sabbath-Day Point

Here historical associations and natural beauties crowd upon us in profusion. Towards the south the view of the Narrows is extremely fine; while to the north we have the broad bay; the landing and hotel at Garfield's; Rogers' Slide, and the precipice of St. Anthony's Nose reflected in the clear water.

In the year 1758 General Abercrombie landed on this fertile point, to rest and refresh his army of 16,000 men, while on his way to attack the French at Ticonderoga. It was Sabbath morning when they landed,—hence the name.** Here, in 1756, a small band of colonists were attached by a party of French troops and Indians, whom they defeated with great slaughter. Again, in 1776, the green sod of this point was stained with blood. A fight took place between a band of Tories, with their Indian allies, and a party of American militia, in which the former were signally defeated.***

The next point of peculiar interest that we come to is

Rogers' Slide,

so named from Major [Robert] Rogers, who, while flying from the Indians in 1758, practised upon them a ruse, by which he persuaded them that he had actually slid down the stupendous declivity, which is about 400 feet high, with a steep front of

---

*One of the deepest areas of the lake lies offshore between Shelving Rock Mountain and Buck Mountain where depths range from 187-195 feet.

**General James Abercromby's forces landed at Sabbath Day Point on Wednesday, July 5, 1758. The name Sabbath Day Point was in use prior to the Abercromby Expedition.

***There are secondary accounts of a 1756 skirmish involving Israel Putnam and provincial troops aboard vessels near Sabbath Day Point.[20] Jeduthan Baldwin described a March 19, 1777, attack on American soldiers at Sabbath Day Point by Native Americans under British command.[21]

naked rock; and well might the savages be surprised at the bold Major's supposed descent, as they stood baffled on the brink of the tremendous cliff.

The lake is narrowed here by Rogers' Slide on the one hand, and St. Anthony's huge Nose on the other.

Prisoners' Island is two miles farther on. Here, during the wars, the prisoners taken by the English were confined; and from this spot some of them escaped by swimming ashore.*

Howe's Landing lies to the west of Prisoners' Island. Here the English army under Abercrombie landed in 1758, previous to attacking Ticonderoga. It is named after Lord [George Viscount] Howe, who fell in that expedition. A little farther and we reach the foot of the lake, and the termination of our pleasant voyage down this beautiful sheet of water.

Steamboat *Minne-Ha-Ha* at Cooks Landing, Ticonderoga.
(Lake George Historical Association)

*The 148 French prisoners who had been captured in the initial battle on July 6, 1758, by British and provincial forces under George Viscount Howe and Robert Rogers were held on Mutton Island (later renamed Prisoners Island). Two days after the engagement, the prisoners were sent to the southern end of Lake George.[22]

Fort Ticonderoga

This fort was built by the French in [1755 and] 1756, and was named by them Carillon. Happily its present beautiful Indian name has entirely supplanted the other. Ticonderoga signifies noisy; and it is the name given by the natives to the falls at the outlet of Lake George.* The fort is a peaceful ruin now; but it was the scene of many a fierce struggle in the warlike days of old.

Before reaching this fortress, however, we have a delightful walk or drive of four miles before us, along the short and sparkling stream that connects Lake George with Champlain, for Ticonderoga belongs to the latter lake.

The turbulent little stream makes a descent of 230 feet, in the course of which there are two series of beautiful cascades, called The Falls of Ticonderoga. The romance of these is done away, however, to some extent, by the manufactories which the good people of the villages of Alexandria and Ticonderoga have erected on the banks.** Through these villages we pass on our way down. The walk is most charming. The scenery varies continually, and openings in the foliage reveal vistas of the distant landscape,—the lake, and the hills and valleys of Vermont beyond; while the riotous stream foams and tumbles beside us, presenting at every turn new and beautiful combinations of rock and water, draped with rich verdure, the colours of which harmonize pleasantly with the bright blue peeps that we obtain of Lake Champlain ever and anon as we jog along.

The Upper Falls, near the village of Alexandria, consists of a succession of bold leaps, which make a descent of 200 feet within the distance of a mile. The water power is unlimited; for which latter utilitarian remark we apologize to the romantic reader.

The Lower Fall descends 30 feet perpendicularly, and is situated near the village of Ticonderoga, where it is turned aside and compelled to work, ere it continues its headlong passage to Lake Champlain.***

In our spirited engraving of the south end of Lake Champlain, Fort Ticonderoga is seen on the left,† with a background of woods; while, on the right, we have the windings of the lake, dotted with small craft.

*According to tradition, Ticonderoga was said to be the Native American name for "two rivers flowing into each other" or "the place of rocks dividing the waters," but "between two great waters" is probably a more accurate derivation.

**A large number of sawmills, several iron forges, a barrel factory, graphite mills, and a shipyard for canal boat construction lined the banks of the Lake George outlet to Lake Champlain.

***A long historical passage on Fort Ticonderoga has been omitted from the text here.

†In 1853 Henry Marvin noted that the "venerable walls[of Fort Ticonderoga] which rise in some places to the height of twenty feet, preserve much of their original appearance."[23] Five years later Flavius Cook provided a detailed description of the barracks: "You stand now in the centre of the fortress, an open square made by two story barracks, substantially built of lime stone. Those to the west, are yet standing; those to the south, partially ruined; those to the east and north, entirely destroyed, except the foundations and cellar walls. . .Roofless, doorless, windowless, the old barracks have a ghastly appearance as they stare at you across the parade ground.——Two stories, each with six ghastly window holes with no panes but air, no sash but spider webs and ivy, remind one strongly of the dilapidating power of time. Yet Fort Ticonderoga is one of the best preserved ruins of its age and material, on the continent. You enter the barracks and find the old plaster firm yet on the walls of the apartments."[24] An 1866 newspaper article reported "that these ruins are still in a tolerable state of preservation is owing more to the extent of the fortifications than to the watchful care of the inhabitants of the vicinity.

Notes

1. Betty Ahern Buckell, *Old Lake George Hotels* (Lake George, N.Y.: Buckle Press, 1986), 17-18.
2. Henry Marvin, *A Complete History of Lake George* (New York: Sibells & Maigne Printers, 1853), 23-24.
3. B. F. DeCosta, *Lake George; Its Scenes and Characteristics* (New York: Anson D. F. Randolph & Co., 1869), 23.
4. Ibid., 36.
5. Amelia M. Murray, *Letters from the United States, Cuba and Canada* (New York: G. P. Putnam & Company, 1856), 376.
6. Ibid.
7. Ibid., 377.
8. Marvin, 49-50.
9. Ibid., 53.
10. T. Addison Richards, "Lake George," *Harper's New Monthly Magazine*, July 1853, 166.
11. Ibid.
12. *Nelson's Guide to Lake George and Lake Champlain* (London: T. Nelson and Sons, 1866), 3-21.
13. Marvin, 52; Richards, 165.
14. Marvin., 32.
15. *Lake George: Complete Report of the New York State Joint Legislative Committee on Lake George Water Conditions* (Albany: New York State Legislature, 1945), 121.
16. Richards, 161; See also Marvin, 33.
17. Flavius J. Cook, *Home Sketches of Essex County: Ticonderoga* (Keeseville, N.Y.: W. Lansing & Son, 1858), 9.
18. Reuben Gold Thwaites, ed., *Travels and Explorations of the Jesuit Missionaries in New France* (Cleveland: The Burrows Brothers Company, 1898), Volume 29, 49.
19. Richards, 164.
20. David Humphreys, *An Essay of the Life of the Honourable Major General Israel Putnam* (1788; reprint, Boston: Samuel Avery, 1818), 31; William Cutter, *The Life of Israel Putnam*, 4th ed. (1850; reprint ed., Port Washington, N.Y.: Kennikat Press, 1970), 61-62.
21. Jeduthan Baldwin, *The Revolutionary Journal of Col. Jeduthan Baldwin 1775-1778*, ed. Thomas Williams Baldwin (Bangor, ME.: Deburians, 1906), 95-96.
22. Samuel Thompson, *Diary of Lieut. Samuel Thompson*, ed. William R. Cutter (Boston: Press of David Clapp & Son, 1896), 9.
23. Marvin, 90.
24. Cook, 118.
25. "Visit to Fort Ticonderoga—Watering Place Letters, July 30, 1866," *The Bulletin of the Fort Ticonderoga Museum*, 9 (Summer 1954): 302-3.

Some of the oldest portions of the fort, and those also which, but a few years since, presented the finest specimens of the architecture of that time, have, by the shocking vandalism of the farmers, been pulled down and carried away for the purpose of building stone fences!. . .A large bow window—the one said to have belonged to the room in which Ethan Allen awoke the British commander when he demanded the surrender of the fort. . .is still standing, as are also the ovens and one or two bastions."[25]

"The Northern Extremity of Lake George" by James David Smillie
shows the Rogers Rock Hotel from the summit of Rogers Rock,
published in *Harper's New Monthly Magazine*, August 1879.

18. S. G. W. Benjamin 1879

By 1879 a myriad of changes had occurred at Lake George as a consequence of the burgeoning tourist trade. Samuel Greene Wheeler Benjamin's description of Lake George, appearing in *Harper's New Monthly Magazine* in August 1879, reflected the widespread interest in the lake as a premier resort area. To Benjamin, "Lake George is, indeed like a work of art of the highest order, for it has the quality of improving the more one studies its attractions."[1] Similarly, the contemporary guidebooks and historical narratives of Benjamin C. Butler, Benjamin F. DeCosta, R. S. Styles, and Seneca Ray Stoddard heightened the allure of Lake George's epic past and beauty.[2]

The most obvious change in the landscape of Lake George after the publication of Thomas Nelson's guide in 1866 involved an expansion of hotels and boarding houses along the shores of the lake. The Lake House, the oldest hotel, was still considered one of the finest hotels at the lake in the late nineteenth century. The 300-foot-long structure was three stories high with large porches on the front and back. Eighty feet from the lake, the Lake House had "a lovely tree-covered lawn" that sloped to the edge of the water.[3] The Fort William Henry Hotel underwent a major reconstruction following its sale in 1868 to T. E. Roessle & Sons of Albany. The building was raised to accommodate a 16-foot-high main floor and a fifth floor was added. A prominent observation deck was affixed to the roof of the building, allowing superb views of the lake as far as the Narrows. Finished in finely carved wood, the 1,000-guest hotel was elegantly decorated and tourists were served in an enormous dining room overlooking the lake.* Other hotels in Caldwell and the

---

*Twelve-year-old Theodore Roosevelt and his family lodged at the Fort William Henry Hotel in the summer of 1871. Roosevelt collected souvenirs at the ruins of Fort George, engaged in shooting matches on the hotel grounds using an airgun, and climbed Prospect Mountain for "a magnificent view of Lake George."[4]

Opposite page, above:
The Central House in Caldwell.
(Fort William Henry Museum)

Opposite page, below:
Glens Falls & Lake George Stage
at the Halfway House tollgate.
Photograph by Seneca Ray Stoddard.
(Richard K. Dean Collection)

Above:
The Fort William Henry Hotel.
Photograph by Seneca Ray Stoddard.
(Fort William Henry Museum)

Right:
The partially constructed cable-inclined railway to the Prospect
Mountain House.
(Fort William Henry Museum)

Prospect Mountain House
(Postcard, author's collection)

southern basin included the Carpenter Hotel (formerly the Caldwell House), Central Hotel, Nelson House, Coolidge House, Echo House, Harris House, Fort George Hotel (on the southeast shoreline), Crosbyside House (formerly the United States Hotel), and in the Kattskill Bay area: the East Lake George House, Trout Pavilion, Grove Hotel, and Kattskill House. The 50-guest Prospect Mountain House, located on the summit of Prospect Mountain, was one of the most interesting new resorts in the late 1870s. The hotel burned in 1880 but was quickly rebuilt. Fifteen years later, the carriage road to the summit was supplemented by an Otis-built, cable-inclined railway.

The Bolton Landing region accommodated travelers at the Mohican House, Wells House, Bolton House, Lake View House, Braley's Inn, and the Locust Grove Cottage. Even the wilderness of the southern Narrows was dotted with sizable hotels by the time of Benjamin's article. The hotels at the Narrows included the 40-guest Fourteen Mile Island House, 150-guest Pearl Point House at Shelving Rock, 100-guest Hundred Island House just south of the Pearl Point House, 50-guest Horicon Pavilion at Black Mountain Point, and the 100-guest Sherman House on the west side of the lake at French Point.[5] A boarding house, the Sabbath Day Point House, and another across the lake, the Hulett's Landing Hotel, provided lodgings for a growing number of tourists on their summer excursions. The hamlet of Hague, noted for its fishing potential, attracted a large number of travelers to its hotels and boarding houses: the Phoenix Hotel (formerly Garfields), Wheeler's Trout House, McClanathan's Hillside House, and the Bay View House.[6] The Rogers Rock Hotel, a first-class inn accommodating 125 guests, was built on a point north of Rogers Rock in 1874 by T. J. Treadway and his brothers (later the owners of the Treadway Inn chain).

The growth of tourism at Lake George was aided by an expansion of transportation facilities in the region. Railroads reached Glens Falls in 1869 which allowed a shorter stagecoach ride to Lake George via the plank road. Tourists often stopped at the Half-Way House, between Lake George and Glens Falls, for meals and lodgings. In 1882 the railroad network was extended to Caldwell, greatly reducing the stagecoach business from Glens Falls.

The steamboat company at Lake George became involved in the movement toward business consolidation during the latter part of the nineteenth century. Following a large purchase of common stock in the Lake George Steam Boat Company, the Champlain Transportation Company consummated a takeover of the Lake George company in 1868. In the same year the Rensselaer and Saratoga Railroad acquired the Champlain Transportation Company, but in 1871 the Delaware and Hudson Canal Company leased in perpetuity all of the assets of the Rensselaer and Saratoga. Subsequently, the Delaware and Hudson coordinated its train and steamboat schedules to allow continuous rail and steamboat service between New York City and Montreal. In 1875 the Delaware and Hudson completed a rail line connecting the Baldwin Landing on northern Lake George to the Montcalm Landing at Ticonderoga on Lake Champlain. Seven years later, the company brought its rail lines from Glens Falls directly to the Caldwell steamboat dock. In 1872 the Champlain Transportation Company received legislative approval of a new charter for its Lake George subsidiary under the slightly modified name, Lake George Steamboat Company.

At the time of the takeover of the Lake George operation, the chief asset of the company was the 140-foot steamboat *Minne-Ha-Ha*, built in 1857. The 400-passenger steamer had been a financial success except for the years of the Civil War when revenues were halved due to the interruption of the tourist trade. As a youngster in 1871, Theodore Roosevelt rode on the vessel from Caldwell to Ticonderoga and noted in his diary that the scenery was "so wild that you would think that no man had ever set his foot there."[7]

Although the financial maneuvering had eclipsed some local control of the Lake George steamboat business, the infusion of capital eventually allowed investment in new vessels. The Champlain Transportation Company provided funds for the 64-foot *Ganouskie* built in 1869 to supplement the service offered by the *Minne-Ha-Ha*. After completion, the *Ganouskie* was assigned a schedule opposite that of the *Minne-Ha-Ha*, departing from the Baldwin Landing in the morning and returning in the early evening. In 1876, as a result of support from the Champlain Transportation Company, the Lake George Steamboat Company began construction of the largest steamer to date on the lake, the 195-foot *Horicon*. The main saloon of the vessel, finished in butternut and black walnut with elegant gas chandeliers, had a length of 108 feet and width of 27 feet. The 643-ton, 1,000-passenger *Horicon* used the engines and boiler salvaged from the steamer *Champlain* which had been wrecked north of Westport on Lake Champlain in 1875. The luxurious *Horicon*, a name derived from James Fenimore Cooper's *The Last of the Mohicans*, would carry tourists for more than three decades on Lake George.

In 1877, after 20 years of service on Lake George, the aging *Minne-Ha-Ha* was retired and her engine and boiler removed at Ticonderoga. Cyrus Butler, owner of the Horicon Iron Company on the Lake George outlet in Ticonderoga and the Horicon Pavilion, subsequently towed the engineless craft to the Narrows with his 51-foot steamer *Meteor*. The *Minne-Ha-Ha* was permanently docked in the bay at Black Mountain Point and functioned as a 25-room hotel and dining facility to

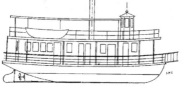

Top: The Horicon Pavilion at Black Mountain Point. Photo by Seneca Ray Stoddard. (Bolton Historical Soc.) *Above:* The 61-foot *Lillie M. Price* and the *Horicon* (1877-1911). Drawings by Ludwig Kasal. *Below:* The *Ganouskie* at Bolton Landing. Photo by S. R. Stoddard. (Lake George Historical Assoc.)

Opposite page, top: The 195-foot steamboat *Horicon.* (Fort William Henry Museum) *Middle:* The *Minne-Ha-Ha* as a floating hotel at Black Mountain Point. (Fort William Henry Museum) *Bottom:* Sunken frames of the steamboat *Minne-Ha-Ha* at Black Mountain Point. (Photo by the author)

supplement Butler's Horicon Pavilion. Butler's resort also offered tourists horse-back and mule rides to the summit of Black Mountain and hiking on his 9,000-acre tract of land. Travelers visiting the rustic Horicon Pavilion noted "its cheery Japanese decorations. . .[and the *Minne-Ha-Ha's*] odd sleeping rooms. . .[and] miniature imitation of the Eastern style of the main hotel."[8] After a fire destroyed the Horicon Pavilion in 1889, the *Minne-Ha-Ha* was left to the elements, and later partially dismantled and dynamited. One may still view the sunken frames of the old steamer from the surface of the bay at Black Mountain Point.

"Cliff near the summit of Black Mountain" by James David Smillie
from *Harper's New Monthly Magazine,* August 1879.

In addition to the steamers *Horicon* and *Ganouskie*, a number of smaller commercial steamboats served excursionists in the 1870s and early 1880s. The 61-foot *Lillie M. Price*, owned by the Lake George Steam Yacht Company, popularized the Paradise Bay tour with two daily trips to the Narrows. The 30-foot, 25-passenger *Owl* and nearly identical *Julia* began charter service on the lake in the 1870s. The 50-foot sidewheeler *H. Colvin* and the 51-foot propeller-driven *Meteor* also provided commercial duty and charters on the lake in the latter years of the decade.

The author of the *Harper's* 1879 Lake George article, Samuel Greene Wheeler Benjamin, had a prolific writing career and a life of extensive travel. Born in Greece on February 13, 1837, S. G. W. Benjamin was the son of Nathan Benjamin, an American missionary, and Mary Gladding Wheeler, a writer. Benjamin's lineage included two great-grandfathers, Captain Nathan Benjamin and Captain Charles Seymour, who had served in the American Revolution. The first 18 years of young Benjamin's life were spent chiefly in Greece where he learned several languages, attended the English College in Smyrna, Turkey, and relished the adventurous life in an exotic land. A passage to America during the winter of 1847-1848 initiated his lifetime fascination with sailing vessels and the sea. After his father's death in 1855, Benjamin and his family returned permanently to the United States. Even before his graduation from Williams College in 1859, Benjamin began writing for magazines. His earliest work, when he was 17, involved marine drawings of the Crimean War for the *Illustrated London News*. Benjamin later worked from 1861 to 1864 as an assistant librarian in the New York State Library in Albany and married Clara Stowell of Brookfield, Massachusetts, in 1863.

Benjamin's career centered on free-lance writing. His 19 books, written between 1860 and 1888, dealt with Europe, Persia, the Atlantic islands, art, literature, ocean sailing, and other topics. From 1863 to 1886, Benjamin also authored numerous magazine articles, including 24 for *Harper's New Monthly Magazine*. Many of his *Harper's* articles were descriptive pieces of various geographical destinations, including the Bahamas, Channel Islands, Gloucester (Massachusetts), Prince Edward Island, the South Shore of Massachusetts, the Magdalen Islands (Gulf of St. Lawrence, Canada), and Lake George.

In 1882, two years after the death of his wife, Benjamin married author Fanny Nichols Weed. Appointed the first American minister to Persia the following year, he proved to be a tenacious and able diplomat. With the end of his tenure as the Persian minister in 1885, Benjamin continued his proliferous writing endeavors. He was exuberant, versatile, and, ultimately, a romantic. Benjamin was also an expeditious writer who could complete a piece in quick order. One of his books, *The Multitudinous Seas*, was written in only four days; some of his magazine articles were dictated while he painted maritime scenes. His love of the sea was evidenced by 45 transatlantic voyages. He was described as never becoming seasick even during the worst weather and "set great store by his use of whiskey and tobacco, and drank water rarely."[9]

Benjamin died at his home in Burlington, Vermont, on July 19, 1914. His final work, *The Life and Adventures of a Free Lance* (an autobiography), was published shortly after his death.

Illustrations by James David Smillie that accompanied S. G. W. Benjamin's "Lake George" in *Harper's New Monthly Magazine*, August 1879.

Above: "Caldwell, at the head of Lake George."
Below: "Black Mountain, from the Narrows"
Opposite page.
Above: "Dome Island."
Below: "The Butler's Pantry, Camp Manhattan."

Lake George[10]

It is a noteworthy fact that the most attractive resorts of tourists in Europe and Asia are rendered doubly interesting by the historic and legendary associations which invest them. Thus the visitor to these noted spots finds himself not only entranced by the loveliness of the scenery, but his imagination is also kindled and his sympathies are aroused by a contemplation of the scenes which have occurred there; a summer trip of pleasure may thus also assume the guise of a pilgrimage to the memory of the men of other days.

In a relative degree the same may be said of the New World, and of this Lake George offers a prominent example. Long before the men of this generation were born, Indians, Frenchmen, and Englishmen, priest, soldier, fair-haired maiden, tawny squaw, and even the deer of the forest, were fighting and acting in the grim tragedy of existence on the shores of Horicon [Lake George], and weaving around its matchless waters associations that would add a pleasant melancholy, a romantic charm, to the enchanting beauty which renders it the most winsome spot in the United States.

It is quite worth one's while to consider how a place of this description should be approached. One goes to it to escape for a few days from the tumultuous influences of the age, by its placid flood to revel in a lotus-eating repose [dreamy contentment from Homer's *Odyssey*],* and with reverential soul to bow at the shrine of nature, and place himself in sympathy with the Great Spirit who limned [painted] those hills, and poured between them molten turquoise, and overarched them with a vault quick with stars; who from the majesty of eternity watched the stirring scenes formerly enacted there, and had imbued us with feelings that lead us forth to enjoy the inexhaustible beauty of a lake which lies among the everlasting hills like a sparkling eye in the smiling face of happy childhood.

Clearly such a spot should be reached with a certain art in the method of approaching it, and therefore it seems proper to take a steamer up the Hudson on a calm summer evening, with the moon at the full. As we glide along by Palisades or beetling [overhanging] Highlands robed in mysterious shadows, the spirit of the past eloquently sings to us the story of the romance and history of the beautiful river. And when, as a concession to the age, we take the [railroad] cars at Albany to Glenn's Falls, we are still gliding among historic scenes. Saratoga, Gansevoort, Fort Edward—what events throng on the memory at the utterance of those names!

At Glenn's Falls we begin the last part of the journey to the lake on one of the stages which run the distance of nine miles between the two places. A better way of reaching the lake could hardly be devised. Seated on the top of the vehicle, one surveys the landscape at his leisure, takes in the various points of interest on the road, and falls into the easy, tranquil frame of mind which prepares him to hail with philosophic rapture the first appearance of the peaceful lake dreaming among the hills. The toll-gates through which one must pass give a sort of quaint old-time effect to the trip, and when, as often happens, a procession of six to ten stages and carriages filled with passengers sweeps along in a continuous line, a certain stateliness is

*In 1854 George William Curtis authored the book *Lotus-Eating: A Summer Book* which included one chapter on Lake George.[11]

Fort William Henry Hotel.
(Postcard, author's collection)

imparted to the ride. The view of the plain and of Glenn's Falls, when one is on an elevation about three miles from the town, is one of the loveliest to be seen in any land. If the horses were trimmed with rosettes[ornamental decorations], and the drivers could blow a horn as the coaches wheel up to the well-known halfway house,* where the host has dispensed admirable lemonades and punches for forty years, or when they finally roll up to the shores of the lake, something would be added to, but entirely consonant with, the other features of this very charming ride.

And thus, by an easy and ever-suggestive transition, one at last finds himself standing on the sandy beach of the magical lake. It is difficult to describe the quiet delight one feels as he gazes on the expanse of tranquil azure spread before him, like a part of the sky inlaid on the emerald bosom of the earth. Peace is in the very air which lazily slumbers over the water, while the monotone of the silvery ripples rolling on the yellow sands, and the musical moan of the breeze in the cone-scented pines, seem to carry the soul back to other days. Lake George is, indeed, like a work of art of the highest order, for it has the quality of improving the more one studies its attractions, and the ever harmonious flow of lines constantly suggests a composition of consummate genius in which every effect has been combined to produce a certain ideal. The lake is about thirty-four miles long, but is so divided by clusters of islets or overlapping promontories as to give the impression of a succession of lakes five in number. It was discovered by Champlain between 1609 and 1613, and

*George Brown had operated the Half-Way House at the foot of French Mountain since 1846. The inn's reception room exhibited a large collection of Native American relics gleaned from the battlefields of the French and Indian War.[12] Dexter Shoes is now located on the former site of the Half-Way House.[13]

was named by Father Jacques the Lake of St. Sacrament.* The Indian name was Andiatarocte, which meant the Tail of the Lake.** Horicon is a fanciful title given to the lake by [James Fenimore] Cooper, who objected to the name it now bears, which was bestowed on it by the English [in 1755]. There is an attempt made on the part of some to abolish the present name of Lake George, but it is too firmly incorporated with our national history to be obliterated at this late day, while it also reminds us of the time when we yet boasted of our English ancestry, and looked with honest and manly pride on the manner which still represents the greatest empire the world has seen.

Caldwell, at the head of the lake, is a leaf-embowered hamlet at the foot of lofty hills. Behind it rises Prospect Mountain, and French Mountain faces it on the east. Between these heights reposes a rolling valley bordering on the lake, which has been the scene of some of the most romantic and thrilling events in our history. The position of Lakes George and Champlain early pointed them out as vastly important in those times as a portage, and this made it essential to hold the head of each lake. The French for a time secured control of the later by a formidable fortress at Ticonderoga, while the English sought to hold Lake George by two forts at the head of the lake, called respectively Fort William Henry and Fort George. The first was built of logs, surrounded by earth-works of some size, directly on the edge of a low bluff washed by the waves. The possession of these forts was a cause of much border warfare, and several severe conflicts occurred in the immediate vicinity.

Little now remains to mark the stirring scenes which occurred there so long ago in the wilderness. Now and then the ploughshare turns up an arrow-head or a bullet, a bit of a flint-lock or a skull. The outline of Fort William Henry is still more or less discernible, especially the salient angles abutting on the lake, and in the water below are fragments of the wharf where boats were moored and loaded.

Fort George, although in a most dilapidated condition, due in part to the disgraceful conduct of the neighboring farmers, who burned part of its walls for lime, yet remains a picturesque ruin, one of the few we still possess. It is starshaped, and stands on a slight eminence in a valley surrounded by lofty hills. It must have been a difficult position to carry by assault in those days. A few years ago the lake could be distinctly seen from the fort, but the pines have since grown up, and form a massive screen, as if to shelter it from further damage from the elements and man. It is a charming spot toward evening, a scene of extraordinary beauty and pastoral repose—velvety moss cushioning the moldering ramparts, ox-eyed daisies speckling the green, and goldenrod softening its gaudy yellow in the delicate rosy light suffusing the landscape. The purple shadows slowly creep up the hill-sides; on the stillness float the far-off crow of the barn-yard fowls, and the tinkle of their bells as

---

*In 1609 Samuel de Champlain accompanied a war party of Algonquin, Huron, and Montagnais as far as Ticonderoga. Champlain noted in his journal that "the Indians told me. . .that we had to pass a rapid [Ticonderoga] which I saw afterwards. Thence they said we had to enter another lake [Lake George] which is some nine or ten leagues in length, and that on reaching the end of it we had to go by land some two leagues and cross a river [Hudson] which descends to the coast."[14] Champlain and his Native American allies battled the Iroquois at Ticonderoga and returned to Canada without entering Lake George. In 1646 Father Isaac Jogues, a Jesuit missionary, named the body of water Lac du Saint Sacrament.

**Translations of seventeenth-century Jesuit writings suggest that the Iroquois name for the lake, "Andiatarocté," means "there where the lake is shut in."[15]

the cattle wend homeward; and nearer by are heard the plaintive, monotonous peep of the phoebe-bird, the buzz of the locust, and the cricket's creaking soliloquy. What does he care what happened at Fort George last century, if you but leave him to chirp away at his own sweet will?

Descending from Fort George to the shore, one comes to a [c]rude bridge over a creek which makes into the land. There a half hour may often be judiciously spent in contemplating one of the choicest scenes on the lake, and with curious fancy endeavoring to picture the further beauties which are yet to be revealed in wandering over it. On either hand are graceful points tufted with Druidic* pine and white-pillared birch, leading up to slopes at once beautiful and majestic. In the dim distance the far-off shores are limned [painted] hazily against the sky while nearer islets, showing darkly against them, serve as a foil to increase the aerial perspective. As seen from here, the lake appears as a sheet of water perhaps ten miles long, and no suggestion of any water beyond is presented to the eye.**

Is yonder graceful form that now poises almost motionless in the blue above, and now swoops majestically northward, an eagle? or is it the spirit of some Indian Chief? or is it the genius of the scene, that bids us launch away in sail-boat, steamer, or canoe to explore the beauties of Lake George? Whichever it be, let us follow in its track, and obey the influences which it suggests. The sail-boat offers a delightful mode of wandering over the blue waters, but the suddenness and violence of the squalls which often occur, and the liability to be struck by a back flaw [gust of wind] from a mountain cliff, make this very hazardous, except to those who possess caution, skill, and experience. The light skiff, easily gliding under the impulse of oars, is better for most, especially if they have time to bestow to paddling among the creeks and coves. The steamer [*Horicon*] is rather for those who are travelling on time, and are anxious to "cram up" about the lake. It is curious to note the impatience of some to get rapidly over the water, even when the steamer is shooting by the shores at the rate of fifteen miles an hour, as if speed were all they desired, while the very scenes they had come to see seem to them to be of secondary importance.

Tea Island—a minute islet a mile from Caldwell—first calls attention after leaving the village. It is a legendary spot, for Abercrombie is said to have buried treasure there. Why he should have done so, and whether he actually did do so, are questions for the curious, but the legends of the lake should not be lightly overthrown.*** They form part of its heritage and attractions. Slipping by Diamond Island, noted for its quartz crystals, and the pine-feathered shores of Long Island,

Overleaf:
Illustrations from *Lake George* by Adolph Wittemann (1885).
(Souvenir book, author's collection)

*Druids refer to pre-Christian Celtic priests who appear in legends as magicians and wizards.

**From his position at the south end of Lake George, Benjamin's view extended only to Tongue Mountain.

***Stories of buried treasure from the French and Indian War have persisted since the nineteenth century. The tales vary as to the location of the treasure and whether the French or English troops buried it.[16] There is no mention of buried payrolls or treasure, however, in military diaries and journals of this period.

Steamer Horicon & R.R. Dock.

The Sagamore.

Fort William Henry Hotel.

Fort George Hotel & Cottages.

Recluse Island.

Lake House & Cottages, Caldwell.

the largest of George's isles, we reach on the eastern shore a finger-like cluster of promontories forming several charming and romantic bays. These are West, Slim, and Sheldon's points, the last forming one side of Sheldon's Bay, which winds in a southerly direction for several miles. The striking woodland at the end of the point is and has long been a favorite camping ground for those who like to rough it. For many years it was the haunt of the Manhattan Lodge of the Alpha Delta Phi Society, but they have recently moved their quarters to Little Green Isle, where, as has been well said, "they have, from long experience and suffering, succeeded in getting at the milk in the cocoa-nut of camping."*

Island excursion.
(Fort William Henry Museum)

No place could be found which more thoroughly fulfill the conditions requisite to camping out than Lake George. Shut in from the boisterous world by surrounding mountains, its shores are fringed by the most fairy-like nooks and sheltered coves, while the islets, which so abound as to be fabled to reach the mystic number of 365, offer the most delicious wooded retreats. Sometimes isolated, sometimes interwoven in a tangled mesh of green intersected by the mottled azure of sheeny waters, the tent or the bark [shelter] of the idler may nestle under pine and birch, almost invisible, while the light skiff is drawn upon the mimic beach, and the hilarious songs and mirth of the sportsmen indicate how successful they are in driving dull care away amid those scenes of enchantment. The waters also abound with fish— bass, trout, and pickerel—and the neighboring thickets afford in the season a sufficient variety of game, including such noble quarry as the bear and the deer. There is also a quality in the air of Lake George which is invigorating and stimulating as an elixir. When the wind is from the north, the atmosphere is so limpid and pure

*In 1875 the Manhattan Club, a college fraternity, had moved its campground from Sheldon Point (Sandy Bay) to Elizabeth Island (Little Green Island).

it seems as if the lake was inclosed within a crystal sphere which shuts out all dust and taint. There are few places where quinine would be so likely to sell at a discount as at Lake George.*

One denizen of this region can not be spoken of without a degree of respect combined with aversion. It is the rattlesnake. He flies the haunts of men, and is gradually disappearing from that vicinage; but, like inferior races of man, which, before they altogether vanish before an advancing civilization, cling desperately to a few strongholds, so this reptile yet retains certain positions around the lake, which are infested in a way that demands caution on the part of the tourist. It is not

Dome Island.
(Postcard, author's collection)

uncommon to see these snakes swimming in the lake, passing from cove to cove or isle to isle. Leaning over a boat one calm day, I saw one swimming under the stern. He raised his head when he saw me, and the expression of his face was neither amiable nor assuring as he darted his head spitefully forward. I hit him with a stick, when he dived and disappeared. Tongue Mountain and Shelving Rock are most infested at present. An old man and woman who occupy a solitary cabin on the former have long made a business of catching rattlesnakes and supplying the market. The demand is much larger than one would suppose on the part of showmen and naturalists, and also from the rustics of the neighborhood, who have the notion that rattlesnake oil is an infallible remedy for the rheumatism. Doubtless this superstition—for it is nothing else—arose in the same way as the belief in former days in a newt's [salamander's] eye, a baby's finger, a sliver from the finger-nail of a mummy, or the

---

*Quinine is a white, water-soluble alkaloid that had been used for various ailments including malaria. The efficacy of quinine was apparently discovered by Jesuit missionaries in Peru and introduced to Europe about 1640. In the nineteenth century the bitter powder was used as a tonic to stimulate the appetite.

baboon's blood—objects remote or difficult to obtain. The quotation for good healthy rattlesnakes at Lake George averages one dollar apiece, caught and delivered. Those who do not mind the trifling annoyance of being bitten by one are allowed the free range of the rattlesnake preserves, and may catch them for nothing.

Leaving the idyllic nooks of Sheldon's Bay [Warner Bay], we make a run across the lake with a flowing sheet, a reef in the mainsail, and a sharp eye to windward, for the flaws are lively. The lake is here four miles wide, or from the bottom of Sheldon's Bay nearly seven miles on a northwest course, heading for Basin Bay [Bolton]. We pass Little Green Island [Elizabeth Island], and have Dome Island, whose vertical sides and top are covered with masses of velvety vegetation, Shelving Rock, and the bold crags of Tongue Mountain on our right, Black Mountain looming up grandly in the distance. Basin Bay is a retired, land-locked, forest-hidden cove, encircled by a sandy beach. On a point at the entrance stands a solitary tree, like a light-house on a jetty. From here it is but a short run to Bolton Bay, around by Recluse Island and an adjacent rocky isle, with which it is connected by a rustic bridge. For some unknown reason the lone house which stands on Recluse Island is at present entirely unoccupied.*

Bolton, among a host of attractive spots on the lake, holds in my opinion a rank among the two or three most interesting points. There is no part of Lake George

The Lake View House at Bolton Landing. Photograph by Seneca Ray Stoddard.
(Bolton Historical Society)

*Located east of Clay Island in Bolton, Recluse Island had one cottage in 1869. Benjamin F. DeCosta noted that "on the sides of this island, facing the Narrows and Bolton, are the remains of some earthworks, which were probably erected by Abercrombie's forces, who, in 1758, were stationed on the lake."[17] DeCosta also mentioned that "numerous relics of the Indians, such as stone knives, hatchets, and arrowheads" had been found on the island.[18]

where the views are so varied or more satisfactory, excepting the one from Sabbath-day Point. At Bolton the islets which dot the surface of a lake whose waters are blue as the sea in the tropics carry the eye to the rosy-tinted range which includes Pilot, Buck, and Erebus mountains, and culminates in the stateliness of Black Mountain. Or, looking northwest, the superb masses of verdure on Green Island are seen mirrored on the burnished surface of the lake. Behind rises the mighty dividing wall called Tongue Mountain, which seems to separate the lake in twain, for Ganouskie, or Northwest Bay, five miles long, is in effect a lake by itself, with its own peculiar features. Free from islands, and of a somewhat severe style of beauty, Ganouskie Bay wins our respect rather than our affection. One can imagine that in the shades of the forests on its shores the Indians of old might have buried their sachems with barbaric pomp at midnight. At certain hours one is reminded of the Tros[s]achs, on Lake Katrine [Scotland], when gazing up the receding waters and dark heights of Ganouskie Bay. Catamount Mountain rises on its western side, like a mighty fortress crowned at one end by a huge bastile. Does one weary of these spacious prospects, and long for bits of nature less fatiguing to the imagination, then Bolton affords the rambler the choicest of nooks, the most enticing little coves, encircled by mossy banks. More than any other resort of the lake does it offer pleasing walks and drives. Of these one of the most charming is from the landing to the village, which is called the Huddle. The name at once suggests some of the closely crowded hamlets of Europe. It is in reality a straggling collection of small farm-houses, including a smithy, two shops, and a post-office, clustered around a brook [Huddle Brook] which foams down from the mountain with a perpetual song of joy as it hies [hastens] on its merry way to merge its sparkling waters with those of the lake, at the head of Bolton Bay. Why the hamlet should have such a preposterous name is purely a matter of conjecture. Possibly in order to indicate what it is not. Perhaps to some of the simple, honest farmers who live lonely lives in solitary houses miles away from any other dwelling, a collection of fifteen or twenty houses might suggest a crowd confusedly huddled. There is a wood on Bolton Bay, reached by a pathway at the Huddle, which is really one of the most exquisite spots on the lake. The entrance faces a mossy bank, which takes the most vivid tints when embroidered with the golden rays of the mid-day sun. One should not leave Bolton without seeing a thunder-storm gathering in the mountains behind it, and gradually overcasting the waters of the lake with a steely gray. The roll of the thunder is very grand at Lake George, with its troop of echoes, and the lightning, blending with the moonlight, produces a weird and indescribable effect. The gentle angler will be pleased to learn that some of the best fishing grounds of the lake are near Bolton.

Skirting the reddish shores of Green Island, we now take a soft summer wind, and quietly steal across to Fourteen-mile Island and Shelving Rock, whose shore abounds in inviting bays. Into the prettiest of these empties a brook. Near by are the Shelving Rock Falls, a lovely cascade. Leaving on our right a miniature archipelago, called the Hen and Chickens, and passing under the beetling [projecting] [scars] of Shelving Rock, we now enter the Narrows, which are well guarded by a string of closely clustered islands tufted with birch, chestnut, and pine. We pass next into another section of Lake George, so shut in at either end by islets and promontories as to seem an entirely distinct sheet of water. This impression is deepened by the different and individual character of its scenery. From a spacious bay four to five miles wide and twelve miles long, we enter a narrow strait swarming with islets both in mid-channel and along the thickly wooded shores, and surrounded by the peaks and precipices of Tongue and Black mountains, which stand face to face in all their majesty. One is here reminded of the Highlands on the Hudson, or of certain parts of the Danube [River].

Leisurely crossing to Hundred-mile Island, and thence to Pearl Point, we arrive at last at the most enchanting nook in the whole lake: it is called Paradise Bay. A small peninsula, joined by a narrow strip to the main-land, makes out from the foot of the mountain. It is quite regularly indented with many coves, and where it ends it is met by a chain of isles, which inclose in their embrace a transparent pool of extraordinary clearness and beauty. These islets are in turn divided by serpentine lanes of crystalline water, and are so densely draped with forest, underwood, and vine, and so royally carpeted with lush moss speckled with bluebells and everlasting flowers, that it is difficult to tell where the land begins and where it ends. Well is it named Paradise Bay. Every moment in the hushed stillness one expects to see sylphids [slender girls] sporting in the thicket, or naiads [nymphs] showing a white shoulder above the tranquil water, which spreads like a variegated, many-colored floor of polished marble, or like an expanse of flowered satin, as it reflects the surrounding scene on its bosom. Overhead in the serene heavens poises the eagle of the forest, as if to see that no one disturbs the glorious solitude of this sylvan retreat. Is it too much to hope that no pickaxe or spade will ever mar the perfect beauty of this lovely spot by the handiwork of man?*

Gliding out of Paradise Bay, quite another scene confronts us when, a short mile beyond, we come to Black Mountain Point, and take a nearer view of the citadel of Lake George. This peak, which is the culminating point of a lofty range of hills, springs from the eastern shore about the middle of the lake. It soars 2340 [2665] feet above the water, and from its commanding form and position easily seems much higher. Inland it is flanked by two prominent truncated cones, which dip suddenly to the plains below toward Lake Champlain. Running westerly from these knobs, the ridge rises into a precipitous dome when it reaches Lake George, and curving gradually but rapidly downward, forms a magnificent descent toward the water, till it reaches a more gentle slope, which again terminates in a precipice, that is washed by the waves of the lake. Such is a general idea of the outline of Black Mountain as seen from its southern approach. It suggests a couchant lion resting his paws in the lake, and serenely gazing in majestic repose over the landscape at his feet. But I know of no mountain that possesses more variety of feature, more diversity of character, than this monarch of the lake, who demands our attention not so much for his size as for his individual traits. By the force and vividness of his form he adds a certain grandeur to almost every prospect of Lake George, and elevates the least interesting view into the realm of the ideal. The absence of trees at the summit, and the warm gray hue of the storm-beaten crags, give to this mountain the most exquisite atmospheric effects, especially when the departing glow of sunset lingers on its brow with a rosy flush long after the lake below is hidden in twilight gloom. It is a peculiar and pre-eminent quality of the scenery of Lake George that while it never startles,

*Paradise Bay, at the foot of 2,533-foot Erebus Mountain, is a scenic enclosed bay with Sarah Island at its mouth, Hazel Island to the north and Artists Rock (Round Rock Island) to the south. By 1879 Paradise Bay had been placed on the itinerary of the smaller steamboats. Other contemporary excursionists described the bay as "a miniature lake, shut out from the main water by barriers of trees and rocks so completely that all consciousness of the proximity to the lake was lost."[19]

Paradise Bay.
(Photo by the author)

overpowers, or wearies the imagination by such stupendous sublimity as that of the Swiss lakes, it is never tame nor monotonous in its beauty. Its charm is rather that of a well-balanced character that presents many phases, and constantly gratifies us by the discovery of some new attraction, or like a carefully studied masterpiece of art, which, without captivating our interest at once, reveals with each inspection truths and beauties unseen before. It grows in importance; it elevates our imagination from day to day. We begin by respectfully but cautiously admiring it; we end by giving it a devoted and unqualified enthusiasm; and inasmuch as we have benefited by a study of its merits, it becomes identified with our moral and intellectual existence. Such is Lake George—a lofty work of art by the greatest artist of all.*

Black Mountain may be ascended from Hulett's Landing or from Black Mountain Point. An excellent zigzag road has been recently opened to the summit from the latter point, and I chose that.** The distance is over three miles, and the last part of the road, winding over the dome, is often very steep. The prospect is one of very

*The main part of this paragraph was later quoted directly in *Possons' Guide to Lake George and Lake Champlain* in 1888.[20]

**The road to the summit was built as a toll walking and bridle path by Cyrus Butler, owner of the Horicon Pavilion at Black Mountain Point. In 1878 the 12-bedroom hotel was supplemented with the remodeled *Minne-Ha-Ha* moored in the bay. Seneca Ray Stoddard described the Horicon Pavilion as "the most striking and picturesque hotel at Lake George, it, with its accessories, is really a work of art, in keeping with the grand and beautiful surrounds."[21] The hotel burned in 1889, and today the land is a state forest preserve. S. G. W. Benjamin chose to focus his observations on the natural beauties of the lake rather than on hotels and other man-made structures.

unusual extent, considering the moderate elevation of the peak, extending from Mount Marcy in the north to Saddleback in the south. The rugged, rolling character of the neighboring counties gives the landscape somewhat the appearance of the ocean when it is seamed with the ridges of the heaving billows of a great storm. This effect is increased when the hazy atmosphere of a southerly wind throws a veil of gray over the scene, through which the hills and mountains are seen rolling away in a sublime, mysterious, and elusive gradation, until they fade into the infinitude of the sky. Nearer at hand repose the winding waters of Lake George, adorned with green islets. As I gazed from that height, with none but the eagle to keep me company, while the soft wind from the south stole by sighing the requiem of the ages, I seemed to see before me again the peerless straits of the Bosporus [connecting the Black Sea and the Sea of Marmara], as they appear when one gazes on them from the Giant's Grave.

Black Mountain Point, site of the wreckage of the steamer *Minne-Ha-Ha*.
(Photo by the author)

Betaking ourselves once more to the boat, we glide along the base of Black Mountain toward Hulett's Landing, and pass two striking cliffs, peeping out from the dense masses of foliage, which have a vertical height of seventy to eighty feet; they are called Cives and Sucker rocks. Hulett's Landing is one of the best spots on the lake for obtaining superior views of Black and Tongue mountains, and the arrangement of coves, islets, rocks, and points, crowned in some cases with kiosks [open summerhouses] or summer cottages, and joined by rustic bridges, is very pleasing.*

---

*The locality included the 50-guest Hulett's Landing Hotel operated by John W. Hall in 1879. The house was built originally by Philander Hulett, who began taking in boarders about 1870.

Reaching thence across the lake, on a [south] westerly course, we enter the labyrinthine mazes of Harbor Islands, a group of islets collected together in bewildering but enchanting confusion. During the border wars the Harbor Islands were the scene of a bloody conflict between the English and the Indians. On the 25th of July, 1757, Colonel John Parker left Fort William Henry on a scouting expedition with 400 men. They had reached the Harbor Islands, amid whose intricate recesses they supposed themselves securely concealed from observation while they snatched a little repose. Suddenly, in the gloom of early morning, canoes filled with swarthy Indians, hideous in their war-paint, darted into the channels among the islands, and the appalling whoop of the savages pierced the still air and aroused the English to a consciousness of their fate. Panic-stricken, the English took to flight, but the fleet canoes easily overtook the heavy barges. It was a slaughter rather than a fight; 131 were killed outright; nearly all the rest were captured alive; only twelve escaped. Of the prisoners, some were rescued by Montcalm; the others were tortured to death.*

Continuing on our course across the lake, we reach the base of Tongue Mountain, with French's Point on our left, and look up at the frowning and tremendous precipice called Deer's Leap, a vertical cliff several hundred feet high.** How many millions of deer roamed through the forests of Lake George for ages, but only one of them ever achieved immortality, and, as often happens with human beings who give rise to some notable event, even the name and race of that deer have not been handed down to us. Such is fame! Like most traditions, this legend is undoubtedly founded upon an actual incident. A poor Indian, half famished perhaps, had hunted this deer half a winter's day; his squaws and papooses in his wigwam cried for food in the savage season of frost. Urged by desperation, he chased the wounded roe from thicket to thicket, until they approached the edge of the precipice. Suddenly the bleeding animal found herself on the edge of the cliff; death was close

---

*This is an often-repeated story, but Benjamin's version differs somewhat from the facts. After a French scouting party led by Lieutenant de St. Ours was attacked on Lake George, a detachment under Lieutenant de Corbière was ordered southward on the lake to lie in ambush for any English parties.[22] In late July 1757, Colonel John Parker with his New Jersey regiment, consisting of 350 men and 10-14 officers in whaleboats and bateaux, were dispatched on a scouting mission and ordered to destroy French outposts on the northern end of Lake George. According to a letter written on July 26, 1757, by an observer at Fort William Henry, the provincial force was sent "to attack the advanced guard at Ticonderoga by water, in whale and bay boats: They landed that night on an island, and sent, before [the] break of day, to the main land three battoes, which the enemy way-laid; and took. These battoes were to land two miles on this side [west]; they being taken, gave the enemy intelligence of [our] design of landing. Our men [the] next morning, at day-break, made for said point, and the enemy, who knew our scheme, contrived, as a decoy, to have three battoes making for the said point, which our people imagining to be the three [English] battoes sent out the evening before, eagerly put to the land, where about 300 men lay in Ambush, and from behind the point came out [in] 40 or 50 canoes, whale and bay-boats, which surrounded [our men] entirely, and cut off every one that was in the circle. . .Parker. . .escaped with about 70 men."[23] The point on the shore where the French and Indian attack occurred was later identified by provincial soldiers as Sabbath Day Point.[24]

**Deer Leap is five miles north of French Point. French Point was the location of the 100-guest Sherman House and cottages built by William Sherman in the 1870s. The two-story hotel was built close to the shoreline with a long open porch facing the islands in the Narrows. A farm adjoined the hotel to supply boarders with fresh vegetables, cream, and milk. The hotel burned in 1889, but one cottage survived and was purchased by General Electric as a vacation camp for employees. The land was later donated to the state by G.E. in memory of George Foster Peabody. Peabody, a noted financier and philanthropist, had given Prospect Mountain and the Hearthstone campground to the state of New York for public use.

on her track; she heard the panting of the hound, the yell of the hunter. It was but a choice of deaths. With a rush and a bound, she leaped into the air, and whirling downward, fell crushed on the rocks far below. Was not the fate of the deer a type of the life of man, hunted down by adverse fortune and despair, until forced to choose between the alternatives of certain ruin or self-destruction?

Nothing better illustrates the inexhaustible variety of the natural attractions of Lake George than the splendor of the scenery on the eastern slopes of Tongue Mountain as seen toward sunset, when the shadows begin to close in upon it. Alternately tender and beautiful, as the slanting rays of evening steal through the gorges and illumine the treetops of the forest and the grass on the slopes, or savage and grand, as the Deer's Leap cliff stands forth in purple gloom, or the Twin Mountain peaks soar 2000 feet, dark and thunderous, against the burning glories of the declining sun, with here and there a fairy-like cove and glen to soften the severity of the crags above, and bring them into harmony with the loveliness of the lake, until almost suddenly the mountains recede to the westward, and we see before us the idyllic meadow-lands of Sabbath-day Point, whose vivid emerald is flooded with the roseate fervor of departing day, and kissed on either shore by the limpid azure of the lake, presenting a scene of alluring and tranquil repose, lovely and enchanting as the Elysian Fields.* Had we to choose one spot on Lake George in preference to any other, this would be the one. Situated like a barrier between two portions of the lake, each of which possesses distinct features, Sabbath-day Point commands on either hand the best possible view of each.** Looking south, one sees the part of the lake we have just described within the Narrows. From a boat half a mile north of the point one is able to make of it a superb foreground, which adapts itself to the flow of lines formed by Black and Tongue mountains. As outlined from that spot, the view has in it a certain something classical that is excessively rare in this country, but quite common in Italy and Greece. It has the quality of satisfying the soul like a lofty strain of music, thoughtful and full of exquisite modulations, and delicate strains, and suggestions of half-suppressed passion. When the air is from the south, and with its ethereal [heavenly] haze gives to each part of the prospect its true relations in subdued gradations, I know of nothing in this country that can equal or surpass this prospect. If we look northward from Sabbath-day Point, the scene is quite reversed. We see before us a broad lake resembling the sea in its hue and expanse. From its shores the hills every where retire, and no islands break the breadth of the view. Miles and miles away in the distant horizon, faintly outlined and tinted with the softest of pearly grays, loom the bold perpendicular cliffs of Rogers's Rock and Anthony's Nose, like the shores of an unknown land which we approach after a long voyage. Here and there a white sail, a mere glistening speck in the distance, lends to the illusion.

It was at Sabbath-day Point that Lord Abercrombie halted on his expedition to Ticonderoga. Here the troops—16,000 in number, in 500 or 600 boats—landed and passed the night.*** One would like to know more about one of the most interesting

*Elysian Fields refers to the classical myth of a blissful abode after death.
**At the time of Benjamin's Lake George article, the 24-guest Sabbath Day Point House was in operation, charging boarders $7-8 a week.[25]
***On July 5, 1758, General James Abercromby's troops landed at Sabbath Day Point at five o'clock in the evening. After the artillery and provision rafts had reached the stopping point, the army, in 900 bateaux, 135 whaleboats, and 3 small radeaux, renewed its voyage northward at about eleven o'clock at night.

and picturesque events in the annals of war: how did the battalions encamp; how long did they linger by the lake, building their bateaux; what stories they told around the camp fires by the wavering, dusky gloom of the primeval forest; the foraging and scouting parties; did ladies accompany the expedition; were the notes of fife and drum heard among the hundred isles, as they swept up the lake in mighty procession, the regimental banners incarnadining the blue sheen of the winding lake, and interweaving their crimson with the plume-like branches of the isles amid which the mighty armament threaded its majestic course with the measured rhythm of ten thousand oars, which startled the eagle screaming from its eyrie [nest]. Mile after mile, hour after hour, the stately host glided along the echoing shores, until they landed on the sward [grassy expanse] of Sabbath-day Point, and, rolled in their blankets, slept deep, many of them for the last time in this world, while the sentinels marched their rounds, and called, through the night-watchers, "All is well," while the Indian scouts prowled in the neighboring forest to spy out the movements of the foe, until the reveille smote sharp on the air of dawn, and the regiments sprang to greet the morning star, and marched to meet their doom.

Proceeding northwest from Sabbath-day Point, we have on our right the spacious waters of Blair's Bay and the gentle slopes of Spruce Mountain. On our left is a settlement called the Hague, on a pretty inlet at the mouth of a cleft among the hills, which carries the eye inland to the ridge called the Three Brothers. Beyond the Hague is Friends' Point, whose beauty is enhanced by a cluster of emeralds called the Waltonian Islands by a fishing club which at one time made it their summer resort.*

We are now drawing near to the striking headland called Anthony's Nose. It dips with considerable abruptness to the water at the end of a long and lofty ridge. Its rocky sides are richly variegated with the vivid tints of lichens and mosses, and the water around it is 400 to 500 [175] feet deep, and of a brilliant sea-green color. Passing Anthony's Nose, we turn a sharp angle and enter into a fourth division of Lake George, which is quite closed in, while no part of the lake has more individual traits of its own. Facing us are the vertical sides of Rogers's Rock, which stands out into the lake, quite isolated, and rises to a height of 640 feet above the water—altogether a very massive and impressive feature of the landscape. The rock is of a rich purple-brown color, and on the south side the precipice is deeply grooved, giving the effect of a fortress of old, supported at the angles by heavy bastions. The vegetation which clothes the lower part of the cliff resembles ivy clambering up a mouldering wall. About four. . .in the afternoon of an August day, the sun so strikes the rock that one side of the bastions is in dark shadow, while the other, smitten by the light, stands out in strong relief. The effect is magnificent.

On the east side of Rogers's Rock is a smooth space entirely bare of vegetation, and sloping to the water at a very sharp angle. This is called Rogers's Slide. It took its name from the circumstance that Major [Robert] Rogers, in the winter of 1757-58, was defeated by the Indians when scouting in the vicinity of Ticonderoga [Benjamin's story of Rogers' escape is omitted here; see chapter 5].

*Waltonian Island was named for the Waltonians, a sportsmen club founded in the 1850s whose members camped each summer on the island until 1870. The Waltonians had adopted the name from the English writer Izaak Walton (1593-1683), known as the "Father of Angling," who had written *The Compleat Angler, or the Contemplative Man's Recreation* in 1653. The book appeared in five editions in Walton's lifetime and was subsequently published more than 100 times.

Above: Phoenix Hotel in Hague.
(Postcard, author's collection)
Below: John Wheeler's Trout House in Hague.
(Hague Historical Society)

Above: Rogers Rock Hotel.
(Postcard, author's collection)
Below: The Burleigh House, Ticonderoga, completed in 1880.
(Ticonderoga Historical Society)

Echo Bay, formed by a beautiful and abrupt promontory jutting out from Rogers's Rock, is a most charming spot, noted, as the name indicates, for its echoes. Inclosed by massive cliffs and leafy underwood, its waters are at once deep and limpid. The rambles up the steep sides of the rock have a singularly wild solitude and picturesqueness, and are well appreciated by the partridges and squirrels. One is often greeted there by the whirring drum of the former and the shrill bark of the latter.

There is a simplicity and a grandeur in the beauty of this part of Lake George which allies it to some of the European lakes. The outlines are drawn with a firm hand in long unbroken curves, and the eye is occupied with masses rather than with details, while the height of the shores and the absence of islands make it seem like the bowl of a vast sunken crater into which the sea has poured. In the distance, far away to the south, the faint lilac-tinted outline of Black Mountain relieves the grand sweep of Anthony's Nose, and gratefully appeals to the fancy. In no part of Lake George is the water more beautifully blue. Thus the lake appears from the promontory alluded to above. But on descending to the water, and following the shore of the lake to its extreme northern limit, it shows still another phase.

Passing Coates Point, we find that the hills recede, and that another geological formation shows a beach different from any other on the lake, while the ripples that curl on the sand indicate that the water is there somewhat colored by the clay against which it dashes, and assumes a pale creamy green. It was on that beach that Lord Abercrombie landed his army. Not far from it is an islet called Prisoners' Island, on which the English who were captured in the battle that followed were confined.* Here Lake George terminates as a lake. But through a narrow winding course of four miles farther it seeks to pour its waters into those of Lake Champlain, dashing down in musical rapids, which caused the French to call the meeting of the waters Carillon.** There in the forest still stand the earthworks which Abercrombie vainly sought to storm. Lord [George Viscount] Howe and 2000 men fell on that memorable day, whose sadness was but partially effaced by the victory of Lord Amherst in the following year. Just beyond are the ruins of Fort Ticonderoga, overlooking Lake Champlain. The fortress is one of the most interesting spots on the continent. A thorn bush, covered with blood-red berries, on the beetling [overhanging] brow of one of the salient angles, is the only semblance of a banner left waving there now,

---

*The British and provincial army held 148 French prisoners on the island following the first skirmish of the ill-fated 1758 Abercromby Expedition. Lord Howe was killed in the first volley of musket fire in the battle (see chapter 6). Howe's body, followed by the French prisoners, arrived by bateaux at the southern end of Lake George on July 8, 1758.[26] Originally called Isle au Mouton (Mutton) by the French, the area near Prisoners Island was the site of the first engagement involving vessels on the lake during the French and Indian War. In early November 1755, when Rogers and his Rangers were caught between the fire of French and Indian forces on land and in canoes, the Rangers used two bateaux, mounting wall-pieces (swivel guns), to pretend to try to pass by the enemy war canoes. The ploy worked as the Indians maneuvered their canoes to head off Rogers and his men. When the canoes were within range of the wall-pieces, the Rangers opened fire, disabling them. The "engagement which I judge was near 2 hours & c." also involved firing on French and Indian shore positions.[27]

**The name Carillon, which translates to a chime in French, was said, according to tradition, to be derived from the cascade of water at the outlet of Lake George. Ticonderoga, or Cheonderoga, was an Indian name for the place "between two great waters." While there is no definitive evidence, the name Carillon may have been derived from Philippe de Carrion, a former officer of the French Carignan Regiment who erected a log shed at Ticonderoga to facilitate the smuggling of furs between Albany and New France.[28]

and the cattle and sheep browsing on the herbage within the glacis around the roofless quarters of the garrison plainly tell us that war has rung its clarion for the last time on those ramparts where Montcalm and Amherst, Ethan Allen and Arnold, St. Clair and Burgoyne, have in turn battled and held sway.

He who has not seen Lake George should no longer defer to cultivate its acquaintance, while he who has once formed a friendship for its attractive beauty feels that he has stored his memory with an enduring treasure of lovely pictures that shall cheer him along the dusty road of life, and lead him to return often to behold the glorious original of his dreams.

Tourists at the ruins of Fort Ticonderoga in the late nineteenth century.
(Fort William Henry Museum)

Notes:

1. S. G. W. Benjamin, "Lake George," *Harper's New Monthly Magazine*, August 1879, 323.
2. Benjamin C. Butler, *Lake George and Lake Champlain*, (Albany: Weed, Parsons and Co., 1868); B. F. DeCosta, *Lake George; Its Scenes and Characteristics* (New York: Anson D. F. Randolph & Co., 1869); R. S. Styles, *A Descriptive and Historical Guide to the Valley of Lake Champlain and the Adirondacks* (Burlington, Vt.: R. S. Styles' Steam Printing House, 1871); S. R. Stoddard, *Lake George; A Book of Today* (Glens Falls, N.Y.: S. R. Stoddard, 1873).
3. Charles H. Possons, *Possons' Guide to Lake George, Lake Champlain and Adirondacks* (Glens Falls, N.Y.: Chas. H. Possons, Publisher, 1888), 37.
4. Theodore Roosevelt, *Theodore Roosevelt's Diaries of Boyhood and Youth* (New York: Charles Scribner's Sons, 1928), 241-42; See also Trip Sinnott, *Tea Island: A Perfect Little Gem*, 10th ed. (Clinton Corners, N.Y.: The Attic Studio Press, 1993), 31-33.
5. For more information on hotels see Betty Ahearn Buckell, *Old Lake George Hotels* (Lake George, N.Y.: Buckle Press, 1986); See also S. R. Stoddard, *Lake George; A Book of To-Day* (Albany: Weed, Parsons and Company, Printers, 1873), 30-42, 118-22; S. R. Stoddard, *The Adirondacks: Illustrated* (Albany: Weed, Parsons & Co., Printers, 1874), 183-88; S. R. Stoddard, *The Adirondacks: Illustrated* (Albany: Van Benthuysen & Sons, Printers, 1879), ix; Elsa Kny Steinback, *Sweet Peas and a White Bridge* (Burlington, VT.: The George Little Press, 1974), 91-101; Styles, 16.
6. *Lake George Mirror*, 20 May 1880.
7. Roosevelt, 243.
8. [J. A. Whiteman], *Camp and Canoe-Chats* (New York: Press of John Rankin, Jr., n.d.), 95.
9. Allen Johnson, ed., *Dictionary of American Biography* (New York: Charles Scribner's Sons, 1929), Volume 2, 189.
10. Benjamin, 321-39.
11. George William Curtis, *Lotus-Eating: A Summer Book* (New York: Harper & Brothers, Publishers, 1854), 127-42.
12. Stoddard, *The Adirondacks: Illustrated* (1874), 182.
13. Robert L. Eddy, *Queensbury's Heritage* (Glens Falls, N.Y.: Robert L. Eddy, 1991), 118.
14. H. P. Biggar, *The Works of Samuel De Champlain* (Toronto: The Champlain Society, 1925), Volume 2, 93-94.
15. Reuben Gold Thwaites, ed., *Travels and Explorations of Jesuit Missionaries in New France* (Cleveland: The Burrows Brothers Company, 1898), Volume 29, 49.
16. Wallace E. Lamb, *Historic Lake George* (Glens Falls, N.Y.: Glens Falls Post Company, 1946), 58; Thomas Reeves Lord, *Stories of Lake George: Fact and Fancy* (Pemberton, N.J.: Pinelands Press, 1987), 20; Thomas Reeves Lord, *More Stories of Lake George: Fact and Fancy* (Pemberton, N.J.: Pinelands Press, 1994), 43-44; Betty Ahearn Buckell, *Stuff* (Lake George, N.Y.: Buckle Press, 1992), 135-41; Sinnott, 60.
17. DeCosta, 24.
18. Ibid., 64.
19. [Whiteman], 70.
20. Possons, 76-77.
21. S. R. Stoddard, *Lake George: A Book of To-Day* (Glens Falls, N.Y.: S. R. Stoddard, 1887), 100.
22. "An Account of the Taking of Fort George, or William Henry, Situated on Lake St. Sacrament, and of Events in Canada This Year [1757]" in *Report of the Public Archives for the Year 1929*, ed. by Arthur G. Doughty (Ottawa: Public Archives of Canada, 1930), 98; See also Louis Antoine de Bougainville, *Adventure in the Wilderness: The American Journals of Louis Antoine de Bougainville 1756-1760*, trans. and ed. Edward P. Hamilton (Norman, OK.: University of Oklahoma Press, 1964), 138, 140.
23. "Extract of a letter from a Gentleman at Fort William-Henry. . .July 26, 1757," *The London Magazine* (September 1757): p.n.a.
24. E. B. O'Callaghan, ed., *Documents Relative to the Colonial History of the State of New York* (Albany: Weed, Parsons and Company, 1858), Volume 10, 734.
25. Stoddard, *The Adirondacks: Illustrated* (1879), ix.

26. Samuel Thompson, *Diary of Lieut. Samuel Thompson*, ed. William R. Cutter (Boston: Press of David Clapp & Son, 1896), 9.

27. E. B. O'Callaghan, ed., *The Documentary History of the State of New-York* (Albany: Charles Van Benthuysen, Public Printer, 1851), Volume 4, 273; See also Robert Rogers, *Journals of Major Robert Rogers* (1765; reprint ed., Ann Arbor, MI.: University Microfilms, Inc., 1966), 5-8; Burt Garfield Loescher, *The History of Rogers Rangers* (San Francisco: Burt Garfield Loescher, 1946), Volume 1, 35-43, 315-18.

28. Roger R. P. Dechame, "Why Carillon"? *The Bulletin of the Fort Ticonderoga Museum* 13 (Fall 1980): 432-46.

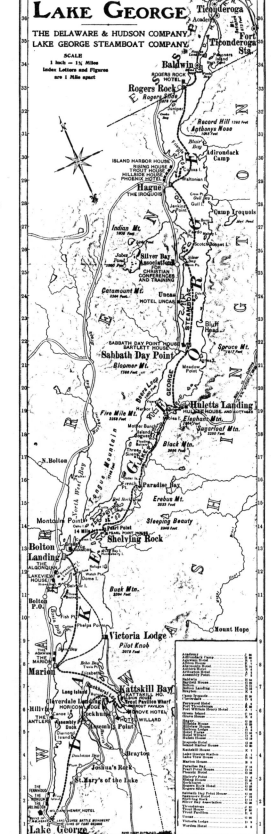

"Lake George." Delaware & Hudson Company map (1906).

(Author's collection)

"A Day on Lake George." Drawn by W. P. Snyder, from *Harper's Weekly*, July 25, 1891.
(Author's collection)

19. Seneca Ray Stoddard 1914

T HE TWENTIETH CENTURY ushered in a new era of change as tourism continued to increase and the automobile hastened new economic development along the lake. Seneca Ray Stoddard, a guidebook author, photographer, mapmaker, and lecturer, was a keen observer of the transformation of Lake George over the four decades that his Lake George guides were published. His photographs, largely taken with heavy, bulky cameras, have provided a lasting legacy in the documentation of both Lake George and the Adirondacks. More importantly, his images of the Adirondacks during his lifetime served as a catalyst for the creation of the Adirondack Park in 1892.

Over the four decades that Seneca Ray Stoddard wrote his Lake George guidebooks a multitude of changes had occurred at the lake. While a few hotels had closed or been destroyed by fire, many new ones had opened since the late 1870s. Enlarged in 1868, the 1,000-guest Fort William Henry Hotel was destroyed by a spectacular fire in 1909. The hotel was rebuilt with private baths and other modern features but on a smaller scale, accommodating only 200 guests. The new Fort William Henry Hotel's advertisement in Stoddard's 1914 guidebook noted in bold type: "Absolutely Fireproof."[1] The rebuilt hotel exhibited an ornate cement-and-marble pergola along the lake connected to the hotel by an elegant archway over the beach road. The 300-guest Lake House, the first large hotel at Lake George and a fixture for three-quarters of a century, was razed in 1904. The land was subsequently purchased by the family and friends of the late Edward Morse Shepard, who donated it to the village as the Shepard Memorial Park in 1917. The Prospect Mountain House, with its inclined railway, closed in 1903 and was later purchased by George Foster Peabody, who donated the land to the state of New York. New hotels at the southern end of the lake included the Arlington, Delevan, Worden, Fernwood, and Woodfin (burned 1899).

The Sagamore Hotel, completed in 1883 on Green Island in Bolton Landing, would have a lasting impact on the area to the present day. Ten years after opening, the rambling hotel burned to the ground but was rebuilt for the next season. The new 400-guest Sagamore offered electric lights, rooms with private baths, steam-powered elevators, a post office, telegraph and telephone, bowling, and a variety of other sports. The hotel description submitted that "laundry and out buildings [are] fire proof" since the fire in 1894 had begun in the laundry.[2] Nevertheless, in 1914 the second Sagamore also burned to the ground. The Sagamore continued accommodating tourists for a number of years in auxiliary buildings that had not been touched by the fire. The hotel was finally rebuilt just at the onset of the Great Depression.

The 100-guest Agawam Hotel in Bolton. Although Seneca Ray Stoddard's
1892 Lake George guide mentioned that the hotel had burned in 1890, a
36-guest Agawam Hotel was in operation after the turn of the century.
(Bolton Historical Society)

New hotels on both sides of the lake offered a diverse package of facilities for the traveling public. After 1879 the new hotels in the Bolton area included the Algonquin, Fenimore, Antlers, Diamond Point House, Wilson's Hotel, and the Agawam. The old Wells House burned in 1890, and two landmarks were razed just after the turn of the century: the Mohican House and the Bolton House. Additions to the hostelry on the east side in the Kattskill Bay area included the Albion House, Horicon Lodge (burned 1911), Victoria Lodge, and Hotel Willard (formerly the

Sheldon House). After 35 years in the tourist trade, the Kattskill House burned in 1908.

In the Narrows only the Pearl Point House was still open for business in 1914. Both the Horicon Pavilion and the Sherman House burned in 1889. The Fourteen Mile Island House, renamed the Kenesaw House, was acquired by the steamboat company in 1888 as a regular stopping "point for excursionists. . .with every facility for recreation and enjoyment," including a shooting gallery.[3] The novelty of the island eventually diminished for tourists; the hotel closed in 1896 and the island was sold for private development in 1905. The Hundred Island House was purchased by George O. Knapp, who closed the hotel just after the turn of the century and built an impressive estate on the mountainside near Shelving Rock.

In terms of hotels and boarding houses, Hague was in its prime on the eve of World War I. The enlarged Sabbath Day Point House accommodated 100 guests while the nearby Bartlett House boarded 20 travelers (later 40). In addition to the Phoenix, Trout House, and Hillside, the new hotels in Hague after 1879 included the 200-guest Hotel Uncas (today's Northern Lake George Resort), 50-guest Island Harbor House, 100-guest Rising House, 95-guest Mohican House, 75-guest Iroquois House, and the 1,000-guest Silver Bay Association. On the east side of the lake tourists found accommodations at the Gull Bay Inn and the Glenburnie Inn.

During the period of the late nineteenth century and early twentieth century, the landscape along the southwestern shoreline was dramatically reshaped by the imposing private residences of the wealthy. While the "Great Camps" of the Adirondacks were rustic in style, the Lake George estates of "Millionaires' Row" reflected the palatial fashion of lower New York state. In an era of conspicuous consumption and no income tax, the proximity and beauty of Lake George were a natural extension for the wealthy of New York City.[4]

A network of railroads, trolleys, and roads significantly changed access to Lake George at the turn of the century. Probably no more singular example of the transformation was the journey between Glens Falls and Caldwell. Early travelers had a long, rough ride by wagon from Glens Falls to the lake. Bloody Pond and the gravesite of Colonel Ephraim Williams (chapter 2) were often stopping points of interest along the way. When W. Max Reid, author of *Lake George and Lake Champlain*, embarked on a trolley at Glens Falls in 1909, the trip to Bloody Pond took only 20 minutes.[5] Railroads went directly to the steamboat landing on Lake Champlain at Ticonderoga. Although there wasn't a road for automobiles for the entire length of the lake in 1914, there was a good thoroughfare from Glens Falls to Bolton Landing. Even by the mid-1920s only a dirt road traversed Tongue Mountain to Sabbath Day Point. In 1926 the New York State Conservation Commission observed that "it is a little traveled mountain road, its use by automobiles beyond the head of the bay [Northwest] is not recommended."[6] A macadam road was completed from Hague to Ticonderoga in 1925 and over Tongue Mountain in 1928. As indicated in Stoddard's 1914 Lake George guidebook, steamboats carried a limited number of automobiles between landings on the lake.

The late nineteenth century inaugurated a new period with respect to land use and conservation at Lake George. A state law in 1876 (c. 297) prohibited any further sale of state islands, and in 1885 they became part of the new state-owned Forest Preserve. The 1885 law (c. 283) which created the New York State Forest Preserve initiated the provision (section 8) that "the forest preserve shall be forever kept as wild forest lands."[7] In the same year, the non-profit Lake George Association was founded. Initially the organization pressed for enforcement of fishing and hunting laws, but later its goals centered on the conservation and protection of the natural purity of the lake. In 1892 the Adirondack Park was created, and two years later the Forest Preserve's "forever wild" clause was incorporated into Article 14 of the New York State Constitution. From 1871 to 1900, the state acquired 3,700 acres at Lake George in tax foreclosure sales. Later the state acquired the Tongue Mountain range and the estate of George O. Knapp in the Shelving Rock area. After the turn of the century, the Forest, Fish and Game Commission (Department of Environmental Conservation today) ordered that all structures on state islands be removed, a ruling that required more than a decade to enforce. In 1917 the state began "rip-rapping" the islands, laying stone around the shoreline to prevent erosion. By then, island camping by the public had become a well-established activity.

Horse-drawn trolley in Caldwell.
(Fort William Henry Museum)

In 1914 steamboats continued as the main method of transportation between communities on the lake. For the rest of the decade (except 1917-1918) and the early 1920s, the Lake George Steamboat Company was at its zenith, carrying over 100,000 passengers per year. Several changes, however, had taken place since Seneca Ray Stoddard's first Lake George guidebooks in the 1870s. After the steamer *Horicon* entered service in 1877, the company built the 172-foot *Ticonderoga* in 1884, the last of the company's wooden steamboats. When the *Ticonderoga* began operation, the smaller *Ganouskie* was retired, later spending a few years as a floating saloon at Big Burnt Island in the Narrows. Several other commercial steamboats also plied Lake George during this period. The 61-foot *Lillie M. Price*, noted for its Paradise Bay cruises, ended service in 1888. Two years later, the 90-foot *Island Queen* (first called the *L.G.A.*) began twice-daily trips to the bay. Following the destruction by fire of the *Island Queen* in 1892, the newly-built 93-foot steamer *Mohican* began Paradise Bay tours (1894). One year later, the Lake George Steamboat Company abandoned plans to build a small steamer and instead purchased the *Mohican* from the Paradise Bay Line.

The 1,000-passenger *Ticonderoga* was remodeled and lengthened 15 feet in 1896, but the elegant craft met its demise only five years later. Early on the morning of August 29, 1901, the steamer departed without passengers from the Baldwin dock headed for Caldwell after a moonlight cruise the previous night. Prior to reaching her first stop at the Rogers Rock Hotel, smoke began billowing from the engine room. Although an earnest attempt was made to extinguish the fire while it was tied to the hotel dock, the vessel could not be saved after the fire spread to the dock and burned the mooring ropes. The crew escaped, but two women employees "driven

The steamboat *Ticonderoga* ablaze near Hawkeye Point on August 29, 1901.
(Dragonfly Books, Ticonderoga)

aft by the fire [were] forced to plunge through the lower deck cabin window. . .and over the rail into the lake" as the flaming steamer drifted northward.[8] One of the women was severely burned in the ordeal. The *Ticonderoga* grounded on Hawkeye reef, north of the Rogers Rock Hotel, and burned to the waterline in two hours. Most of the wreckage was removed from the lake in the winter of 1902.*

---

*Although the remaining pieces of the steamer *Ticonderoga* became the object of souvenir hunters for decades, the nine-by-six-foot rudder lay undisturbed in eight feet of water near the reef. In 1948 two young summer residents raised the rudder. Eventually the rudder was varnished for display in the clubhouse of the Northern Lake George Yacht Club, but the relic instead became an outside picnic bench and disintegrated.[9]

The 1,500-passenger *Sagamore* entered service on Lake George in 1902.
(Postcard, author's collection)

One year after the destruction of the *Ticonderoga*, the Lake George Steamboat Company launched the first steel-hulled sidewheeler on the lake, the 203-foot *Sagamore*, a name popularized by James Fenimore Cooper's reference to Chingachgook in *The Last of the Mohicans*. The lavishly-furnished vessel had monogrammed china and silver, gold-leaf decorated ceilings, electric lights, a barbershop, plush carpeting and furniture, mirrored hallways, and a cherry- and hazel-trimmed interior. The 1,125-ton steamer was lengthened 20 feet in late 1902 to improve directional stability. Six years later, the steamboat company replaced the *Mohican* with a second steel-hulled vessel, the 115-foot *Mohican II*. Of the large steamboats on Lake George, only the *Mohican II* would survive the Great Depression. Redesigned twice, the *Mohican II* is the oldest commercial vessel still in service on Lake George today. In 1911 the aging *Horicon* was retired and succeeded by the new 230 1/2-foot, steel-hulled *Horicon II*. The steamer's main saloon, quarterdeck, and 100-seat dining

Pampero on the shore of Lake George in 1990.
(Photo by the author)

Horicon II, 1911-1939.
(Lake George Historical Association)

room were finished elegantly in butternut wood with cherry trim and equipped with luxurious furniture.

In this period, the Lake George Steamboat Company also began regularly-scheduled tours in the southern basin with gasoline yachts. The service began with the 45-foot *Mercury* in 1909, but the 54-foot *Pampero* replaced the vessel in the following year. With the financial success of the *Pampero*, the company contracted to have the 70-foot *Mountaineer II* built for Lake George. In addition to the Lake George Steamboat Company's yachts, other small commercial vessels competed for the tourist trade, including the regularly-scheduled 75-foot *Scioto* of the Kattskill Bay Line and several others which operated in various years during the first two decades of the new century: the 80-foot *Ellide*, 75-foot *Iroquois*, 67-foot *Locust*, 45-foot *Uncas* and a number of smaller boats.

The broadening of the tourist business at Lake George during the period from the 1870s to the eve of World War I was due in part to the influence of Seneca Ray Stoddard's guidebooks. Of the writers included in *Chronicles of Lake George*, only

In 1915 Captain Frank Hamilton (Kattskill Bay Line)
began tours with the 75-foot steam yacht *Scioto*.
(Postcard, author's collection)

Stoddard was a native of the region. Stoddard was born on a farm in Wilton, New York, on May 13, 1843, to Charles and Julia Ray Stoddard. The Stoddard family were descendants of Anthony and Mary Stoddard, who had emigrated from England in 1639. When he was 19 years old, Seneca Ray Stoddard left the family farm and worked as an ornamental painter on the interior of railroad passenger cars in Troy, New York. From this experience Stoddard moved to Glens Falls in 1864 and started a decorative and sign painting business. He was soon dabbling in landscape painting and the fledgling art of photography. A short time later, Stoddard abandoned painting for the photography business, which he located in a modest store at his Elm Street home. He began making photographic forays to Lake George, Lake Champlain, and other nearby lakes. By then Stoddard had married 18-year-old Helen Augusta Potter (1868), and in November of the following year his first son was born.

On the heels of William H. H. Murray's popular *Adventures in the Wilderness; or Camp-Life in the Adirondacks*, Stoddard produced his first viewbook (1872), which depicted 11 scenes at Lake George. He had his eye on the rest of the Adirondacks as well, making his first long trek into the region in 1870, accompanied by his brother-in-law, Charles Oblensis. Three years later Stoddard and Oblensis again traveled through the Adirondacks, meeting the famous guides and characters of the region: Orson Schofield Phelps ("Old Mountain Phelps"), Alvah Dunning, Mitchell Sabattis, Mart Moody, Bill Nye, and Paul Smith. His research travels resulted in the first edition of *The Adirondacks: Illustrated*, a practical as well as entertaining guidebook published in 1874. The guidebook covered a trip on Lake Champlain to Plattsburgh then inland to all of the well-known areas of the Adirondacks and contained information on guides, routes, distances, hotels, canoe trips, walking trails, and an abundance of descriptive details. Stoddard's early guidebooks relied on etchings and drawings for illustrations, often based on the photographs that he had taken in the region.

Although subsequent guidebooks by other authors may have involved more substantive information, Stoddard's *Adirondacks: Illustrated* was much more popular. Biographer Maitland C. De Sormo attributed the guide's success to humor and better illustrations. Stoddard "was a wittier writer as well as an artist and photographer. Therefore his illustrations were more original, authentic and effective."[10] Stoddard's humor, perhaps inspired by Mark Twain, was dispersed throughout his guidebooks. For example, he referred to Samuel de Champlain's historic voyage as the first visit of a "sporting man. . .who, in 1609, joined a company of native tourists on a gunning expedition to the southern borders of the future state park, where he fell in with a party of Iroquois and succeeded in bagging a satisfactory number."[11] Stoddard's narrative included the purported idiosyncrasies of his traveling companion (brother-in-law): "the professor. . . abstains from the absorption of that mysterious compound known as hash, on account of the uncertainty of its origin. Revolts at [the] sight of sausages, as it is unpleasantly suggestive of a dear little dog that he once loved."[12] Although Stoddard relied less on a humorous narrative style in his Lake George volumes, he did poke fun at the tourist business. His description of the Lake House wryly noted its "magnificent collection of relics, consisting of a piece of bomb shell, Indian pestle [pounding tool], and a tumbler of tooth-picks."[13] "When the source of revenue [from tourists] is removed and cold weather sets in," according to Stoddard, "it is *said* that the inhabitants imitate the example of bruin [a bear], who retires to some den. . .until awakened by the breath of spring, when he wanders forth, seeking whom he may devour."[14] In later editions of his guidebooks, Stoddard deemphasized humor and his narrative style and provided more travel information. However, some of his favorite vignettes, such as the story of Captain Sam Patchin's sleigh ride, were carried in all subsequent editions of the Lake George guide.

His first guidebooks had few maps, largely because not many up-to-date maps existed at the time. Stoddard's remedy was to learn the art of cartography; in the process he evolved into a celebrated mapmaker of the region. Stoddard acquired his foundation in surveying from an apprenticeship with Hiram R. Philo, an accomplished surveyor from Glens Falls and his brother's father-in-law. His 1880 "Map of the Adirondack Wilderness," which took almost four years to complete, was highly praised by outdoor magazines and sportsmen. Stoddard relied on official surveys, earlier maps, local authorities, guides, hotelkeepers, and his own detailed observations. His famous map of Lake George was based on his field work at the lake in 1880, using the 30-foot steamer *Owl* to make the triangulations. The multi-colored chart, reprinted many times, showed steamboat routes, hotels, roads, cottages, mountains, and islands, and included eight enlarged maps of the towns, the Narrows, and Fort Ticonderoga. In 1890 Stoddard produced a similar chart of Lake Champlain. A hydrographic chart of Lake George, based on his exacting survey work from 1906 to 1908, was a significant navigation aid for boaters well into the twentieth century. Stoddard was always willing to change with the times, as evidenced by his use of an automobile to evaluate road conditions for his illustrated auto road maps published between 1908 and 1915.

The steamer *Owl*. Photograph by Seneca Ray Stoddard.
(Lake George Historical Association)

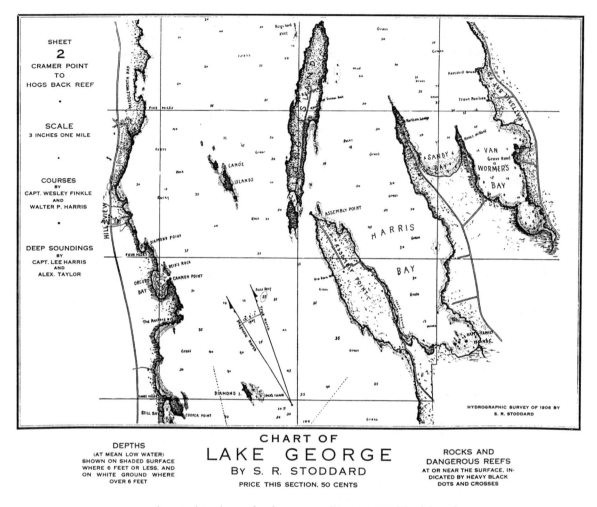

Hydrographic chart of Lake George by S. R. Stoddard (1907).

While Stoddard may be remembered for his guidebooks and maps, his most significant legacy is the thousands of pictures taken during four decades in the Adirondacks. Biographer William Crowley of the Adirondack Museum submitted that Stoddard "produced outstanding photographs when he turned the camera's eye upon the Adirondack landscape, and he was among a generation of American photographers who pioneered in the field of landscape photography."[15] Many of his photographs remain the representative illustrations of the Adirondacks in the late nineteenth and early twentieth century. Stoddard's photography has been linked to the "Hudson River School" because of its emphasis on the natural landscape and to "Luminism," which emphasized the effects of varying light on realistic scenery. His views of the glassy stillness of Lake George are "characteristic of the smooth surfaces of Luminist painting."[16]

Seneca Ray Stoddard created his images at a time when photography was an arduous task. Prior to the use of dry plates in the 1880s, wet-collodion negatives had to be processed on site in a tent. Even with dry plates, photography involved heavy cumbersome equipment, and good photographs were as much a science as an art. Stoddard was quick to adopt the use of powdered magnesium metal as a flashlight powder for night exposures. Some of Stoddard's remarkable campfire scenes in the Adirondacks were taken in 1888, only a year after the new flash powder was introduced by German chemists. His most extraordinary night photographs, using multiple flashes, were taken of the Washington Square Arch in New York City, the Statue of Liberty, and the Chicago World's Fair. Stoddard's skill led to his engagement as the photographer for the American Canoe Association, Delaware and Hudson Company, Central Vermont Railway, and the Adirondack Railroad. He was also employed by Verplank Colvin as head of the photographic section for the state topographical survey of the Adirondacks, producing stunning panoramic views from the summits of the mountains.

Stoddard's photographs won instant acclaim, including laudable comments on his display at the 1876 Philadelphia Centennial Exhibition. His work was marketed through the largest retailer of photography in the country, E. & H. T. Anthony & Co. of New York City, and sold on steamboats, in bookstores, several hotels, including the Fort William Henry Hotel, and advertised in his guidebooks.[17] The job of producing the prints was largely relegated to his wife and other female employees at the Glens Falls office. Unfortunately, Stoddard's prints are often used today without a credit line since the information on the origin of the photographs has been lost over the years.

Stoddard's reputation was enhanced by lecture/slide shows on the Adirondacks. His shows, involving over 200 tinted lantern slides shown on a huge 30-foot square canvas, were given during the winter in cities and at hotels in the Adirondacks during the summer. Stoddard's most consequential lecture was before the New York State Assembly in Albany on February 25, 1892. The head of the Forestry Commission introduced Stoddard to a packed Assembly with the explanation that the presentation was on behalf of the pending legislation to create an Adirondack Park. The following day the *Albany Evening Journal* noted Stoddard's conservationist message, which decried the ruthless exploitation of the forest and suggested that the purpose of the lecture was to show the "public that great and beautiful natural park to the north of us, to the end that the interests of the people might be awakened to the idea of protecting the forest and keeping it in its natural state."[18] Over the next few months, Stoddard replicated the show, including his appeal for preservation, for audiences in many of the cities in the state. On May 20, 1892, the New State Assembly passed the bill to establish the Adirondack Park. Stoddard's preservationist views were later reflected in his publication, the *Northern Monthly Magazine* (1906-1908).

In addition to his travels in the Adirondacks, Seneca Ray Stoddard journeyed to many parts of the Northern Hemisphere. He completed a 2,000-mile trek in a sailing canoe, the *Atlantis*, from Glens Falls south on the Hudson River and along the Atlantic coast to Truro, Nova Scotia. The voyage, requiring five summers from 1883 to 1887, tested the sailing skills of Stoddard and his varying sailing mates on the open sea in an 18-foot canoe. In 1892 Stoddard traveled to Alaska, hauling the largest camera in the world, built under his supervision to capture the Alaskan landscape. The huge camera used 20-by-49 1/2-inch negatives but failed to work, forcing Stoddard to use smaller cameras. His first lecture upon his return was before an audience of 1,000 at the Glens Falls Opera House. In the winter of 1894 he traveled with his cameras to Florida and Havana, and during the summer made a grand tour of the American west, producing 700 negatives. The following year Stoddard toured the Mediterranean and the Near East; in 1897 he traveled to England, Scotland, the Scandinavian countries, Russia, and the Atlantic islands; and in 1900 to France and Germany. Stoddard always used innovative financial arrangements to defray the expenses of his trips—either exchanging passage for ads in his guidebooks, photographing passengers and crew members for cash, or selling souvenir photo albums of the voyage to passengers.

Stoddard's wife died in 1906. Two years later he married Emily Doty, who lived until 1936. His oldest son, a prominent lawyer, had served as a military officer in the Spanish-American War, the Philippine-American War (1898-1902), and World War I; his youngest son, born in 1876, became a doctor. Both sons died in 1943. Seneca Ray Stoddard, the indomitable traveler, was confined to his bed in late 1916, suffering from arteriosclerosis. On April 26, 1917, Stoddard died, and with him an era in the documentation of Adirondack history ended.

Over the years Seneca Ray Stoddard's publishing endeavors have left their mark on the Adirondacks. Both his *Adirondacks: Illustrated* and *Lake George; A Book of To-Day* spanned four decades of publication. Stoddard also produced a dozen picture albums of Adirondack destinations, hotel brochures, booklets, postcards, maps, and 10,000 photographs of the region.

The following narrative is a condensed version of Stoddard's 1914 guide to Lake George.

Self-Portrait, Seneca Ray Stoddard.
(Richard K. Dean Collection)

Lake George[19]

Lake George! How the heart bounds and the pulse quickens at [the] sound of the words that bring with them thoughts of the "Holy Lake." In fancy again we breathe the air, heavy with the odor of pines and cedar, or fragrant with the breath of blossoming clover. Again we wander among the daisies and buttercups that gem the hill-side sloping so gently down to where the wavelets kiss the white beach or, floating among the verdant islands, watch the sunlight and shadow chase each other over the mountain.

A memory of the past comes to me as I write of good old days now past and gone; when lumbering coaches toiled heavily along where now go swiftly glancing trains; of tally-ho, now crowded out by monsters breathing fire and smoke; of sounding plank in place of shining lines of steel. More comfortable now undoubtedly are its luxurious cars, but the poetry has gone with the dear old stages, and the new things of the day have made the going commonplace. Changes about its shores have also come with time, but in changeless form the hills still hang above it and rightfully and becomingly it still holds its proud title "Queen of American Waters."

Fort William Henry was built of pine logs and covered with sand. The ruins are in the sandy, tree-covered bluff west of the railroad depot, between it and the Fort William Henry Hotel. The outline is still preserved, showing the form of the old fort, nearly square, flanked on the west, south, and a part of the east side, by a ditch, and on the north by the lake. The "Old Fort Well" was within the fort and still remains near the east side, partially filled with stones and rubbish. Where the fence which now incloses the grounds on the east would run, if continued out into the lake deep under water, is the old Fort dock. Outside the dock a little way, may be seen an old hulk,* with blackened ribs and keel half hidden in the sand, which is

Forty-four-foot sloop raised near the site of Fort William Henry. (Lake George Hist. Assoc.)

*Stoddard was repeating a story from earlier editions of his guidebook; the shipwreck had been removed from the lake after the turn of the century. Almost a half century earlier, Benjamin F. DeCosta noted "the hull of a large vessel is still seen in fair, calm weather, and appears to be nearly full of cobble-stones, probably ballast. There the old craft has lain for an entire century. . . The spot where this hulk may be seen is near the steamboat landing."[20] Burned to the water's edge and laden with military relics, the 44-foot sloop was raised on July 2, 1903, by William S. Tuttle and sold for souvenirs.[21] Several frames from this historic vessel are on exhibit at the Lake George Historical Association.

supposed to have been one of the number sunk by Vaudreuil in [March] 1757.* Shell and cannon balls have been taken from it at different times and in 1820 two small cannon were removed from the wreck.

Fort George is east of old Fort William Henry, on the low bluff, around which the railroad swings as it turns away from the lake. It was built in 1759, by General Amherst (the portion completed being but a bastion of what was then designed for an extensive fortification) and was occupied as a military post while the necessity for one lasted. It is now but a great heap of earth held in place by the walls, which are quite well preserved on the east side and sloping off from edge toward the centre and north. The greater portion of the stonework has been removed, and burned to make lime.** On the table land, a little to the southwest of the fort, was the old entrenched camp, the scene of the engagement between [Baron de] Dieskau and General [William] Johnson in 1755.

The Battle Monument stands on the open ground [erected by the] Society of Colonial Wars of the State of New York and unveiled with imposing civic and military ceremonies [on] September 8, 1903. The figures, representing Gen. Sir William Johnson and the Mohawk Chief King Hendrick, are of bronze, 9 feet high, standing on a pedestal of Barre [VT.] granite 12 feet in height.

Lake George is the name of the village at the south end of St. Sacrament in place of the time-honored old one of "Caldwell,"*** and it is in order for people who live at various points to explain that they are not at Lake George really, but only encamped round about the waters thereof. It is a comely village awakened to the newer life of thrift and enterprise in place of the slumbrous past, with growing civic pride and independence in its modern ways and belongings, yet delightful in its combination of the old and new and restful in its shaded streets and beautiful mountain setting.

Opposite page:
Top: "Steam Yacht Landing" at Lake George Village.
(Postcard, author's collection)
Middle: "Boat Landing, Fort William Henry Hotel" (ca. 1904).
(Postcard, author's collection)
Bottom: The Fort William Henry Hotel II opened in 1911 after a fire had destroyed the original hotel in 1909. The second hotel was razed in 1969, but the dining room on the west side of the building was saved.
(Postcard, author's collection)

---

*In March 1757 a French force of 1,600 men under the leadership of Francois-Pierre de Rigaud de Vaudreuil attacked the garrison at Fort William Henry. Although the French and Indians were unsuccessful in destroying the fort, they did burn the outer fort structures, bateaux, and a few of the larger vessels.

**Original plans obtained from England were used in the partial reconstruction of Fort George in the 1920s. According to a 1921 newspaper report. "The east wall has been entirely refaced and the excavation of the interior has been started. . .with the exception of the upper parts, the stone walls of the various rooms are in an excellent state of preservation."[22] Noting the 80,000 visitors yearly to Fort Ticonderoga, an editorial in the *Lake George Mirror* in 1930 called for "the rebuilding of these historic ruins. Hundreds of relics, cannon balls, muskets, Indian arrowheads. . .are scattered about this section, and most of them could be obtained in a museum in the park grounds."[23]

***Lake George Village was incorporated in 1903; the Caldwell township, however, existed until 1962 when the town also adopted Lake George Village as its name.

Hotels and boarding houses are varied and sufficient ordinarily for all occasions, the price ranging from $1 to $4 a day, according to season and accommodations.

Fort William Henry Hotel is at the head of Lake George just west of the ruins of that famous old fort after which it was named. It looks out northward, commanding one of the most beautiful of the noted views of this most beautiful lake. It stands centrally on a bluff in the pathway of the winds that draw through the notch north and south between the mountains and out over the surface of the lake. High mountains rise east and west but gradually in gentle lines that make for restfulness, casting long shadows in the dewy mornings and glorious afternoons. Broad piazzas and northern windows and balconies reveal miles of receding shores that stretch to where verdant islands close the narrowing way and the big mountains stand guard above the Narrows. The house is built and furnished in old colonial style. Stone and slate and concrete give it an air of substantiality that appeals to such as prefer substance to display and flowering shrubs soften all.

The house is modern in all its fittings, modern in all appointments. It should meet all reasonable requirements of young and old in its admirable combination of luxuries and conveniences that have now become necessaries to the discerning traveller. Amusements will be found fitted to languid and strenuous alike, riding, driving, motoring, motor-boating, sailing, rowing—each has its votaries [enthusiasts] and here all may find satisfactory means of enjoying their own. It is simply to touch a button at the office and the thing is done.

A new resort feature of this section is the opening of the house for winter guests. For such entertainment was it built and equipped and amply meets all requirements at all times. Its initial season was a great success as evidenced by an overflowing house. Later experience under the general manager, Albert Thieriot, has demonstrated that season has little to do with success where seasonable sports are offered and an all-the-year house has no reason to lament the passing of the summer where the winter's guests are provided with such comforts as may be had at home. With winter come winter's amusement, snowshoeing, skeeing, curling, toboganing and kindred sports, for which visitors journeyed to Montreal, are here in perfection, less than an afternoon's trip from the great metropolis.

The Carpenter House is on the main street of the village, which continues northward along west of Fort William Henry Park. This house will provide for about 50 people.

The Worden is at the north end of the village, facing east, the north piazza looking out on the Lake, where the street descends to Pine Point, a favorite resort for guests of the house. The Worden will accommodate about 100 guests. An omnibus runs to all trains and boats, free for guests of the house. The house is substantial and convenient. There are bath and toilet rooms on upper floors. It has

Opposite page:
Top: Southern view of Lake George with the Fort William Henry Hotel II in the foreground.
(Postcard, author's collection)
Middle: Rowing crew from the Worden Hotel in 1911.
(Lake George Historical Association)
Bottom: "East end of pergola and steamboat landing." (Postcard, author's collection)

The Worden Hotel in Lake George Village.
(Postcard, author's collection)

electric bells, the best of modern spring beds. There is a fine piazza along the front, and balconies on the first floor, facing the north and west.

The Arlington House adjoins the Worden on the south. A free 'bus runs to all trains.

The smaller hotels and boarding houses are to be found in and about the town.

Driving, Autoing and Trolleying

The Bolton Road is the most picturesque and one in which the lake is the ever-present and evervarying feature. It may be continued up past Northwest Bay and indefinitely among the mountains beyond and still be found interesting. Lateral roads lead from this up the western hills and offer a variety of interesting if somewhat laborious ways.

The East Side drive is an interesting one for those who enjoy woods and partially cultivated country. It follows eastward along the beach at the south end of the lake, then turning north passes Fort George cottages and numerous picturesque summer cottages and finally the Paulist Fathers "St. Mary's of the Lake," then rising to the cleared space around the north side of French Mountain, overlooks a great expanse of the lake. A branch road may be followed along the shore to "Lake George Park," on Dunham's Bay, notable as the summer place of the late Edward Eggleston, novelist and historian.*

*Edward Eggleston (1837-1902) was a noted historian and novelist and a writer for *Scribner's Monthly*, *Century*, and other periodicals. Although he never attended college, he became president of the American Historical Association. His brother, George Cary Eggleston (1839-1911), was also a writer who summered at Lake George.

To Prospect Mountain, seen prominently at the west, is an interesting wood and field excursion. The drive is by the Warrensburg road to the first toll-gate, thence around the mountain, approaching the summit point finally from the southwest, by which the ascent is gradual. From the observatory here fully one-half of the lake can be seen, and the main peaks of the Adirondacks easily distinguished.

The Ruins of Fort Gage are about one mile south of Fort William Henry, where the trolley cuts through the big hill. The lines of earthworks may still be traced through the pines that now cover them.*

Steamboats

The *Sagamore* was built at Baldwin by the W. & [A.] Fletcher Co., of Hoboken, N.J., in 1902. The boat is thoroughly up to date in its fittings. Its dimensions are 224 feet length over all, 30 feet moulded beam, 54 feet beam over all. The hull is of steel divided into three water-tight compartments by bulkheads. It has a vertical beam engine, cylinder 44 inches in diameter, 10 feet stroke of piston, has Morgan feathering wheels and will make 20 miles an hour. It has steam steering gear; is lighted by electricity, and has a 14-inch search light. The hurricane deck is arranged for the convenience of passengers, and is accessible aft by companionways leading from the deck below. The dining room is on the main deck.

The *Horicon* (new) was built at Baldwin during the winter of 1910-1911. It is 231 feet long, 59 feet beam, has three decks with passenger accommodations for 1500 people; dining room located on main deck aft, seating capacity 100 persons. The hull and engine were contracted. . .through the well known shipbuilding firm, W. & A. Fletcher Co., Hoboken, N.J. The hull was launched December 1st, 1910. The boat is provided with two boilers 10 feet 6 inches wide, 26 feet long; the engine is the jet condensing beam type, diameter of cylinder 52 in., stroke of piston 10 ft. Patent feathering wheels 22 1/2 ft. diameter, 8 ft. 9 in. wide, with curved steel buckets. The dining cabin, quarter-deck and main saloon is finished in butternut with cherry trimming to show the natural wood. The boat will develop a speed of 21 miles an hour.

The *Horicon* leaves Lake George (south end of the lake), at about 10:00 a.m. (on arrival of the train from Albany and Troy and connection from the Hudson River night boats and N.Y. through sleeping cars), and touching at the various landings reaches Baldwin about noon, where passengers are transferred by rail to the Champlain boat at Montcalm Landing. In the afternoon the *Horicon* returns from Baldwin with passengers from the Champlain boat, connecting at Lake George station with trains south to Troy, Albany and New York. Fare through the Lake $1.50 either way. Excursion tickets good on date of sale only. The *Sagamore* runs [daily and] on Sundays, during July and August. The dining room is on the main deck. Dinners are served going north and immediately after leaving Baldwin, going south. Price $1.00. The table is wholesome, substantial, and of the best material and served in good manner. To feast the eye on the beauties of Lake George and satisfy the craving of a healthy appetite, such as Lake George air usually brings is a happy combination of good things.

---

*Constructed on a hill southwest of Lake George, Fort Gage was a stockaded redoubt (small fort) that protected the military road to Fort Edward. In 1975 a salvage excavation of the fort occurred after the site had been twice bulldozed for a motel; today the area is covered by the Ramada Inn.[24]

The *Mohican*, new (built in 1908), length over all, 115 feet; 26 1/2 ft. beam outside the guards, twin screw propeller. Her regular trip is between Lake George, Pearl Point and Paradise Bay during July and August.

The boat is subject to charter when not running on regular trips. During May, before the larger boats are in service, and in October, after they have been withdrawn, the *Mohican* makes the round trip daily, Sundays excepted, leaving Baldwin at about 7 a.m. Returning leaves Lake George station about 2:40 p.m. or on arrival of train from the south.

The 115-foot *Mohican II* (ca. 1919). The vessel began
operation in 1908 and is still in service today.
(Postcard, author's collection)

Built in 1912, the 70-foot gasoline yacht *Mountaineer II* was one of the vessels owned
by the Lake George Steamboat Company at the time of Stoddard's 1914 guidebook.
(Postcard, author's collection)

During July and August the fast power boat, The *Mountaineer* (new), leaves Lake George station at 10:00 a.m., 3:00 p.m., 5:00 p.m. and 8:00 p.m., making signal landings along the west shore as far as [Hotel] Marion, thence across to Victoria Lodge and Kattskill Bay, returning by the east shore.

Down the Lake

Tea Island is a little gem by the west shore, somewhat resembling the crater of an extinct volcano, with the rim broken away on the east side, forming a beautiful harbor in miniature. Tradition says Abercrombie buried gold and valuables here. [See note chapter 18.]

A little further north where the road runs well up the side of the rising ground at the west is the summer home ["Abenia"] of George Foster Peabody, philanthropist of national fame.

St. Mary's of the Lake, on the east side, is the summer place of the Paulist Fathers [Roman Catholic missionary priests], who also own Harbor Islands, camping there occasionally in the summer time.

Plum Point, a half-mile north of the St. Mary's received its name, it is said, because of the large quantities of plums once raised here. The casual observer will see no plums, and may not see the point. Dunham's Bay opens up on the right.

Diamond Island, near the centre of the lake, three miles from its head, was so named because of the quartz crystals once found here in considerable quantities. It was fortified and used as a military depot by [General John] Burgoyne after his capture of Ticonderoga in 1777, and the same year was the scene of an engagement between the English then in possession and a party of Americans under Col. John Brown, resulting in the defeat of the latter. [See chapter 10.]

Cramer's Point (west side two and three-fourths miles) was an island when the islands all belonged to the state, but it is said that a former owner of the adjoining shore looked upon it with longing eyes, and one night the kind waves, or something equally efficacious, filled up the intervening space with earth, the island and the main land clasped hands across the muddy chasm and the two were made one so that thereafter no law was found to put them asunder.*

The Antlers [Hotel] is the large building on the west (three and one-half miles).

Reid's Rock is just north of Cannon Point (west three and three-quarters miles). A man named [Rud] Reid, whose love for rum had taken him across the lake one stormy night in late autumn, was found on this rock in the morning frozen stiff, and covered with ice from the dashing spray.

Orcut Bay is entered between Reid's Rock and Cannon Point. "The Healing Spring" is just over the ridge west of this bay, and may be reached along shore.

Diamond Point (west 4 miles) comes next. The quartz here, like that of Diamond Island, occasionally yields very pretty crystals. Sampson Paul, an Indian, who flourished over half a century ago, once with a common fishing spear here, killed a panther as he was coming out of the water benumbed with cold.** Diamond Point

---

*George H. Cramer, one-time president of the Rensselaer and Saratoga Railroad, was said to have hired Edward N. Sanderson to dump 40 loads of rock and soil to fill in the channel between Cramer Island and the shore, thus annexing land that would have been a state island.[25]

**The story of "Old Samson Paul" was first published in *Lake George* by J. P. Sweet in 1863.[26]

Wreckage of the 75-foot steamer *Scioto* at Canoe Island.
(Photo by the author)

House—boats do not land. Reached by carriage from Lake George, or by small steamers. Canoe Islands (west 4 1/2 miles), east of Diamond Point House, about midway between it and Long Island. Here in 1880 the American Canoe Association was organized.

Long Island is the largest island at Lake George, being something more than a mile in length.

South Island [Speaker Heck Island], separated by a shallow strait from Long Island, usually displays two or three model Canvas camps occupied by free permission of the owner.

Assembly Point is at the right, 4 1/2 miles from Caldwell, beyond, is Harris Bay, about three-quarters of a mile in width, extending south more than 1 1/2 miles, at one place almost making an island of Assembly Point. Near its head [Harris Bay] is the Happy Family group of four pretty little islands. This section is quite noted for pickerel fishing.

Ripley's Point [Cleverdale Point] extends northward about a mile east of Assembly Point (right 5 1/2 miles from Caldwell). It is a pleasant colony of cottage camps, popular and populous during the summer, with Glens Falls, Hudson Falls and Fort Edward people.

Horicon Lodge, which stood on Ripley's Point, was destroyed by fire in 1911. The landing is maintained for the accommodation of cottagers.

Hotel Willard is on Sheldon's Point with capacity for about 100 guests.

Grove Hotel (right 7 miles), is among the trees on the east shore of the bay that makes deep down into Harrisena [area named for the Harris family]. Capacity of the house and cottages about 75.

Trout Pavilion is on the east side of Kattskill Bay, seven miles from Caldwell as the boat runs. Its pleasant grouping of hotel and cottages among the trees impress one favorably. Accommodations are here afforded for nearly 100 guests. Water comes from a mountain spring and a farm connected with the house supplies fresh vegetables. All steamers land. The place is quite noted as a fishing resort. All necessaries of the sport with guides and boats are supplied. George H. Cronkhite, who as boy and man, has resided here all his life, is proprietor. Long distance telephone in office.

Elizabeth Island appears as a point of the shore north of the Kattskill House.

Pilot Mountain (right, 7 miles, air line from Caldwell), nearly sharp at its summit, descends steeply to the Lake at points where we touched. Buck Mountain (right, 9 miles), a grand rocky, round-featured dome on the east, rising 2,000 [2,334] feet above the lake. With Pilot Mountain on its south flank it is locally known as the "deer pasture."

Hotel Marion is on the west side of the lake, 5 1/2 miles north of the steamboat landing, at its head. All line boats land on their trips north and south. Accommodations are offered for 250 guests. A regular postoffice, telegraph and telephones are in the house. Golf, tennis and croquet grounds are on the hotel preserve. Boat and carriage liveries supply all needs. Picturesque roads along shore and backward over the mountains invite. . .riding and driving, and shaded walks to that best of exercise for which nature has made provision. About the house are a variety of native trees—oak, pine, birch and butternut. Directly west is a bluff, with forest at base and summit and in the depths good hunting for the smaller game. The house has

The Marion House (later Hotel Marion) from *Caldwell, Lake George*
(Lake George Printing Company, 1901.)

communicating rooms and rooms with private baths. Guests of the Marion have golf privileges on the Lake George club course subject to N.Y. rules governing kindred organizations. The proprietor is a member of the American Motor League and the needs of the motorists have been anticipated in a new garage with necessaries and supplies.

The Lake George Club [built in 1909] has its home in the fine building, modern in every feature, a little way south of the Marion. W. K. Bixby is president.* The club is composed of men who are recognized as having the best interests of Lake George at heart. It has been called the "Millionaires' Club" but you can stop for $50 a year if you are all right otherwise.

Victoria Lodge is on the east side, about 8 miles from the head, with a number of lesser cottages scattered along at the foot of Buck Mountain.

Northward from Hotel Marion are a number of pretty little islands and the fine sweep of Basin Bay. The Three Brothers' Islands, now united by a continuous bridge, were owned and during the season occupied by the late Spencer Trask.**

Belvoir Island [Clay Island], seeming a point of the main land until a narrow passage way reveals the open bay [Huddle Bay] at the west, belongs to Rev. Geo. W. Clow of White Plains. A number of modest cottages are here among the trees. Recluse Island is just east of Belvoir Island, the steamer passing on the east and circling round it toward the west to make Bolton Landing. This island was the subject of the "earthquake hoax" of 1868, at which time it was reported in the New York papers as having sunk 80 feet below the surface. A graceful bridge connects it with what was once known as Sloop Island. Dome Island is nine miles from Caldwell, near the centre of the lake. Seen from the north or south, it has the appearance of a huge emerald dome, somewhat flattened, but bearing enough of the appearance to justify the name. This island was purchased from the State in 1856, for $100.*** It is also the property of the owner of Recluse Island. A gold mine is in the side of Buck Mountain†, near the water's edge, easterly across the lake from Dome Island. It is said that gold is here in paying quantities and that platinum is also found. The Calf Pen is a notable notch in the rock along shore near the gold mine. The section between this Dome Island is noted as deep water fishing grounds.

*William Keeney Bixby, president of the American Car and Foundry Company, purchased the famous Mohican House in Bolton Landing at the turn of the century. The old hotel was razed and a stately white mansion constructed on the site in 1901-1902. His son Harold was among the sponsors of Charles Lindbergh's transatlantic flight and was responsible for naming the plane *The Spirit of St. Louis*. One of William K. Bixby's boats, the 45-foot gasoline launch *Forward*, built in 1906, is presently a New York State Submerged Heritage Preserve in 40 feet of water on the east side of Diamond Island.

**Spencer Trask, a successful financier who backed Thomas A. Edison, later became president of the New York Edison Company and served on the executive committee of General Electric. In 1902 Trask and his wife Katrina purchased the former Crosbyside Hotel and subsequently donated the property to the Girls' Friendly Society to use for affordable vacations for working women. Although the original Crosbyside structure burned, the Wiawaka Hotel continued the mission of the Girls' Friendly Society. Near the present Wiawaka docks lie seven French and Indian War bateaux in a New York State Submerged Heritage Preserve.

***Shortly after Stoddard finished his last Lake George guidebook, Dome Island was purchased by John S. Apperson in order to forestall economic development. The island was donated to the Nature Conservancy in 1956 and remains one of the most primitive islands on the lake.

†After one purported find of gold in 1884, many people futilely searched for the precious metal on Buck Mountain.

The Lake View House is on Bolton Bay, westward from Belvoir Island [Clay Island]. Capacity about 100. The house stands on a point of land projecting from the west shore, surrounded by a grove of native trees affording the maximum of breeziness with a minimum of exposure to the sun. The grounds are picturesque and the effort has been quite successfully made of leaving nature's perfect work comparatively untouched while relieving the place of unsightly objects and making all trim and accessible. The outlook is unsurpassed anywhere for quiet and beauty as revealed in retreating headlands and pretty grouping of island forms and gate-like openings in the distant Narrows, beyond which rises giant Black Mountain. A pleasant feature is the tennis court among the trees completely shaded from morning and afternoon sun. All the amusements common to summer places may be enjoyed here. A large room for hops, etc., affords opportunity for evening gatherings. A dark room on the grounds is a convenience appreciated by amateur photographers. A small steamboat built under Mr. J. Brown's directing hand, makes regular trips to and from the public landing on the arrival of the regular steamers. Guests of the house are welcome to free transportation whenever the boat runs.

Sweet Brier Island, north of the Lake View, [is] at the entrance of Phantom Bay.

The Algonquin [Hotel] is on the west shore of the little bay back of Sweet Brier island with capacity for 75 guests. Its furnishings are up-to-date and the house presents an attractive appearance with its surroundings of locusts and maples.

Bolton Landing is a little north of the old landing place, the dock building gabled and shingled on roof and sides. The Church of St. Sacrament is on a spur of the hill southwest of Bolton Landing, its bell tower, like some dwarf lighthouse, standing in front. A little to the north is the Roman Catholic Church. A Baptist Church is at the village, still further along. The village of a single street, lies back a little way—a picturesque and pretty hamlet, restful, drowsy even, calm and attractive.

Wilson's [Hotel] is a comfortable house on the west side of the village street, with accommodations for about 30. The Stewart House, a little farther north, takes boarders during the summer.

Motorists bound north should take steamer here at Bolton Landing for Sabbath Day Point, Hague or Rogers Rock landing. Fare to Sabbath Day Point $2.50 to $3.50, according to rating of car. Driver free. The drive over Hague Mountain is difficult and should not be undertaken except by the surest of hill climbers.

The Fenimore is at the west end of the bridge that connects with Green Island.

The Sagamore, which stood at the south end of Green Island,* was totally destroyed by fire April 12, 1914. Its rebuilding is uncertain. The cottages surrounding are owned by members of the club and occupied by them pending decision.

From the Sagamore dock the boat runs almost due east toward the Narrows, about two miles distant. Crown Island (west 10 miles), [is] but a little distance from Green Island. Northwest Bay (or "Ganouski," as the Indians called it) extends northward about four miles beyond Crown Island. When midway of the lake notice in the abrupt termination of the long mountain extending southerly beyond

*Before the Sagamore Hotel, Green Island may have played a role in the French and Indian War. According to an early newspaper report, "near the north end of Green Island and on its west side a formation which is evidently artificial, and designed for defense [was discovered]. . .On the main shore, and in different places from 200 to 300 yards from the water have been found various relics indicating an old encampment, or a battle ground. These have been hatchets of French manufacture, a Bayon[e]t, etc."[27]

Shelving Rock, the Sleeping Beauty, in fine profile against the sky, with face thrown backward and chin uprising from the lower forests at the south. The Bungalow Islands [Hen and Chickens Islands] form a pretty group near the east shore in the bay south of Shelving Rock. On one, the late Delevan Bloodgood, medical director U. S. Navy, has built picturesquely after the fashion of the East Indian bungalow.* Along the rocky shore of the mainland are many pretty bays and headlands. At one point a little brook makes out over a beach; up this stream, a little way, is a little gem, among cascades, called Shelving Rock Falls. Turning toward the west we see Tongue Mountain, rugged and broken, west of the Narrows, which sloping gradually southward, terminates in Montcalm Point, owned by Mr. J. Buchanan Henry. West of the mountain is Northwest Bay. "Green Oaks," the summer place of E. Corning Smith, of Albany, is on Turtle Island, lying within the Narrows northeast of Montcalm Point. Nearer is Oahu Island [also called Flora Island] (west 11 miles), the property of Gen. P. F. Bellinger, of Elizabeth, N. J. Gen. Bellinger occupies the cottage toward the south, while the one near the north end is the summer place of J. W. Moore, Chief Engineer U. S. Navy. Fourteen Mile Island is on the east. Why called Fourteen Mile Island the oldest inhabitant does not pretend to say. It is presumed, however, that fourteen miles was the estimated distance from Fort William Henry before actual measurement demonstrated it to be less. The island has an area of twelve acres. On the east side of the island, separating it from the mainland, is a narrow and deep channel, through which the largest steamers can pass. Here is another dock where excursion steamers land.** This island belongs to W. H. Beardsley, of the Florida East Coast Railway.

Mr. George O. Knapp of Chicago, whose summer place stands back on higher ground against Shelving Rock, owns the main land and shore from Shelving Rock Bay to Black Mountain Point.***

The Pearl Point House, standing on the extreme point of land projecting from the east shore out into the Narrows, is the only hotel in this part of the lake.

Rambling, quaint and profusely ornate in architecture, Pearl Point attracts much attention and admiration. It has piazzas on all sides resulting in cozy nooks with choice in wet or dry, sun or shade, heat and cold. The abundance of native trees that crowd close about almost hides it from view, yet with clear space below, admits free passage to every breeze that comes to it over the surrounding water. Including nearby cottages, it will provide for 100 guests. Boating is possible in nearly all weathers, even in winds, which might interfere in the more open lake. Fishing is equal to the best grounds of the Narrows. Long distance telephone brings the outside world near.

*The Forest Commission required the removal of private cottages from public islands. Bloodgood's bungalow was moved in sections over the ice to the private shoreline.

**On the night of August 3, 1893, tragedy struck after 27 passengers boarded the 55-foot steamboat *Rachel* at the Kenesaw House dock on Fourteen Mile Island. Bound for the Hundred Island House on the eastern shore of the Narrows, the steamer hit the submerged remains of an old pier just south of the hotel. The vessel capsized in the darkness, trapping some the passengers under the shade deck; nine lost their lives.[28] The *Rachel* was raised four days later. Both the Kenesaw House and the Hundred Island House closed after the turn of the century.

***In 1902 George O. Knapp, co-founder of the Union Carbide Corporation, finished a palatial estate on the side of Shelving Rock Mountain. An electric cable railway connected the boat dock to the basement of the main house. In 1917 a "defective wire" in the basement, related to the electric cable car, caused a fire that entirely destroyed the summer home.[29] In 1941 Knapp's extensive parcel of land was acquired by the state for public use.

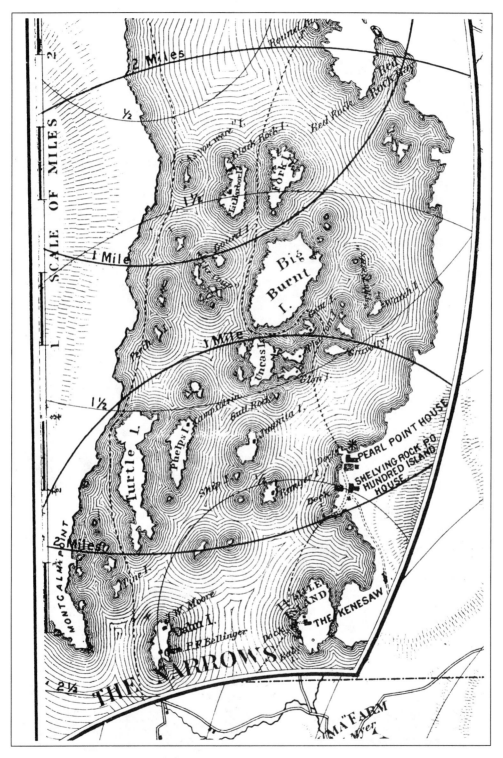

Detail of S. R. Stoddard's 1889 Lake George map.

The islands of the Narrows are best seen from the rocky outlook a little way up on the side of Shelving Rock. West is Ranger Island [once occupied by Judge F. E. Ranger of Glens Falls], with the pretty cottage and sharp-peaked tower. Next toward the north is Juanita. On Glen Island, next at the north, the "Cold Water Club," composed of solid men from Glens Falls, become boys again every year. The pretty cottage on Phantom Island is owned by J. A. Holden, State Historian, of Glens Falls, and will be occupied by himself and family during the season. Gravelly Island is the nearest to Pearl Point at the north. Over toward the west shore, between Ranger and Juanita Islands, can be seen parts of big Turtle and Phelps [Mohican] Islands. All of these islands except Turtle belong to the State.*

Burnt Island is the largest of the Hundred Island group, and occupies a central position toward the north. As-You-Are Island is the last of the group near the west shore. Once an old hunter who had been a soldier snapped his flintlock musket at a deer that had taken refuge here but missed fire, and he cried excitedly, "As you are 'till I prime." The frightened creature, not knowing which way to turn, stood until a second snap rendered flying impossible.** Little Harbor Island, east of the last named, has on its north border one of the curious holes in the rock caused by the action of moving water and bowlders [boulders] kept turning until they [wear] their way down into the softer rock. Fork island, its shape suggesting its name, terminates the cluster at the northeast. French Point projects from the west shore, 13 miles north of Caldwell and is owned and occupied during the summer by Mr. W. Stanford of Schenectady [now state forest].

Paradise Bay, on the east side, opposite French Point, is usually the objective point in the excursions made from the head of the lake. It is separated from Red Rock Bay on the south by Paradise Point. At its northern entrance are a number of pretty islands. There are other islands about here, some rising abruptly from the depths, moss-draped and thicket-crowded, while others only see the light when the water sinks to its lowest level. All around are treacherous shoals and reefs, and when

Opposite page: **Launches of Lake George**

Top left: The 47-foot *Oneita.* (Hague Historical Society)

Top right: The 75-foot steam yacht *Iroquois*, built in 1902, became the tour boat for the Silver Bay Association in the 1920s. (Postcard, author's collection)

Second: The 67-foot *Locust* was operated from Caldwell as a tour boat during the 1890s and after the turn of the century. In later years the vessel towed coal barges for the graphite operation in Hague. (Dragonfly Books, Ticonderoga)

Third, left: The launch *Uncas*, built in Hague, provided scheduled passenger service in the southern basin in 1912. (Hague Historical Society)

Third, right: The 80-foot *Fanita*, built in 1890. (Bolton Historical Society)

Fourth, left: The 80-foot, 800-horsepower *Ellide* broke the world speed record for a steam launch at 40 miles per hour. During the 1920s the "speed yacht" *Ellide* was used as a tour boat on Lake George.

Fourth, right: The 55-foot *Pocahontas*, built in 1885, burned at her dock on Three Brothers Island in 1913.

*All of the islands mentioned in this paragraph, including Turtle Island, are state property today. All private residences on state islands were removed in the twentieth century.

**The story of As You Were Island first appeared in print in 1863.[30]

Paradise Bay.
(Postcard, author's collection)

the light is right and the water rough, you may see the surface checked and spotted by the bright green that marks their position, while the little steamer with many a graceful turn, threads the labyrinth as the verdant gateways open and close along her course.

Black Mountain stands on our right, the "Monarch of the Lake." It stretches away to the north, seeming to recede as we approach and to travel with us, its granite crest lifted over two thousand feet above us, its rocky sides seamed and scarred and reddened by fires that have swept over it in times past. A sentinel, it seems, overlooking the whole lake and mountains round about; the first to welcome the rising sun, and at evening, glowing in the splendor of the dying day, while the valleys below are misty with the shadows of coming night. From its summit, 2,661 feet above tide, and 2,315 above Lake George, nearly the entire lake may be seen. To the north is Lake Champlain; at the east lie the Green Mountains; on the west and north the Adirondacks rise one above another, while away toward the south, like a thread of silver, stretches the mighty Hudson. If you make the ascent don't forget the luncheon. From Black Mountain Point a road ascends to the top of Black Mountain.

Half Way Isle is under the west shore, the centre of a circle, of which the circumference is the rim of a mountain that rises, amphitheater-like, around its western side. The Three Sirens, lovely and inviting, but surrounded by dangerous shoals and reefs, are near the middle of the lake nearly opposite Half Way Island. Hatchet Island is one of the same chain; the derivation of the name is unknown, but tradition connects it with an Indian hatchet which some one found there some time.*

---

*In 1853 Henry Marvin submitted that "some years ago a hatchet was found upon one of these islands, supposed to belong to one of the chiefs of the Mohicans, and from this circumstance they derived their name."[31]

One Tree Island is just west of the channel usually followed, which here runs close under the east shore. The stump is all that remains of that "one tree." Floating Battery is north of One Tree Island. It is the southernmost large island of the group lying along the east shore opposite the highest point of Black Mountain. In the little bay at its south end is the remains of what is said to be one of the two "castles" (floating batteries, or gunboats), built to accompany Abercrombie down the lake in his advance on Ticonderoga, in 1758.* The name is sometimes applied to the entire group, as it stretches northward. Mother Bunch is the name given to the northernmost member of the group, because, it is said, of a fancied resemblance between a rock standing on the east shore of one of the islands and an old woman. The name is a beautiful tribute to the memory of the old lady anyway, while the classic elegance and appropriateness of the term only fell short of absolute inspiration in that it was not advanced a step farther to "Grandmother" Bunch, and done with it. The Cives Rock is a solid wall, breaking off perpendicular; from the mountain slope on the right, at the north end of Mother Bunch group. Water constantly drips over its face, and c[h]ives (a species of garlic growing in tufts), spring spontaneously from its fissures. The largest boats can be laid up along side of this rock in still weather.

The Harbor Islands are near the center of the lake, the west channel passing close by their western border. They are owned by the Paulists, who received a title to them from the State in 1872, and who occupy them occasionally as a camping place. The group is the first of any considerable size on the west side, north of the Narrows, and was once the scene of one of the bloodiest engagements in the history of the lake. On the 25th of July, 1757, a party of between three and four hundred English, commanded by Col. John Parker, left Fort William Henry, and under cover of the darkness proceeded down the lake on a scout. When near this place, at dawn of the next morning, dark objects shot out from among the islands to meet them, while the savage war-whoop sounded on all sides. As the yelling horde advanced the English became panic-stricken and sought safety in flight, but their clumsy barges were no match for the light canoes of the enemy. Some threw themselves into the lake and succeeded in reaching the shore and were there pursued and struck down by the savages. One hundred and thirty-one English were killed outright, twelve escaped, and the rest were taken prisoners. Father Roubaud, a Jesuit priest, says in his "Relations": "The first object which presented itself to my eyes on arriving there was a large fire, while the wooden spits fixed in the earth gave signs of a feast—indeed, there was one taking place. But oh, Heaven, what a feast! The remains of the body of an Englishman were there, the skin stripped off and more than one-half of the flesh gone. A moment after I perceived these inhuman beings eat, with famishing avidity, of this human flesh; I saw them taking up this detestable broth in large spoons and, apparently, without being able to satisfy themselves with it; they informed me that they had prepared themselves for this feast by drinking from skulls filled with human blood, while their smeared faces and stained lips gave evidence of the truth of the story." The good father attempted to reason with them, but to no avail. One said to him: "You have French taste; I have Indian; this food is good for me," offering at the same time a piece of the human flesh to the horrified priest.**

*The few scattered remains of this wreck seem to correspond to an eighteenth-century vessel.

**The story of the annihilation of Colonel John Parker's expeditionary force began appearing in guidebooks after the publication of Benjamin C. Butler's *Lake George and Lake Champlain* in 1868,

Vicar's Island is just north of the Harbor Islands. Here, on its northern border, an affecting incident transpired once, of which Captain Sam Patch[i]n, who lived at Sabbath Day Point at the time, was the hero. One winter's day the Captain conceived the idea of sailing his grist to Bolton mill on the ice, so, piling the bags of grain into the old cutter, and with a pitchfork held firmly in his hands for a rudder, he hoisted sail and sped away before a strong north wind. The old man was, it is said, given to spiritual things and had, on this occasion, hoisted in rather too much rye in the liquid form to conduce to the safe transportation of that in the bags. The ice was "glare," and the cutter sailed well—remarkably well; but there was not so much certainty about the satisfactory behavior of the steering apparatus. The craft insisted on heading directly for the island, and could not be diverted from its course. An idea now occurred to the veteran. The cutter was of the kind called "jumper," a mettlesome old jumper at that, and the captain had great confidence in its ability to do whatever it undertook, so he decided to jump the island. He tried it! It was not, strictly speaking a success, for when the cutter reached the shore it paused against a rock, while Sam who seemed anxious to get along continued on some distance with the bags and finally brought up deep in a snow drift. Captain Sam was always dignified, but on this occasion it is said his manner of resting on that snow-drift was remarkably impressive. Even the snow felt moved, and the island itself was touched. When finally he came out and set his radiant face homeward, the records say that it was not a Sam of joy or a Sam of thanksgiving, but a Sam abounding in language that would have set a mule driver up in business, and brought despair to the boss canvasman of any circus that ever was.*

Deer's Leap Mountain is on the west, a little way north of Vicar's Island. The top is rounded, the side facing the lake a perpendicular wall of rock. At its foot are great fragments of rock, that have fallen from time to time, said to be the home of the rattlesnake. Here, once on a time, a buck, pursued by hunters, was driven and reached the brow of the precipice with a pack of yelling hounds close at his heels. . .but leaping for life, far out over the giddy height fell and was impaled on the point of a tree below.

Hulett's Landing is north of Black Mountain at the base of the mountain known as the Elephant, 18 miles from Caldwell. The main group of buildings, with the various cottages and bungalos, accommodate 250 guests.**

[continued from page 391] which described the battle.[32] A number of statements in Stoddard's version of the story need clarification. Although an attack by English provincial troops on a French reconnaissance party led by Lieutenant de St. Ours had occurred a few days earlier at "Isle de la Barque," Colonel Parker's force was ambushed at Sabbath Day Point.[33] The provincials were not in "clumsy barges" but in whaleboats and some bateaux; bateaux and whaleboats were called "barges" in translations of French military journals.[34] Sixty to 100 provincial troops escaped and returned by whaleboat or land to Fort William Henry.[35] The Indian camp where Father Roubaud observed the cannibalism was located near Fort Carillon (Ticonderoga).[36]

*Captain Samuel Patchin, a Revolutionary War veteran, built a home on Sabbath Day Point just before 1800. Francis Parkman (chapter 16) visited Patchin in 1842. On March 18, 1844, Patchin died and was buried in a cemetery adjacent to Route 9N in Hague. The story of Patchin's sleigh ride, repeated in more than 40 editions of Stoddard's guidebooks, was first published in J. P. Sweet's *Lake George* in 1863.[37]

**In 1909 the 200-guest Hulett House used the eclectic advertisement "Amusements are, hunting and fishing with dancing."[38]

The Hulett House.
(Postcard, author's collection)

Meadow Point, with a cluster of pretty cottages, is north of Hulett's on the same shore.

Hog's Back is the rugged mountain extending along on the east. Near its highest point [Israel] Putnam and [Robert] Rogers once came upon an Indian encampment, and, after the heroic manner of warfare in those days left none to tell the tale.* North of Hog's Back stretches Spruce Mountain—strikingly bold and precipitous. Bluff Head is the long point extending out from the east shore.**

From Hulett's Landing we run diagonally across the lake to Sabbath Day Point, about two miles distant.*** As we draw near to the point glance backward toward Black Mountain and note how the old giant asserts his supremacy, rising up to overtop his less stately supporters. A little further along and he is again the stately center of the picture. The Elephant stands back there at the north end of Black Mountain. Note his well formed head toward the west; his eye; the rift that marks the outline of his massive jaw; the wrinkled neck and great rounded back with scattered bristles of dead pines clearly defined against the sky beyond. Sugar Loaf Mountain is over at the left of the Elephant. Its summit, viewed from a little distance

*Robert Rogers and his Rangers had a secret passage between Lake George and Lake Champlain, thought to be the valley between Hogback and Spruce mountains.[39] Many tales of the Rangers are difficult to pinpoint geographically.

**Writing in 1853, Henry Marvin recounted an incident in which a gale struck a sailing "bark," causing the vessel to capsize "and all on board were entombed in a watery grave."[40] The accident occurred north of Bluff Head and Odell Island.

***On July 15, 1909, the 32-foot gasoline yacht *Ruth-Allan* was being towed from Hulett's Landing to the western shore due to an engine failure. As the *Ruth-Allan* approached Sabbath Day Point at 6:48 in the evening, the tow line snapped during a sudden storm, causing the vessel to plunge to the bottom. The side curtains from the canopy top had been hooked down, drowning three men aboard, including the young mechanic trying to restart the engine. The vessel was subsequently towed to shore and the bodies found with grappling irons.[41]

Sabbath Day Point House.
(Postcard, author's collection)

north of Sabbath Day Point, looks very like a pig lying down, with his sharp nose pointing east. These animals were undoubtedly of the lot created "in the beginning." Twin Mountains are seen in the southwest from Sabbath Day Point. The southern most one is the Deer's Leap, the other known locally as Bloomer Mountain.

Sabbath Day Point (west, about 19 1/2 miles from Caldwell) has been the scene of many stirring incidents in the history of Lake George. It commands the approach by water on either hand and would naturally be selected for a camping place by parties who might have reason to expect the advance of an enemy. Here, in 1756, a body of provincials, under Putnam and Rogers repulsed a superior force of French and Indians.* On the 5th of July, 1758, Abercrombie, with his splendidly equipped army of over fifteen thousand men, landed for rest and refreshment, remaining until near midnight, when he moved down the lake, leaving immense fires burning, to give his watchful enemy the impression that he was still there.

Concerning the first settler, the following documentary evidence [dated June 20, 1764] is found in the office of the Secretary of State, at Albany: "That your petitioner [Samuel Adams] hath been Encouraged to Erect a house of Entertainment for the Convenience and accommodation of Passengers on Sabbathday Point on Lake George in the County of Albany and hath resided there for the space of Two years last past. . .[patent granted June 3, 1766]."

In 1798, Captain Sam Patch[i]n (hero of the cutter ride to Vicar's Island) built a log-house near the site of the present building, since which the point has never been without its resident family.

Sabbath Day Point House, enlarged since the old days, is a wholesome and attractive place with all a farm's welcome and surroundings. Accommodations are

---

*There is a scarcity of firsthand sources for this story. The incident was mentioned in a 1788 biography of Israel Putnam, in an annotated version of Anthony Wayne's orderly book (1859), and in Benjamin C. Butler's *Lake George and Lake Champlain*.[42]

here in house and cottages, for 100 guests. F. A. Carney, proprietor. There are cosy parlors, dainty home-like guests rooms and a table exceedingly wholesome and of immaculate neatness. The farm of 500 acres furnishes fresh vegetables, butter, cream and eggs. All steamers land at the dock. There is a telegraph and long distance telephone in the house. Electric lights and garage are among modern necessities.

A recent addition provides a large dining room with windows opening east, west and south, and a number of very desirable sleeping rooms increasing the accommodations to 100. In the words of the proprietor, "We do not have many rules. Guests are allowed to do anything that ladies or gentlemen would care to do." There is a fine bathing beach here sloping gradually from the lawn into deep water and another on the circling bay at the west. The books found on the shelves are wholesome and suggestive of a high intellectual standard. Row boats may be had here at $3.00 per week. Southbound autoists are advised to take the steamer from Sabbath Day Point to Bolton Landing to avoid difficult mountain climb.

Grace Memorial Chapel, just north of the Point was erected in 1885, in memory of the wife of Mr. Norman Dodge, daughter of Rev. A. D. Gillette, D. D. It is undenominational. Services are held during the season by visiting clergymen.

Hotel Uncas [Northern Lake George Resort in 1995] is on the west shore a little more than a mile north of Sabbath Day Point.

The Mohican is on higher ground just north of Uncas landing.

Silver Bay is on the west, 22 miles from the head of the lake. It owes its existence as a resort to Mr. Silas H. Paine of New York, who, as a summer resident, occupies the large cottage on high point just north of the landing.

Construction and painting crew at the Silver Bay Hotel (ca. 1898).
(Hague Historical Society)

"The Silver Bay Association for Christian Conference and Training" owns buildings and land consisting of nearly 1500 acres with a half-mile of lake shore.

The equipment includes a large main building (186 rooms), Forest Inn (76 rooms), Overlook, nine cottages, eight furnished cottages for housekeeping, Memorial Building with auditorium (seating 1,000), six class room buildings, boat house, bath house, athletic field, general store and gymnasium.

"Scotch Bonnet" is the name given to a little island lying just west of the steamboat channel, a mile north of Silver Bay. It was so named because of a tree which once grew upon it, resembling in shape a Scotch cap or bonnet.

Moving the 30-passenger launch *Uncas* from Jesse Sexton's boat shop to the lake in Hague (1910). The Hillside House can be seen on the right.
(Hague Historical Society)

Camp Iroquois is at Glen Eyrie [south of Gull Bay] on the east shore a little more than two miles north of Silver Bay. Originally planned as a camp for Manly Young Men it has outgrown the original design and become a colony giving room for half a thousand with a liberal sprinkling of substantial families.

Hague is situated on a broad, sweeping bay, at the west side of the lake, 28 miles from its head.* The general character of its scenery is peaceful, lacking the grandeur of the Narrows, but possessing a great variety of foliage, with graceful elms whose slender branches droop and sway like the weeping willow, the like of which is seen nowhere else at the lake. A walk up the valley road, leading west, gives a number of the most charming bits of scenery imaginable.

The Phoenix Hotel is a large white three-story building seen just a little way north of the steamboat landing. Lawn and meadowland belonging to the house reach

---

*Beginning in 1888, Hague became known for its annual regattas. At the turn of the century, the regatta events included a procession of decorated yachts, numerous races, and a speed demonstration by the 80-foot steam yacht *Ellide*, which held the world's speed record at the time.[43]

Tourism at Hague-on-Lake George.

Clockwise from bottom left:

Rising House (Postcard, author's collection)
"Steamer *Sagamore* at Hague" (ca. 1909). (Postcard, author's collection)
"Hotels at Hague-on-Lake George." (Postcard, author's collection)
Steamboat landing. (Postcard, author's collection)
Phoenix Hotel. (Hague Historical Society)
Guests at the Trout House. (Hague Historical Society)
Island Harbor House. (Postcard, author's collection)

out to the bathing beach on the water front. It is homelike and attractive, with a good table supplied with vegetables, milk and eggs from the hotel farm.

The Hillside is where a brawling brook comes down a few rods north of the Phoenix. Capacity about 80. Location, grounds and outlook are exceedingly picturesque while the house and proprietor have an excellent reputation and a host of friends.

The Iroquois (color olive) is third of the notable hotels. It has capacity for about 75.

The Trout House, three stories, painted white, is partially hidden among the trees. Capacity about 120 guests. Open all the year. Richard J. Bolton, proprietor. A free carriage runs to and from the steamboat landing during July and August. The outlook from the Trout House is charming, and often painted by artists. A pretty sand beach circles along in front of the house. The changed road and rearrangement of grounds with modern improvements and additions to the hotel make it one of the handsomest in all the northern parts of the lake while under its present management it has gained a reputation for spreading one of the very best of tables. That Mr. [Richard] Bolton has the confidence of his fellow citizens is expressed in the fact that he was recently made a sheriff of his county by a large majority.

The Rising House, a short distance north, is on the flank of a hill crowding close against the road well shaded from the afternoon sun, with piazza on the front which under the protecting trees affords a fine extended lookout east and south. It is three stories in height, accommodating 100 guests. It has hot and cold water baths and whatever is considered essential in modern fittings. Necessary supplies for hunting, fishing, [tele]graph office is in the house.

On the west side of the mountain beyond are the graphite works belonging to the Dixon Crucible Company of Jersey City.*

The mill in Graphite (ca. 1915).
(Hague Historical Society)

*A large mining complex was situated west of Hague in an area called Graphite (north side of present-day Route 8). The mine closed on April 1, 1921, due largely to import competition.[44] The ruins of the mill, various buildings, and homes are still visible in the forest today. A smaller graphite mine, Lake Shore Mines, was located on the mountainside above the Rising House.

Continuing northward the road winds along the shore, passing Calamity Point where, embedded in the white sand, lie the remains of the steamboat *John Jay*, destroyed by fire here July 29, 1856. It burned to the water's edge and six lives were lost. [See chapter 17.]

Back in the bight [bend] of the bay, nearly hidden among the trees, is the picturesque cottage of Harry W. Watrous, the artist, and Mrs. Watrous, the novelist.

Island Harbor (west, 1 mile north of Hague Landing), was the name given to the cozy hotel and cluster of cottages on the west shore of the bay formed by the enclosing group known as Cook's Islands. It is much frequented by sportsmen and has a record for big fish, approached by few resorts along the Lake. During the past winter additions and many improvements have been made. The water supply is from a spring 1000 feet above the lake. A bathing beach is in the closed harbor. Altogether it is wholesome, attractive and delightfully informal. The location shows lovely vistas through the islands and affords safe boating in covered waters even in the roughest of weather. The drives and foot-paths through the shady woods nearby are exceedingly picturesque. Island Harbor has accommodations in house and four cottages for 100 guests. It has modern conveniences and is lighted by acetylene gas. A glass-enclosed dining room overlooking the lake is a delightful place. Home-cooking of the best type, wholesome and sweet, is a notable feature.

Waltonian Isle is the outermost and largest of the group of nine islands lying outside Island Harbor, state land, preempted and occupied during the summer by that princely squatter and royal entertainer and promoter of sports—Col. W. D. Mann of "Town Topics."* Ten miles away at the south, the "Elephant" stretches his huge bulk across; over his head Black Mountain stands guard, growing misty along the distant narrows. At the north is Friend's Point, a pleasant tree-bordered meadow, quiet and beautiful enough now, but of old the scene of many bloody engagements, being then, as now, a favorite camping ground.**

Blair's Bay sets well back into the eastern shore south of Anthony's Nose.

"Adirondack Camp" is on a commanding point reaching out from the east shore, south of Blair's Bay and directly across the lake from Friend's Point. Here Dr. Elias G. Brown of New York has established a camp for boys and fitted it up to delight the youthful mind. Dr. Brown has had large experience in the care and training of boys and has enlisted college men as counsellors and assistants. Practical camping, woodcraft and nature study are taught; and an important feature of the summer's outing is the attention paid to physical development. There is every kind of sport—tramping with an Adirondack guide, mountain climbing and canoeing, tennis, baseball, basketball, tether-ball and kindred games. The boys sleep in tents.***

Glenburnie Inn and Cottages are on the east at head of Blair Bay with accommodations for 80. Two minutes' walk from Steamboat Landing. All line boats land.

*After the state ordered William D'Alton Mann's summer home removed from Waltonian Island, the house was hauled across the ice (1917) to the shoreline, where it remains today. In 1904 Mann was the object of a hoax by Harry Watrous involving a wooden lake monster.

**An often repeated story of Friends Point, involving the near skirmish between two English scouting parties, was popularized in 1853 by Henry Marvin in his book *A Complete History of Lake George*.[45] The point was actually named for William Friend who received a land grant in 1771.

***Now co-ed, the Adirondack camp is still in operation.

Anthony's Nose extends west along the north side of Blair's Bay. It is heavily wooded, excepting in spots where a cliff is presented or where its western point rounds over sharply into the lake. From a position well back on the south side of Blair's Bay can be seen a perfect face in profile, with smooth brow, Roman nose, firm lips and bearded chin looking out toward the west from the perpendicular wall at the second mountain step. In passing we run close to the point of the mountain, so near at times that a stone could be easily tossed against its iron-stained sides.*

Rogers' Slide is toward the west, a mountain nearly a thousand feet high, with smoothly rounded top and precipitous sides. Nearly half of its entire height is a smooth wall of rock descending at a sharp angle to the water's edge. It is rich in minerals. [See chapter 5 for the story of Rogers Rock.]

The Rogers' Rock Hotel stands on a promonitory just north of the Slide. This property was bought in 1903 by the Rogers' Rock Hotel Company. The grounds have a lake frontage of over one mile and extend backward fully a half mile to include Rogers' Rock mountain. Near by are deep waters and running brooks. From its commanding position it looks out over the narrowing waters of the outlet and south to where Black Mountain stands guard over the way. A road winds through the wood and up the mountain, and woodland paths run here and there to retired nooks, or views of vantage, with guideboards pointing the way. The steamboats all land on regular trips. Small boats in variety give facilities for fishing or pleasure excursion. A cottage about 150 feet above the house, and another at lake shore, give guests a choice in altitudes afforded by no other hotel at Lake George. The house abounds in quaint, old-fashioned furniture and bric-a-brac. Electric bells connect office with guests rooms, which are of good size and fitted with comfortable beds and plenty of linen. A never failing mountain spring furnishes a bountiful supply of pure water. A large greenhouse and ample spaces are devoted to flowers and lawns. Gardens aggregating more than five acres, furnish the table with fresh vegetables in variety and abundance. Meals are served at small tables daintily appointed. Fresh vegetables, meats, fish, milk, cream, butter and eggs are given special attention. The billiard room and bowling alleys removed from the house to the landing are in perfect order. The fleet of new rowboats, equipped with spoon oars, cushions, back rests, etc., should meet the requirements of the most exacting. Capacity of house, 100 guests. Postoffice in the hotel.

Rogers' Rock Mountain may be ascended by a good path leading from the hotel. From the top may be had a view of surprising grandeur and extent. On its summit, appearing as a tiny bird cage from below, is seen a summer house built by Boston's celebrated divine, the Rev. Joseph Cook, whose birth-place is just over the other side of pleasant Trout Brook Valley.

He will see the lake and Black Mountain at the south, the hills and valleys of Vermont and Massachusetts on the east, at the north the valley of Lake Champlain, and on the north and west the foothills of the Adirondacks.

---

*During a dense fog on July 1, 1927, the steamboat *Sagamore* crashed head-on into the rock ledges of Anthony's Nose. The stricken vessel successfully navigated to the Glenburnie dock where the passengers were unloaded. The vessel sank in 18 feet of water on the north side of the dock but was raised and subsequently refurbished at great expensive at the company's Baldwin shipyard. Seven years later, during the Great Depression, the vessel was retired and then scrapped a short time later.

North from Rogers' Rock Hotel is a beautiful bay [Hearts Bay], stretching in a broadening curve to a sharp, sandy point, its abrupt shores dotted by a number of pretty villas. Beyond the point is Baldwin.

Baldwin is thirty-four miles from Caldwell. Here the steamboat trip ends. Of old the steamers ran nearly a mile farther [to Cooks Landing], but the channel was winding and uncertain. Here the morning boat from the south delivers up its passengers to the waiting train which conveys them overland to Ticonderoga, where the steamer, *Vermont*, is taken for points north on Lake Champlain. The Lake George boat, after taking on board the passengers brought from the north starts on its return trip through the lake.

Ice harvest on Lake George at Ticonderoga.
(Ticonderoga Historical Society)

Mount Defiance, a little elevation east of the outlet, commands Fort Ticonderoga, lying over beyond and received its name when, in 1777, [General John] Burgoyne, from its summit, trained guns on the old fort.

Prisoners' Isle is out in the lake north of the steamboat landing.* [See also chapter 18 note, page 356.]

Howe's Landing is the bit of circling beach west of Prisoners' Isle, where Abercrombie, with his army of 15,000 men, landed, on the 6th of July, 1758, and advanced toward Ticonderoga. Toward the north, the lake rapidly narrows to a mere creek and hastens to its fall, the crystal water discolored by the clay of the bottom.

The Upper Falls of Ticonderoga may be seen on the left as we approach to cross the outlet. Pulp mills, etc., here, give employment to a large number of operatives.

---

*In 1903 Captain Elias S. Harris noted that Prisoners Island was "about half the size it was when I first saw it [around 1843]" due to erosion.[46]

Toward the north where the waters of the outlet circling to the east are joined by those of Trout Brook from the valley of the west Lord [George Viscount] Howe, the idol of the English army and the life and actual leader of Abercrombie's unfortunate expedition in 17[5]8, was killed. A stone bearing a rudely scratched inscription recently discovered, marked a grave believed to have been that of the young nobleman.*

Ticonderoga (village), three miles from Baldwin and two from Lake Champlain, is a prosperous village of 6,000 inhabitants. The water power is considerable. The town has made rapid strides in improvements and growing wealthy in manufacturing interests. The Burleigh House is the best hotel.

The Lower Falls of Ticonderoga at the lower edge of the village, are picturesque as well as utilitarian where they make their last leap to the level of Lake Champlain. From this point the stream is navigable for small steamers down to where it empties at last at the base of the historic promontory. Montcalm Landing is at the east foot of Mt. Defiance, five miles from Baldwin. Here Lake George trains connect with the Champlain steamer and with cars north and south. The old fort can be seen at the north, about a mile distant from the landing.

The Ruins of To-day

The old battery on the bluff, above the fort steamboat landing, is said to have been the original Carillon.** Back on the higher ground are the barrack walls, trenches and bastions.

The Old Fort and Garrison grounds consisting of about 700 acres were ceded by the state toward the close of the [eighteenth] century to Columbia and Union Colleges, and in [1820] purchased by William Pell, the great-grandfather of the present owner, Stephen H. P. Pell. Efforts have been repeatedly made to interest both the state and national governments in the care of the old fort, the owners expressing a willingness to sell at a nominal price if the preservation could be guaranteed, but in vain. They have now undertaken the restoration of the old building as nearly on original lines as can be determined.

Opposite page:
  Top: Fort Ticonderoga (ca. 1920). (Postcard, author's collection)
  Bottom: The restored West Barracks of Fort Ticonderoga. (Postcard, author's collection)

---

*Contrary to nineteenth-century stories that Lord Howe had been buried in Ticonderoga, Samuel Thompson on July 8, 1758, recorded that "they brought [the body of] Lord How[e]" to the southern end of Lake George.[47]

**Stoddard is referring to the Lotbinière Battery, also called the Grenadier's Battery, located on a promonitory at the lakeshore. Because Fort Carillon had been built a considerable distance from the lake, the French subsequently constructed this redoubt or smaller fort to defend the narrows.

Notes:

1. S. R. Stoddard, *Lake George and Lake Champlain: A Book of To-Day* (Glens Falls, N.Y.: S. R. Stoddard, 1914), 185.
2. W. H. Tippetts, *Lake George: The Queen of American Lakes* (Caldwell, N.Y.: W. H. Tippetts, Publisher, 1901), 27; Betty Ahern Buckell, *Old Lake George Hotels* (Lake George, N.Y.: Buckle Press, 1986), 47.
3. Charles H. Possons, *Possons' Guide to Lake George; Lake Champlain and Adirondacks* (Glens Falls, N.Y.: Chas. H. Possons, Publisher, 1888), 64; Ogden J. Ross, *The Steamboats of Lake George 1817 to 1932* (Albany: Press of the Delaware and Hudson Railroad, 1932), 103.
4. Kathryn E. O'Brien, *The Great and the Gracious on Millionaires' Row* (Sylvan Beach, N.Y.: North Country Books, 1978).
5. W. Max Reid, *Lake George and Lake Champlain* (New York: G. P. Putnam's Sons, 1910), 316-17.
6. A. S. Hopkins, *Lake George* (Albany: State of New York Conservation Commission, 1926), 8.
7. William H. Brown, ed., *History of Warren County* (Glens Falls, N.Y.: Board of Supervisors of Warren County, 1963), 98-99; See also Philip Terrie, "Behind the Blue Line," *Adirondack Life*, January/February 1992, 49; Elsa Kny Steinback, *Sweet Peas and a White Bridge* (Burlington, VT.: The George Little Press, 1974), 87.
8. *Lake George Mirror*, 31 August 1901; See also *Glens Falls Daily Times*, 29 August 1901.
9. George Chapman Singer, letter, 17 July 1975; See also Jane M. Lape, ed., *Ticonderoga: Patches and Patterns from Its Past* (Ticonderoga, N.Y.: The Ticonderoga Historical Society, 1969), 208.
10. Maitland C. De Sormo, *Seneca Ray Stoddard: Versatile Camera-Artist* (Utica, N.Y.: North Country Books, Inc., 1972), 39.
11. S. R. Stoddard, *The Adirondacks: Illustrated* (Albany: Weed, Parsons & Co., Printers, 1874), 9.
12. Ibid., 37.
13. S. R. Stoddard, *Lake George; A Book of To-Day* (Albany: Weed, Parsons and Company, Printers, 1873), 39.
14. Ibid., 46.
15. William Crowley, *Seneca Ray Stoddard: Adirondack Illustrator* (Blue Mountain Lake, N.Y.: Adirondack Museum, 1982), 21.
16. John Fuller, *Seneca Ray Stoddard: In the Adirondacks With Camera* (Syracuse, N.Y.: Robert B. Menschel Photography Gallery), p.n.a.; See also Crowley, 16, 18; See also forthcoming Joseph Cutshall King and Winston Adler, *Seneca Ray Stoddard* (Boston: David R. Godine, Inc., 1996).
17. Stoddard, *The Adirondacks: Illustrated* (1874), 200.
18. De Sormo, 70; See also John Mitchell, "Spirits of the Mountains," *Adirondack Life*, March/April 1992, 53-54.
19. Stoddard, *Lake George* (1914), 5-6, 18-21, 36-118, 135-39.
20. B. F. DeCosta, *Lake George; Its Scenes and Characteristics* (New York: Anson D. F. Randolph & Co., 1869), 63; See also Elizabeth Eggleston Seelye, *Lake George in History* (Lake George, N.Y.: Elwyn Seelye, 1896), 105.
21. *Lake George Mirror*, 11 July 1903; Captain E. S. Harris, *Lake George: All About It* (Glens Falls, N.Y.: Glens Falls Republican, 1903), 27; Ross, 33.
22. *Lake George Mirror*, 13 August 1921.
23. Ibid., 5 July 1930.
24. Lois M. Feister and Paul R. Huey, "Archaeological Testing at Fort Gage, A Provincial Redoubt of 1758 at Lake George, New York," *The Bulletin and Journal of Archaeology for New York State* 90 (Spring 1985): 40-59; See also Archelaus Fuller, "Journal of Col. Archelaus Fuller of Middleton, Mass., in the Expedition Against Ticonderoga in 1758," *The Essex Institute Historical Collections* 46 (1910): 215; Caleb Rea, "The Journal of Caleb Rea," *The Essex Institute Historical Collections* 18 (1881): 181; Abel Spicer, "Diary of Abel Spicer," in *History of the Descendants of Peter Spicer*, comp. by Susan Spicer Meech and Susan Billings Meech (Boston: F. H. Gilson, 1911), 398.
25. O'Brien, 246.
26. J. P. Sweet, *Lake George* (New York: J. P. Sweet, 1863), 20-21.
27. *Lake George Mirror*, 5 June 1897.
28. *Lake George Mirror*, 12 August 1893; *Glens Falls Daily Times*, 4 August 1893.

29. *Lake George Mirror*, 11 August 1917; Steinback, 72.
30. Sweet, 31.
31. Henry Marvin, *A Complete History of Lake George* (New York: Sibells & Maigne, Printers, 1853), 60.
32. B. C. Butler, *Lake George and Lake Champlain* (Albany: Weed, Parsons and Co., 1868), 152-54; See also DeCosta, 98-100.
33. Louis Antoine de Bougainville, *Adventure in the Wilderness: The American Journals of Louis Antoine de Bougainville 1756-1760*, trans. and ed. Edward P. Hamilton (Norman, OK: University of Oklahoma Press, 1964), 132; "Extract of a Letter from a Gentleman at Fort William Henry. . .July 26, 1757," *The London Magazine* (September 1757): p.n.a.; E. B. O'Callaghan, ed., *Documents Relative to the Colonial History of the State of New York* (Albany: Weed, Parsons and Company, 1858), Volume 10, 734; Seth Tinkham, "Diary of Seth Tinkham," in *History of Plymouth County, Massachusetts*, comp. D. Hamilton Hurd (Philadelphia: J. W. Lewis & Co., 1884), 996; Samuel Hazard, ed., *Pennsylvania Archives* (Philadelphia: Joseph Severns & Co., 1853), Volume 3, 472.
34. James Montresor, "Journal of Col. James Montresor," *Collections of the New-York Historical Society* 14 (1881): 22.
35. *London Magazine* (September 1757): p.n.a.; Ian K. Steele, *Betrayals: Fort William Henry & the "Massacre"* (New York: Oxford University Press, 1990), 217 n. 47.
36. Reuben Gold Thwaites, ed., *Travels and Expeditions of the Jesuit Missionaries in New France* (Cleveland: The Burrows Brothers Company, 1900), Volume 70, 124-29.
37. Sweet, 34-36.
38. Reid, 343.
39. Burt Garfield Loescher, *Rogers Rangers: The First Green Berets* (San Mateo, Ca.: Burt Garfield Loescher, 1969), Volume 2, 238-39, n. 114; E. B. O'Callaghan, ed., The *Documentary History of the State of New York* (Albany: Charles Van Benthysen, Public Printer, 1851), Volume 4, 285.
40. Marvin, 66-67.
41. *Lake George Mirror*, 16 July 1909; 23 July 1909.
42. David Humphreys, *An Essay of the Life of the Honourable Major General Israel Putnam* (1788; reprint, Boston: Samuel Avery, 1818), 31; [Anthony Wayne], *Orderly Book of the Northern Army at Ticonderoga and Mt. Independence* (Albany: J. Munsell, 1859), 67; Butler, 2d ed., 145-46; Another account used the date 1758, see Hugh Maxwell, "Memoir of Hugh Maxwell," in *The Christian Patriot* (New York: p.n.a., 1833), 101; See also Sweet, 39.
43. *Lake George Mirror*, 29 August 1901; See also Harris, 23.
44. Wilford C. Ross, *The History of Graphite, New York* (Glens Falls, N.Y.: Ridgecraft Books, 1976), 17-25; Robert Gordon, "Days of Ore," *Adirondack Life*, July/August 1990, 38.
45. Marvin, 68.
46. Harris, 26.
47. Samuel Thompson, *Diary of Lieut. Samuel Thompson*, ed. William R. Cutter (Boston: Press of David Clapp & Son, 1896), 9.

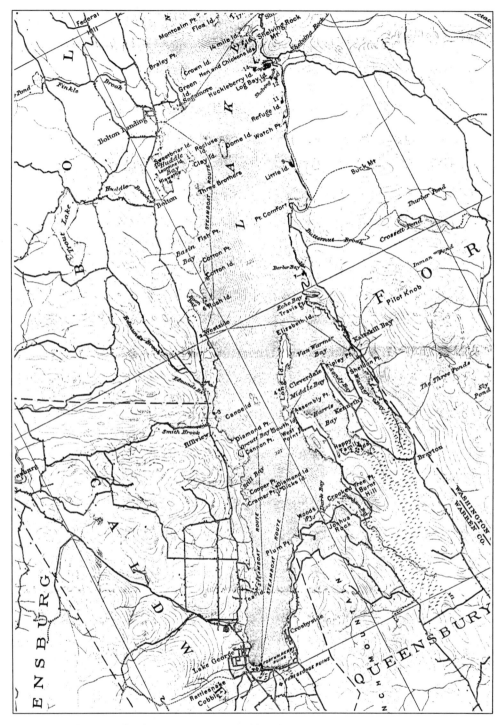

Detail of "Map of Lake George" prepared by the Conservation Commission, 1926.
A. S. Hopkins, State Forester.

(Author's collection)

Index

Praise for Russell P. Bellico's first book, also published by Purple Mountain Press:

SAILS AND STEAM IN THE MOUNTAINS
A Maritime and Military History of Lake George and Lake Champlain

"Bellico fully traces the roles played by Lake George and Lake Champlain in the French and Indian War, the American Revolution, and the War of 1812, then moves beyond to the canal boats and steamships that plied them in more peaceful pursuits during the nineteenth and twentieth centuries."—*American History*

"What makes Bellico's work stand out from the literature in the subject is his extensive use of original diaries and journals of the soldiers who fought the battles at the lakes. At points it achieves the narrative flow and high drama of the new hit movie *The Last of the Mohicans*." —*Times Union*, Albany

"Bellico draws on a vast fund of research and documentation to bring to life the early explorations, naval and military actions of the French and Indian wars, the Revolution, and the War of 1812. . . . This massive work is substantiated by an impressively extensive bibliography."—*Vermont Sunday Magazine*

"Attractively illustrated, handsomely printed and bound, this new history of maritime and military affairs on Lake Champlain and Lake George gives a thorough review of the exploration and early, crucially important military history of the Champlain Valley." —*Vermont Life Magazine*

"No one who claims interest in the history of the Lake George/Lake Champlain region, who expresses a fascination with the richness of underwater history and a desire to see it preserved, or who just enjoys envisioning the past in modern landscape, should find their library without this book."—*Sea History Magazine*

"Now in its second printing in two years, this popular and very readable history of two significant Adirondack lakes and the events and ships involved through the years is the most comprehensive account of the area. Meticulously documented, it takes the reader into the early history of the strategic waterway into Canada, and right down to present time and the boats currently plying the lakes."—*Steamboat Bill* (Journal of the Steamship Historical Society)

"Offering a wealth of new details culled mainly from primary sources: journals, orderly books, letters, newspaper reports, etc.—this book provides a fresh retelling of the 17th, 18th, and 19th century battles waged along the 152-mile water chain linking what is now the United States and Canada. . .author Bellico has laced the book not infrequently with colorful anecdotes, observations by participants, and sections discussing archaeological discoveries related to the campaigns."—*Military Collector and Historian*

"The maritime and military history of Lake George and Lake Champlain springs to life in the pages of this compelling reference."—*Adirondack Life Magazine*

"Bellico's book meticulously traces the history of these two lakes. In all of this material Bellico presents much primary data as well as a complex synthesis of events. . .the volume also offers copious textual and citation footnotes and additional page-end comments. . .Exquisite photographs provide a counterpoint to the historical illustrations in the text." —*American Neptune: A Quarterly Journal of Maritime History*